LEARNING **JAVA**
THROUGH GAMES

LEARNING JAVA
THROUGH GAMES

LUBOMIR STANCHEV

CRC Press
Taylor & Francis Group
Boca Raton London New York

CRC Press is an imprint of the
Taylor & Francis Group, an **informa** business

CRC Press
Taylor & Francis Group
6000 Broken Sound Parkway NW, Suite 300
Boca Raton, FL 33487-2742

First issued in hardback 2017

© 2014 by Taylor & Francis Group, LLC
CRC Press is an imprint of Taylor & Francis Group, an Informa business

No claim to original U.S. Government works

Version Date: 20130715

ISBN-13: 978-1-4665-9331-2 (pbk)
ISBN-13: 978-1-138-42803-4 (hbk)

Library of Congress Cataloging-in-Publication Data

Stanchev, Lubomir, 1975-
    Learning Java through games / Lubomir Stanchev.
        pages cm
    Includes bibliographical references and index.
    ISBN 978-1-4665-9331-2 (pbk.)
    1. Java (Computer program language)--Problems, exercises, etc. 2. Java (Computer program language)--Textbooks. I. Title.

QA76.73.J38S758 2013
005.2'762--dc23   2013027590

Visit the Taylor & Francis Web site at
http://www.taylorandfrancis.com

and the CRC Press Web site at
http://www.crcpress.com

To all my teachers and to my loving and supporting family.

Contents

Preface

Java is a programming language that was originally developed in 1995 by James Gosling at Sun Microsystems, which later became part of Oracle Corporation. Since then, seven major revisions of the language have been introduced and thousands of textbooks that describe every nitty-gritty detail of the language have been published. At the same time, many computer science departments of universities throughout the world have adopted Java as their introductory programming language. The reason is that Java is a strongly typed language that is easy to learn and apply. The language also helps identify erroneous code early in the coding process. The popularity of Java as an introductory programming language has led to the publication of thousands more textbooks that use the Java language to introduce the reader to basic programming principles.

This textbook stands somewhere in the middle. It tries to cover as much material as possible from the latest Java standard (Java SE 7). At the same time, it is a textbook that is aimed at readers with no previous programming background. It not only teaches how to use the different features of the language, but it also teaches the reader how to program. What makes this textbook unique is its application-motivated approach. The textbook contains a plethora of games. Almost all Java constructs are introduced as a necessity to implement different game features. Most chapters start with a description of a game. Next, different Java constructs that can be used to implement the features of the game are introduced on need-to-use bases. The textbook reads similar to a mystery novel. The reader must read through the whole chapter in order to understand all the features that are needed to implement the game.

The second strength of the textbook is that, unlike most existing Java textbooks, it spends a lot of time preaching good software development practices. Martin Fowler once famously wrote, "Any fool can write code that a computer can understand. Good programmers write code that humans can understand." This textbook tries to teach the reader not only how to write code that works, but also how to follow good software practices. All sample programs in the textbook strive to achieve low cohesion and high coupling, which is the marksmanship of well-designed code. Many programs in the textbook are refactored multiple times in order to achieve code that is easy to understand, reuse, and maintain. The author of this textbook firmly believes that even novice programmers should be taught good programming practices. The reason is that if one does not develop good programming habits from the outset, then it is more difficult to develop them afterwards.

The textbook is split in two parts. Chapters 1–7 cover basic programming techniques, such as conditional statements, loops, methods, arrays, and classes. Chapters 8–15 cover more advanced topics, such as class inheritance, recursions, sorting algorithms, GUI programming, exception handling, files, and applets. The textbook is designed to be either used by a reader who wants to learn the language on their own or as part of a two-course introduction to programming sequence. Most chapters build on each other and the best way to read the textbook is from start to finish. A dependency diagram of the chapters is shown in Figure 0.1.

Chapter 1 introduces basic computer concepts, such as main memory, hard disk, operating system, and binary numbers. It should be read by readers that have little computer

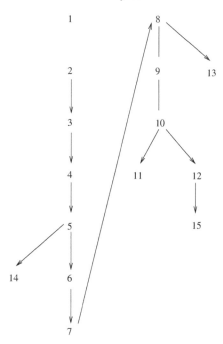

FIGURE 0.1: Chapter sequence.

experience. Chapter 2 introduces variables and conditional statements. These are the building blocks of any program. Chapter 3 introduces loops. Loops allow us to execute the same piece of code multiple times. Chapter 4 introduces methods. Methods allow the programmer to divide the code into smaller segments, which can shorten the program and eliminate redundant code. Chapter 5 introduces arrays. These allow us to create numerous pieces of data of the same type in a single statement. Chapter 6 introduces classes, which are the pivot of any object-oriented programming language. Classes are introduced late in this textbook because they are a more advanced concept that requires understanding of basic programming principles. Chapter 7 combines two independent topics: the utility `ArrayList` class and the Java `enum` keyword. An `ArrayList` is a more powerful version of an array that provides more capabilities. Conversely, the `enum` keyword stands for *enumerate* and allows the programmer to enumerate the values of a user-defined type.

The second part of the textbook contains advanced programming techniques. Chapter 8 revisits classes and introduces more advanced topics, such as inheritance and polymorphism. Chapter 9 shows the basics of displaying text and drawings inside a window. Chapter 10 describes how events can be handled in Java. Concepts from Chapter 9 are used as examples. Chapter 11 presents the `Breakout` game. The chapter shows how programming techniques can be applied on a non-trivial project. If the reader is in a hurry, the chapter can be skipped because it is not a prerequisite for any other chapter. Chapter 12 describes basic graphical user interface (GUI) components, such as windows, panels, buttons, combo boxes, and so on. Chapter 13 describes files and exception handling. It requires, as a prerequisite, mainly the understanding of classes and class inheritance. Chapter 14 covers recursion and requires, as a prerequisite, the understanding of methods and arrays. Chapter 15, which is an optional chapter, shows the reader how to program Java Applets.

Book resources, including Java code from the examples in the textbook and slides, can be found at http://softbase.ipfw.edu/~lubo/LearningJava. Please e-mail typos or suggestions for book improvement to stanchev@gmail.com.

About the Author

Lubomir Stanchev is an associate professor in the Department of Computer Science at Indiana University – Purdue University Fort Wayne. He got his Ph.D. degree from the David R. Cheriton School of Computer Science at the University of Waterloo in Canada. He has taught introductory programming courses and software engineering courses about fifteen times in the past eight years. He has published more than five journal articles and more than twenty conference proceedings in the area of computer science. He has been writing software code for over thirty years and he has worked as a software developer in four different companies.

List of Figures

List of Tables

Part I

Basic Principles

Chapter 1

Computer Hardware and Software

This chapter introduces the basic components of a computer: its hardware and software. After all, this is a computer programming textbook and we need to have a basic understanding of how the computer works before we can start developing software for it. For completeness, some historical information about computers and computer games is also included in the chapter.

1.1 Brief History of Computers

Computers are electronic devices that can perform calculations. The first electronic digital computer was built by physics professor John Atanasoff and his graduate student Clifford Berry in 1937. The computer could not be programmed and could be used only to solve linear equations. Six years later, in 1943, the first programmable electronic computer was built by Tommy Flowers; see Figure 1.1.

As you can see in the picture, the first computers took a lot of space. Different components, such as secondary storage and main memory, were in separate racks. Early computers could easily fill a present-day classroom. Colloquial expressions such as: "I will go to check on the memory" were common in those days. Even the term "bug", which is commonly used to describe a software error, derives from the days when actual rodents were roaming around the different components of a computer. As time progressed, computers became smaller and cheaper. The personal computer was introduced in the late 1970s and early 1980s by the likes of Hewlett Packard, Apple, and IBM.

1.2 Hardware Components of a Computer

The brain of a computer is the *Central Processing Unit (CPU)*; see Figure 1.2 . It is a device that can perform simple calculations. These include addition, deletion, subtraction,

3

FIGURE 1.1: A Colossus Mark 2 computer. Artwork created by United Kingdom Government.

FIGURE 1.2: An Intel 80486DX2 CPU from above. Photographed by Andrew Dunn. The picture is licensed under the Creative Commons Attribution-Share Alike 2.0 Generic license.

and multiplication. The speed of a CPU is measured in *hertz*, which is a measure of frequency in cycles per second. In one cycle, the CPU can perform one instruction. Typical CPU speeds of modern computers are around 2 GHz, which corresponds to 2 gigahertz, or 2 billion instructions per second. The actual data on which the operations are performed is stored in main memory; see Figure 1.3. The main memory is where both the programs and the data are stored.

The main memory contains both the application data and the commands that manipulate the data. The commands from the main memory are loaded on the CPU. The CPU then reads data from main memory, performs the operation that is requested, and saves the result back into main memory. Therefore, all a computer can do is to move data from one spot to another in main memory and perform arithmetic computations.

The main memory of a computer consists of a sequence of cells, where every cell can take one of two states: 0 or 1. The different values are usually represented by different voltage. For example, 0.8 volts or below may denote 0, while 2.2 volts or above can denote the number 1. In computer science, this single cell is referred to as a *bit*. Table 1.1 shows common units for measuring the size of memory (i.e., number of bits).

In modern computers, the main memory of a computer is typically between 1 and 16 GBs, while the hard disk can typically store anywhere between 256 GB and 1 TB. Moore's law is the observation that over the history of computing hardware, the number of transistors

FIGURE 1.3: DDRAM memory modules for desktop computers. Picture is from Wikipedia commons.

TABLE 1.1: Memory units.

(Unit)	(Size)	(Approximate size in bytes)
byte (B)	8 bits	1
kilobyte (KB)	1024 bytes	1,000
megabyte (MB)	1024 KBs	1,000,000
gigabyte (GB)	1024 MBs	1,000,000,000
terabyte (TB)	1024 GBs	1,000,000,000,000

on integrated circuits doubles approximately every two years. This means that with time, both main memory and CPUs become cheaper.

Note that there is a significant difference between the hard disk and the main memory of a computer. When the computer shuts down, everything that is written in main memory disappears. This is why the main memory of a computer is referred to as *volatile* memory. Alternatively, the data on the hard disk is persistent even after the computer shuts down and there is no power. Usually, magnetic fields are used to store the data permanently. This is why hard disks are referred to as *persistent* storage. Since the hard disk of a computer contains physical components, such as moving heads and rotating platters, accessing data from the hard disk is significantly slower than accessing data from main memory. Since the hard disk contains moving components, Moore's law does not apply to it. Main memory is significantly more expensive than hard disk memory. For example, currently one can buy a 1 TB hard disk for around $100. Buying that much main memory costs more than 10 times more. Note that the CPU cannot directly access data from the hard disk. The data needs to be first brought into main memory before it can be accessed by the CPU.

Main memory is often referred to as *Random Access Memory (RAM)*. This means that it takes exactly the same time to access any cell of the main memory. Alternatively, accessing different parts of the hard disk can take different time. For example, the sector (unit of division of the hard disk) that is the closest to the reading head can be accessed the fastest. Accessing a sector that is far away from the reading head will incur *rotational delay*. This is the time that is needed for the reading head to reach the sector.

Input devices and *output devices* can be connected to a computer. Examples of input devices include keyboard, joystick, mouse, and microphone. Examples of output devices include monitor, speakers, and printer. An Internet connector can be considered to be both an input and output device. The CPU communicates with devices though main memory reads and writes. For example, a program can display an image on the screen by writing the image to the video card of the display. Similarly, information from an Internet connector can be received by reading the data from shared main memory.

1.3   Binary Representation of Numbers

It is important to understand the fact that a computer can store only zeros and ones. Consider the integer 423. It is equal to $4 \cdot 10^2 + 2 \cdot 10^1 + 3 \cdot 10^0$. This is known as *base 10 representation* because every digit is between 0 and 9. Similarly, there is base 2 representation that uses only 2 digits: 0 and 1. This is also referred to as the *binary* representation of the number. For example, the binary number 01010010 represents the decimal number $0 \cdot 2^7 + 1 \cdot 2^6 + 0 \cdot 2^5 + 1 \cdot 2^4 + 0 \cdot 2^3 + 0 \cdot 2^2 + 1 \cdot 2^1 + 0 \cdot 2^0 = 82$.

There is also an easy algorithm for converting a decimal integer to a binary number. Consider the decimal integer 134. The conversion algorithm keeps dividing the number by 2 and records the remainders.

```
134 /2 =   67 remainder 0
67 / 2 = 33 remainder 1
33 / 2 = 16 remainder 1
16 /2 = 8 remainder 0
8 / 2 = 4 remainder 0
4 / 2 = 2 remainder 0
2 / 2 = 1 remainder 0
add a 1
```

The binary number is created by starting with the number 1 and then taking the remainders in reverse order. For example, the decimal number 134 is equal to the binary number 10000110. To verify our work, we can try to convert the number back to a decimal number. It will be equal to: $1 \cdot 2^7 + 0 \cdot 2^6 + 0 \cdot 2^5 + 0 \cdot 2^4 + 0 \cdot 2^3 + 1 \cdot 2^2 + 1 \cdot 2^1 + 0 \cdot 2^0 = 134$.

Sometimes, data that is stored in computers is represented using hexadecimal numbers. These are numbers in base 16. Table 1.2 shows the hexadecimal digits. The first 10 digits are the same as the decimal digits. Then the letters A–F are used to represent the numbers 10–15. Consider the hexadecimal number 4F1A. Since a hexadecimal digit takes 4 bits to represent, the number will be 16 bits or 2 bytes long. To convert it into a binary number, we can just use Table 1.2 as a reference and convert every digit individually. In binary, the number will be: 0100 1111 0001 1010. Since the hexadecimal representation of a number is much shorter than the binary representation, it is often used to represent binary data, such as main memory addresses.

1.4   Software Creation and Types of Software

Software is usually written by *software programmers* using a *programming language*, such as Java or C. It is then converted into binary code that the CPU can understand. A *compiler* will directly translate the program code into binary (or executable) code, which can be later executed. For example, in Windows executable files have the extension .exe. Conversely, an *interpreter* interprets the program. It translates every line of code into executable code, which is then executed. A file that contains the executable code is not created. An interpreter is usually slower than a compiler because each line of code needs to be translated into executable code before it can be executed.

Java takes an approach that uses both a compiler and interpreter. Java code is compiled into Java binary code, which is different than the binary code that the CPU can understand. This binary code can be later executed by a *Java Virtual Machine (JVM)* interpreter. This

TABLE 1.2: Hexadecimal digits.

(*Hexadecimal digit*)	(*Decimal number*)	(*Binary number*)
0	0	0000
1	1	0001
2	2	0010
3	3	0011
4	4	0100
5	5	0101
6	6	0110
7	7	0111
8	8	1000
9	9	1001
A	10	1010
B	11	1011
C	12	1100
D	13	1101
E	14	1110
F	15	1111

is the reason why Java programs can run slower than programs that are directly compiled, such as programs written in the C programming language. Alternatively, the Java Virtual Machine may be physically coded as part of the CPU. For example, some cell phones have CPUs that can execute Java binary code.

There are two general types of software: *operating system software* and *application software*. Operating systems software provides the interface between the hardware of the computer and the application software. For example, the operating system of a computer allows programs to access input and output devices, such as the keyboard, the hard disk, the mouse, and the monitor. Most modern operating systems also provide Graphical User Interface (GUI) to the system. A different responsibility of the operating system is to allow programs to execute concurrently and share resources, such as the main memory and the hard disk. The application software in a computer is made up of the programs that are run by the end users. These include games, office software, and web browsers.

1.5 Type of Programming Languages

Computer software can be written using different programming languages. A programming language of first generation is machine code. To put it differently, this is a sequence of zeros and ones that the computer can understand. Such code can be represented, for example, in hexadecimal notation. A typical example of a machine instruction is to read data that is stored in a location of main memory. The problem with machine code is that it is low level and it is difficult for humans to interpret. A second-generation programming language is referred to as *Assembly language*. Now the instructions are written using English words (e.g., add, sub, move, etc.). There is a straightforward mapping between code written in an Assembly language and machine code. The disadvantage of Assembly is that it is a very low level language and writing Assembly code is difficult. A third-generation programming language provides high-level access to the data. Examples of third-generation programming languages include C, C++, and Java. An advantage of using a high-level programming language is that the programmer does not need to deal with physical main memory addresses. A compiler can translate a third-generation program into machine language. Alternatively, the programming code can be interpreted by an interpreter. There is also a fourth-generation programming language where the programmer describes the desired result without specifying how to retrieve it. Database languages, such as SQL, are typical examples of a fourth-generation programming language.

1.6   Brief History of Computer Games

One of the first computer games was developed in the Brookhaven National Laboratory in 1958. The name of the game was "Tennis for Two". A knob was used to define the trajectory and a button was used for hitting the ball. An oscilloscope was used for displaying the ball on the screen. A screen shot of the game is shown in Figure 1.4.

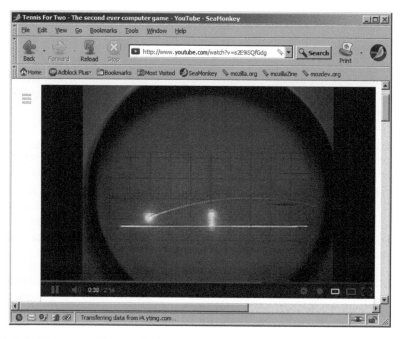

FIGURE 1.4: The game Tennis for Two. The screen shot is taken from a video made by the Brookhaven National Laboratory, a United States Government laboratory.

Later on, in 1971, the game Spacewar! was introduced. It is considered to be one of the first commercial games. It is a two-player game. Each player has control of a spaceship and attempts to destroy the other player. One thousand and five hundred coin-operated game consoles were created and placed in malls throughout the United States. See Figure 1.5 for a screen shot.

One year later, in 1972, the game Pong was introduced to the general public. It is widely believed to be the first mass video game and 19,000 consoles were sold. The game is played by two players. It has a moving ball and players try to keep the ball inside the playing area using a paddle. A screen shot of the game is shown in Figure 1.6.

One of the first color games was Space Invaders and it was produced by Atari in 1978. It involves defending the Earth from alien invaders by shooting rockets at them.

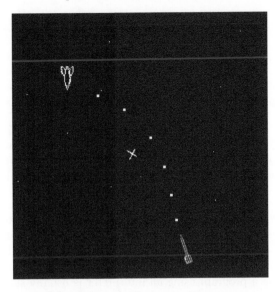

FIGURE 1.5: The game Spacewar.

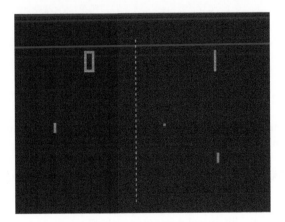

FIGURE 1.6: The game Pong.

Of course, no overview of computer game history will be complete without the legendary Pac-Man. The game was introduced in 1980 as a coin-operated game console and it was one of the most popular computer games of its time. It is one of the icons of the 1980s and it can still be found in 1980-style diners. The player controls Pac-Man through a maze, eating pac-dots. Of course, the Pac-Man had to run away from the bad guys that can eat him.

1.7 Summary

The chapter introduced basic computer concepts, such as the different types of hardware and software. It also described the different types of computer programming languages and different ways a computer program can be executed. The chapter finished with a brief overview of historical computer games.

1.8   Important Points

1. A computer consists of hardware and software. While the software can be easily changed by a programmer, the hardware of the computer can only be physically modified.

2. There are two types of software: application software and operating systems software. The operating system helps the application software communicate with the hardware. It also allows the application software to run smoothly by providing features, such as concurrent program execution and graphical user interface.

3. There are two ways to execute a program: using a compiler and using an interpreter. A compiler translates the program into executable code that can be later executed by the CPU. An interpreter, on the other hand, both translates and executes the program in real time. Since an interpreter needs to perform the additional task of translating the code, running a program using an interpreter is usually slower.

1.9   Exercises

1. Explain how a Java program is executed.

2. Convert the number 1353 to an 8-bit binary number. Next, convert the number to a hexadecimal number.

3. Convert the binary number 10101001 to decimal.

4. Convert the hexadecimal number 2FA3 to decimal.

5. What is your favorite historical computer game?

Chapter 2

Data Types and Conditional Statements

The chapter introduces the basic structure of a Java program. The main method is where the program starts executing. For now, we will use the console for reading and displaying data. Most programs will read data from the console and save it in main memory. The memory in a Java program is accessed through variables. These variables can be used to store integers, real numbers, and strings, among others. The chapter shows how to read data from the keyboard, save it in variables, manipulate the data, and then display the result. The chapter also shows how the keywords if and switch can be used to interrupt the sequential execution of a program.

2.1 Our First Java Program

Java code can be written using any editor, including Notepad. However, using an *Integrated Development Environment (IDE)* simplifies things. For example, an IDE can highlight in red Java code that has a syntactic error. It can also auto-format the code for us and can execute our code in a single click of the mouse. Lastly, an IDE gives us the ability to *debug* the code. Debugging allows us to execute Java code line by line. This allows one to monitor how the data changes as the program executes and helps isolate errors. This section will provide a quick overview of NetBeans, which is an IDE that is supported by Oracle, the same company that supports the Java language.

In most programming textbooks, the very first program displays "Hello World!" Let us follow this tradition and see how we can write this program in NetBeans. Before you continue reading, make sure you download and install the latest version of Java and then the latest version of NetBeans. Luckily, both Java and NetBeans are freely available for most operating systems. Next, start NetBeans and use the menu to create a new project. Select Java Application; see Figure 2.1.

On the next screen, see Figure 2.2, type in the name of the project, for example, HelloWorld. Under Project Location, NetBeans will show you the folder where the IDE will store the files. Make sure Create Main Class is not selected. If it is, then NetBeans

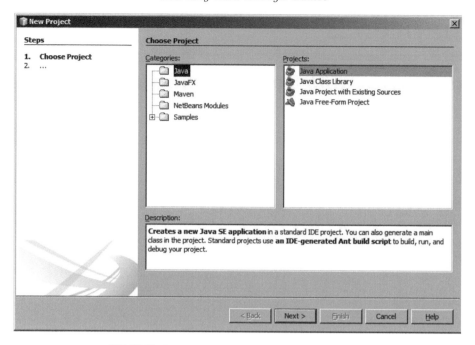

FIGURE 2.1: Creating a new Java project.

will create some default code. However, we will write all the code from scratch. Also, please make sure that `Set As Main Project` is selected. This will guarantee that the new project is the main project (i.e., the project that will be executed when the green forward arrow is clicked). As a last step, click the `Finish` button.

Next, we need to create the Java files. For now, our code will consist of a single file. In the project menu, expand the project `HelloWorld` and right-click on `Source Packages`. Select `New` and then `Java Class`. Type `Main` as the name of the class. Enter `helloworld` as the package name; see Figure 2.3. Click the `Finish` button.

A new file is created. It should contain roughly the following text.

```
package helloworld;

public class Main {

}
```

The only difference between this file and the file you will see will be the *comments*. Comments are usually written in a natural language, such as English. They are meant to be read by other humans and not by computers. Comments have no effect on how the program is executed. There are two ways to create comments. A one-line comment is created by typing // followed by some text description. Consider the following code.

```
package helloworld;

public class Main {
  public static void main(String args[]){ //start of program


  }
}
```

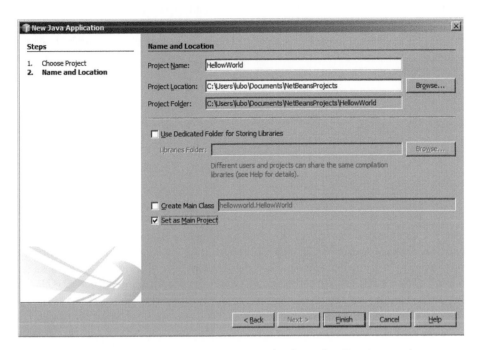

FIGURE 2.2: Setting the properties of a Java Application project.

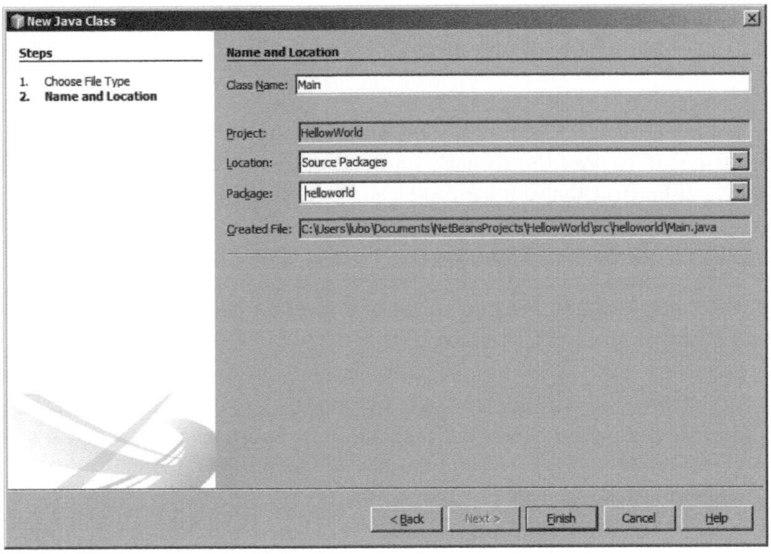

FIGURE 2.3: Creating a new Java class.

The comment describes the point where the program starts executing. Note that the //
comment syntax specifies that everything till the end of the line is a comment. However,
sometimes we want to specify a multi-line comment. In this case, we can use the following
syntax: /* ... */. The sequence /* is used to denote the start of the comment section and
the sequence */ is used to denote the end of comment section. Using the new syntax, our
previous comment can be rewritten as follows.

```
package helloworld;

public class Main {
    public static void main(String args[]) {/* your program starts
        executing here */


    }
}
```

Next, let us examine the code. The code `package helloworld` means that the file belongs to the package `helloworld`. One can think of a package as a software library that
contains several programs that are packaged together. If we did not select a package name
when creating the `Main` class, then this line would have been omitted and the class would
belong to the default package. Note that we created a class that is called `Main`. As a result,
a file `Main.java` was created.

> All Java files have extensions .java. Java requires that a file that is called `Main.java`
> contains a `public` class called `Main`. Every Java file contains exactly one public class.
> This class has the same name as the name of the file. All class names (and therefore
> Java file names) should start with a capital letter.

Packages are broken down into classes. For now, we can think of a class as an independent
part of the program, where more information will be provided in Chapter 6. Classes contain
methods and variables. The code in our example `Main` class contains the `main` method.

> Every Java application contains the `main` method. This is where the program
> starts executing. It is possible to have multiple `main` methods. In this case, however,
> one needs to explicitly specify which `main` method should be the starting point of the
> program.

Every method has a name. We can think of a method as "hired help". For example, we
can ask Joe to add two numbers. Similarly, we can ask a method to add two numbers. When
the method finishes executing, it can return some information. For now, we will assume that
the `main` method always has the syntax: `public static void main(String[] args)`. The
text in the parentheses means that the `main` method can take as input a set of strings. A
full overview of methods is presented in Chapter 4. More information about the parameters
of the `main` method are presented in Chapter 5.

Note that there is an opening brace (a.k.a., curly bracket) after the definition of the class
and after the definition of the method in our example code. Braces in Java are used to define
the beginning and end of a block. For example, all the code inside the `main` method (or any
other method) should always be delimited by an opening and closing brace. Similarly, the
start and end of a class is represented by an opening and closing brace, respectively.

The closing brace of a block is tabulated exactly under the statement that contains the opening brace. NetBeans formats the code automatically as you type. However, if for some reason the code is not formatted, you can auto-format it. Simply go to the menu **Source** and select **Format**.

Next, we will modify our code to print "Hello World!" To do so, simply type a statement that does the printing in the **main** method.

```
package helloworld;

public class Main {
  public static void main(String args[]){
    System.out.println("Hello World!");
  }
}
```

The statement: `System.out.println("Hello World!")` does the printing. The `println` method stands for print and then print new line. Alternatively, the statement `System.out.print("Hello World!")` will just print `Hello World` without moving to the next line. In Java, the symbol "\" is used to display a special character. For example, `System.out.print("Hello World!\n")` will display `Hello World` and then a new line. The reason is that the character "\n" displays a new line. For example, the statement `System.out.print("Hello\n World\n")` will display `Hello` on the first line and `World` on the next line.

Note that NetBeans supports auto-complete. For example, we can write **Sys** and press **Ctrl+Space**. **System** will automatically be displayed. We just need to press **Enter** to select it. The semicolon at the end denotes the end of the statement. Note that the statement will be underlined with a red line if we forget the semicolon. This is NetBeans's way of telling us that something is wrong. If we hover over the red line, we will see the message: ';' **expected**. Note that one needs to resolve all errors before the program can be executed.

In Java, spacing and new lines are not always important. For example, ten commands can be put on the same line. This is why putting semicolon after every statement is crucial.

A *literal* in Java is a constant that is specified in the code. For example, 2 is an example of an integer literal and 2.33 is an example of a literal that is a real number. Note that in the program the string `"Hello world!"` is surrounded by double quotes. All string literals in Java are surrounded in double quotes. Conversely, as we will see later, single characters are surrounded in single quotes. The `ptintln` line does the printing. Note that the line calls the `println` method. As a parameter to the method, the string `"Hello World!"` is passed. Note that every time we call a method, we need to specify in parentheses the parameters of the method. If the method takes as input no parameters, then we should type only the opening and closing parenthesis.

The first time that we run the program, we need to right-click on **Main.java** in the **Projects** view and select **Run File**. For sequential executions of the program, we can just click on the green arrow above the code. Note that the first time that we click the green arrow, it will ask us where the **main** method is. The reason is that there can potentially be multiple main methods. Figure 2.4 shows the result of executing the program. Note that one can run the program by clicking on the green arrow only if the correct project is selected

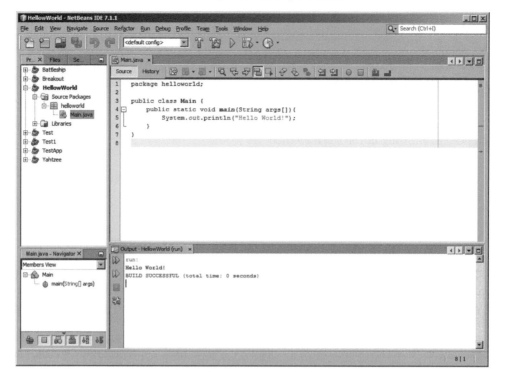

FIGURE 2.4: Example program execution.

as the main project. For example, one can change the main project by right-clicking on the project in the `Projects` view and selecting `Set as Main Project`.

2.2 Variables

Next, let us consider a more useful program. The user enters the temperature in degrees Celsius and the program converts the temperature to degrees Fahrenheit. Before implementing any program, we need to design an *algorithm* that solves the problem. An algorithm is a sequence of steps that provides a recipe that addresses the problem at the logical level. For our problem, an example algorithm can include the following steps.

1. Prompt the user to enter temperature in Celsius.

2. Read an integer form the keyboard and save it in memory location x.

3. Calculate the result of $y = 32 + (9/5) * x$, that is, the temperature in Fahrenheit, and save y in memory.

4. Print the value of y on the screen.

Before transforming the algorithm into Java code, we need to learn about variables in Java. Variables are a way of referring to cells in main memory. Java supports the primitive types that are shown in Table 2.1. A variable name should always start with a lowercase

TABLE 2.1: Java primitive types.

(*Type*)	(*Size*)	(*Values*)
byte	1 byte	−128 to 127
short	2 bytes	−32,768 to 32,767
int	4 bytes	−2,147,483,648 to 2,147,483,647
long	8 bytes	−9,223,372,036,854,775,808 to 9,223,372,036,854,775,807
float	4 bytes	-10^{96} to 10^{96}
double	8 bytes	-10^{384} to 10^{384}
boolean	1 bit	true of false
char	2 bytes	0 to 65,535

letter. For example, the following code declares, sets, and prints the value of an integer variable.

```
int i;
i = 3;
System.out.println(i);
```

The first line declares the variable i to be of type integer. The second line assigns the number 3 to the variable. The third line prints the value of the variable. The first two lines can be combined as follows.

```
int i = 3;
```

Note that several variables can be declared on the same line. For example, the following is a valid statement.

```
int i=3, j =4;
```

However, we can define multiple variables in a single line only when all the variables are of same type.

Note that a computer is not all powerful, that is, it cannot represent an arbitrary number. For example, we all know that there are infinitely many real numbers, while the main memory of a computer is finite. This is why Java defines *primitive variable types* that take a fixed amount of memory. For example, the byte type can be used to store a small integer, while the long type can be used to store up to a 19-digit integer. Most of the time, we want to store an integer that is not very big (less than 10 digits) and we will use the type int. Note that most types allow for both negative and positive integers to be stored. Usually, the first bit of the binary representation of a number indicates if the number is positive or negative.

There is a special syntax that is needed in Java to represent a long number. The letter "L" must be appended to the end of the number. For example, a variable of a long type can be defined as follows.

```
long ssn = 999333222L;
```

A float and a double must have a decimal point. For example, the number 3 is perceived as an int, while the number 3.0 is considered a double. A float must also have the letter F after it. Here is an example of declaring a variable of type float.

```
float pi = 3.1415F;
```

A byte is a number that is represented by a single byte (8 bits). A hexadecimal number can be specified by using the 0x prefix. For example, consider the following code snippet.

```
byte x = 0x2F;
System.out.println(x);
```

The hexadecimal number "2F" represents the binary number 0010 1111. If we convert this to an integer, we will get the number 47. Therefore, the program will print 47.

The `float` and `double` types can be used to represent a real number. What Table 2.1 does not show is that precision can be lost as the number is saved in main memory. For example, a `float` stores only the first few digits after the decimal dot. If we care about precision, then we are better off using a `double` (called double because it uses twice the size). Consider the following code snippet.

```
float x = 1/3F;
System.out.println(x);
```

It prints 0.33333334. Note that dividing an integer by a float gives us a float. As you can see, the result is not exactly 1/3. Alternatively, suppose we save the value of the division in a `double`.

```
double x = 1/3.0;
System.out.println(x);
```

We will now get 0.3333333333333333, which shows much better precision. Note that 1/3 is an irrational number and as such cannot be precisely stored using a `float` or a `double`. Throughout the book, we will not be concerned in saving main-memory space and therefore we will always use a `double` instead of a `float`. Similarly, we will always use an `int` instead of a `short`.

The second-to-last primitive type is `boolean`. It uses only one bit that can take the values `true` or `false`. The last primitive type `char` represents a character. It is used to store a character. About sixty-five thousand characters can be stored, which allows support for different international alphabets. Let us go back to our four-step algorithm. The first step involves printing a message to the screen. Here is one possible implementation.

```
System.out.print("Please enter temperature is Celsius: ");
```

> The instruction `System.out.print("...")` prints the string in the double quotes. If we want to print a string and then go to a new line, then we should use the syntax: `System.out.println("...")`.

The second step of the algorithm requires several commands. First, we need to allocate space to save the keyboard input. We can do that using the following syntax.

```
int x;
```

The statement allocates four bytes in main memory (i.e., enough space to store an integer) and makes x reference the location; see Figure 2.5. Next, we want to read an integer from the keyboard and save it in the variable x. We need to perform the following two operations in order to do that.

```
Scanner keyboard = new Scanner(System.in);
x = keyboard.nextInt();
```

The first line creates the `keyboard` object. The syntax for creating a new object is a little involved and is discussed in detail in Chapter 6. Note that `keyboard` is the name of a variable and it can be replaced with a variable name of our choice. The second line calls the `nextInt` method on the `keyboard` object. Note that a method is a routine that one can call. It is similar to calling a friend of yours and asking them to do you a favor. In this case, the "favor" will be reading an integer from the keyboard and returning the result. There are different methods that can be called on a `Scanner` object. For example, `nextDouble` reads

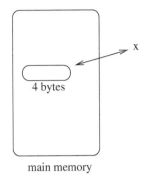

4 bytes

main memory

FIGURE 2.5: Allocating integer in main memory.

a double from the keyboard. Note that when we call a method, we can specify additional parameters inside the parentheses. However, even if no additional information is included, we still need to type the opening and closing parenthesis. This tells Java that we are calling a method and not simply referring to a variable.

Next, let us concentrate on the third step of the algorithm. The variable y is created and its value computed. Here is a possible implementation of the step.

```
double y;
double c = 9/5;
y = 32 + c*x;
```

Note that multiplication in Java is denoted by the character "*", while division is denoted by the character "/". This is standard for most programming languages. The second line of code calculates the value of the coefficient by which we will multiply the temperature in Celsius. Note that the command does two things: it declares the variable c as a double (i.e., a real number with double precision) and it sets the value of c. Note that every variable must be declared before it can be referenced. It is also the case that every variable can be defined only once. The third line sets the value of y. Note that Java allows arbitrary arithmetic expressions. Since multiplication has higher priority than addition, the multiplication of c and x will be done first and then the number 32 will be added, Conversely, if we wanted the addition to be done first, we could have used braces as follows.

```
y = (32 + c)*x;
```

Since parentheses have the highest precedence, the addition will be performed first and then the multiplication.

It is worthwhile to examine the assignment operator (a.k.a., =) in greater details. The left-hand side must always be a variable. Writing the following code simply does not make sense.

```
3 = x;
```

The right-hand side can be an expression that evaluates to a value. Of course, the type of this value must be compatible with the type of the left-hand-side variable. The assignment operator actually returns a value. This means that you can write Java code as shown below.

```
x=y=z=4;
```

This code will be executed from right to left. First, z will become equal to 4. The expression $z = 4$ will return the new value of z, that is, the number 4. Next, y will become equal to 4 and the assignment operator will return the new value of the variable y, that is, 4. Lastly, x will become equal to 4.

The final step of the algorithm is to display the value of y. This can be achieved by the following two lines.

```
System.out.print("The temperature in Fahrenheit is: ");
System.out.println(y);
```

The first line prints the string that is specified in the double quotes. Note that all string literals in Java need to be surrounded by double quotes. The second line prints the value of y. Note that the **print** method can take any input: for example, integer, double, character, and even an object. The second line of the code uses the **println** method instead of the **print** method because we want to print a new line at the end.

With small modifications, our degree Fahrenheit to degree Celsius program will look as follows.

```
1   package helloworld;
2   import java.util.*;
3
4   public class Main {
5     public static void main(String args[]){
6       int x;
7       double y,c;
8       System.out.print("Enter temperature is Celsius: ");
9       Scanner keyboard = new Scanner(System.in);
10      x=keyboard.nextInt();
11      c = 9/5;
12      y = 32+c*x;
13      System.out.print("The temperature in Fahrenheit is: ");
14      System.out.println(y);
15    }
16  }
```

Let us first examine the program line by line. Line 1 defines the package. From now on, for simplicity, we will create the programs in the default package and omit the package line. Note that defining the package is a statement and, as such, is followed by a semicolon. If we delete the semicolon, NetBeans will underline the whole line in red. If we hover over the red line with the mouse, it will tell us that we have forgotten the semicolon. Line 2 tells Java that we want to use the `java.util` library. This is where most of the utility classes are stored. For example, we need this library in order to read input from the keyboard. Since this is such an important library, we will include it in almost every program. Note that some of our example programs will skip the `import` section. In order to see how to reproduce the `include` lines, delete the second line of the code. The `Scanner` class will now be underlined in red indicating an error. Right-click on the code that is underlined in red and select **Fix Imports**. You will be given a chance to add the import that you need. In our case, we can select `java.util.Scanner`. Note that `import java.util.*` imports all classes from the library `java.util`. Conversely, the statement `import java.util.Scanner` imports only the `Scanner` class library.

A class that is underlined in red can mean that we have forgotten an import. The easiest way to fix the error is to right-click on the red code and select `Fix Imports`. When you have a program that does not compile, hover with the mouse over the red parts of the program and see what the errors are. If NetBenas reports that a class is undefined, you may have misspelled the class or simply forgotten to include an import. In the second case, selecting `Fix Imports` will solve the problem. If the line is still underlined in red after selecting `Fix Imports`, then the error is not forgetting to import a library.

Lines 4–16 define the `Main` class. The opening brace at Line 4 defines the beginning of the class, while the corresponding closing brace at Line 16 represents the end of the class. In every class, we can include one or more methods. Inside the `Main` class, we have a single `main` method: Lines 5–15. Every program must have a main method; this is where the program starts executing. Note that we have moved the definitions of the variables to the top of the method. In Java, variables can be declared anywhere throughout the code. However, it is good software practice to define them at the beginning of a block. Blocks in Java are defined by opening and closing braces.

Every variable has a *scope*. This is the context in which the variable is valid. After a variable goes out of scope, it is no longer valid and it cannot be referenced. The reason is that the memory for the variable is freed after the variables goes out of scope. The score of a variable is defined by the inner-most pair of opening/closing braces surrounding the variable. Of course, the life of a variable starts with its definition and it cannot be referenced before it is defined.

For example, the scope of the variables x, y, and c is the `main` method. This is the inner-most pair of opening/closing braces surrounding the variable definition. Note that a variable definition must also precede the first use of the variable. For example, we cannot write the statement `c = 9/5` before the statement `double y`.

The variables y and c are defined on the same line (Line 7). One can define several variables in the same statement as long as all the variables are of the same type. Line 8 asks the user to enter the temperature in Celsius. Line 9 declares a `Scanner` object, that is, an object that is needed to read input. Line 10 reads an integer from the keyboard and saves it in the variable x. Lines 11–12 compute the value of c and y, respectively. Note that the order of the two lines matters. One should not use the variable c before its value is initialized. Line 13 prints a statement that the temperature in Fahrenheit will be displayed and Line 14 displays the temperature.

Let us run the program. If we enter 0 degrees Celsius, then we get 32.0 degrees Fahrenheit. It seems that our program works correctly. Just to be sure, let us run the program again. If we enter 40 degrees Celsius, we get 72 degrees Fahrenheit. This, however, is incorrect output. We can calculate that $32 + \frac{5}{9} \cdot 40 = 104$. This means that our program has a bug. Fortunately, we do not have to physically search for the rodent. Instead, we can *debug* the program.

Debugging is executing a program line by one. This allows us to examine how the variables change as the program progresses.

Before we can debug a program in NetBeans, we need to set a *breakpoint*. A breakpoint is a place where the program will stop executing. After the breakpoint, we can debug the program line by line. In order to set a breakpoint, click on the number of the line. In our case, we will set a breakpoint at Line 8. After we set a breakpoint, we will see a red circle at the line of the breakpoint. Note that we can only set a breakpoint at a line that performs an operation, that is, Line 8 is the first line where we can set a breakpoint. We can also set a method breakpoint at Line 5. We will then see a red triangle instead of a circle. This is called a method breakpoint and the program is interrupted for debugging before the method is executed.

In order to debug the program, we will select **Debug** and then **Debug Main Project** from the menu. We will see Line 8 marked in green. This is the line that is currently been executed. We will press F8 to move to the next line. Next, we will press F8 two more times and enter the temperature in Celsius. Now we are at Line 11. We will press F8 again to move to Line 12. We will hover with the mouse over the variable c and we will see that c is equal to 1.0. However, we expected that c will be equal to $\frac{9}{5} = 1.80$. We have *isolated* the error. We will press the square red button at the bottom of the screen to stop the debugger. Our error is due to *integer division*.

> The result of dividing two integers is always an integer. The result is always rounded down to the lowest number. For example, 8/9 is equal to 0.89, which is rounded down to 0. In other words, Java calculates 8/9 as 0. If we want the result to be a double and not an integer, we need to convert one of the two arguments to a double before performing the operation.

There are two popular ways to convert an integer to a double. The first way is to write **(double)** before the integer. This is called a *casting* operation and it converts the integer to a double. In our example, we can fix our program by rewriting Line 11 as follows.

```
c=9/((double)5);
```

In this case the number 5 is converted to a double. Alternatively, we can simply divide 9 by 5.0 and write the following code.

```
c=9/5.0;
```

Note that when we divide two variables, we cannot simply put .0 at the end of the variable. We need to either cast the variable to a double or multiply it by 1.0. For example, Line 11 can also be rewritten as follows.

```
c=(9*1.0)/5;
```

The result of an arithmetic operation that takes as input two integers is always an integer. However, an operation that takes as input an integer and a double will return a double. This is why multiplying by 1.0 is a common way of converting an integer to a double.

Correct Line 11 and run the program again. Now it should be working. We have learned several valuable lessons. First, just because the program works on one example does not mean that it is correct. We need to run multiple tests to convince ourselves that the program is working. Even then, we can never be 100% sure that the program works. However, performing multiple tests can give us some confidence in the correctness of the program. When we find a test case for which the program fails, we need to debug the program line by line and isolate the error. Once the error is isolated, fixing it is not that difficult. It is common for a novice programmer to spend a lot of time debugging. As you get more experienced, the debugging time will decrease.

Note that Lines 11 and 12 can be merged into the following single line.

```
y = 32 + (9.0/5)*x;
```

Recall that the left side of the assignment operation must always be a single variable. The right side of the assignment operation can be any expression that involves the four basic arithmetic operations: +, -, *, and /. Parentheses are used to define the order of operations. In the above example, the parentheses were used to specify that the division should be performed before the multiplication. Note that division and multiplication have higher precedence than addition and subtraction. This is why the multiplication in our example is performed before the addition. Operations with the same precedence (e.g., multiplication and division) are performed left to right. Therefore, we could have actually omitted the parentheses and rewritten the code as follows.

```
y = 32 + 9.0/5*x;
```

2.3   Random Numbers and the `if` Statement

Converting degrees Celsius to degrees Fahrenheit was not a real game. However, we needed this rudimentary example in order to set the stage. We are now ready to create our first game. Of course, we cannot start right off the bat with a cool game that has graphical user interface and moving objects; we will save such examples for later. Instead, we will create a game that helps elementary school students learn the multiplication table. The program will create two random one-digit numbers and ask the user to multiply them. If the user gives the correct answer, then the program will congratulate them. However, if the user does not type the correct response, then the program will suggest that they study harder. Here is an outline of the steps of the program.

1. Create two random numbers x and y.

2. Display the two random numbers and ask the user to enter the result of $x * y$.

3. Read the user input in the variable z.

4. If $z = x * y$, then congratulate the user. Otherwise, ask the user to study harder.

Note that this program is different from our first program in two ways. First, it involves the generation of a random number. Second, it contains a decision point. Depending on the user input, the program will take one of two possible routes. In other words, the program is not going to execute sequentially as our first program.

Create a new project and a new class called **Arithmetic**. This time, define the class to be part of the default package. Add the **main** method and import the library **java.util**. You should have the following code.

```
import java.util.*;

public class Arithmetic {
  public static void main(String[] args){

  }
}
```

Type `Math.random` inside the `main` method (i.e., inside the braces that surround the body of the method). You will see a description of the method. It returns a double between 0 and 1, where the method can return 0 but it will never return 1. If we multiply this number by 10, then we will get a number between 0 (inclusive) and 10 (exclusive). If we cast this number to an integer, then we will get an integer between 0 and 9, which is exactly what we want. Here is the implementation of Step 1 of the algorithm.

```
int x = (int) (Math.random()*10);
int y = (int) (Math.random()*10);
```

Note that the class `Math` provides other useful functions. For example `Math.abs(-3)` will return the absolute value of a number. Alternatively, `Math.sqrt(2.3)` returns the square root of a number. Note that the input and the output of the function is of type `double`. The `Math.max` and `Math.min` functions are also useful for finding the max and min of two numbers.

Note that the first line performs two tasks. It declares the variable x to be an integer and it sets the value of x. Note that a variable cannot be used before its value is initialized. Therefore, it is common to declare a variable and set its initial value in the same statement. The expression `(int)` converts (or *casts*) the double to an integer. Note that the casting operation always rounds down the number. For example, if the parentheses are missing, then the cast will apply to the result of `Math.random()`. Since this number is always greater than or equal to 0 and smaller than 1, casting it to an integer will return 0. In other words, omitting the parentheses will make x equal to 0.

Step 2 asks the user to compute `x*y`. It can be coded as follows.

```
System.out.print(x+"*"+y+" = ");
```

Note that the parameter to the `println` method contains several expressions connected with "+". The operator "+" is used to `concatenate` two strings. Of course, one of the parameters must be a string. If the other parameter is not a string, then it is automatically converted to a string. For example, if $x = 5$ and $y = 6$, then the above statement will print "5*6= ".

Step 3 reads an integer from the keyboard. It can be implemented as follows.

```
int z;
Scanner keyboard = new Scanner(System.in);
z = keyboard.nextInt();
```

The last step needs to check if the user entered the correct number. Here is the implementation.

```
if(z == x*y){
    System.out.println("Congratulations!");
} else {
    System.out.println("You need more practice");
}
```

The implementation uses a new `if-else` structure; see Figure 2.6. An opening and closing parentheses always follow an `if` statement. If the condition inside the parentheses evaluates to true, then the first block is executed (a block is defined by opening and closing braces). As the figure suggests, after the first block is executed the flow of control jumps to the line after the end of the `else` block. Conversely, if the condition in the parentheses is false, then the second block (i.e., the block after the `else` statement) is executed. The `==` operator is used to compare two numbers. It returns `true` when the numbers are the same and `false` otherwise. Java provides additional comparison operators; see Table 2.2. The `==` and the `!=` operators may be new to the reader.

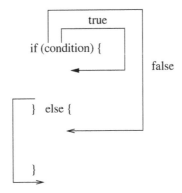

FIGURE 2.6: The `if-else` construct.

TABLE 2.2: Java comparison operators.

Operator	Meaning	Example
==	equal	$3 == 3$
>=	greater or equal	$3 >= 3$
>	greater	$4 > 3$
<	smaller	$3 < 5$
<=	smaller or equal	$3 <= 3$
!=	different	$5! = 3$

The operators = and == are very different. For example, the statement i = 3 assigns the value of 3 to the integer i. Conversely, the condition (i == 3) checks if the value of i is equal to 3. Remember to never use a single equality inside a condition. Inside a conditional statement, always use double equality.

The operator == returns `true` when the two operands are equal. Conversely, the operator != returns `true` when the two operands are distinct. For example, the last two lines of our code can be rewritten as follows.

```java
if(z != x*y){
  System.out.println("You need more practice");
} else {
  System.out.println("Congratulations!");
}
```

Note that it is not required that an `if` statement has an `else` part; see Figure 2.7. For example, the last two lines of our program can be rewritten as follows.

```java
if(z == x*y){
    System.out.println("Congratulations!");
    return;
}
System.out.println("You need more practice");
```

The statement `return` simply terminates the method. A return statement inside the `main` method terminates the program. Therefore, the last line of code in the above code snippet will only be executed when z is different from $x * y$. The `if-else` construct may become difficult to understand when there are multiple `if` and `if-else` statements nested

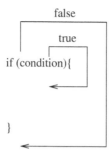

FIGURE 2.7: The if construct.

in each other. Using the above trick and avoiding the else part altogether is preferred when possible.

In general, it is not required to start a new block after an if statement. For example, here is perfectly valid Java code.

```
if(z == x*y)
    System.out.println("Congratulations!");
    return;
System.out.println("You need more practice");
```

However, this code is not equivalent to the previous snippet of code and does not accomplish our goal. Since the braces are missing, the if statement is applied only to the first statement that follows. Therefore, the return statement will always be executed (regardless of whether $z = x * y$) and the last line of code becomes unreachable. It is good software practice to always create a block after an if statement by typing opening and closing braces. This will eliminate mistakes as shown above. Another common mistake by novice programmers is to add a semicolon after an if statement. Consider the following code snippet.

```
if(z == x*y);
{
    System.out.println("Congratulations!");
    return;
}
System.out.println("You need more practice");
```

The semicolon will terminate the if statement. The code will print Congratulations! and exist the program regardless of the value of the condition inside the if statement. Therefore, it is a good idea to put the opening brace at the same line as the if statement to remind us that we should never put a semicolon after an if statement.

> Always crate a new block after an if statement. Never put a semicolon after an if statement.

Below is a listing of our program. Run it and make sure it works correctly. Remember to run it several times. Note that testing a program that generates random numbers is a little tricky. You can get different data every time you run the program.

```
import java.util.*;
public class Arithmetic {
    public static void main(String[] args) {
```

```
int x = (int) (Math.random() * 10);
int y = (int) (Math.random() * 10);
Scanner keyboard = new Scanner(System.in);
System.out.print(x + "*" + y + " = ");
int z = keyboard.nextInt();
if (z == x * y) {
  System.out.println("Congratulations!");
} else {
  System.out.println("You need more practice");
}
}
}
```

Note how the start of a block and the closing brace at the end of the block should be aligned. Remember that we can always select the `Source-Format` menu in NetBeans to format our code.

2.4   Combining Conditions

Our next program calculates the grade of a student. It takes as input the student's numerical grade and it converts it to a letter grade. Here is the algorithm that we will use.

1. Ask the user to enter grade as number.

2. Read the number in variable x.

3. Declare a variable *grade*.

4. If $x >= 90$ and $x <= 100$, then set grade to be equal to 'A' .

5. If $x >= 80$ and $x < 90$, then set grade to be equal to 'B' .

6. If $x >= 70$ and $x < 80$, then set grade to be equal to 'C' .

7. If $x >= 60$ and $x < 70$, then set grade to be equal to 'D' .

8. If $x < 60$, then set grade to be equal to 'F'.

Steps 1–3 are easy. A possible implementation follows.

```
System.out.print("Enter numeric grade: ");
int x;
Scanner keyboard = new Scanner(System.in);
x = keyboard.nextInt();
char grade;
```

Next, we need to check if the grade is between 90 and 100. We can do this using two nested `if` statements.

```
if (x >= 90){
  if(x <= 100){
    grade = 'A';
  }
}
```

TABLE 2.3: Java operators on Boolean values.

Operator	Meaning	Example
&&	and	T&&T=T T&&F=F F&&F=F
||	or	T||F=T T||T=T F||F=F
!	negation	!T=F, !F=T

Note that a character literal, such as 'A' , is enclosed in single quotes. Conversely, a string value, such as "cat", is enclosed in double quotes. The above implementation is not optimal. The second if statement can be misleading. A user may interpret it that grade='A' when $x <= 100$. However, x must be also greater or equal to 90. Nested if statements can quickly get confusing to interpret. Therefore, a good programming practice is to never have too many nested if statements and avoid them if at all possible. A better implementation is to combine the two if statements into a single if statement. Here is how this can be done.

```
if (x >= 90 && x <= 100){
    grade = 'A';
}
```

The "&&" operator is an operator that works on boolean values (i.e., true/false values). It is the logical "and". For example, the "+" operator can be used to add two integers and return an integer. Conversely, the "&&" operator takes as input two boolean values and produces a boolean value. Java supports three operators on Boolean values; see Table 2.3.

For example, if we want to give a letter grade of 'O' (i.e., other) when the numeric grade is smaller than 0 or bigger than 100, we can write the following code.

```
if (x > 100 || x < 0){
    grade = 'O';
}
```

The operator "——" is the logical or operator. Note that the condition (x>100 && x<0) is not meaningful because x cannot be bigger than 100 and smaller than 0 at the same time. The next statement is a rewrite of the last code snippet that uses the negation operator.

```
if !(x <= 100 && x >= 0){
    grade = 'O';
}
```

We will go inside the if statement when it is not true that x is between 0 and 100. Note that the following code snippet will not compile.

```
if !(0 <= x <= 100){
        grade = 'O';
}
```

The reason is that $0 <= x <= 100$ is not a valid condition. This is a statement that can be written in math, but it is not recognized by the Java compiler. One rule to remember is that the condition of an if statement must always be surrounded by parentheses. For example, the following code snippet will produce a syntax error.

```
if x < 60{
    grade = 'F';
}
```

Our complete program is shown next.

```java
import java.util.*;

public class Grade {
  public static void main(String[] args) {
    int x;
    char c='0';
    System.out.println("Enter numeric grade: ");
    Scanner keyboard = new Scanner(System.in);
    x = keyboard.nextInt();
    if(x <= 100 && x >= 90){
      c = 'A';
    }
    if(x < 90 && x >= 80){
      c = 'B';
    }
    if(x < 80 && x >= 70){
      c = 'C';
    }
    if(x < 70 && x >= 60){
      c = 'D';
    }
    if(x < 60 && x >= 0){
      c = 'F';
    }
    System.out.println("Your letter grade is: "+c);
  }
}
```

Note that the variable c needs to be given a default value. If it is not, then the last line of the code (i.e., the line that does the final printing) will have an error. The reason is that it is possible that not a single **if** condition fires. In this case, the value of c will not be defined and Java will not know what to print. Note as well that the Java compiler is not very smart. Even if it is logically the case that one of the if conditions must always be true, Java will not be able to determine this. Therefore, it is a good idea to give a default value to every variable. The above program will report grade of 0 when the grade is not between 0 and 100.

2.5 The String Class

Next, let us consider the reverse problem. The user enters the letter grade and the program presents the numeric grade. Here is a possible algorithm to solve the problem.

1. Ask the user to enter the grade as a string.

2. Save the result in the string s.

3. If s is equal to "A", then tell the user the grade is between 90 and 100.

4. If s is equal to "B", then tell the user the grade is between 80 and 90.

5. If s is equal to "C", then tell the user the grade is between 70 and 80.

6. If s is equal to "D", then tell the user the grade is between 60 and 70.

TABLE 2.4: Comparison of `String` elements.

What we want to write	*What we must write*
s1==s2	s1.equals(s2) or s1.compareTo(s2)==0
s1>s2	s1.compareTo(s2)>0
s1<s2	s1.compareTo(s2)<0

7. If `s` is equal to `"F"`, then tell the user the grade is lower than 60.

The first two lines of the algorithm can be implemented as follows.

```
System.out.print("Enter letter grade: ");
Scanner keyboard = new Scanner(System.in);
String s = keyboard.next();
```

The code uses the `next` method. It returns the next string that is typed. Note that Java does not have a `nextChar` method that reads a single character from the keyboard. The `next` method reads characters from the input until a delimiter, such as space or new line, is reached. If we want to read a whole line from the keyboard, then we can call the `nextLine` method. Note as well that a `String` behaves similar to a primitive type (e.g., integer). We can define the string variable *s* by simply typing the following command.

```
String s;
```

Similarly, we can assign a value to a string as follows.

```
s = "cat";
```

Remember that string literals are surrounded by double quotes. One major difference between a `String` and the other primitive types is that strings cannot be compared the same way as integers. You can still compare two strings for equality, but you need to use the `equals` method instead of "==". Similarly, you can compare two strings relative to their lexicographical ordering. A lexicographical ordering of two strings relates to how they will appear in a dictionary. For example, the string `"abc"` will appear before the string `"de"`. Note that every character has an ASCII code; see Figure 2.8. Two strings are compared by comparing the ASCII code of their first character. If the first characters have the same code, then the ASCII code of the second characters are compared and so on. The `compareTo` method is used to compare two strings. Table 2.4 summarizes the two methods.

Note that the `compareTo` method returns a positive integer when the first string is bigger, 0 when the two strings are the same, and a negative integer when the first string is smaller. Therefore, in order to check if two strings are the same, we can either write `s1.equals(s2)` or `s1.compareTo(s2) == 0`.

Going back to our original problem, we can check the value of the string `s` as follows.

```
if(s.equals("A")){
   System.out.println("Your grade is between 90 and 100");
}
if(s.equals("B")){
   System.out.println("Your grade is between 80 and 89");
}
if(s.equals("C")){
   System.out.println("Your grade is between 70 and 79");
}
if(s.equals("D")){
    System.out.println("Your grade is between 60 and 69");
}
```

Dec	Hex	Char	Dec	Hex	Char	Dec	Hex	Char	Dec	Hex	Char
0	00	Null	32	20	Space	64	40	@	96	60	`
1	01	Start of heading	33	21	!	65	41	A	97	61	a
2	02	Start of text	34	22	"	66	42	B	98	62	b
3	03	End of text	35	23	#	67	43	C	99	63	c
4	04	End of transmit	36	24	$	68	44	D	100	64	d
5	05	Enquiry	37	25	%	69	45	E	101	65	e
6	06	Acknowledge	38	26	&	70	46	F	102	66	f
7	07	Audible bell	39	27	'	71	47	G	103	67	g
8	08	Backspace	40	28	(	72	48	H	104	68	h
9	09	Horizontal tab	41	29	)	73	49	I	105	69	i
10	0A	Line feed	42	2A	*	74	4A	J	106	6A	j
11	0B	Vertical tab	43	2B	+	75	4B	K	107	6B	k
12	0C	Form feed	44	2C	,	76	4C	L	108	6C	l
13	0D	Carriage return	45	2D	-	77	4D	M	109	6D	m
14	0E	Shift out	46	2E	.	78	4E	N	110	6E	n
15	0F	Shift in	47	2F	/	79	4F	O	111	6F	o
16	10	Data link escape	48	30	0	80	50	P	112	70	p
17	11	Device control 1	49	31	1	81	51	Q	113	71	q
18	12	Device control 2	50	32	2	82	52	R	114	72	r
19	13	Device control 3	51	33	3	83	53	S	115	73	s
20	14	Device control 4	52	34	4	84	54	T	116	74	t
21	15	Neg. acknowledge	53	35	5	85	55	U	117	75	u
22	16	Synchronous idle	54	36	6	86	56	V	118	76	v
23	17	End trans. block	55	37	7	87	57	W	119	77	w
24	18	Cancel	56	38	8	88	58	X	120	78	x
25	19	End of medium	57	39	9	89	59	Y	121	79	y
26	1A	Substitution	58	3A	:	90	5A	Z	122	7A	z
27	1B	Escape	59	3B	;	91	5B	[	123	7B	{
28	1C	File separator	60	3C	<	92	5C	\	124	7C		
29	1D	Group separator	61	3D	=	93	5D	]	125	7D	}
30	1E	Record separator	62	3E	>	94	5E	^	126	7E	~
31	1F	Unit separator	63	3F	?	95	5F	_	127	7F	□

FIGURE 2.8: ASCII code table.

```java
if(s.equals("F")){
    System.out.println("Your grade is below 60");
}
```

The full program is listed below.

```java
import java.util.*;

public class Grade {
    public static void main(String[] args) {
        System.out.print("Enter letter grade: ");
        Scanner keyboard = new Scanner(System.in);
        String s = keyboard.next();
        if (s.equals("A")) {
            System.out.println("Your grade is between 90 and 100");
        }
        if (s.equals("B")) {
            System.out.println("Your grade is between 80 and 89");
        }
        if (s.equals("C")) {
            System.out.println("Your grade is between 70 and 79");
        }
        if (s.equals("D")) {
```

```
      System.out.println("Your grade is between 60 and 69");
    }
    if (s.equals("F")) {
      System.out.println("Your grade is below 60");
    }
  }
}
```

2.6 The switch Statement

It may get tedious to write code that compares a variable to one of several possibilities using if statements. To simplify the process, Java supports the switch statement. The rewrite using the switch statement is shown next.

```java
import java.util.*;

public class Grade {
  public static void main(String[] args) {
    System.out.print("Enter letter grade: ");
    Scanner keyboard = new Scanner(System.in);
    String s = keyboard.next();
    switch(s) {
      case "A":
        System.out.println("Your grade is between 90 and 100");
        break;
      case "B":
        System.out.println("Your grade is between 80 and 89");
        break;
      case "C":
        System.out.println("Your grade is between 70 and 79");
        break;
      case "D":
        System.out.println("Your grade is between 60 and 69");
        break;
      case "F":
        System.out.println("Your grade is below 60");
        break;
      default:
        System.out.println("I have no idea what is your grade!");
    }
  }
}
```

The general structure of the switch statement is shown in Figure 2.9. Note that the default part is optional. In the figure, if the variable is equal to 2, then the control flow jumps to the line "case 2: ...". Note that this is the only jump that occurs in the switch statement. After the program jumps to that line, it will continue executing. If there is nothing to change the control flow again, the program will execute the code for "case 3: ..." and "default: ...".

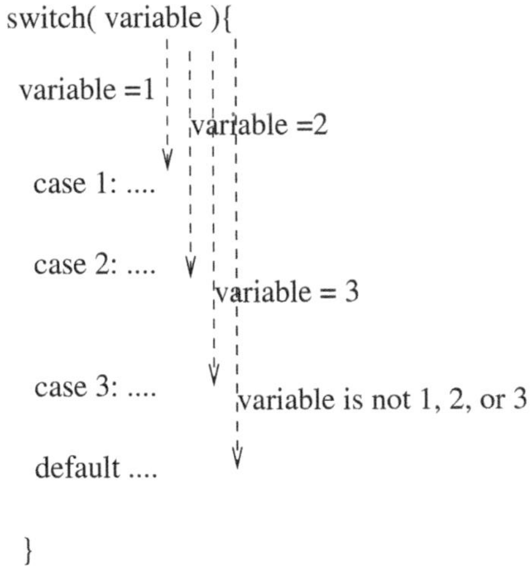

FIGURE 2.9: The switch statement.

A switch statement can only be used to substitute a set of if statements that check for **equality**. We cannot use an if statement to check for inequality (e.g., $>= 3$). Java supports a switch statement only on variables of type int, char, and String. Java does not support a switch statement on doubles.

A switch statement checks the value of the variable inside the parentheses. If it is equal to the first case value, then the program jumps to this case and continues executing. Usually, a break statement is put at the end of every case block in order to guarantee that only one case statement is executed. For example, if the break statements are removed from the above code and the user enters the string "A", then all print statements will be executed.

The break statement exits out of the current switch statement and goes to the first line immediately after the switch block. Usually, a break statement is required at the end of each case block in order for the switch statement to work properly. A break statement is not required after the last switch block (assuming there is no default block) because the program exits the switch statement after that anyway.

Note that the switch syntax allows a default option. In the above code, if the input string is not equal to "A","B", "C", "D", or "F", then only the last print statement will be executed.

2.7   The Conditional Operator

It seems tedious to use an if-else construct even when we have a single line in both the if and else blocks. In some cases, Java allows us to substitute the if-else statement with a one-liner. We can do that when we assign different values to the same variable based on the validity of a condition. Recall our arithmetic game example.

```
1   import java.util.*;
2   public class Arithmetic {
3     public static void main(String[] args) {
4       int x = (int) (Math.random() * 10);
5       int y = (int) (Math.random() * 10);
6       Scanner keyboard = new Scanner(System.in);
7       System.out.print(x + "*" + y + " = ");
8       int z = keyboard.nextInt();
9       if (z == x * y) {
10        System.out.println("Congratulations!");
11      } else {
12        System.out.println("You need more practice");
13      }
14    }
15  }
```

We will rewrite the code to use the new construct. We will create a variable output of type String. The value of the output will depend on whether the user guessed the correct result. Now Lines 9–13 can be rewritten as follows.

```
String output;
if (z == x * y) {
  output = "Congratulations!";
} else {
  output = "You need more practice";
}
System.out.println(output);
```

Now, we can use the "?:" constructor to rewrite the code as follows.

```
String output;
output = (z == x * y) ? "Congratulations!" : "You need more practice";
System.out.println(output);
```

> The general syntax of the conditional operator is x = (condition)? value1 : value2. If the condition is true, then x becomes equal to value1. Otherwise, x is assigned the value of value2.

The rewritten game follows.

```
import java.util.*;
public class Arithmetic {
  public static void main(String[] args) {
    int x = (int) (Math.random() * 10);
    int y = (int) (Math.random() * 10);
    Scanner keyboard = new Scanner(System.in);
    System.out.print(x + "*" + y + " = ");
    int z = keyboard.nextInt();
    String output;
    output = (z == x * y) ? "Congratulations!" : "You need more
        practice";
    System.out.println(output);
  }
```

}

As you can see, the new version is more compact and does not use an `if-else` construct. However, the rewrite only applies when one of two different values is assigned to the same variable based on the validity of a condition.

2.8 Summary

The chapter presented an introduction to Java programming. Using an integrated development environment, such as NetBeans, simplifies the development process. NetBeans not only helps us identify compiler errors instantly, but also allows us to execute our program line by line and monitor how the variables change (a.k.a., debug the program).

The cornerstones of any program are the variables. They can be thought as the "memory" of the program. Throughout the execution of the program, we use variables to save important data. Java allows us to create variables that store characters, integers, reals, and strings, among others. Note that every type has a restriction. For example, we cannot store a number that is bigger than three billion inside a variable of type `int`. Similarly, we can only store a finite number of different real numbers inside a variable of type `double` and loss of precision is common. Sometimes, the value of a variable can be supplied from the keyboard. In other cases, the value of a variable can be the result of some computation. As we saw, we can even assign a variable to be equal to a random number.

Managing the control flow is an important part of every program. For example, sometimes we want to branch our program based on the value of a condition. In this case, we can use an `if` statement. Similarly, we can use a `switch` statement when we want to check if a variable is equal to one of several values, where a `switch` statement can only be used on integers, characters, and strings. A conditional operator is used when we want to assign one of two values to a variable based on the validity of a Boolean condition.

2.9 Syntax

- `int i` ⇒ Declares the variable i to be an integer.

- `i = 3` ⇒ Assigns the value 3 to the variable i.

- `double d` ⇒ Declares the variable d to be a double.

- `d = 32.22` ⇒ Assigns the value 32.22 to the variable d.

- `char c` ⇒ Declares the variable c to be a character.

- `c = 'a'` ⇒ Assigns the value 'a' to the variable c.

- `long l = 2342412L` ⇒ Declares the variable l to be of type `long` and assigns the value 2342412 to it.

- `float f = 22432.222F` ⇒ Declares the variables f to be of type `float` and assigns the value 22432.222 to it.

- `String s` ⇒ Declares the variable `s` of type String.

- `s = "abc"` ⇒ Assigns the value `"abc"` to the variable `s`.

- `d = Math.random()` ⇒ Assigns a random number between 0(inclusive) and 1(exclusive) to the variable `d`.

- `s1.compareTo(s2)` ⇒ Returns a positive integer if `s1 > s2`, 0 if `s1 = s2`, and a negative integer if `s1 < s2` (the string order is lexicographical).

- `s1.equals(s2)` ⇒ Returns `true` when the strings are the same and `false` otherwise.

- `if(a > b) {...}` ⇒ If `a > b`, then the block is executed.

- `if(a > b) {...} else {...}` ⇒ If `a > b`, then only the first block is executed. Otherwise, only the second block is executed.

- `a==b` ⇒ True when `a = b`.

- `a!=b` ⇒ True when `a ≠ b`.

- `a>=b` ⇒ True when `a ≥ b`.

- `a<=b` ⇒ True when `a ≤ b`.

- `a>b && c>d` ⇒ True when `a>b` and `c>d`.

- `a>b || c>d` ⇒ True when `a>b` or `c>d`.

- `!(a==b)` ⇒ True when the variables `a` and `b` are different.

- `switch(i) { case 4: ... break; case 5: ... break; ... default: ... }` ⇒ If `i=4`, then the statements for the first case are executed. If `i=5`, then the statements for the second case are executed. If `i` is not equal to any of the case values, then the statements for the default case are executed.

- `System.out.println("hello")` ⇒ Prints `hello` followed by a new line.

- `System.out.print("hello\n")` ⇒ Prints `hello` followed by a new line.

- `System.out.print("hello")` ⇒ Prints `hello`.

- `Scanner keyboard = new Scanner(System.in)` ⇒ Creates a scanner object.

- `int i = keyboard.nextInt()` ⇒ Reads the next integer from the keyboard into the variable `i`.

- `double d = keyboard.nextDouble()` ⇒ Reads the next double from the keyboard into the variable `d`.

- `String s = keyboard.next()` ⇒ Reads the next string from the keyboard into the variable `s`.

- `String s = keyboard.nextLine()` ⇒ Reads the next line from the keyboard into the variable `s`.

- `x = (a>b) ? y : z` ⇒ If `a>b`, then `x` becomes equal to `y`. Otherwise, `x` becomes equals to `z`.

- `int i = (int) 32.94` ⇒ Converts the number 32.94 to an integer. The result is always rounded down. The integer `i` will become equal to 32.

- `int i = 2/3` ⇒ The result of integer division is an integer. The result is rounded down. Therefore, the variable `i` will become equal to 0.

- `double f = 2/3.0` ⇒ The variable `f` will become equal to approximately 2/3. The reason is that the result of dividing an integer by a double is a double.

- `return` ⇒ Exists a method.

- `int a = Math.max(b,c)` ⇒ Finds the max of two numbers.

- `int a = Math.min(b,c)` ⇒ Finds the min of two numbers.

- `int a = Math.abs(b)` ⇒ Finds the absolute value of a number.

- `double a = Math.sqrt(d)` ⇒ Finds the square root of a double.

2.10 Important Points

1. A file called `Foo.java` must include exactly one public class called `Foo`.

2. Every Java program has a `main` method where the program starts executing.

3. *Debugging* is executing a Java program line by line and monitoring the values of the variables. Use debugging to isolate errors in your code. Before debugging in `NetBeans`, first set a *breakpoint*. This is where the program will stop executing and where the debugging will start.

4. The block of every method starts with an opening brace and finishes with a closing brace.

5. The closing brace of a block should appear exactly under the line of the opening brace. Select the `Source-Format` menu in NetBeans to auto-format the code.

6. Add a semicolon (a.k.a., ;) after every statement. However, do not add a semicolon after an `if` or a `switch` statement.

7. Give thought to variable names. Do not name variables `x` and `y` when less generic names are more appropriate.

8. Every variable must start with a lowercase letter. Conversely, the name of every class starts with a capital letter.

9. Every variable has a *scope*. This is where the variable is defined. The scope of a variable starts from the point where it is defined and ends with the end of the innermost block. The start of a block in Java is denoted by an opening brace, while its end is denoted by a closing brace.

10. The left side of an assignment operator (i.e., =) must be a variable. For example, $x = 4$.

11. Distinguish between "=" and "==". The first operator is used to perform assignment, while the second operator is used to check for equality.

12. The result of dividing two integers is an integer, where the result is rounded down. For example, writing $x = 8/9$ is equivalent to writing $x = 0$.

13. Always include a `break` statement at the end of each `case` block inside a `switch` statement.

14. Use the `equals` and `compareTo` methods to compare strings.

15. Use the statement `return` to exit any method, including the `main` method. Use this statement instead of using the `else` part of an `if` statement where possible. In general, avoid creating nested `if` statements and using the `else` construct where possible. This makes the code easier to read.

16. Surround string literals in double quotes and character literals in single quotes.

2.11   Exercises

1. Write a program that prints your name and address. Feel free to use a fake address.

2. Write a program that reads two integers from the keyboard and prints their average. Do not forget that dividing two integers always returns an integer.

3. Write a program that checks if the user is underage. If they are, then the program should tell them not to go to the bar. If they are over 21, then the program should print that they are allowed to go to the bar, but they should drink responsibly.

4. Write a program that prints two random integers (smaller than 100 and bigger than 0). The program should ask the user to multiply the numbers and read the result from the user. If the user has done the multiplication correctly, then the program should print "Congratulations!" Otherwise, the program should print "Better luck next time."

5. Write a program that reads an integer. If the integer is between 1 and 4, then the program should print `one`, `two`, `three`, or `four`, respectively. If the integer is not between 1 and 4, then the program should print `Number not between one and four`. Use a `switch` statement.

6. Write a program that chats with you. If you type `Hi`, then the program should print `Hi` and terminate. If you enter `Bye`, then the program should print `Bye` and terminate. If you enter anything else, the program should respond `And how do you feel about this?` and terminate. Use a `switch` statement.

7. Describe how the computer executes the following Java statement.

   ```
   int i = 5;
   ```

8. Rewrite the following code using the conditional operator.

```
if (x>3){
    a = 5;
} else {
    a = 7;
}
```

9. Consider the following code.

```
if (true){
    int i = 3;
}
System.out.println(i);
```

What is the scope of the variable i? Why will the program not compile? How can the program be changed to compile.

10. Consider the following code.

```
int i=6;
if (false)
    i = 3;
    System.out.println(i);
```

What will the program do? Why is the `println` line not part of the `if` statement?

11. Suppose x = 3 and y = 4. Which of the following conditions are true.

   (a) (x==3 && y >2)
   (b) (x< 5 || y > 7)
   (c) !(x>3) || (y > 4)
   (d) !(x > 3 || y < 7)

12. Write a program that reads two strings from the keyboard and prints the largest (relative to lexicographical order). Use the `compareTo` method to compare the strings.

2.12   Lab

Write a program that prints the following diamond.

```
    1
  2 3 4
1 2 5 7 4
  2 3 5
    4
```

The printed numbers are random digits between 0 and 9. In Java, `Math.random()` returns a random **double** that is greater than or equal to 0 and smaller than 1. The method is defined in the library `java.math.*` (use `import java.math.*`) . Multiply this number by something to get a digit between 0 and 9. Use `int i = (int) d;` to convert a **double** to an **int**.

Chapter 3

Loops

In the previous chapter, we showed how to use the if and switch statements in order to choose from several possible program execution paths. In this chapter, we present different types of flow control structures that are called *loop* structures. These structures allow the same code segment to be executed multiple times. There are three loop structures in Java: while, do, and for. The while structure allows us to repeatedly execute the same block of code until a condition is met. The do structure is similar, but it guarantees that the code will be executed at least once. The for structure is best suited when we know how many times we want to execute a particular code segment. The chapter also covers the modulus operator.

3.1   The while Statement

First, we will improve on the multiplication game from the last chapter. If the user entered the wrong number, then we will give the user the option to enter the correct result. The program should continue asking the user for an answer until the correct answer is entered. The code from last chapter is shown below.

```
1   import java.util.*;
2   public class Arithmetic {
3     public static void main(String[] args) {
4       int x = (int)(Math.random() * 10);
5       int y = (int)(Math.random() * 10);
6       Scanner keyboard = new Scanner(System.in);
7       System.out.print(x + "*" + y + " = ");
8       int z = keyboard.nextInt();
9       if (z == x * y) {
10        System.out.println("Congratulations!");
11      } else {
12        System.out.println("You need more practice");
13      }
```

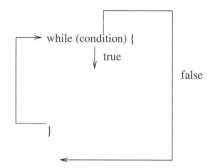

FIGURE 3.1: The while construct.

```
14    }
15  }
```

In the new code, we will eliminate Lines 9–13. We will execute Lines 7–8 multiple times until the correct answer is given by the user. Lines that need to be executed multiple times can be surrounded by a while block. The new code for Lines 7–8 is shown next.

```
int z;
while (...) {
  System.out.print(x + "*" + y + " = ");
  z = keyboard.nextInt();
}
```

If the condition in the while statement parentheses is true, then the while statement block is executed. Otherwise, the block is skipped and the program continues executing with the first line after the while block; see Figure 3.1.

> A while statement allows the same block that is surrounded by braces to be repeatedly executed. The block can be executed zero or more times. The program will stop repeatedly executing the block and move to the line immediately after the block when the condition inside the parentheses of the while statement becomes **false**.

In other words, we need to have a condition that should be **true** when we want to execute the block and should become **false** when we want to move on. Maybe in our case we can rewrite the code as follows.

```
int z;
while (z!=x*y) {
  System.out.print(x + "+" + y + " = ");
  z = keyboard.nextInt();
}
```

If z is not equal to x*y, then this means that the user did not answer the question correctly. In this case, we will go ahead and ask them for input again. The only remaining caveat is that we need to insure that the while statement is executed at least once. We can assure that by setting the variable z initially to a value that is different from x*y. The rewritten program follows.

```
import java.util.*;
public class Arithmetic {
  public static void main(String[] args) {
```

```
  int x = (int) (Math.random() * 10);
  int y = (int) (Math.random() * 10);
  Scanner keyboard = new Scanner(System.in);
  int z=x*y+1;
  while(z!=x*y){
    System.out.print(x + "*" + y + " = ");
    z = keyboard.nextInt();
  }
  System.out.println("This is correct!");
  }
}
```

Note the last printing statement in the code. It will only be executed when the `while` condition becomes false. In other words, it will only be executed when `z` is equal to `x*y`. At this point, we know that the user entered the correct guess and we can let them know.

3.2 The do-while Construct

In the previous code we needed to put in extra effort to ensure that the code in the `while` block is executed at least once. Setting the value of `z` to `x*y+1` is not an elegant solution. This is a common scenario and giving fake values to variables in order to ensure that the `while` loop is executed at least once is not the best option. Alternatively, we can use a `do-while` loop, which ensures that the body of the loop is executed at least once. Here is how the program can use the `do-while` statement.

```
import java.util.*;
public class Arithmetic {
  public static void main(String[] args) {
    int x = (int) (Math.random() * 10);
    int y = (int) (Math.random() * 10);
    Scanner keyboard = new Scanner(System.in);
    int z;
    do{
      System.out.print(x + "*" + y + " = ");
      z = keyboard.nextInt();
    } while (z!=x*y);
    System.out.println("This is correct!");
  }
}
```

One needs to insert a semicolon at the end of a `do-while` statement. This happens to be the only Java construct that requires a semicolon at the end.

The structure of a `do-while` statement is shown in Figure 3.2. As the figure suggests, a `do-while` statement works very similar to a `while` statement. When the condition is true, the block is executed again. The block stops being executing when the condition becomes false. The only major difference is that a `do-while` statement guarantees that the block is executed at least once. A minor difference is that a `do-while` statement must always end with a semicolon. Interestingly, this is the only Java structure that ends with a semicolon.

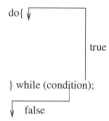

FIGURE 3.2: The do-while construct.

> A do-while statement is similar to a while statement. The difference is that a do-while statement is always executed at least once. The while statement is at the end of the block and is followed by a semicolon.

Note that one may be tempted to rewrite the code as follows.

```
1   import java.util.*;
2   public class Grade {
3     public static void main(String[] args) {
4       int x = (int) (Math.random() * 10);
5       int y = (int) (Math.random() * 10);
6       Scanner keyboard = new Scanner(System.in);
7       do{
8         System.out.print(x + "*" + y + " = ");
9         int z = keyboard.nextInt();
10      } while (z!=x*y);
11      System.out.println("This is correct!");
12    }
13  }
```

This, however, is the wrong approach and the rewrite will generate a compiler error. The reason is that every variable has a scope. The scope of a variable is defined by the innermost *block* (opening-closing braces) where the variable is defined. In the above example, the variable z is not defined after the closing brace at Line 10 and therefore cannot be referenced in the while condition.

Note that both the while and do-while loops can be applied on a single statement. For example, consider the following code.

```
while(true) System.out.println("Hi");
```

The code will keep printing Hi indefinitely. Although creating such loops is possible, this is a bad programming practice because it is error prone. For example, if we want the loop to print two lines, we may modify the code as follows.

```
while(true)
    System.out.println("Hi");
    System.out.println("What is your name? ");
```

However, the while statement applies only on the first line and the second print statement will never be executed.

The astute reader may wonder what the reason is for allowing the statement while(true) { ... }. Does this not mean that the loop will continue executing forever? The answer is no. One can insert inside a while block the *break* statement. It causes the program to jump to the line immediately after the `while` statement regardless of the value of the `while` condition. For example, our multiplication program can be rewritten as follows.

```java
import java.util.*;
public class Arithmetic {
  public static void main(String[] args) {
    int x = (int) (Math.random() * 10);
    int y = (int) (Math.random() * 10);
    Scanner keyboard = new Scanner(System.in);
    int z;
    do{
      System.out.print(x + "*" + y + " = ");
      z = keyboard.nextInt();
      if(z==x*y){
        break;
      } else {
        System.out.println("This is incorrect!");
      }
    } while (true);
    System.out.println("This is correct!");
  }
}
```

The program checks if the variable `z` is equal to `x*y`. If it is, the program breaks out of the `do-while` statement. Otherwise, it prints that the guess was wrong and starts executing the loop again. Note that the `break` statement can be used to escape from both `while` and `do-while` loops and from a `switch` block. In general, the `break` statement can be used to escape from any loop or a `switch` block. However, the `break` statement cannot be used to escape from any other block, including an `if` block.

3.3 The `for` Loop

Next, let us play a guessing the game. The computer will think of a random number between 0 and 999. We will have 10 tries to guess the number. Every time we guess, we will be told if the number is lower or higher. In this program, we need to perform a task at most 10 times. One way to do so is to use a `while` loop that keeps track of the number of guesses. A `break` statement can be executed when the number is guessed before the tenth try. Here is a code snippet of the program.

```java
...
int numTries = 0;
while(numTries <= 9){
    ...
    numTries = numTries+1;
}
...
```

The `while` statement will be executed for `numTries` = 0 to 9, that is, a total of 10 times. In general, the easiest way to execute something 10 times is to create a counter that keeps track of how many times it is executed. One needs a loop that keeps executing the block until the counter reaches a predetermined value. This is similar to going to the gym and running ten laps. You need to keep track of how many laps you have run and stop when this

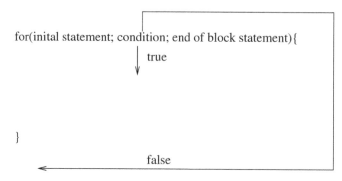

FIGURE 3.3: The `for` statement.

number reaches ten. Note that in the above code we started counting at 0. We could have started counting at 1 and kept counting until we reached 10. However, computer scientists often like to start counting at 0. For example, if a computer scientist counts tree apples, he or she will most likely count: apple 0, apple 1, apple 2.

Counting is such a common operation when programming that Java supports a special kind of loop just for counting that is called the `for` loop. The structure of the `for` loop is shown in Figure 3.3. The `for` loop has three parts that are separated by semicolons. The first part is executed at the beginning of the loop and it is executed only once. The second part (a.k.a., the condition) is checked before the block of the loop is executed. If the condition is true, then the block is executed. Otherwise, control jumps to the line immediately after the `for` loop block. The third part of the `for` loop is executed after the block is executed and before the condition is checked again. For example, our last code snippet can be elegantly rewritten using a `for` statement as follows.

```
for(int numTries = 0; numTries <= 9; numTries = numTries+1){
    ...
}
```

The `for` block will be executed for `numTries` = 0 to 9. At the end of the tenth execution, the statement `numTries = numTries + 1` will be executed and `numTries` will become equal to 10. Then the condition `numTries <= 9` will become false and the program will jump to the line immediately after the `for` loop.

The variable `numTries` is only valid inside the `for` loop. It we want to examine the value of the variable `numTries` after the `for` loop, then we need to define it before the `for` loop as shown next. In most cases, the counter is only used to keep track of how many times the `for` loop block is executed and the first syntax is used.

```
int numTries;
for(numTries = 0; numTries <=9; numTries=numTries+1){
    ...
}
System.out.println(numTries);
```

The above program will print the number 10 if the `for` loop does not contain a `break` statement. The variable `numTries` is referred to as the *counter variable*.

Java allows us to modify the value of the counter variable inside the `for` loop. However, this is *cheating*. After running one lap, you can move the counter to ten and say that you have run ten laps. In general, modifying the counter variable inside the `for` block is considered poor programming practice.

TABLE 3.1:
Increment/decrement Java
shortcuts.

(*Expression*)	(*Meaning*)
$i++$ or $++i$	increment i by 1
$i--$ or $--i$	decrement i by 1
$i+=5$	increment i by 5
$i-=5$	decrement i by 5

Incrementing or decrementing a variable by one (or more) is a very common operation. This is why Java has several shortcuts for these operations; see Table 3.1.

Note that there is a difference between $i++$ and $++i$. Consider the following code.

```java
int i = 3;
int a = i++;
```

In this case, the operation increment by one will be performed *after* the value is assigned. In other words, ++ after the variable means: use the current value of the variable in the calculations and perform the increment by one later. In the above example, at the end i will be equal to 4 and a will be equal to 3. The variable i will be equal to 4 because the statement i++ incremented i by one. The variable a will be equal to 3 because the old value of the variable i was assigned to the variable a. Alternatively, consider the following code.

```java
int i = 3;
int a = ++i;
```

Now, "++" means increment by one and use the new value. At the end of the code, the variable i will again be 4, but this time a will be also equal to 4. The reason is that the new value of the variable i is assigned to the variable a. In general, if the "++" is after the variable, then this means perform the increment by one later. Conversely, if the ++ is before the variable, then this means perform the increment by one first and use the new value of the variable in the expression. The operation "−−" works in the same way, but it decrements the value of the variable by one. Next, let us examine a more interesting example.

```java
int i = 5;
int a = i++ + ++i;
```

The question is what will the value of the variable a be after the code is executed? The expression i++ + ++i will be executed from left to right. First, i++ will be executed. This will make the value of i equal to 6. However, since the "++" is after the variable, the old value 5 will be used for the calculation. Next, the expression ++i will be evaluated. Now the value of i will become 7. Since the "++" is before the variable, the new value 7 will be used in the computation. Therefore, Java will add 5 and 7 and assign 12 to the variable a. Such code is considered "tricky" and should not be part of your program. In general, avoid using more than one of the arithmetic shortcuts close to each other when the meaning is not obvious. However, one should be able to understand how tricky code works. For example, you may have to edit tricky code that is written by someone else.

The last two lines of Table 3.1 show examples of incrementing/decrementing by more than 1. For example, i + =a is equivalent to writing i = i + a. Similarly, one can write a *= 3 to multiply the value of a by 3 or a /= 3 to divide it by 3. It is typical to use the "++" shortcut in the third part of a `for` loop. For example, consider the following code.

```java
int numTries;
```

```java
for(numTries = 0; numTries <=9; numTries++){
   ...
}
System.out.println(numTries);
```

The code in the block will be executed 10 times. Let us next show an implementation of our game using the `for` loop.

```java
1   import java.util.*;
2
3   public class GuessGame {
4     public static void main(String[] args) {
5       int number = (int) (Math.random() * 1000);
6       Scanner keyboard = new Scanner(System.in);
7       for (int numTries = 0; numTries < 10; numTries++) {
8         System.out.println("Enter your guess: ");
9         int guess = keyboard.nextInt();
10        if (guess == number) {
11          System.out.println("You got it!");
12          return;
13        }
14        if(guess > number){
15          System.out.println("Go lower");
16        } else {
17          System.out.println("Go higher");
18        }
19      }
20      System.out.println("You ran out of guesses");
21      System.out.println("My number was: "+number);
22    }
23  }
```

Line 5 creates a random number between 0 and 999. Lines 7–19 create a `for` loop that is executed 10 times. If the player enters the correct guess (Line 10), then we print an appropriate message (Line 11) and terminate the program (Line 12). Otherwise, we compare the player's guess with the chosen number and tell the player to go higher or lower. Note that Lines 20–21 will only be executed if the **return** statement on Line 12 is never executed, that is, the player was unsuccessful in guessing the number in ten tries.

Sometimes, we may want to execute more code after the game ends (e.g., start a different game). In this case, exiting the program when the user enters the correct guess is not the right option. An alternative implementation that does not use the **return** statement is shown next.

```java
1   import java.util.*;
2
3   public class GuessGame {
4     public static void main(String[] args) {
5       int number = (int) (Math.random() * 1000);
6       Scanner keyboard = new Scanner(System.in);
7       int numTries;
8       for (numTries = 0; numTries < 10; numTries++) {
9         System.out.println("Enter your guess: ");
10        int guess = keyboard.nextInt();
11        if (guess > number) {
12          System.out.println("Go lower");
13          continue;
```

```
14              }
15              if (guess < number) {
16                  System.out.println("Go higher");
17                  continue;
18              }
19              System.out.println("You got it!");
20              break;
21          }
22
23          if(numTries == 10){
24              System.out.println("You ran out of guesses");
25              System.out.println("My number was: " + number);
26          }
27      }
28  }
```

This time, we need the value of the counter variable after the `for` loop is executed. This is why Line 7 declares the variable *numTries* before the loop. The `for` loop uses two interesting commands: `continue` and `break`. While we have seen the `break` command before, the `continue` command is new. The command `continue` means: stop executing this iteration of the `for` loop and go to the next iteration. In our program, the statement `continue` means: jump to the third part of the `for` loop, that is, to the expression `numTries++`. If we have determined that the guess is too high or too low, then we simply let the player know that and execute the `continue` statement in order to jump to the next iteration. If Line 19 is being executed, then this means that neither condition is true, that is, the player guessed the number correctly. In this case, we let the player know that they won and exit the `for` loop using the `break` statement.

In the new version of the program, we are not sure if the player guessed the number correctly at Line 23. We could have terminated the `for` loop because the counter reached 10 or because the player guessed the correct number. Therefore, we need to check the value of the counter variable at Line 23. If it is equal to 10, then this means that the player was unsuccessful in guessing the number and we need to print an appropriate message.

3.4 Nested `for` Loops

No game is complete without some good artwork. Drawing graphics involves advanced programming techniques and it and will be covered in Chapter 9. For now, we need to content ourselves with drawing ASCII art, that is, pictures from characters. Our next task is to create a program that displays a diamond of stars.

```
    *
  * * *
* * * * *
  * * *
    *
```

The size of the diamond (i.e., the number of stars in the middle line) will be a parameter of the program. In the above picture, the size of the diamond is equal to 5. Note that the size of the diamond must be an odd number.

We will solve the problem by using the popular *divide-and-conquer* approach. The first part of the program will print the top half, while the second part of the program will print the bottom half. We divided the program into two parts because the number of stars keeps increasing initially, but then it starts decreasing after the middle line. The *pseudocode*[1] for our algorithm follows.

```
let n be the size of the diamond
nSpaces = n-1;
nStars = 1;
for every line in the first half {
   print nSpaces spaces;
   print nStars stars;
   print new line;
   increment the number of stars by 2;
   decrement the number of spaces by 2;
}
nSpaces = 2;
nStars = n-2;
for every line in the second half {
   print nSpaces spaces;
   print nStars stars;
   print new line;
   decrement the number of stars by 2;
   increment the number of spaces by 2;
}
```

We know how many lines are in the first and second half of the diamond. We also know how many stars and spaces to print at every line. Therefore, we are ready to implement our program. Note that the program will involve *nested* **for** loops. A nested **for** loop is a loop inside a loop. For example, we will create one loop to iterate over the lines. Then, for every line, we will create inner **for** loops to print the spaces and stars. The code of the program follows.

```java
1   import java.util.*;
2
3   public class Diamond {
4     public static void main(String[] args) {
5       Scanner keyboard = new Scanner(System.in);
6       System.out.print("Enter size of diamond: ");
7       int size = keyboard.nextInt();
8       int numStars = 1;
9       int numSpaces = size - 1;
10      for (int line = 0; line < size / 2 + 1; line++) {
11        for (int i = 0; i < numSpaces; i++) {
12          System.out.print(" ");
13        }
14        for (int i = 0; i < numStars; i++) {
15          System.out.print("* ");
16        }
17        System.out.println();
18        numSpaces -= 2;
19        numStars += 2;
20      }
21      numStars=size -2;
22      numSpaces = 2;
```

---

[1]Pseudocode is a description of an algorithm that uses a language that is similar, but not identical, to a programming language.

```
23        for (int line = 0; line < size / 2; line++) {
24          for (int i = 0; i < numSpaces; i++) {
25            System.out.print(" ");
26          }
27          for (int i = 0; i < numStars; i++) {
28            System.out.print("* ");
29          }
30          System.out.println();
31          numSpaces += 2;
32          numStars -= 2;
33        }
34      }
35   }
```

Lines 8–20 print the top part of the diamond, while Lines 21–33 print the bottom half. Note that the variable i is used as a counter. Traditionally, the counter is referred to as an *iterator* by programmers and, as a consequence, i is a common name for the counter variable. The first part of the code tells the computer to print $\frac{size}{2} + 1$ lines. The variable *line* is used as the counter variable. When printing a line, we print numSpaces spaces and numStars stars. Next, we update the value of the variables. Note that Line 17 prints a new line. The println method does not require a parameter. If it is called without a parameter, then just a new line is printed.

An experienced programmer probably will not introduce the variable line. The reason is that either the variable numSpaces or the variable numStars can be used to decide when to stop the for loop. We will keep executing the first for loop while the numSpaces is greater or equal to 0. We will keep executing the second for loop while the numStars is greater or equal to 0. Note that the condition inside the for statement is exactly the opposite (or the negation) of the loop terminating condition.

```
import java.util.*;

public class Diamond {
  public static void main(String[] args) {
    Scanner keyboard = new Scanner(System.in);
    System.out.print("Enter size of diamond: ");
    int size = keyboard.nextInt();
    for (int numStars =1, numSpaces = size -1; numSpaces >=0; numSpaces
        -=2, numStars+=2) {
      for (int i = 0; i < numSpaces; i++) {
        System.out.print(" ");
      }
      for (int i = 0; i < numStars; i++) {
        System.out.print("* ");
      }
      System.out.println();
    }
    for (int numStars=size -2, numSpaces = 2; numStars >0; numSpaces+=2,
        numStars-=2 ) {
      for (int i = 0; i < numSpaces; i++) {
        System.out.print(" ");
      }
      for (int i = 0; i < numStars; i++) {
        System.out.print("* ");
      }
      System.out.println();
```

```
      }
    }
}
```

Note that one can define and initialize several variables in the first part of the `for` statement. However, all the variables that are defined must be of the same type and the variables are separated by commas. Remember that the first part of the `for` statement is executed exactly once when the `for` loop starts executing. The second part of the for statement must contain a single condition (if the condition is missing, then `true` is the default value). The third part of the `for` statement can contain several commands separated by commas. The third part of the `for` loop is always executed after the body of the `for` loop is executed. Note that the first and/or the third part of the `for` statement can also be missing. In particular, the following `for` statement defines an infinite loop: `for(;;){` ... `}`.

The first outer `for` statement first initializes the variables `numSpaces` and `numStars`. The middle part of the `for` statement tells us that we will keep going while the variable `numberOfStars` is greater or equal to zero. The third part of the `for` statement tells us that at the end of every iteration we will increase the number of stars by 2 and decrease the number of spaces by 2. The inner `for` loop simply prints the required number of stars and spaces. The second outer `for` loop is similar. The difference is that now the variable `numStars` is initially set to `size-2` and the variable `numSpaces` is initially set to 2. After the body of the loop executes, the variable `numSpaces` will now be increased by two, while the variable `numStars` will now be decreased by two. The body of the `for` loop will keep executing while the number of stars to be printed is a positive number, that is, there are stars to be printed.

Adding several counter variables to a single `for` loop is not uncommon. For example, you may count the number of laps you have run and the number of times your shoe unties. For example, you may want to keep running until you complete 10 laps or your shoe unties 3 times. In this case, the `for` statement may be: `for( laps = 0, unties = 0; laps <10 && unties < 3 ; laps++){` ... `}`. Note that several conditions can be combined in the middle part of a `for` loop using binary operators. However, the middle part of a `for` loop must still be a single condition.

3.5   The Modulus Operation

In this last section of the chapter, we will cover the *remainder* (a.k.a., *modulus*) operation. In math, when two integers are divided, there is a remainder. For example, when the number 25 is divided by the number 3, the result is 8 and the remainder is 1. In Java, the operator % is used to represent the remainder operator. For example, 25%3 will give us the number 1. Note that 25/3 is equal to 8 because Java implements integer division. In other words, $25 = (25/3)*3+1$. Therefore, another way to think about the remainder operation is to ask, what is the difference to the closest number that is equal to or less than the dividend and is divisible by the divisor. In other words, writing `n%a` is equivalent to writing `n - (n/a)*a`.

In order to demonstrate how the modulus operation works, let us create a simple application that converts a decimal number into a hexadecimal number. The program will take a number as input and will keep dividing the number by 16. Every time the division is performed, the remainder will be saved as a character in the `String` variable `result`. If the remainder is bigger than 9, then the corresponding letter will be saved. After the loop, the string will be printed in reverse order. Here is the implementation of the program.

```java
import java.util.*;

public class Test {
  public static void main(String[] args){
    System.out.println("Please enter a decimal number: ");
    Scanner keyboard = new Scanner(System.in);
    int number = keyboard.nextInt();
    String result = "";
    while(number > 0){
      int remainder = number % 16;
      if(remainder <= 9){
        result = result + remainder;
      } else {
        result = result + (char)('A'+remainder-10);
      }
      number/=16;
    }
    System.out.print("The number in hexadecimal is: ");
    for(int i=0; i < result.length(); i++){
      System.out.print(result.charAt(result.length()-i-1));
    }
    System.out.println();
  }
}
```

The program first reads the number from the keyboard. Then there is a `while` loop. In the loop the number is divided by 16 and the remainder is concatenated to the variable `result`. This continues until the number becomes 0. Note that the line: `number/=16` divides the number by 16. As explained in Chapter 1, this algorithm will give us the number in hexadecimal representation, but the digits will be reversed.

Note that when the remainder is bigger than 9, it needs to be converted to a character. For example, if the remainder is 12, then $12 - 10$ will be equal to 2. Looking at Figure 2.8, we can see that the ASCII code of 'A' is 65. When we add 2 to 65 we will get the number 67. The ASCII code of 67 is 'C' and therefore 'C' will be concatenated to the variable `result`. In general, Java treats characters and integers similarly. For example, if we try to add a character to an integer, then the result will be an integer. The character will be converted to an integer using the ASCII table and then the addition will be performed. Conversely, the ASCII table is also used when an integer is cast to a character. Adding a number to the character 'A' is a common trick. For example, `(char)('A'+23)` will give us the 24nd letter of the English language (i.e., the letter 'X').

The code after the `while` loop displays the `String` variable `result` in reverse order. The `length` method returns the length of the string. The `charAt` method gives us the character at the specified position. Note that the first character of the string is at location 0. This is why the last character of the string is at location `result.length()-1`. When i is equal to 0, the character at position `result.length()-1` will be displayed. When i is equal to 1, the second to last character will be displayed and so on.

Note that we did not really have to create the string in reverse order. Alternatively, we could have added every new digit of the string to the beginning of the string and eliminated the code that reversed the string. Here is the rewrite.

```java
import java.util.*;
```

```java
public class Test {
  public static void main(String[] args){
    System.out.println("Please enter a decimal number: ");
    Scanner keyboard = new Scanner(System.in);
    int number = keyboard.nextInt();
    String result = "";
    while(number > 0){
      int remainder = number % 16;
      if(remainder <= 9){
        result = remainder+result;
      } else {
        result = (char)('A'+remainder-10)+result;
      }
      number/=16;
    }
    System.out.println("The number in hexadecimal is: "+result);
  }
}
```

Examine the code: `result = remainder+result`. This means that the value of the character `remainder` will be added at the beginning of the string.

3.6 Summary

The chapter introduced the three loop types in Java: `while`, `do-while`, and `for`. The two while loops are used when we want to keep repeating the same list of operations until some event happens. For example, we may want to read input from the keyboard until a positive number is entered. The difference between the two while loops is that the `do-while` loop guarantees that the body of the loop will be executed at least once. Conversely, if the condition inside a `while` statement is initially false, then the body of the `while` loop will never be executed.

The `for` loop is perfect when counting is involved. For example, one can use a `for` loop to print the numbers from 1 to 10. A `for` loop usually has one or more counter variables that change after every execution of the body of the loop. When the middle condition of the `for` loop becomes false, the body of the loop stops repeating and the program continues from the line that is immediately after the `for` loop.

The chapter also introduces the modulus (a.k.a., remainder) operator. It is used to calculate the remainder of dividing two integers.

3.7 Syntax

- `i++;` ⇒ Increment i by one.

- `i--;` ⇒ Decrement i by one.

- `a = i++;` ⇒ Make a equal to i and then increment i by one.

- a = i--; $\Rightarrow$ Make a equal to i and then decrement i by one.

- a = ++i; $\Rightarrow$ Increment i by one and then make a equal to the new value of i.

- a = --i; $\Rightarrow$ Decrement i by one and then make a equal to the new value of i.

- a+=b; $\Rightarrow$ Equivalent to a=a+b.

- a-=b; $\Rightarrow$ Equivalent to a=a/b.

- a*=b; $\Rightarrow$ Equivalent to a=a*b.

- a/=b; $\Rightarrow$ Equivalent to a=a-b.

- a%=b; $\Rightarrow$ Equivalent to a=a%b.

- for(int i=0; i < n; i++) { ... } $\Rightarrow$ Execute the body of the for loop n times.

- for(int i=0,j=0; i < n; i++,j+=5) { ... } $\Rightarrow$ Execute the body of the for loop n times. The variable j starts at 0 and is incremented by 5 at every iteration of the loop.

- while(*condition*) { ... } $\Rightarrow$ Keep executing the body of the while loop until the *condition* becomes false.

- do { ... } while(*condition*); $\Rightarrow$ Keep executing the body of the loop until the *condition* becomes false. The body of the do-while loop is always executed at least once.

- some loop { ... break; ... } $\Rightarrow$ The break statement forces Java to stop executing the loop and transfer control to the first line after the loop.

- some loop { ... continue; ... } $\Rightarrow$ The continue statement forces Java to stop executing the current iteration of the loop and proceed to the next iteration. If the loop is a for loop, then the continue statement jumps to the third part of the for loop. If the loop is a while or do-while loop, then control jumps to the condition of the loop.

- a = 103%20 $\Rightarrow$ The value of the variable a will become equal to 3 because this is the remainder when one divides the number 103 by 20.

- s.length() $\Rightarrow$ Returns the length of the String s.

- s.charAt(3) $\Rightarrow$ Returns the character at position 4 of the string s. Note that counting starts at 0.

3.8 Important Points

1. All three loops are similar to an if statement. If the condition is true, then the body is executed. The difference is that the body of an if statement is executed at most once. The body of a while statement is executed 0 or more times. The body of a do-while statement is executed 1 or more times.

2. A `for` statement contains three parts. The first part is executed once at the beginning. Then the condition in the middle is checked. Similar to an `if` statement, the body is executed when the condition is true. The third part of a `for` statement is executed after every execution of the body of the loop. The first part of a `for` loop can define and initialize multiple variables of the same type. The variables must be separated by commas. Similarly, the third part of a `for` loop can perform several actions that are separated by commas. Each of the parts of a `for` loop can be missing. If the middle of a `for` loop is missing, the Boolean value `true` is used.

3. The operation `i++` means use the current value of the variable `i` in the calculations and then increment `i` by 1. Conversely, `++i` means increment the variable `i` by 1 and then use the new value of the variable `i` in the expression.

4. Do not forget to add a semicolon after a `do-while` statement. This is the only loop that requires a semicolon at the end.

5. The `continue` statement can be used inside any of the three loops. It forces Java to skip the rest of the body of the loop and start a new iteration. In a `for` loop, the statement will make the program jump to the third part of the `for` loop. For a `while` and `do-while` statement, the program jumps to the condition. If the condition is true, then the body is executed again. If it is not, then the loop is terminated.

6. The `break` statement can be used in any kind of a loop or a `switch` construct. The statement instructs Java to jump to the line that is immediately after the body of the construct.

7. The counter variable should usually not be modified inside the body of a `for` statement. It should only be modified in the third part of the `for` statement, which is executed immediately after the body of the `for` statement.

8. Always create a block for a loop by inserting opening and closing braces. Although Java allows the body of a loop to be a single statement without surrounding braces, doing so is bad programming practice.

9. The operator `%` is used to calculate the remainder of dividing two integers.

3.9 Exercises

1. Improve the multiplication game from the previous chapter. We will randomly ask the player to either add, multiply, or subtract one-digit numbers (we skip division because the result of dividing two numbers is not an integer). The game should ask 10 math questions and record the answers. At the end, the game should tell the player how well they did, that is, how many questions they answered correctly.

2. What is the result of executing the following statements?

```
int i = 5;
i— + ++i;
System.out.println(i);
```

Compile and run the program to check your answer.

3. What will be printed by the following code snippet?

```
int i=0;
for( i=2;i<25;i+=2){
    if(i%7==0) {
        break;
    }
}
System.out.println(i);
```

4. What will be printed by the following code snippet?

```
int i=0;
for( i=2;i<25;i+=2){
    if(i%7==0) {
        continue;
    }
}
System.out.println(i);
```

5. Rewrite the following code to use a **while** statement instead of the **for** loop.

```
for(int i=0,j=0;i<10;i++){
    j++;
    System.out.println(i+j);
}
```

6. Write a program that persistently asks the user to enter a positive number. The program should only terminate when a positive number is entered. Use a **do-while** loop.

7. Rewrite the program from Question 6 to use an infinite **while** loop. That is, **while(true)** {...} structure. Use a **break** statement to terminate the loop when a positive number is entered.

8. Write a program that reads an integer from the keyboard and tells the user if the number is prime. Use a **for** loop to check if the number is divisible by the numbers from 2 up to the value of the input number minus 1.

9. Write a program that reads an integer from the keyboard and prints the corresponding binary number.

10. Write a program that reads an integer from the keyboard and prints the factorial of the input. Use a variable of type **long** to store the result.

11. A palindrome is a string that reads the same forward and backward. Write a program that reads a string from the keyboard and tells the user if the string is a palindrome.

3.10 Lab

You will create a two-player version of the Hangman game. The program should first ask for the first player to enter a word and save the word. Next, the second player should be allowed to guess letters. If a letter appears in the word, then they should be told at what position. After 6 guesses, the player has one shot of guessing the word. A possible run of the program follows (user input is in italic).

Player 1 enter word: *mississippi*
Player 2 enter guess: *c*
No letter c
Player 2 enter guess: *d*
no letter d
Player 2 enter guess: *e*
no letter e
Player 2 enter guess: *m*
at position: 1
Player 2 enter guess: *a*
no letter a
Player 2 enter guess: *i*
at position 2 5 8 11
Enter word: *mississippi*
This is correct!

Use a **for** loop to iterate through all the guesses. Use a nested **for** loop to iterate through all the characters of the word. When there is a hit (i.e., the user character matches a word character), report the value of the index of the character in the word. Do not forget to add one to the result because the characters of a string are counted starting at index 0.

3.11 Project

The game of Nim is played as follows. You have **n** toothpicks to choose from. Player A can remove 1, 2, or 3 toothpicks. Player B can then remove 1, 2, or 3 toothpicks. This process repeats, alternating between players A and B, until there are no more toothpicks left. The player who removes the last toothpick is the loser. Assume that one of the players is human and the other player is the computer (your program).

Use a random generator to decide who goes first. The player that goes second chooses the value of **n**, where **n** must be bigger than 20 and smaller than 30 (if this is the computer, then use a random generator to determine the value of **n**). Remember to print the remaining number of toothpicks on the screen after every move. If it is the human's turn, then ask him or her how many toothpicks he or she wants to remove. After the last toothpick is removed, print "YOU WIN" or "YOU LOSE".

Example program run (player input in *italic*) follows.

Welcome to my game of Nim.
This time you are going to go first.
I choose the total number of toothpicks to be 21.
Your Turn. There are 21 toothpicks left. How many toothpicks do you want to remove? *2*
My turn. There are 19 toothpicks left. I, the Computer, will remove 3 of them.
Your Turn. There are 16 toothpicks left.

How many toothpicks do you want to remove? *3*

My Turn. There are 13 toothpicks left. I, the Computer, will remove 3 of them.

Your Turn. There are 10 toothpicks left. How many toothpicks do you want to remove? *3*

My Turn. There are 7 toothpicks left. I, the Computer, will remove 3 of them.

Your Turn. There are 4 toothpicks left. How many toothpicks do you want to remove? *3*

My Turn. There is 1 toothpick left. I, the Computer, will remove it.

YOU WIN!

Try to design your program to play as smart as possible.

Chapter 4

Methods and Formatted Output

So far, we have written all the code in the `main` method. Although this is fine for small programs, it is impractical for larger ones. Consider a program that consists of ten thousand lines of code. Scrolling through all the lines to find an error is not a viable option. To avoid this scenario, Java allows us to modularize our code into *methods*. Good software practices call for every method to perform a single task. For example, a method that reads an integer from a file and multiplies it be a constant will not be very reusable. The chance that one will require these two operations in the same order again is very low. However, a method that reads an integer from a file has a good chance of being reused. Similarly, a method that multiplies an integer by a constant also has a high probability of being reused. As a rule of thumb, a method should not be very complicated and it should rarely take more than 50 lines of code. If a method is longer than that, we should consider breaking it down into smaller methods.

Formatted printing allows us to print the result in any format that we want. For example, we can justify the output to the right or to the left. We can also specify the number of digits after the decimal dot that will be displayed for doubles.

4.1   Introduction to Methods

You can think of a method as a "friend" that does you a favor. During the execution of a program, you can ask your friend to do something for you. When you do that, you can send your friend some information. Your friend will perform the required task and may return some result. After calling a method, the program usually waits for the method to do its job before continuing. For example, suppose you have two friends called Bob and Peter. Bob is a good painter and Peter is an excellent carpenter. If you want a room remodeled, then you can call Bob to paint the walls. You will call Peter to put in the hardwood floor only after Bob has finished painting. Similar to your friends, methods also have names. Our fictitious example can be implemented as follows.

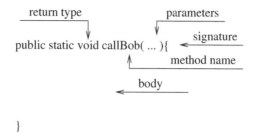

FIGURE 4.1: The different parts of a method.

```java
import java.util.*;
public class Remodel {
  public static void main(String[] args) {
    callBob();
    callPeter();
  }

  public static void callBob() {
    System.out.println("Paint room");
  }

  public static void callPeter() {
    System.out.println("Install hardwood floor");
  }
}
```

Note that method names should always start with a lowercase letter. The program will print `Paint room` followed by `Install hardwood floor`. Note that one needs to use the syntax: `methodName(...)` to call a method. In other words, we always need to use parentheses when calling a method. The reason is that if we do not use the parentheses, then the compiler will think that we are referring to the variable `callBob` and not the `callBob` method. For now, all methods will be `public` and `static`. A `public` method means that the method can be access from everywhere (i.e., a friend that can be called by anyone). A `static` method means that the method does not have any hidden parameters. More information on both keywords will be presented in Chapter 6.

The different parts of a method are shown in Figure 4.1. The parameters of the method go between the parentheses. This is the information that is sent to the method. In our example, nothing is sent to both methods. A return type of void means that the method does not return anything. The first line of the method definition includes the name of the method, the parameters of the method, and the return type. This line is sometimes referred to as the *signature* of the method.

Next, we will show how data can be passed between methods. We will keep the same example, but now the width and length of the room will be passed to Bob and Peter. Our friends will paint and put hardwood floor in the room and will send us the bill (they are our friends, but they will not work for nothing). Here is the modified version of the code.

```java
import java.util.*;

public class Remodel {
  public static void main(String[] args) {
    double bobPrice = callBob(8, 12);
    double peterPrice = callPeter(8, 12);
```

```
    double totalPrice = bobPrice + peterPrice;
    System.out.println("Total price for the project: $" + totalPrice);
  }

  static double callBob(int width, int length) {
    System.out.println("Paint room");
    double pricePSF = 0.80;
    return pricePSF * width * length;
  }

  public static double callPeter(int width, int length) {
    System.out.println("Install hardwood floor");
    double pricePSF = 3.20;
    return pricePSF * width * length;
  }
}
```

Now we send the dimensions of the room to our friends. Bob charges 80c/foot for painting, while Peter charges \$3.20 for hardwood flooring. Note that the variables `width` and `length` are *local* variables for both methods. That is, these variables are only defined inside the methods. When the `callBob` method is called, `width` becomes equal to 8 and `length` becomes equal to 12. The two values are used to calculate the total cost of the job. After the method terminates, the variables are destroyed. These variables are called `automatic` because space for them is automatically created at the beginning of the method and they are automatically destroyed at the end of the method in which they are defined.

> A *formal parameter* of a method is a variable that is defined between the parentheses in the signature of the method. An actual parameter of a method is the value that is passed to the method.

In the `callBob` method, the variables `width` and `length` are the formal parameters. Consider the following code.

```
int x = 3;
int y = 5;
callBob(x,y);
```

The variables `x` and `y` are the actual parameters. The values 3 and 5 are passed to the `callBob` method. Note that the `callBob` method cannot change the values of the variables `x` and `y` because it does not have access to them. The `callBob` method only has access to their values.

> Any changes to the value of the formal parameters of a method do not affect the actual parameters. The reason is that in Java, methods are called by value. Only the values of the actual parameters are sent to a method.

After Bob finishes painting the room, he will send us the bill. He does that by calling the `return` command. Note that the command performs two tasks. First, as we have seen before, it terminates the current method. Any code after calling the `return` statement will not be executed. The control is transferred back to the calling method (in this case, the `main` method). Second, the `return` method can send back information. In this case, the method will send back 76.80, which is the price that is charged by Bob.

Every time we call a method, we need to check if the method returns data. If it does, we need to save the result somewhere. For example, the following code will compile.

```
callBob(8, 12);
```

However, we never save the result of calling the method. Bob would paint the room, which is good. However, he will send us the bill and we are not saving the amount anywhere. As a result, we will not know how much to pay Bob.

> When calling a method, we always need to check the return type. If the return type is not void, then we need to save the result that is returned by the method in a variable for future reference.

Type and execute the program. You should get: $384.00000000000006, not bad for a small project. Note that if you do the math by hand, the result is exactly 384 dollars and 0 cents. Java prints the 6 as the fourteenth digit after the decimal dot because computers are not very good at working with real numbers. Java can only store a finite number of real numbers (i.e., 2^{64}) using a double (i.e., 8 bytes). If the real number cannot be exactly represented, then the closest real number is chosen.

4.2 Formatting Output

It will be nicer if we get the program to print $384.00 instead of $384.00000000000006. When it comes to currency, we probably want to see only two digits after the decimal dot. Java has the printf method (stands for formatted printing) that supports formatted output. Accidentally, there is a format method that can be called on a System.out object and that does exactly the same thing. We can print a number with two digits after the decimal dot as follows.

```
System.out.printf(" $%.2f on painting and"
         + " $%.2f on hardwood for total of $%.2f,",
         bobPrice, peterPrice, totalPrice);
```

The printf method is interesting because it takes as input a variable number of arguments. The first argument is always a string. This is the string that is displayed. The string can contain zero or more % constructs. An argument needs to be specified for every such construct. In our example, the first string contained three % constructs. This means that we need to specify three additional parameters. Every time a % construct is seen in the string, it is substituted with the next argument of the method. In our case, bobPrice is equal to $76.80, peterPrice is equal to $307.20, and totalPrice is equal to $384.00. The f after the % sign means that a floating point number will be printed next (either a float or a double). A list of some possible characters that can be used after the % sign is shown in Table 4.1.

Between the % sign and the character, one can specify the size of the output using two numbers separated by a dot. To the right of the dot, one can specify the number of digits after the decimal dot to be displayed. To the left of the dot, one can specify the total number of characters to be displayed. For example, the following statement displays 3 digits after the decimal dot.

```
System.out.printf("%.3f",23.3228);
```

TABLE 4.1: Examples using `printf`.

`printf("%d",3)`	prints integer
`printf("%f",3.233)`	prints real number
`printf("%s","abc")`	prints string
`printf("%c",'a')`	prints character

The result will be 23.229. The reason is that the result is rounded to three decimal places after the decimal dot. For a second example, consider the statement.

```
System.out.printf("%3d",23);
```

This means display the number using **at least** three characters. Therefore, "23" will be printed. By default, the result is right justified. If we want the result to be left justified, then we should specify a negative formatting number.

```
System.out.printf("%-10d",23);
```

The code will display the number 23 followed by eight spaces. Next, consider the following example.

```
System.out.printf("%6.2f",23.24999);
```

This means that a real number will be printed with 2 digits after the decimal dot and at least 6 total characters. The result will be 23.25, where there will be a single space in front of the number. The space will guarantee that there are at least 6 characters displayed. Note that, unlike casting, here the number is rounded. In other words, Java will display 2 digits after the decimal dot and will try to make the output as close as possible to the original number.

Lastly, suppose we want to display the total cost of the project, but we want to display it in the following format: $325,365.34. Here is an example of how this can be done.

```
import java.text.*;
public class Test {
  public static void main(String[] args){
    DecimalFormat myFormatter = new DecimalFormat("$###,###.00");
    System.out.println(myFormatter.format(325365.34));
  }
}
```

The `DecimalFormat` class is defined in the `java.text.*` library. Note that if the price of the project is 2.23, then the string $2.23 will be displayed. In other words, the symbol # is used to represent a character only when the respective digit exits. Conversely, 0 is used to represent a filler. For example, if the cost of the project is $43, then $43.00 will be printed. Alternatively, consider the following code.

```
import java.text.*;
public class Test {
  public static void main(String[] args){
    DecimalFormat myFormatter = new DecimalFormat("$000,000.00");
    System.out.println(myFormatter.format(2.23));
  }
}
```

Now the result will be $000,002.23 when the cost of the project is 2 dollars and 23 cents. The reason is that 0 means that 0 will be displayed if there is no digit at the specified position.

In both cases, a `DecimalFormat` object is created. The format of the object is specified as input. Then the `format` method is called to format the output. Finally, the `print` or `println` method needs to be called to display the result.

4.3   Code Refactoring

Methods have two main advantages. First, they make the code shorter by allowing us to place repeating code inside a method and call the method when we want to execute the code. Second, they allow us to break our program into modules and make it more manageable.

Let us reexamine the code for drawing a diamond of stars from the last chapter.

```
for (int numStars =1, numSpaces = size −1; numSpaces >=0 ; numSpaces−=2,
        numStars+=2){
    for (int i = 0; i < numSpaces; i++) {
        System.out.print(" ");
    }
    for (int i = 0; i < numStars; i++) {
        System.out.print("* ");
    }
    System.out.println();
}
for (int numStars=size −2, numSpaces = 2; numStars >=0 ; numSpaces+=2,
        numStars−=2 ) {
    for (int i = 0; i < numSpaces; i++) {
        System.out.print(" ");
    }
    for (int i = 0; i < numStars; i++) {
        System.out.print("* ");
    }
    System.out.println();
}
```

As you can see, the code for printing spaces and printing stars repeats twice. In order to simplify the code, we will *refactor* it. Refactoring means restructuring the code without changing its behavior. Of course, we can create a method that prints a number of stars and a method that prints a number of spaces. An even better design would be to generalize the task further and create a method that prints a bunch of characters. In other words, we want to create a friend that can help us when we want to print characters. Unlike our friends Peter and Bob, this friend will not charge us. A possible implementation of the method is shown next.

```
public static void printStrings(String s, int n){
    for(int i=0; i < n; i++){
        System.out.print(s);
    }
}
```

Note that the method prints a number of strings instead of a number of characters because we want to print the string "* " multiple times. If we did not want to create a space between the stars, then we could have created the following method.

```
public static void printChars(char c, int n){
```

```
    for(int i=0; i < n; i++){
      System.out.print(c);
    }
}
```

Now we can rewrite our code for printing a diamond as follows.

```
import java.util.*;

public class Diamond {
  public static void printStrings(String s, int n){
    for(int i=0; i < n; i++){
      System.out.print(s);
    }
  }
  public static void main(String [] args) {
    Scanner keyboard = new Scanner(System.in);
    System.out.print("Enter size of diamond: ");
    int size = keyboard.nextInt();
    for (int numStars =1, numSpaces = size -1; numSpaces >=0 ; numSpaces
        -=2, numStars+=2) {
      printStrings(" ",numSpaces);
      printStrings("* ",numStars);
      System.out.println();
    }
    for (int numStars=size -2, numSpaces = 2; numStars >=0 ; numSpaces
        +=2, numStars-=2 ) {
      printStrings(" ",numSpaces);
      printStrings("* ",numStars);
      System.out.println();
    }
  }
}
```

The code is not necessarily shorter, but it is easier to understand. When we want to print a number of characters, we simply call our friend `printStrings`. He will print as many strings as we want for free! Next, note that we print a line in the same way when we print the top and the bottom of the diamond. Therefore, we can create a method that prints a line.

```
public static void printLine(int numSpaces, int numStars){
      printStrings(" ",numSpaces);
      printStrings("* ",numStars);
      System.out.println();
}
```

Now, our main method will call the `printLine` method when we want to print a line. The number of spaces and stars in the line are specified as parameters. The `printLine` method in turn calls the `printStrings` method twice to print the spaces and stars, respectively. The new version of the code is shown below.

```
import java.util.*;

public class Diamond {
  public static void printStrings(String s, int n) {
    for (int i = 0; i < n; i++) {
      System.out.print(s);
```

```java
      }
  }
  public static void printLine(int numSpaces, int numStars) {
    printStrings(" ", numSpaces);
    printStrings("* ", numStars);
    System.out.println("");
  }
  public static void main(String[] args) {
    Scanner keyboard = new Scanner(System.in);
    System.out.print("Enter size of diamond: ");
    int size = keyboard.nextInt();
    for (int numStars = 1, numSpaces = size - 1; numSpaces >= 0;
        numSpaces -= 2, numStars += 2) {
      printLine(numSpaces, numStars);
    }
    for (int numStars = size - 2, numSpaces = 2; numStars >= 0;
        numSpaces += 2, numStars -= 2) {
      printLine(numSpaces, numStars);
    }
  }
}
```

Now the code is much easier to understand. If we look at the code, we will see that we first print a bunch of lines with stars, where every time the number of stars increases by two. Then, we print a bunch of lines, where every time the number of stars decreases by two. One may even be able to guess that we are printing a diamond just by examining the code. This code is an example of *self-documenting* code. The above example shows the importance of giving appropriate names to methods and variables. It also shows how creating compact methods that perform a single task can make the code easier to write, understand, and modify.

4.4   Documenting Methods Using JavaDoc

Note that after you type: "`printLine(`" in your program in NetBeans, you can press Ctrl+Space for auto-completion. NetBeans will show you that there is a method that takes as input two variables of type int and the name of the variables. However, it will not give you any additional information and it will show `JavaDoc missing`. Conversely, if you type "`printf(`" and press Ctrl+Space, then you will see a detailed description of the method. The reason is that someone went through the trouble of writing documentation for the `printf` method. It will be nice if we can do the same for the methods that we write.

JavaDoc is the de facto standard for documenting Java code. It allows the automatic creation of web pages (i.e., HTML files) that describe the methods of a program. For example, type in your favorite search engine: "Java Scanner". Select the first answer. It will take you to a web page that describes the `Scanner` class and its methods. Believe it or not, this page is automatically created from JavaDoc. Whoever wrote the `Scanner` class used JavaDoc to document their code. Then they compiled the code into an HTML file and posted it on the Internet.

Let us go back to our example of printing a diamond. Type /** on a separate line immediately before the `printStrings` method. Press Enter on the keyboard. The following template will be automatically generated by NetBeans.

```
/**
 *
 * @param  s
 * @param  n
 */
```

As you can see, JavaDoc is a way to document your code using a special automatically generated template. On the second line, we need to specify the description of the method. On the next lines, we will describe the meaning of each of the method's parameters. Here is a possible version of the JavaDoc documentation.

```
/**
 * Prints  a  string  multiple  times  on  the  same  line.
 * @param  s  The  string  to  be  printed.
 * @param  n  The  frequency.
 */
```

Fill in the JavaDoc for the rest of the methods. Now we are ready to compile our JavaDoc. Note that the JavaDoc compiler does not work if you have used the default package for your class. Go to the menu **Run** and select **Generate JavaDoc**. A new Web page with the JavaDoc of your program should automatically open. Moreover, the JavaDoc will be automatically displayed by NetBeans when you need it. For example, type "**printStrings(**" in the **main** method and press Ctrl+Space. Now you will see a description of the method and each of the parameters.

> Creating and using JavaDoc is an important part of writing a program. It helps us prevent errors that are caused by using methods incorrectly, passing the wrong arguments to methods, or passing the arguments in the wrong order.

As a general rule, add JavaDoc before every method and before every class. Use additional comments sparingly. For example, only code that performs a non-trivial task needs to be explicitly documented. Remember to always give appropriate names to both methods and variables. Just because a method is documented, it does not mean that its name can be counterintuitive.

4.5 Sending Data between Methods

By now, we have a basic understanding of how methods work. They are like friends. We send them some information and we ask them to do something. They perform the task and present us with the result. Look at the following simple program and see if you can figure out what it prints.

```java
import java.util.*;

public class Example{
    public static void inc(int i){
        i++;
    }
    public static void main(String[] args) {
        int i = 3;
```

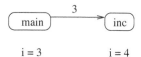

i = 3   i = 4

FIGURE 4.2: Passing parameters between methods.

```
    inc(i);
    System.out.println(i);
  }
}
```

If you guessed 4, you guessed incorrectly. Look at Figure 4.2. The `main` method declares the variable `i`. This variable is local to the `main` method and is only defined inside the `main` method. When the `inc` method is called, the value of the variable and not the actual variable is passed to the `inc` method. In other words, the `inc` method only gets as input the number 3. Now, the `inc` method has a local variable of its own, which also happens to be called `i`. This variable is modified from 3 to 4. After the method terminates, the variable `i` of the `inc` method is automatically deleted. This is done by the Java *garbage collector*. The Java garbage collector looks at main memory that cannot be referenced and it frees it so it can be allocated again. Next, control is passed back to the `main` method. The variable `i` inside the `main` method has not changed and it is still equal to 3.

> In Java, variables of primitive type (e.g., `int`, `double`, `char`, etc.) are passed by value when methods are called. This means that any modification to the variables of the method will not be seen by the calling method.

Next, suppose that we want to rewrite the program in a way that allows us to change the value of `i`. We have two options. First, the new value of `i` can be sent back as a return value of the method. The rewritten code follows.

```
import java.util.*;

public class Example{
  public static int inc(int i){
    i++;
    return i;
  }
  public static void main(String[] args) {
    int i = 3;
    i = inc(i);
    System.out.println(i);
  }
}
```

Now, the `inc` method sends back the new value of the variable `i` in the `inc` method (i.e., the value 4). The assignment operator changes the variable `i` in the `main` method to 4. Alternatively, the variable `i` can be defined as a global variable as shown next.

```
import java.util.*;

public class Example{
  static int i;
  public static void inc(){
```

```
      i++;
  }
  public static void main(String[] args) {
      i = 3;
      inc();
      System.out.println(i);
  }
}
```

Unlike the two previous examples where there were two variables i (one in the **main** method and one in the **inc** method), now we have a single variable i. No information is passed between the methods. The **main** method tells the **inc** method to update the global variable i. The **inc** method updates it and returns control to the **main** method. At this point, the **main** method prints the value of the global variable i. For now, we will declare all global variables as **static**, where the meaning of the **static** keyword will be discussed in Chapter 6. Note that even global variables have scope. The scope of the variable i is the block in which it is defined. Therefore, its scope will be the **Example** class. Remember that the innermost block in which a variable is defined determines its scope. The innermost block for the variable i is the **Example** class.

Comparing the two solutions, the first one is preferable. Good programming practices call for global variables to be used sparingly. The reason is that if a global variable has an incorrect value, then it is difficult to isolate the error. If your class contains ten methods, then any of these methods could have changed the value of the global variable.

Note that a method can return only a single piece of information. For example, a method that returns two integers cannot be created. Global variables are one way to solve this problem. The method can simply modify two global variables and have **void** return type. An example is shown next.

```
import java.util.*;
public class Example{
    static int firstNumber, secondNumber;
    public static void main(String[] args){
        readTwoIntegers();
        System.out.println(firstNumber);
        System.out.println(secondNumber);
    }

    public static void readTwoIntegers(){
        Scanner keyboard = new Scanner(System.in);
        firstNumber = keyboard.nextInt();
        secondNumber = keyboard.nextInt();
    }
}
```

This is a bad design. Global variables should not be declared just because the **readTwoIntegers** method needs to return two integers. A much better approach is to avoid using methods that return two integers. A program with an improved design is shown next.

```
import java.util.*;
public class Example{
    public static void main(String[] args){
        int firstNumber, secondNumber;
        firstNumber = readInteger();
        secondNumber = readInteger();
```

```
    System.out.println(firstNumber);
    System.out.println(secondNumber);
  }

  public static int readInteger(){
    Scanner keyboard = new Scanner(System.in);
    return keyboard.nextInt();
  }
}
```

As a general rule, declare every variable in the innermost scope that you can live with. Variables with a large scope make the program prone to errors. The second program is also preferred because the `readInteger` method performs a single task. It is very likely that a method that reads a single integer from the keyboard will be reused. However, we will rarely need a method that reads two integers. This follows the rule that methods should be simple and perform a single task.

4.6   The Trading Game

We will conclude this chapter with the first non-trivial game. We will create a *Trading Game*. The game consists of 10 days. Every day, the player will be given the opportunity to buy or sell apples and pears. The price of apples and pears will be determined using a random number. The buying and selling will occur through a menu. We will add checks to make sure the player cannot sell product they do not have or buy product they cannot afford. The objective of the game is to make as much money as possible.

The game has some constants. For example, the number of days the game takes should be a constant. Similarly, the numbers that are used in determining the price of apples and pears should be constant. In general, your program should not have numerical numbers, such as 10, inside the code. These are called *magic numbers* and are considered bad programming practice. The reason is that one needs to search for them inside the code in order to change them. Alternatively, these numbers can be defined as constants at the beginning of the program. This is a better solution. You can think of constants as parameters to your program that you can easily change.

Constants in Java are defined using the `final` keyword. For example, the following code will define the number of days.

```
class TradingGame{
  static final int NUMBER_OF_DAYS = 10;
  ...
}
```

The convention is that constants in Java are defined using all capital letters. Constants are usually initialized at the time of declaration. The reason is that the value of a constant cannot be modified.

We will use a *top-down* approach to design the program. We will start with the `main` method. Inside it, however, we will call other methods that we will implement later. Here is one possible implementation of the `main` method.

```
import java.text.*;
import java.util.*;
public class TradingGame {
```

```java
static final int NUMBER_OF_DAYS=10;
static final double BASE_PRICE = 10;
static final double VARIATION = 5;
static final double INITIAL_CASH=100;

static double cash = INITIAL_CASH;
static int appleInventory = 0;
static int pearInventory = 0;
static double applePrice, pearPrice;


public static void main(String[] args) {
  for (int day = 1; day <= NUMBER_OF_DAYS; day++) {
    applePrice = computePrice(BASE_PRICE, VARIATION);
    pearPrice = computePrice(BASE_PRICE, VARIATION);
    System.out.println("Day: " + day + " out of 10");
    int choice;
    do{
      printMenu();
      choice = getChoice();
      switch (choice) {
        case 1: // Print cash balance and inventory
          System.out.println("Cash: " + currencyFormatter(cash));
          System.out.println("Apple inventory: " + appleInventory);
          System.out.println("Pear inventory: " + pearInventory);
          break;
        case 2: //Print today's prices
          System.out.println("Price of apples is: "+
              currencyFormatter(applePrice));
          System.out.println("Price of pears is: "+ currencyFormatter
              (pearPrice));
          break;
        case 3: { //Buy apples
          int amount = getQuantity("apples", "buy");
          if (!buyApples(amount)) {
            System.out.println("You don't have enough money");
          }
          break;
        }
        case 4: { // Sell apples
          int amount = getQuantity("apples", "sell");
          if (!sellApples(amount)) {
            System.out.println("You don't have enough apples");
          }
          break;
        }
        case 5: { // Buy Pears
          int amount = getQuantity("pears", "buy");
          if (!buyPears(amount)) {
            System.out.println("You don't have enough money");
          }
          break;
        }
        case 6: { // Sell Pears
          int amount = getQuantity("pears", "sell");
```

```
            if (!sellPears(amount)) {
               System.out.println("You don't have enough pears");
            }
            break;
         }
      }
   } while (choice != 7);


   }
   System.out.println("You finished with:" + currencyFormatter(cash));
   }
   ...
}
```

Note that the constants are defined at the beginning of the `TradingGame` class. It is pretty common for constants to be defined at the beginning of a class so that they can be easily changed. The price of apples and pears will be computed as a random number in the range (BASE_PRICE−VARIATION, BASE_PRICE+VARIATION).

The variable `cash` keeps track of the amount of cash available to spend. Note that most of the variables are defined as global and are accessible by several methods. Consider for example the variable `cash`. The `buyPears`, `buyApples`, `sellApples`, and `sellPears` methods all need to update this variable. Remember that a method can just perform a calculation and cannot modify an input variable of primitive type, such as a `double`. Therefore, the easiest choice here is to make the variables global. It makes sense to define a variable that is updated by several methods as global. Note that the methods could not simply return the new value of the modified variable because most methods update two variables (e.g., `appleInventory` and `cash`) and a method cannot return two values.

Next, let us examine the `main` method in details. Our program needs to do something every day. Therefore, we create a `for` loop that iterates through the days. At the beginning of every day, we will set the apple price and the pear price using the `computePrice` method. The method will compute a random price using the input parameters. Next, we will print the current day and the menu. Here is the menu.

```
1. Print cash balance and inventory
2. Print today's prices
3. Buy apples
4. Sell apples
5. Buy pears
6. Sell pears
7. I am done for today
```

Note that we have combined some choices in some menu items. For example, Choice 1 prints both the balance and the inventory. From psychology, we know that humans have hard time keeping track of more than 7 items. Therefore, creating a menu that has 10 or more items usually signals a bad user interface.

We next need a loop that allows the player to enter her or his menu choice multiple times. After the player enters her or his choice, we need to perform the operation that the player requested. Since this sequence will always be executed at least once, we are using a `do-while` loop. The loop will keep iterating until the user selects Choice 7.

Note that we have broken the choice selection into two methods. The `printMenu` method prints the available choices, while the `getChoice` method gets input from the player. We have created two methods because creating a single method that performs multiple tasks signals a poor design. Such a method contains more complex logic, which makes it more error-prone. Moreover, methods that perform multiple tasks are rarely reusable.

A `switch` statement handles the possible choices. Note that, as required, there is a `break` at the end of every `case` block except for the last one. Remember that if the `break` statements are missing, then the code will execute several `case` statements at once, which is undesirable behavior. Note that some of the `choice` blocks are surrounded by braces. The reason is that we define the variable `amount` and we want this variable to be local for the block. In other words, there are four variables `amount` that are declared. They happen to have the same name, but they are different variables because they are defined in different blocks and have different scopes. As a general rule, define every variable in the innermost scope that you can.

If Choice 1 is selected, then the program prints the available cash and inventory. Note that the `currencyFormatter` method is used to format the cash amount. Choice 2 prints the prices of apples and pears, where the `currencyFormatter` method is used again to format the prices. One may consider putting the code for Choice 1 or for Choice 2 in a separate method. However, such a method will be custom designed and not reusable. In general, try to create methods that will be called multiple times and will therefore make the program shorter.

Choices 3–6 are similar to each other. First, a method is called to get the quantity of product to be bought or sold. Then a method to do the transaction is called. The method will modify some global variables (e.g., `cash`, `appleInventory`, etc.) and will return `true` if the transaction is successful. Note that it is a bad programming practice for methods that perform sale transactions to print to the screen. Their job is to just perform the transaction and report whether the transaction was successful or not. If they also print to the screen, then this will significantly reduce their reusability. If one of the transaction methods returns `false`, then the `main` method prints the appropriate error message.

Note that the code for Choices 3-6 is pretty similar. The astute reader may wonder if we can put this code in a method and just call the method 4 times. This is certainly a possibility. However, such a method will have an `if` statement that checks the input parameters and will call different methods based on the value of an input parameter. In other words, there will be no significant reduction in the number of lines of code. In general, a method that executes different code based on the value of an input parameter is considered bad programming practice. It is much simpler to just create a separate method for every possibility.

The code for the `printMenu` method is shown next. It simply prints the menu.

```java
public static void printMenu() {
    System.out.println("1. Print cash balance and inventory");
    System.out.println("2. Print today's prices");
    System.out.println("3. Buy apples");
    System.out.println("4. Sell apples");
    System.out.println("5. Buy pears");
    System.out.println("6. Sell pears");
    System.out.println("7. I am done for today");
}
```

The `getChoice` method is shown next.

```java
public static int getChoice() {
    Scanner keyboard = new Scanner(System.in);
    int choice;
    do {
        System.out.print("Your choice: ");
        choice = keyboard.nextInt();
    } while (choice > 7 || choice < 1);
    return choice;
```

```
}
```

It prompts the player to enter a choice and repeatedly reads the choice until a valid choice is made. One may ask if the number 7 is a magic number. If it is, should it not be declared as a constant? The answer is that declaring the number 7 as a constant will not be very helpful here. We cannot change the number of choices just by changing this number. Therefore, the number of choices is not really a parameter of the program and it does not need to be declared as a constant. You can think of this as being an exception when it is allowable to create a magic number.

The `currencyFormatter` method is shown next. It uses the `DecimalFormat` class to format the dollar amounts in a pretty way.

```java
public static String currencyFormatter(double amount) {
    DecimalFormat myFormatter = new DecimalFormat("$###,###.00");
    return myFormatter.format(amount);
}
```

Note that the two zeros after the decimal dot mean that two digits will always be displayed after the decimal dot. If the amount is 32 dollars, for example, then $32.00 will be displayed. Conversely, the character # is non-imposing and suggests that there can be up to 6 digits, but missing digits will not be filled with zeros.

The `computePrice` method is shown next.

```java
public static double computePrice(double basePrice, double variation) {
    double result = basePrice;
    if (Math.random() > 0.5) {
        result += Math.random() * variation;
    } else {
        result -= Math.random() * variation;
    }
    return ((int)(result*100))/100.0;
}
```

It starts with the `basePrice`. Then a random number is used to decide if we want to add or subtract from it. Up to the value of the variable `variation` can be added or removed from the variable `result`. Recall that `Math.random` returns a number between 0 inclusive and 1 exclusive. After executing the first 6 lines, the value of the variable `result` can be 10.32544, for example. However, we want the number to have only 2 digits after the decimal dot because it must be of type currency. If we multiply the number by 100, we will move the decimal dot two places to the right. For example, we may get the number 1032.544. Now, we can convert the result to an integer and remove everything after the decimal dot. We will get the number 1032. Finally, we can convert the number back to decimal by dividing it by 100.0. We will get 10.32, which is exactly what we wanted. Note that we need to divide by 100.0 and not by 100. If we divide by 100, we will get the result 10 because the result of dividing two integers is always an integer. Note that the whole method can be rewritten in a single line as follows.

```java
public static double computePrice(double basePrice, double variation) {
    return ((int)((basePrice + (Math.random() > 0.5 ? 1 : -1) * variation
    )*100))/100.0;
}
```

However, this syntax uses the conditional operator and is less intuitive. In general, avoid writing code that is non-trivial to understand.

The `getQuantity` method is shown next. The method is very general in that it can be used to ask for any product and any action. Creating a method that is as reusable as possible is a good idea. An extra advantage is that the increased reusability of the method does not increase its complexity.

```java
public static int getQuantity(String product, String action) {
    System.out.print("How many " + product + " do you want to " + action
        + "? ");
    Scanner keyboard = new Scanner(System.in);
    return keyboard.nextInt();
}
```

Lastly, consider the four transaction methods.

```java
public static boolean sellApples(int amount) {
    if (amount > appleInventory) {
        return false;
    }
    cash += amount * applePrice;
    appleInventory -= amount;
    return true;
}

public static boolean sellPears(int amount) {
    if (amount > pearInventory) {
        return false;
    }
    cash += amount * pearPrice;
    pearInventory -= amount;
    return true;
}

public static boolean buyApples(int amount) {
    if (amount * applePrice < cash) {
        cash -= amount * applePrice;
        appleInventory += amount;
        return true;
    }
    return false;
}

public static boolean buyPears(int amount) {
    if (amount * pearPrice < cash) {
        cash -= amount * pearPrice;
        pearInventory += amount;
        return true;
    }
    return false;
}
```

The methods are very similar. However, combining them in a single method is not easy, as explained earlier. The buy methods check to see if the player has enough money to complete the transaction. If this is the case, then the purchase is complete and the cash and inventory are adjusted accordingly. Similarly, the sell methods check to see if the player has enough inventory. If this is the case, then the cash and the inventory are updated appropriately. Note that defining the variables `cash`, `pearInventory`, `appleInventory`, `pearPrice`, and `applePrice` as global variables significantly simplifies the four methods.

Compile and run the complete program. See how much money you can make in 10 days.

4.7 Summary

This chapter covered two topics: methods and formatted printing. Methods are used to break a big program into small manageable pieces. When calling a method, one can send several parameters to the method. A method can return at most one piece of data. When a method needs to return multiple pieces of data, global variables can be used. However, a better approach is to avoid using global variables when possible.

Java supports the `printf` method (inherited from the C programming language). It allows us to display formatted output. For example, it allows us to justify the output to the left or to the right, insert leading or trailing spaces, or specify the precision with which to display a real number. Similarly, Java supports formatted printing through the `DecimalFormat` class. You can specify a pattern and the result will be printed according to the pattern template.

4.8 Syntax

- `System.out.printf("%.2f",a)` ⇒ Prints a double formatted two digits after the decimal dot.

- `System.out.printf("%5d",3)` ⇒ Prints the integer using 5 spaces and right justified.

- `System.out.printf("%-4d",3)` ⇒ Prints the integer using 4 spaces and left justified.

- `System.out.println(new DecimalFormat("$###,###.##").format(3365.34))` ⇒ Prints $3,365.34.

- `System.out.println(new DecimalFormat("$000,000.00").format(3365.34))` ⇒ Prints $003,365.34.

- `static final int DAYS = 10` ⇒ Defines the constant `DAYS` and sets it to be equal to 10.

- `public static void m(...) { ... }` ⇒ Method with no return type.

- `public static int m(...) { ... }` ⇒ Method that returns an integer.

- `public static int m(int i, int j) { ... }` ⇒ Method that returns an integer and takes as input two integers. The input is saved in the variables `i` and `j`, which are local for the method.

4.9 Important Points

1. Every method must have a return type. When this type is `void`, the method does not return anything. When this type is not `void`, the calling method needs to save the result of calling the method for future use. It does not make sense to ask a method to calculate something and then not save the result after calling the method.

2. Every method should perform exactly one task. If a method becomes too big, try breaking it down into several methods.

3. Avoid methods that contain a *switch* parameter. That is, a method that can perform one of several tasks based on the value of an input parameter. Instead, create a separate method for every task.

4. Any modification to the value of the input parameters of a method that are primitive types (e.g., `int`, `double`, etc.) will not be seen by the calling the method. The reason is that the input parameters are local variables for the method. Java uses pass-by-value for primitive-type parameters.

5. Use global variables sparingly. Only define them when you need them. As a general rule, define every variable in the innermost scope that you can live with.

6. Good programming practices call for every method to have an appropriate JavaDoc.

7. Use `printf` to produce formatted output. Remember that "%d" stands for decimal (a.k.a., integer) and not double. Use "%f" to display a `double`.

8. Use the `DecimalFormat` class to specify a pattern for formatting a real number. For example, the class can be used to display currency values.

9. Magic numbers are any numerical literals, such as 42, that appear in your program. Avoid using magic numbers and define such numerical literals as constants at the beginning of the class. For example, `public static int MEANING_OF_LIFE = 42`.

10. Names of constants should be in all capital letters.

4.10 Exercises

1. Write a method that takes in three integers and returns the biggest.

2. Write a method that takes in three integers and returns the average as a `double`.

3. Write a method that takes as input a `double` and prints it to the screen formatted to two digits after the decimal dot.

4. Write a method that takes as input an integer **n** and returns the sum of the first **n** numbers. For example, if the input is 10, the method will return 55 because $1+2+\ldots+10 = 55$.

5. Consider sales tax of 7%. Write a method that takes as input the price of an item and returns the sales tax for that item. Both input and return value should be of type `double`.

6. Write a method that computes the amount of a tip. The method should take as input the total price for the meal. The method should return the amount for the tip. The tip should be between 10% and 20%, where the program should use a random number to determine the exact amount.

7. Write a method that takes as input the speed of a car and the duration of the trip. The method should return the distance that is traveled.

8. Consider the following definition:

```
double x = 32.3947;
double y = 11.82714;
```

What is the result of executing the following statements?

(a) System.out.printf("%.3f\n", x);

(b) System.out.printf("%.3f\n", y);

(c) System.out.printf("%.1f\n", x);

(d) System.out.printf("%.1f\n", y);

9. Write a method that computes the nth Fibonacci number.

10. Write a method that computes $n!$, that is n factorial.

11. Write a method that takes as input a **double** and prints the value in the format $\$***,***.**$. If a digit is not present, do not display anything.

4.11 Lab

Write a program that displays a triangle of random numbers (each number should be between 0 and 9). The height of the triangle should be user specified.

Here are two example runs of the program, where user input is in italic.

```
Enter height of triangle: 5
4
3 3 4
4 6 7 5 4
3 4 5
5
Enter height of triangle: 3
1
2 3
6
```

Create several methods. You should have a method that returns a random digit. You should also have a method that prints a line, where the size of the line should be a parameter.

4.12 Project

Modify the *Trading Game* and add two cities: New York and Los Angeles. The price of apples and pears changes every day in both cities. The player can only buy or sell goods from one of the cities every day. Extend the game by adding inventory of apples and pears for both cities. The inventory changes randomly every day. The player can only buy apples or pears if there is sufficient inventory in the city. The goal of the game again is to make as much money as possible after ten days. You are allowed to introduce new global variables as needed. Try to create as many new methods as needed and follow good software engineering practices.

Chapter 5

Introduction to Arrays

So far, we have examined how variables are declared, initialized, and manipulated. Remember that space in main memory is allocated for every single variable. If we want to create space in main memory for one hundred integers, then we need to declare one hundred distinct integer variables. Although this approach is certainly plausible, it is not very practical. As an alternative, one can declare an array of one hundred integers in a single statement. This makes the program shorter and easier to write and maintain. Moreover, Java allows the creation of variable-sized arrays. In other words, we can use an array to allocate as much main memory as we deem necessary during the execution of a program.

5.1   One-Dimensional Arrays

Yahtzee is a popular dice game. Players roll five dice and try to get different combinations. If a player is not satisfied with her or his dice, then he or she is allowed to reroll some or all of the dice up to two times. A player gets a Yahtzee when all five dice show the same value.

We will next show how to create a simplified version of the game, where the only combination that the player is interesting in achieving is Yahtzee. We will use a data-driven approach to design our program. The reason is that the variables are the pillar of any program. In the Yahtzee case, we need to create five variables for the five dice. The skeleton of the program can look as shown below.

```
class Yahtzee{
  static int d1,d2,d3,d4,d5; // the five dice
  public static void main(String[] args){
    ...
  }
  ...
}
```

We defined the five dice as global variables for the class because most of the methods in the class will access them. For example, consider the method that generates the initial values for the five dice.

```java
public static void rollDice(){
    d1 = getRandomDieValue();
    d2 = getRandomDieValue();
    d3 = getRandomDieValue();
    d4 = getRandomDieValue();
    d5 = getRandomDieValue();
}
```

Since arguments in Java are passed by value and every method can return at most one entity, it is not obvious how to write a method that returns five values. This is the reason why the variables for the dice are declared as global variables.

The `getRandomDieValue` method simply returns a random number between 1 and 6 (the value of the die). It can be implemented as shown below.

```java
public static int getRandomDieValue(){
    return (int)(Math.random()*6+1);
}
```

Recall that `Math.random()` returns a random **double** between 0 (inclusive) and 1(exclusive). Multiplying it by 6 will give us a **double** in the range [0,6). Adding one will shift the range to [1,7). When a double in this range is cast to an integer, then the result will be an integer between 1 and 6.

Our code so far has one major drawback: it is not versatile. For example, suppose that we decide to modify the game to include four instead of five dice. Then a significant portion of the code will need to be rewritten. A different shortcoming of our code is that we need to duplicate some of the code five times: once for every die (e.g., the `rollDice` method).

It will be beneficial if we can somehow combine the variables d1, d2, d3, d4, and d5 so that we can declare them in a single statement and we can manipulate them using a single loop. This will make the code more compact. More compact code is usually not only easier to write, but also easier to maintain (on average, 70% of the cost to develop commercial software goes into maintenance). Fortunately for us, *arrays* come to the rescue!

An array allows us to declare multiple variables of the same type in a single statement. In our example, if we need to create one hundred instead of five dice, then defining one hundred variables will surely be impractical. However, using an array we can create as many dice as we need in a single statement.

In Java, an array is allocated using the **new** keyword.

```java
new int[100];
```

The above line creates an array of one hundred integers. Initially, the array will be populated with zeros. In general, the **new** keyword is used to create a new object, where an array is a special kind of an object. The operator **new** returns a *reference* to the object. The best way to think of this reference is as a unique identifier of the object. This identifier can be used by the Java Virtual Machine to quickly locate the object. The **new** keyword does not return the address of the object because the Java Virtual Machine may move the object during the execution of the program, while the unique identifier remains constant. Consider the following code.

```java
System.out.println(new int[100]);
```

A possible result is: "[I@3e25a5". This means that the allocated space is for an array of integers. **3E25A5** is the hexadecimal representation of the result of applying a function to

FIGURE 5.1: Example array.

the identifier of the object. Note that the 64-bit Java Virtual Machine can support more than 2^{32} objects. However, printing the result of the operator **new** always results in a 32-bit number. Therefore, it is possible that the same value is printed for two distinct objects. We believe that this is an implementation detail and should not affect the way we write our code.

> The operator **new** returns a unique object identifier or a *reference* to an object. When we try to print this value, a function of this identifier is printed. Although this identifier is different from the address of the object, we will consider it to be the address of the object. This assumption will in no way affect our code. However, it will help us better understand how to work with object references.

So far, we have declared variables that belong to primitive types (e.g., **int**, **double**, **char**, etc.). Next, we are going to declare a variable that has type that is an array of integers. Such a variable can be declared as follows.

```
int [] a;
```

Note that it is also legal for the square brackets to appear after the variable. In other words, the above statement is equivalent to the following statement.

```
int a [];
```

The first statement can be read as "the variable a is of type array of integers". This syntax seems more intuitive and will be used throughout the textbook. The second syntax is supported mainly for historical reasons (e.g., in the C language an array is declared as: **int** a[10]). Note that, also for historical reasons, a, b, c, and d are common names for arrays. Of course, the name of an array should be less generic and more descriptive whenever possible.

The declaration of an array and its memory allocation can be combined in a single statement.

```
int [] a = new int [100];
```

This will allocate memory for one hundred integers. Remember that an array is just a sequence of variables of the same type that are allocated simultaneously. The elements of an array of 100 elements are: a[0],a[1], ..., a[99]. Note that the counting always starts at 0 and goes up to the length of the array minus one (this is analogous to the British system for counting floors). If you try to access the element at position 100, you will get an **ArrayIndexOutOfBoundsException**. The reason is that the element at position 100 is not part of the array.

Figure 5.1 shows an example array. In the figure, we assume that the array is allocated at address 1000. Since the size of an integer in Java is four bytes, the array will take 4*5 = 20 bytes. The code to create the array can be written as follows.

```
int [] a = new int [5];
a [0] = 2;
a [1] = 4;
a [2] = 6;
```

```
a[3] = 8;
a[4] = 10;
```

Again, note that counting starts at 0. The reason is that Java will search for the element `a[k]` at address `a+k*4` (assuming that the array contains four-byte elements).

It seems tedious to use six lines of code to define and populate an array of five elements. Fortunately, in Java these lines can be merged into a single line as shown below.

```
int[] a = {2,4,6,8,10};
```

The above line is a shorthand that performs three operations: allocates twenty consecutive bytes to store five integers, makes the variable `a` equal to the address of the allocated memory, and finally populates the array with the numbers {2,4,6,8,10}.

Next, consider an array that contains the numbers: {2,4,6,8,...,1000}. Of course, we can go ahead and explicitly write all 500 numbers that initially populate the array. However, there is a more compact way to perform the initialization. In particular, note that arrays and loops go together like ham and eggs (or peanut butter and jelly if you happen to be vegetarian). If you go to a play and see a gun in the props, odds are that it will be fired by act three. Similarly, if you see an array declaration, odds are that there will be a loop that traverses through its elements. The most popular and easy way to traverse through the elements of an array is using a `for` loop, although using a `while` loop can also be warranted in some rear cases. An array with elements: {2,4,6,8,...,1000} can be populated in Java using the following code segment.

```
int[] a = new int[500];
for(int i=2, j=0; i<=1000; i+=2, j++){
  a[j] = i;
}
```

The code performs the operation `a[j] = i` multiple times. The value of `i` starts at 2 and goes up to 1000 in increments of 2. The value of `j` starts at 0 and goes up to 499 in increments of 1. We therefore have two conditions: $i <= 1000$ and $j <= 499$. Note that we only need to include one of the two conditions in the second argument of the `for` statement because when `i` becomes 1000, `j` will become equal to 499. Note as well that, while the first and third part of a `for` statement can contain multiple statements, the second part of a `for` statement can contain at most one condition.

Let us go back to the Yahtzee game. Now that we know more about arrays, we can declare the dice as an array of integers as shown below.

```
class Yahtzee{
  static int[] dice = new int[5];
    ...
}
```

Although this declaration is correct, it has one minor drawback. The number 5 is a *magic number*. It comes from thin air and it is not clear why we chose 5. A better solution would be to define the number of dice as a constant. The convention is that constants are written in all capital letters.

```
class Yahtzee{
  static final int NUMBER_OF_DICE = 5;
  static int[] dice = new int[NUMBER_OF_DICE];
    ...
}
```

Remember to use the `final` keyword to define a variable as a constant. Constants can be assigned once and cannot be modified after that. Good software practices call for all numerals (e.g., magic numbers, such as 5) to be defined as constants at the beginning of the code.

Note that Java is lenient as to what can go in the size of an array. In particular, the size of an array can be a variable that is initialized from keyboard input and does not need to be a constant. The only restriction is that once an array is created, its size cannot change. Therefore, make sure that you have enough space to store your data when you declare an array.

The `rollDice` method can now be rewritten to use a **for** loop.

```
public static void rollDice (){
  for(int i = 0; i < NUMBER_OF_DICE; i++){
    dice[i] = getRandomDieValue();
  }
}
```

The elegancy in the new approach is that we only need to change the constant `NUMBER_OF_DICE` when we want to change the number of dice. Nothing else needs to be changed. Next, consider a method that modifies only some of the dice. Remember that in the Yahtzee game a player is allowed to change some of his or her dice up to two times. Which dice to change can be specified as a parameter to the method. One possible implantation of the method follows.

```
public static void rollDice (int [] diceToChange){
  for(int i=0; i < ?; i++){
    dice[diceToChange[i]]=getRandomDieValue();
  }
}
```

Note that it is perfectly fine to have two methods that are named `rollDice`. If the `rollDice` method is called without a parameter, then the first implementation will be called and all the dice will be rerolled. Conversely, if the method is called with an array of integers as a parameter, then the second method will be called and only the chosen dice will be rerolled. The question mark in the above code is not a new Java feature. The size of the array `diceToChange` should appear there, but how can we find the size of the array? Fortunately, Java allows us to find the size of the **a** array by writing **a.length**. Therefore, the code should actually read as shown below.

```
public static void rollDice (int [] diceToChange){
  for(int i=0; i < diceToChange.length; i++){
    dice[diceToChange[i]]=getRandomDieValue();
  }
}
```

An example invocation of the method is: `rollDice(new int[] {0,2,4})`. This code will change the value of the first, third, and fifth die (remember that the first element of an array is at index 0). The code is an example of creating an *anonymous array*. The statement `new int[] {0,2,4}` creates an array of three integers with values {0,2,4}. However, this array is not saved in a variable and we cannot refer to it. It is simply passed as an argument to the method.

If we are more comfortable counting dice starting with die 1, rather than die 0, then we can rewrite the method as follows.

```
public static void rollDice (int [] diceToChange) {
  for(int i = 0; i < diceToChange.length; i++) {
    dice[diceToChange[i]-1] = getRandomDieValue();
  }
}
```

Now the call `rollDice(new int[] {1,2})` will change the first two dice, which seems to be a more intuitive behavior for the method.

When our program is complete, it should run as demonstrated by the following example (user input is in italic).

```
Your dice are: 3,2,5,5,1
Which dice do you want to reroll: 1 2 5
Your dice are: 6,5,5,5,4
Which dice do you want to reroll: 1 5
Your dice are: 5,5,5,5,5
You got Yahtzee!
```

Therefore, we need a method that parses user input and converts it into an array of integers. For example, when the user enters: 1 2 5, we want to create the array {1,2,5} and send it to the `rollDice` method. Fortunately, a string tokenizer class is part of the Java library `java.util.*`. Below is an example use of the class.

```
1  public static int[] convert(String s) {
2     StringTokenizer st = new StringTokenizer(s);
3     int[] a = new int[st.countTokens()];
4     int i = 0;
5
6     while(st.hasMoreTokens()) {
7        a[i++] = Integer.parseInt(st.nextToken());
8     }
9     return a;
10 }
```

The first line of the code creates a new string tokenizer object from the string `s`. The name of the tokenizer is `st`. The `countTokens` method returns the number of tokens in the string. The `while` loop goes through all the tokens. The `nextToken` method returns the next token from the string as a `String`, where the `Integer.parseInt` method converts the string to an integer. The `hasMoreTokens` method returns true when there are more tokens in the string tokenizer. The `convert` method creates an array of integers and returns the array. For example, the call `covert("1 2 3")` will return the array of integers {1,2,3}.

Note that the above code makes a clever use of the `++` operator. Line 7 uses the syntax `i++`. This means use the current value of `i` and then increment `i` by one later. The first time Line 7 is executed, the variable `a[0]` will be assigned and `i` will change to 1. This is exactly the desired behavior.

Our next method will check to see if the dice form a Yahtzee. The method will go through all the dice and check if they are equal to the first die. If one of the die is not equal to the first die, then we know that the dice are not all the same and the method will return `false`. If we go through all the dice and they are all the same, then the method will return `true`.

```
public static boolean isYahtzee(){
   for(int i = 0; i < NUMBER_OF_DICE; i++){
      if(dice[i] != dice[0]){ //evidence that the dice are different
         return false;
      }
   }
   return true;
}
```

Novice programmers are sometimes tempted to use the `if-else` construct when writing similar methods. For example, note that the following rewrite is not correct.

```
public static boolean isYahtzee(){
  for(int i = 0; i < NUMBER_OF_DICE; i++){
    if(dice[i] != dice[0]){ //evidence that dice are different
      return false;
    } else {
      return true;
    }
  }
}
```

There are two problems with this rewrite. First, Java will give you a compile error because the method is not guaranteed to return a value. For example, if NUMBER_OF_DICE is equal to zero, then the body of the for loop will not execute. Second, even if you remove this error by placing "return true;" at the end of the method, the method will not return the correct result. When i is equal to 0, the condition in the if statement will fail and the method will always return true.

Lastly, we need to write a method that converts the dice to a string. This method is necessary so that the values of the dice can be displayed. The method starts with the string "Your dice are: " and then it concatenates all the dice to the string. The implementation follows.

```
public static String diceToString(){
  String result="Your dice are: ";
  for(int i=0; i < NUMBER_OF_DICE; i++){
    result +=dice[i]+" ";
  }
  return result;
}
```

We have followed good software practices because the method does just one thing: it calculates a string representation of the dice. Creating string and printing it in a single method would be an inferior design because the latter method is more prone to errors and less reusable.

So far, we have seen a familiar pattern. Every time we want to iterate through the array of dice, we use the following template.

```
for(int i=0; i < NUMBER_OF_DICE; i++){
  do something with dice[i];
}
```

Although the variable i is local to the for loop (it is not defined outside it), it seems tedious to have to introduce a new variable every time that we want to iterate through the elements of an array. Defining the variable i globally is an inferior design because it violates a rule of good software practices: *Every variable should be defined only in the block where it is being used.* For convenience, Java supports an alternative way of iterating through the elements of an array using a *for-each* for *loop*. For example, the diceToString method can be rewritten as follows.

```
public static String diceToString(){
  String result="Your dice are: ";
  for(int el: dice){
    result +=el+" ";
  }
  return result;
}
```

The statement for(int el: dice) means: iterate through all the elements of the dice array. The first time the `for` loop is executed, the variable `el` will be assigned the first element of the array. The second time the `for` loop is executed, the variable will be assigned the second element of the array and so on. The new code seems cleaner and easier to write and understand. The only caveat is that a for-each `for` loop can be used to read an array of elements, but not to populate it. For example, it is tempting to apply our new knowledge of the for-each `for` loop and rewrite the `rollDice` method as follows.

```java
public static void rollDice() {
  for (int el: dice) {
    el = getRandomDieValue();
  }
}
```

Unfortunately, this rewrite is wrong. It modifies the variable `el` multiple times, but it does not change the array in any way. As a general rule, a for-each `for` loop cannot be used to modify an array; it can only be used to examine its content. The reason is that it iterates through an array and it assigns the elements of the array to a variable. Obviously, this in no way changes the content of the array.

As a different example, the `isYahtzee` method only examines the dice without modifying them. Therefore, it can be rewritten as follows.

```java
public static boolean isYahtzee() {
  for (int el: dice) {
    if (el != dice[0]) {
      return false;
    }
  }
  return true;
}
```

As a general rule, use the for-each `for` loop when you want to examine the content of an array but you do not want to modify the array. Most of the time, the for-each `for` loop is preferred to the regular `for` loop because it makes the code cleaner and easier to understand.

We are finally ready to present the first iteration of the Yahtzee game.

```java
import java.util.*;

public class Yahtzee {
  static final int NUMBER_OF_DICE = 5;
  static final int NUM_REROLLS = 2;
  static int[] dice = new int[NUMBER_OF_DICE];

  public static void main(String[] args){
    Scanner keyboard = new Scanner(System.in);
    rollDice();

    for (int i = 0; i < NUM_REROLLS; i++){
      if (isYahtzee()){ // no need to continue if we got Yahtzee
        break;
      }
      System.out.println(diceToString()); //prints the dice
      System.out.print("Which dice do you want to reroll: ");
```

```java
      rollDice(convert(keyboard.nextLine())); //reads the dice
          //to reroll and rerolls them
   }
   System.out.println(diceToString()); //prints the dice
   if (isYahtzee()) {
      System.out.println("You got Yahtzee!");
   } else {
      System.out.println("Sorry, better luck next time!");
   }
}

public static String diceToString() {
   String result = "Your dice are: ";
   for (int el : dice) {
      result += el + " ";
   }
   return result;
}

public static boolean isYahtzee() {
   for (int el: dice) {
      if (el != dice[0]) {
         return false;
      }
   }
   return true;
}

public static void rollDice(int[] diceToChange) {
   for (int i: diceToChange) {
      dice[i - 1] = getRandomDieValue();
   }
}

public static void rollDice() {
   for (int i = 0; i < NUMBER_OF_DICE; i++) {
      dice[i] = getRandomDieValue();
   }
}

public static int getRandomDieValue() {
   return (int) (Math.random() * 6 + 1);
}

public static int[] convert(String s) {
   StringTokenizer st = new StringTokenizer(s);
   int[] a = new int[st.countTokens()];
   int i = 0;

   while (st.hasMoreTokens()) {
      a[i++] = Integer.parseInt(st.nextToken());
   }
   return a;
}
}
```

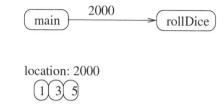

FIGURE 5.2: Passing an array to a method.

Although not perfect, the above code demonstrates a clean design. Every method is short and does exactly one thing. The major shortcoming is that methods that do not need to have access to the array of dice, such as the **convert** method, do anyway. This shortcoming comes from declaring the array of dice a global variable. As an alternative, the array of dice can be declared as a local variable in the **main** method and passed to methods that need it. The new version of the **main** method is shown next.

```java
public static void main(String [] args) {
  int [] dice = new int [NUMBER_OF_DICE]; // the dice
  Scanner keyboard = new Scanner(System.in);
  rollDice(dice);

  for (int i = 0; i < NUM_REROLLS; i++) {
    if (isYahtzee(dice)) {// if we got Yahtzee
      break;
    }
    System.out.println(diceToString(dice)); //prints the dice
    System.out.print("Which dice do you want to reroll: ");
    rollDice(dice, convert(keyboard.nextLine()));
  }
  System.out.println(diceToString(dice)); //prints the dice
  if (isYahtzee(dice)) {
    System.out.println("You got Yahtzee!");
  } else {
    System.out.println("Sorry, better luck next time!");
  }
}
```

Note that arrays in Java are passed to/from methods using their address. Therefore, the **rollDice** method can and does change the value of the input array. An implementation of the method is shown below.

```java
public static void rollDice(int [] d) {
  for (int i = 0; i < NUMBER_OF_DICE; i++) {
    d[i] = getRandomDieValue();
  }
}
```

Figure 5.2 shows an example of passing the array to the **rollDice** method. As the figure suggests, only the number 2000 is passed to the method. This is the location of the array. Since the **rollDice** method knows this location, it can go to it and modify the content of the array. Note that this contrasts the way primitive types (e.g., integers, doubles, and characters) are sent to methods. The latter cannot be modified by a method. For example, consider the following version of the **rollDice** method.

```java
public static void rollDice(int d0, int d1, int d2, int d3, int d4){
```

```
d0=getRandomDieValue ( ) ;
d1=getRandomDieValue ( ) ;
d2=getRandomDieValue ( ) ;
d3=getRandomDieValue ( ) ;
d4=getRandomDieValue ( ) ;
}
```

This version of the method falls short because it only changes the local variables d0, d1, d2, d3, and d4. If you call the method as follows: `rollDice (d[0],d[1],d[2],d[3],d[4])`, then this will not work because the array will remain unchanged after the execution of the method. Yet another implementation of the `rollDice` method is shown below.

```
public static int [] rollDice () {
    int [] d = int [NUMBER_OF_DICE];
    for (int i = 0; i < NUMBER_OF_DICE; i++) {
      d[i] = getRandomDieValue ( ) ;
    }
    return d;
}
```

This implementation is similar to the implementation that takes a single array as input. However, the new implementation makes it clear that method generates a new array of dice and does not read the old array of dice. Therefore, this last implementation of the method is preferred. The method can be called from the main method as shown below.

```
dice = rollDice () ;
```

5.1.1 Deep versus Shallow Array Copy

One needs to be very careful when copying arrays. Consider the following example.

```
public class Test {
  public static void main(String [] args){
    int a[]= new int [] {2,234,14,12,23,2};
    int b[]=new int [6];
    b=a ;
    b[3]=7;
    System.out.println (a[3]) ;
  }
}
```

This looks like a very simple program. First, the arrays a and b are created. Then all the elements of the a array are copied to the b array. The fourth element of the b array is then changed (remember that index counting for arrays starts at 0). This should have no effect on the a array and the number 12 should be printed (the fourth element of the a array). However, we you run the program, then we will see that the number 7 is printed.

In order to understand this counterintuitive behavior, consider Figure 5.3. It shows the initial setup. The variables a and b point to two different arrays. The line b = a is going to make b equal to 1000. In other words, after the assignment both a and b will be equal to 1000. Then when the line b[3]= 7 is executed, both the value of b[3] and a[3] will change. Nothing will now point to the array at position 2000 and it will be purged by the garbage collector. This type of array copy is known as *shallow copy*.

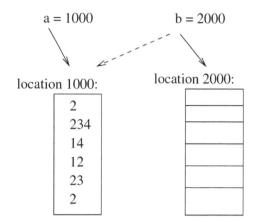

FIGURE 5.3: Example of shallow copy.

Shallow copy is when you copy the address of an array, but not the array itself. The result is having two variables that point to the same array. Any change to the array using one of the variables will affect the other variables. This behavior is undesirable and shallow copying should be avoided.

Next, let us fix the program and make sure that changes to the b array do not affect the a array. Below is a possible solution.

```java
public class Test {
   public static void main(String[] args){
      int a[] = new int[] {2,234,14,12,23,2};
      int b[] =new int[6];
      for(int i= 0; i < a.length; i++){
        b[i] = a[i];
      }
      b[3]=7;
      System.out.println(a[3]);
   }
}
```

Now, as expected, the final value of a[3] will be 12. The only way to make a and b independent arrays, where modifying an element in one of the arrays does not affect the other array, is to use a for loop. The loop copies all the elements from the a array to the b array one by one. After the for loop executes, the value of a is still 1000 and the value of b is still 2000. In other words, the for loop does not change the value of b. It simply copies the elements from a to b one by one. This type of array copying is known as *deep copy*.

Deep copy of arrays is when the elements of the array are copied one by one. This type of copying is preferred to shallow copy because the two arrays will be independent and modifying an element in one of the arrays will not affect the other array.

Since deep copy is such a common operation, Java supports the `Arrays.copyOf` method, which performs a deep copy of an array. Here is an example of how the method can be used.

```java
public class Test {
```

```
public static void main(String[] args){
    int a[] = new int[] {2,234,14,12,23,2};
    int b[] = Arrays.copyOf(a, a.length);
    b[3]=7;
    System.out.println(a[3]);
}
}
```

The `Arrays.copyOf` method creates a new array. The size of the new array is defined as the second parameter of the method. The first parameter of the method specifies the original array from which elements are copied one by one.

5.1.2 Deep versus Shallow Array Comparison

Similar to copying arrays, comparing arrays for equality is not trivial. Consider the following simple program.

```
public class Test {
    public static void main(String[] args){
        int[] a = {2,234,14,12,23,2}
        int[] b = {2,234,14,12,23,2}
        System.out.println(a==b);
    }
}
```

The program creates two identical arrays and compares them for equality. The reader might expect that the arrays should be equal and **true** should be printed. However, if we run the program, we will see that **false** is printed. The reason is that the operator "==" compares the locations of the arrays and not their content. For example, the a array can be stored at location 1000, while the b array can be stored at location 2000 (see Figure 5.3). Since the numbers 1000 and 2000 are different, the program will print **false**.

> One can use the operator "==" to compare two arrays for equality. This will compare the addresses of the two arrays and not their content. This is referred to as *shallow copy*.

If we want to properly compare the content of the two arrays, then we need to use a **for** loop. Here is an example.

```
public class Test {
    public static void main(String[] args){
        int[] a = {2,4,6,8,10};
        int[] b = {2,4,6,8,10};
        System.out.println(compare(a,b));
    }
    public static boolean compare(int[] a, int[] b){
        if(a.length!=b.length){
            return false;
        }
        for(int i=0; i < a.length; i++){
            if(a[i]!=b[i]){
                return false;
            }
        }
    }
}
```

```
        return true;
    }
}
```

Comparing the content of two arrays and not only their location is referred to as *deep comparison*.

> Comparing two arrays using the "==" operator is wrong. This will only tell us if the arrays have the same location. In order to compare the content of two arrays, we need to use a **for** loop that performs deep comparison of the arrays.

Since deep array comparison is such a common operation, there is a method that performs it for us. Here is an example of how the method works.

```java
import java.util.*;

public class Test {
    public static void main(String[] args){
        int[] a = {2,4,6,8,10};
        int[] b = {2,4,6,8,10};
        System.out.println(Arrays.equals(a, b));
    }
}
```

The `Arrays.equals` method uses a **for** loop that iterates through the two arrays. It returns **true** exactly when the two arrays have the same number of elements and all the corresponding pairs of elements in the two arrays are equal.

5.2   The Trading Game Revisited

Let us use our newly acquired knowledge of arrays and refactor the trading game from the previous chapter. Now, we will allow the trader to buy or sell multiple products. Consider the following declaration.

```java
class TradingGame{
    static final int ITEM_COUNT = 2;
    static final String[] item = new String[]{"apples", "pears"};
    static double price[] = new double[ITEM_COUNT];
    static int inventory[] = new int[ITEM_COUNT];

}
```

Now the products, their price, and the available inventory are all defined using an array. This allows us to quickly introduce more items, if needed, by only changing the variables `ITEM_COUNT` and `item`.

The new code for the `main` method follows.

```java
import java.text.*;
import java.util.*;
public class TradingGameArrays {
    static final int NUMBER_OF_DAYS = 10;
    static final double BASE_PRICE = 10;
```

```
static final double VARIATION = 5;
static final double INITIAL_CASH = 100;
static final int ITEM_COUNT = 2;
static final String[] item = new String[]{"apples", "pears"};

static double price[] = new double[ITEM_COUNT];
static int inventory[] = new int[ITEM_COUNT];
static double cash = INITIAL_CASH;

public static void main(String[] args) {
  for (int day = 1; day <= NUMBER_OF_DAYS; day++) {
    for (int i = 0; i < ITEM_COUNT; i++) {
      price[i] = computePrice(BASE_PRICE, VARIATION);
    }
    System.out.println("Day: " + day + " out of 10");
    int choice;
    do {
      printMenu();
      choice = getChoice();
      switch (choice) {
        case 1: // Print cash balance and inventory
          System.out.println("Cash: " + currencyFormatter(cash));
          for (int i = 0; i < ITEM_COUNT; i++) {
            System.out.println(item[i] + " inventory: " + inventory[i
              ] + " Price: " + currencyFormatter(price[i]));
          }
          break;

        case 2: { //Buy Product
          int itemID = getProductID();

          int amount = getQuantity(item[itemID], "buy");
          if (!buy(itemID, amount)) {
            System.out.println("You don't have enough money");
          }
          break;
        }
        case 3: {  // Sell Product
          int itemID = getProductID();
          int amount = getQuantity(item[itemID], "sell");
          if (!sell(itemID, amount)) {
            System.out.println("You don't have enough "+ item[itemID
              ]);
          }
          break;
        }
      }
    } while (choice != 4);

  }
  System.out.println("You finished with:" + currencyFormatter(cash));
}
```

Note that we have simplified the menu. The new `printMenu` method is shown next.

```
public static void printMenu() {
```

```
System.out.println("1. Print cash balance, inventory, and prices");
System.out.println("2. Buy product");
System.out.println("3. Sell product");
System.out.println("4. I am done for today");
}
```

The new menu is much more intuitive and easy to use. Let us examine the different menu items. For Choice 1, the program prints the cash reserves and information about all the items. A `for` loop is used to iterate through the items. Note that we cannot use a for-each `for` loop here because for every index we want to retrieve the item name, inventory, and price. For Choices 2 and 3, the program calls the `getProductID` method. The method asks the user to enter the name of the product and returns the index of the product. The implementation is shown below.

```
public static int getProductID() {
  String s;
  Scanner keyboard = new Scanner(System.in);
  while (true) {
    System.out.print("Enter product name: ");
    s = keyboard.next();
    for (int i = 0; i < item.length; i++) {
      if (item[i].equals(s)) {
        return i;
      }
    }
  }
}
```

The `getProductID` method asks the user to type in the name of the item. Textual input is preferred when there are multiple items that are being traded. The method tries to match the user input to one of the item names. If it is successful, it returns the index of the item. Otherwise, it asks for user input again. Remember that we need to use the `equals` method to compare strings.

Next, note that we have substituted the `buyApples`, `buyPears`, `sellApples`, and `sellPears` methods with just two methods: `buy` and `sell`. The introduction of arrays has allowed us to simplify the design. The two methods are shown next.

```
public static boolean sell(int itemID, int amount) {
  if (amount > inventory[itemID]) {
    return false;
  }
  cash += amount * price[itemID];
  inventory[itemID] -= amount;
  return true;
}
```

```
public static boolean buy(int itemID, int amount) {
  if (amount * price[itemID] < cash) {
    cash -= amount * price[itemID];
    inventory[itemID] += amount;
    return true;
  }
  return false;
}
```

The novelty is that now the `itemID` is passed as a parameter. As a result, we do not have to create separate methods for every item that is being traded. In summary, introducing

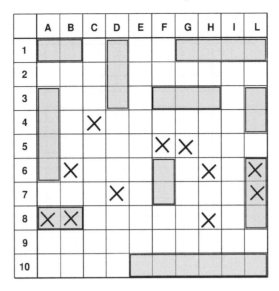

FIGURE 5.4: Example Battleship board.

arrays has allowed us to shorten our code and make it more versatile. We can easily extend the game and add more items to trade. At the same time, the code is more compact and isolating errors is simpler. The menu is also more compact and more user friendly.

5.3   Two-Dimensional Arrays

You have probably played the popular game Battleship. The game was invented by Clifford Von Wickler in the early 1900s. Each player has a ten-by-ten board on which they can place different types of ships.

The board of a player can be represented as a two-dimensional array. The objective of the game is to sink the ships of the other player. Look at Figure 5.4. All attacked spots are marked with an "X". You can see that the player was successful in sinking a patrol boat (a two-cell ship) and significantly damaging a destroyer (a three-cell ship).

Consider the following definition.

```
boolean board [][] = new boolean[10][10];
```

This creates a two-dimensional array of Boolean values. Initially, a default value of false is used for all the elements of the array. Note that the first index represents the number of rows in the table, while the second index represents the number of columns in the table. We will set an element of this array to true when there is a ship that crosses the cell.

Table 5.1 shows an example of representing a battleship on the board. Note that we will use numbers instead of letters to identify the columns. In a two-dimensional array, the row is represented first followed by the column. For example, B7 from Figure 5.4 corresponds to the element at position (6,1) in Table 5.1. A position on the board is accessed using the syntax: board[row][column]. For example, the battleship (a four-cell ship) that is shown on the board in Table 5.1 can be described by the following sequence of statements.

```
board [3][3] = true;
```

TABLE 5.1:   Example
two-dimensional array.

	0	1	2	3	4	5	6	7	8	9
0										
1										
2										
3				X	X	X	X			
4										
5										
6										
7										
8										
9										

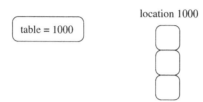

location 1000

table = 1000

FIGURE 5.5: Initial array.

```
board[3][4]=true;
board[3][5]=true;
board[3][6]=true;
```

Here is the place to discuss that Java does not have a native support for two-dimensional arrays. In fact, it stores a two-dimensional array as an array of one-dimensional arrays. In order to demonstrate this point, consider the following code.

```
int [][] table = new int[3][];
for(int row = 0; row <= 2; row ++){
   table[row] = new int[row +1];
   for(int col = 0;col < row+1; col++){
     table[row][col]=col+1;
   }
}
```

The first line creates an array of 3 elements, where every element is an array of integers. Pictorially, this can be represented as shown in Figure 5.5. The three elements of the array will be initially empty. After the code segment is executed, the array will now look as shown in Figure 5.6. For example, when `row=0`, a one-dimensional array is created and the first element of the `table` array is directed to point to it.

> A two-dimensional array in Java is implemented as an array of arrays. When the first array contains arrays of different sizes, the array is called *ragged*.

An array in which rows have different lengths is called a *ragged array*. The advantage of using a ragged array is that it saves space. Without doubt, knowing how to create ragged arrays is one reason for understanding the internals of how a two-dimensional array is created in Java. Another advantage of knowing how a two-dimensional array is stored is

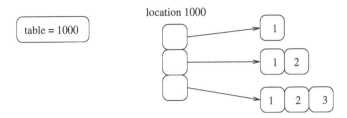

FIGURE 5.6: Example of ragged array.

being able to easily manipulate it. For example, consider a method that takes as input a two-dimensional array and computes the sum of the elements in it. Here is one possible implementation.

```
public static int sum(int [][] a){
    int sum = 0;
    for(int row = 0; row < a.length; row++){
        for(int col = 0; col < a[row].length; col++){
            sum += a[row][col];
        }
    }
    return sum;
}
```

The first `for` loop iterates through all the rows. Note that `a.length` will return the number of rows. Alternatively, `a[0].length` returns the numbers of elements in the first row of the two-dimensional array. Therefore, the above code will compute the sum of the elements in a two-dimensional array even when the array is ragged. Remember that every time we are only reading an array without modifying it, we can use a for-each `for` loop to access it. Accordingly, the above code can be rewritten as shown below.

```
public static int sum(int [][] a){
    int sum = 0;
    for(int [] row: a){
        for(int element: row){
            sum += element;
        }
    }
    return sum;
}
```

Now the first loop iterates over all rows. This is possible because the rows in a two-dimensional array are stored as arrays themselves. The second loop simply iterates though all the elements of the current row. Note that both implementations perform correctly on ragged arrays.

Recall that a one-dimensional array can be declared and populated in a single statement using the following syntax.

```
int [] a = {5,8,7};
```

The same applies for a two-dimensional array. For example, the ragged array from Figure 5.6 can be created using the following statement.

```
int [][] table = {{1},{1,2},{1,2,3}};
```

Here, `table.length` will return 3 because there are three rows. Conversely, `table[1].length` will return 2 because there are two elements in the second row of the table (remember that index counting for arrays starts at 0).

Note that Java supports arrays of any number of dimensions. For example, a three-dimensional array of integer can be defined as follows.

```
int [][][] table;
```

Of course, this three-dimensional array is stored in Java as an array of two-dimensional arrays. As we explained earlier, a two-dimensional array is represented, in turn, as an array of arrays.

5.4   Variable Argument Methods

Java allows us to write a method that takes as input a variable number of arguments. You have seen the `printf` method, which can take as input any number or parameters. Such a method is written using an array. For example, consider a method that takes as input a variable number of strings and returns the result of concatenating the strings. It can be implemented as shown below.

```
public static String concat(String ... strings){
  String result = "";
  for(String s: strings){
    result += s;
  }
  return result;
}
```

Note that the declaration `String ... strings` denotes that the method takes as input a variable number of strings. Theses strings are processed in the method as an array of strings. For example, suppose that the method is called as follows.

```
System.out.println(concat("cat","dog","fight"));
```

Java will create the string array: `{"cat","dog","fight"}` and pass it as input to the `concat` method. In order for this to work in unambiguous fashion, it must be the case that the variable number of arguments is always the last parameter of the method. For the example, the return value will be the string `"catdogfight"`. Note that the operator "+=" means use the string on the left and append the string on the right to it.

An array can also be passed as a parameter to a method that takes as input a variable number of arguments. The following code will also print `catdogfight`.

```
System.out.println(concat(new String[] {"cat","dog","fight}));
```

Lastly, note that a variable number of arguments includes sending no parameters to the method. For example, the following code will just print a new line.

```
System.out.println(concat());
```

5.5 Command Line Arguments

Another place where arrays are used is when a program (this is correct: a program and not a method) is called with a variable number of arguments. Consider the following program.

```java
public class Concat{
  public static void main(String[] args){
    String result="";
    for(String s: args){
      result+=s;
    }
    System.out.println(result);
  }
}
```

The program examines the input to the program, which is stored in the array of strings `args`. It then concatenates all the elements of the array and prints the result. In order to test the program, we can compile it by writing the following line at the command prompt.

```
javac Concat.java
```

This will produce the file `concat.class`, which will contain the Java binary code for the program. We can then execute the program by writing the following line at the command prompt.

```
java Concat Hi There!
```

The result of the program will be the message: "`HiThere!`" Note that in order for the example to work, proper environment variables need to be set so that the operating system knows where to find the executables `java` and `javac`. Alternatively, the statements can be executed in the directory that contains the two Java binaries. In this case, however, the directory of the Java files must be specified.

5.6 Summary

This chapter introduced one and two-dimensional arrays. Arrays are useful for allocating storage for more than one element of the same type in a single statement. A one-dimensional array allocates contiguous space that is referenced using a single index. Conversely, a two-dimensional array declares space in main memory in the form of a table that is referenced using two indices. Later on, in Chapter 7, we will explore additional array topics, such as arrays of objects and the `ArrayList` class.

5.7 Syntax

- `int[] a;` ⇒ Declares the variable `a` to be of type array of integers. We can declare an array of any primitive type or class.

- `a = new int[10];` ⇒ Allocates in main memory space for 10 integers.

- `a[i]` ⇒ Returns the ith element of the array, where counting starts at 0.

- `a.length` ⇒ Returns the length of the array.

- `int [] a ={2,4,6,3};` ⇒ Creates and populates the array.

- `for(int element: a)` ⇒ A for-each `for` loop that iterates through the elements of an array of integers.

- `m(new int[] {2,3,4});` ⇒ Passes an anonymous array of integers to the method.

- `int[][] a = new int[10][20];` ⇒ Creates a two-dimensional array of integers with 10 rows and 20 columns.

- `a[2][3]` ⇒ Refers to the element at row 2 and column 3. Both row and column counting starts at position 0.

- `a[0].length` ⇒ Number of columns in row 0 of the two-dimensional array.

- `a.length` ⇒ Number of rows in a two-dimensional array.

- `int[][] a = {{1,2}, {2}};` ⇒ Creates a two-dimensional ragged array. The first row has the numbers {1,2}, while the second row has the number {2}.

- `int[][][] a;` ⇒ Creates a three-dimensional array.

- `StringTokenizer st = new StringTokenizer(s)` ⇒ Creates a new string tokenizer from the `String s`.

- `st.countTokens()` ⇒ Returns the number of tokens in the string tokenizer. Space and new line are used as the default delimiters.

- `st.hasMoreTokens()` ⇒ Returns `true` if there are more tokens.

- `st.nextToken()` ⇒ Returns the next token as a `String`.

- `public static void m(int ... a)` ⇒ The signature of a method that takes as input a variable number of integers. In the method, the variable `a` is used as though an array was passed to the method. An array of integers can also be passed to the method.

- `public static void main(String[] args)` ⇒ The variable `args` is the array of strings that is passed as input to the program.

- `int[] b = Arrray.copyOf(a,a.length);` ⇒ Makes a deep copy of the `a` array and saves it in the `b` array.

- `Arrays.equals(a,b);` ⇒ Returns true if the two arrays have the same size and elements.

5.8   Important Points

1. An array stores a number of elements of the same type.

2. Once an array is created, its size cannot be changed.

3. A method that receives an array as a parameter can modify it. These changes will be seen by the calling method. Alternatively, a method that takes as input a variable of primitive type, such as an integer, cannot make changes to the variable that will be seen by the calling method.

4. A two-dimensional array is stored as an array of one-dimensional arrays. These arrays do not need to be of the same size, but must contain elements of the same type.

5. The `new` operator needs to be called to create an array. The operator allocates memory and returns an identifier (or reference) of the memory location. Although the address of the array can change during the execution of a program, the programmer will be unaware of this change and the array reference that is returned by the operator `new` will not change.

6. An array is usually traversed using a `for` loop.

7. Use the for-each `for` loop to examine the content of an array. The loop cannot be used to modify the array. When we need to modify an array, or we want to examine the indices of the elements in the array, we need to use the regular `for` loop.

8. Arrays can be used to describe parameters to a program that are defined as constants. For example, an array of strings is used in the *Trading Game* application to describe the commodities that can be traded in the game.

9. An array can be copied using deep or shallow copy. A deep copy copies the content of the array, while a shallow copy just makes the two arrays point to the same content. As a general rule, always use deep copy to copy arrays.

10. Use the `Arrays.equals` method to compare arrays. This will perform deep comparison. Alternatively, using the "==" operator will perform shallow comparison. That is, it will just compare the addresses of the two arrays.

5.9   Exercises

1. Write a method that takes as input an array of integers and returns the third smallest number. Write a full program to test the method.

2. Write a method that takes as input an array of strings and returns the longest string. Write a full program to test the method. Remember that `s.length()` will return the length of the string `s`.

3. Write a method that takes as input a string and returns the array of characters that compose the string. Write a full program to test the method. The expression `s.charAt(i)` returns the character at position `i` of the string `s`.

4. Write a method that finds the number of occurrences of the integer specified as the first parameter in the array of integers that is specified as the second parameter. Write a full program to test the method.

5. Write a method that takes as input a variable number of integers. The method should return the average of the integers as a `double`. Write a full program to test the method.

6. Write a method that takes as input a two-dimensional square array of integers. The method should return the sum of the elements of the top-right to bottom-left diagonal. Write a full program that tests the method.

7. Write a method that takes as input a two-dimensional array of integers. The method should return a one-dimensional array of elements of type `double` that contains the average for each row. Write a full program that tests the method.

8. Write a method that takes as input a two-dimensional array of integers. The method should return a one-dimensional array of elements of type `double` that contains the average for each column. You can assume that the array is non-ragged. Write a full program that tests the method.

9. Write a method that tests if the two-dimensional array that is specified as a parameter is ragged. Write a full program that tests the method.

10. Write a method that takes as input a two-dimensional array of integers. The method should return the biggest integer in the array. Write a full program that tests the method.

11. Write a method that takes as input an array of integers. The method should reverse the array. Write a full program that tests the method.

12. Write a method that takes as input an array of doubles. The method should return the second largest double in the array. Write a full program that tests the method.

13. Write a method that takes as input an array of integers and returns an array of three integers. You can assume that the input array contains at least three elements. The returned array should contain the three consecutive elements in the input array with the biggest sum. For example, if the input array is {3,6,5,2,6}, then the output array should be: {3,6,5} because 3+6+5=14, which is bigger than 6+5+2=13 and 5+2+6=13. Write a full program that tests the method.

5.10   Lab

The bubble sort is the simplest kind of sort. Given an array, the bubble sort goes through the array from left to right and compares consecutive numbers. If two numbers are in the wrong order, then it swaps them. Consider the following example:

```
10 7 6 3 2 1
The bubble sort will first swap 10 and 7 and
create the new array that is shown below.
7 10 6 3 2 1
```

Next, it will swap 6 and 10 and produce the array.
7 6 10 3 2 1
After the first pass of the sort is complete,
the array will be as follows.
7 6 3 2 1 10.

The second pass of the sort will work exactly the same way as the first pass (i.e., going from left to right swapping numbers), but it will stop one number short of the end (i.e., it does not have to read the number 10 because we know that 10 is the biggest number in the array). If the input contains **n** numbers, then **n-1** passes of the array will sort it.

Write a method that sorts an array of integers using bubble sort. The method can use an auxiliary method that swaps two entries in the array. Use a nested **for** loop to implement the bubble sort. The method should modify the input array and have **void** return type. Test your method with different inputs.

5.11   Project

Extend the Yahtzee game to include the combinations that are shown in Table 5.2. The user has seven sets of rolls and the goal is to complete as many of these combinations as possible.

If the user rolls a combination that fits in more than one category, then the program should chose in the following order: Yahtzee, Four-of-a-Kind, Large Straight, Full House, Three-of-a-Kind, Small Straight, Chance. Here is part of an example run of the program (user input is in italic).

```
Your dice: 2 3 4 3 5
Do you want to reroll (Y/N): Y
Which dice: 2
Your dice: 2 4 4 3 5
Do you want to reroll (Y/N): Y
Which dice: 2
Your dice: 2 6 4 3 5
Congratulations, you got a Large Straight that counts for 40 points!
```

When the program finishes, it should print the total point score of the player. The program consists of seven rolls, where every roll can have up to two sub-rolls. If the dice that are rolled do not fit in any combination and chance is already used, then the program should not assign the dice to any combination and give score 0 for the roll.

TABLE 5.2:   Yahtzee game combinations.

Category	Description	Score	Example
Three-of-a-Kind		Sum of all dice	{2,3,4,4,4}
Four-of-a-Kind		Sum of all dice	{4,5,5,5,5}
Full House	3-of-a-kind and a pair	25	{2,2,5,5,5}
Small Straight	4 sequential dice	30	{1,3,4,5,6}
Large Straight	5 sequential dice	40	{1,2,3,4,5}
Yahtzee	All the same	50	{1,1,1,1,1}
Chance	Any dice	Sum of all dice	{2,3,5,5,2}

Chapter 6

Introduction to Classes

A major problem with the original solution to the Yahtzee game was the use of global variables for the dice. Several methods that did not need access to these variables still had access. If the value of one of the die is wrong (e.g., equal to −3), then the bug may lie in any of the methods. The modified solution fixed this problem, but it was based on the premise that the dice were stored as an array of integers. Classes provide an even better solution. The dice can be *encapsulated* inside a class. This means that the code outside the class will not have direct access to the dice. Only the interface of the class (e.g., a set of methods) will be exposed to the outside world. As a result, the class can change how the dice are stored without affecting any code outside the class (e.g., a new implementation can store the dice as an array of short integers). This is referred to as *data abstraction* (i.e., the way the data is stored inside the class is abstracted). Data encapsulation and data abstraction are the pillars of the object-oriented paradigm.

6.1 Classes and Objects

Consider the following definition.

```
int i;
```

The variable i is declared of type integer. The int keyword refers to the type, while i is the variable name. Similarly, an object can be declared as follows.

```
Person p1 = new Person("John");
```

The declaration creates a new person with name John. **Person** is the name of the class and **p1** is the name of the object. A class contains variables and methods that manipulate these variables. For example, the **Person** class may contain the variable **name** and the getName and setName methods. Objects are *instances* of classes. For example, the **p1** object is instance of the `Person` class. Do not forget that object variables always start with a lowercase letter, while class names always start with a capital letter.

> *Instance variables* are associated with the objects of a class. Every instance of a class can have different values for the instance variables.

For example, we can create a new person as follows.

```
Person p2 = new person("Bob");
```

Now `p1` and `p2` are two objects of the `Person` class that have a different value for the instance variable `name`. An instance variable of a class is a variable that is associated with every object of the class. For example, if there are 100 objects of type `Person`, then 100 variables `name` will be created, one for every object.

6.2 Class Interaction and Data Encapsulation

Let us revisit the Yahtzee game from the previous chapter, but this time build a better design that utilizes the object-oriented paradigm. When creating an object-oriented solution, we try to build classes and objects that model real-world entities. For example, if we are building bank software, then we may identify the classes: `BankAccount`, `Customer`, `Teller`, and so on. The customer Peter is an example of an object that belongs to the `Customer` class.

If we go back to the Yahtzee game, a die is an example of a real-world entity that we would like to model. We will create a `Die` class, where a particular die will be an object (or instance) of the class. The pillar of every class is its data. The data inside a class represents the variables of each object in the class. In our case, every die has a `dieValue` that is an integer. Next, the methods of the class need to be identified. Usually, only methods that access or manipulate the data of the class belong to the class. In our case, this can be a method that sets and a method that reads the value of the die. A first iteration of the `Die` class follows.

```java
class Die{
  private int dieValue;
  public void setValue(int value){
    dieValue = value;
  }
  public int getValue(){
    return dieValue;
  }
}
```

The variable `dieValue` is defined as a `private` variable. This means that it is only accessible inside the class in which it is defined. Nobody outside the `Die` class knows about its existence. The `setValue` and `getValue` methods are defined as `public`. This means that they can be accessed from everywhere in our program.

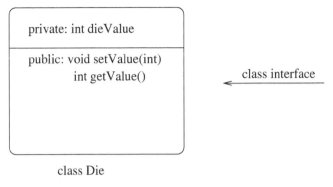

class Die

FIGURE 6.1: Interface of a class.

> Good software design practices call for all instance variables to be defined as `private`. This will hide the internal data structure of a class from the rest of the world. As a consequence, this structure can change without the rest of the world being affected. A second advantage is that the integrity of the data is better guarded because only the methods inside the class have access to the `private` data.

Figure 6.1 shows a pictorial representation of the `Die` class. As a general rule, all variables should be defined as `private`. In other words, the variables should be hidden from the outside world. The variables can be indirectly manipulated through the *interface* of the class, that is, the class's public methods.

Note that the variable `dieValue` is the first variable in this book that is defined without using the `static` keyword. The reason is that the variable belongs to each object of the `Die` class. In other words, every `Die` instance will have its own variable `dieValue`. If we create 100 dice, then 100 variables `dieValue` will be created, one for every object.

> Instance variables can have a different value for every object. They are defined without using the `static` keyword. Conversely, `static` variables are associated with the whole class. A single instance of a `static` variable is created regardless of the number of objects that are created from the class. Memory for a `static` variable is created even when there are no instances (i.e., objects) of the class.

The `getValue` and `setValue` methods are called *getter* and *setter* methods, respectively. Since the variable `dieValue` is private, it can be indirectly accessed through them. Once Alfred Aho, a major contributor to the programming languages field, said during a lecture that getter/setter methods should not be used because they circumvent the access control rules and allow access to private variables. However, when these methods do more than just return the value and set the value of a variable, respectively, their inclusion is warranted and convenient. Through this textbook, we will try to avoid the use of getter/setter methods when possible. An improved implementation of the `Die` class that does not provide direct access to the private variable follows.

```
class Die{
  private int dieValue;

  public void rollDie(){
```

```
      dieValue = getRandomDieValue();
   }

   public int getValue(){
     if(dieValue >=1 && dieValue <=6){
       return dieValue;
     } else {
       return 0;
     }
   }

   private static int getRandomDieValue() {
     return (int) (Math.random() * 6 + 1);
   }
}
```

The `setValue` method is substituted with the more appropriate `rollDie` method. In other words, we do not allow someone from the outside world to set the value of a die. They can only call the `rollDie` method to change the value of a die to a random number. The `getValue` method is changed to return the value of the variable `dieValue` only when it is in the correct range. Note that in the above example it is obvious that `dieValue` will always be between 1 and 6. However, as more methods are added to the `Die` class, this does not need to be the case.

> Every class can contain two types of methods: *static* and *instance*. A method is defined as static by adding the **static** keyword to its definition. The absence of the **static** keyword in the definition of a method implies that the method is instance. Static methods are called on the class and have access only to the static variables of the class. Instance methods are called on an object of the class and have, in addition, access to the instance variables of the object on which they are called.

For example, if `d` is a `Die` object, then `d.rollDie()` will change the state of the die object. When we refer to the variable `dieValue` in the `rollDie` method, we are actually referring to `d.dieValue` (i.e., the variable `dieValue` for the `d` object). We will sometimes refer to the object on which the method is called (e.g., `d` in the above example) as the *hidden parameter* of the method. An instance method uses this object as a parameter without the object being directly passed as a parameter.

Static methods do not possess a hidden parameter. They are called on the whole class and not on a particular object. From within the class, a static method can be invoked just by referring to its name. This is the case inside the `rollDie` method, where the static `getRandomDieValue` method is directly invoked. From outside the class, the `getRandomDieValue` method can be invoked as follows: `Die.getRandomDieValue()`. However, this will only work as long as the declaration of the `getRandomDieValue` method is changed to **public**. Remember that **public** data and methods can be accessed from everywhere. Conversely, **private** data and methods can only be accessed within the class in which they are defined.

Note that a static method **can** be invoked on an object. However, this call is rewritten to call the method on the class that the object belongs to. For example, if `Die` is a public method and `d` is an object of type `Die`, then

System.out.println(d.getRandomDieValue());

will be rewritten by Java as follows.

TABLE 6.1: Access matrix for `static/instance` for methods.

(*Has access to*)	(*Static method*)	(*Instance method*)
Static variables and methods	YES	YES
Instance variables and methods	NO	YES

```
System.out.println(Die.getRandomDieValue());
```

> Good software practices call for static method to be invoked on classes and not objects. Invoking a static method on an object gives the false illusion to the human reader of the code that the method is instance.

The new version of the `Die` class demonstrates *data encapsulation*. This means that the data is only accessible from within the class in which it is defined and therefore we do not need to worry that someone from outside the class can assign an incorrect value to an instance variable. Note that the reason that the variable `dieValue` cannot be accessed from outside the class is because it is defined as a `private` variable. If the variable `dieValue` were defined as a `public` variable, then the following code will be valid.

```
Die d = new Die();
d.dieValue = -4;
```

However, this code allows direct access to the instance variables of the class and therefore makes the methods in the `Die` class obsolete. This is the reason why all variables will be declared as `private` throughout the book. The only exception is constants (i.e., `static final` variables). They can be declared as `public` because nobody can change their value.

The `getRandomDieValue` method is defined as `private` because we desire that it only be called from within the `Die` class. In general, methods that are part of the interface of the class (i.e., can be called by the outside world) will be defined as `public`. Utility methods that are only needed within the class should be defined as `private`. The `getRandomDieValue` method is defined as `static` because it is not related to a particular instance of the class and does not access the instance variable `dieValue`.

Data abstraction is another important feature of the object-oriented paradigm. Data abstraction means that the details of how the data is physically stored are abstracted. For example, someone may decide to store the variable `dieValue` in a `byte` instead of an `int`. However, the interface of the class (i.e., its public methods) does not need to change and therefore all the methods that interact with the `Die` class will remain the same. In other words, we can make changes to the class that will not affect how the outside world interacts with the class. Similarly, changes to the outside world will not affect the behavior of the class.

> We can think of a class as being its own silo that contains `private` variables and `public` interface to these variables. The code inside a class should be self-contained. Changing it should not affect code outside the class. Similarly, changing code outside the class should not affect the code in the class. Unless there is a good reason not to do so, all the variables inside a class should be defined as `private`.

Consider Table 6.1. It is a matrix that tells us which methods have access to which data and methods inside a class. For example, a static method has no direct access to instance methods and variables because there is no current instance of the class. For example, since the `main` method is static, it can only call static methods in the same class. This is the template that we have seen before this chapter.

6.3 Default Constructor

Next, let us examine how the outside world can interact with a class through its interface (i.e., `public` methods). The following code creates a die, rolls it, and prints its value.

```
Die d = new Die();
d.rollDie();
System.out.println(d.getValue());
```

The `new` keyword is used to create a new object. As is the case with arrays, `new` returns a reference to the object. Java actually treats arrays as special types of objects that support the index operation through the use of the square brackets syntax.

Note that the `new` keyword returns a reference to an object that does not change during the life of an object. Alternatively, the address of an object can change as the object is moved. However, this distinction is beyond of the scope of this book and does not affect the way in which we write our programs. Therefore, for simplicity, we assume that `new` returns the address of an object and this address does not change during the life of the object.

The first line in the above code can be split into two lines.

```
Die d;
d = new Die();
```

The first line defines the variable `d` to be of type `Die`, while the second line creates a new object and makes `d` point to it; see Figure 6.2. You may have noticed that the parentheses after `Die` look as though we are calling a method and this is not far from truth.

> Every class has one or more *constructor methods* (or *constructors* for short). The purpose of a constructor is to instantiate a new object of the class. If a constructor is not defined for a class (e.g., it is not defined in the `Die` class), then a default constructor that takes no arguments and that does nothing is created.

Therefore, the class Die is actually rewritten as follows by Java.

```
class Die{
    private int dieValue;
```

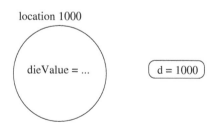

FIGURE 6.2: Example of object.

```
public Die(){} //automatically created if not present
   ...
}
```

The constructors inside a class are easily identifiable because they have the same name as the name of the class and they have no return type (not even **void**). They can be called only through the **new** keyword (i.e., they cannot be called directly as other methods). A constructor can be defined as **private**, but it is usually **public**. The job of the constructor is to assign initial values to the instance variables of the object that is being created.

In our case, the default constructor does not initialize the variable `dieValue` and therefore our initial design of the `Die` class can be improved. The next version of the class that includes a proper constructor follows.

```java
class Die{
  private int dieValue;

  public Die(){
    dieValue = getRandomDieValue();
  }

  public int getValue(){
    if(dieValue >=1 && dieValue <=6){
      return dieValue;
    } else {
      return 0;
    }
  }

  public void rollDie(){
    dieValue = getRandomDieValue();
  }

  private static int getRandomDieValue() {
    return (int) (Math.random() * 6 + 1);
  }
}
```

An example use of the class is shown next.

```java
Die d = new Die();
System.out.println(d.getValue());
for(int i = 0; i<1000; i++){
  d.rollDie();
  System.out.println(d.getValue());
}
```

The code creates a new `Die` object and prints its value. Then it rolls the die one thousand times and prints the value of the die after every roll. Note that this design shows good separation of responsibility. The `getValue` method is only responsible for returning the value of the die, while the `println` method does the printing. Combining the two activities in a single method is an inferior choice because this will reduce the reusability of the method and make it more prone to errors.

6.4 The `toString` Method

It seems tedious to write `System.out.println(d.getValue())` every time we want to print the value of the die d. Can we just write `System.out.println(d)` and expect Java to automatically convert the die d to a string? Surprisingly, the answer is yes. The `toString` method is defined for every Java object. For example, we can always send an object to the `print` and `println` methods. The object is automatically converted to a string by calling the `toString` method.

The default implementation of the `toString` method does not do much: it just returns the name of the class and the address (or the reference, to be more precise) of the object (we saw this behavior when we tried to print an array). To demonstrate this behavior again, let us rewrite our code as follows.

```
Die  d = new Die ();
System.out.println(d);
for(int  i=0;i<1000;  i++){
  d.rollDie();
  System.out.println(d);
}
```

One possible output is: `Die@42e816` one thousand and one times. In order to get meaningful output, we need to add the `toString` method to the `Die` class. One possible implementation follows.

```
public String toString(){
  return dieValue+"";
}
```

Note that the `Die` class contains the value of the die as an integer. We can use the trick of adding an integer and an empty string to convert the integer to a string. We will make one more modification to the `Die` class and make the number of sides on the die a parameter. Note that the above `toString` method actually overrides an existing `toString` method. Therefore, if we want the printing of a die to work properly, we cannot change the name of the `toString` method or its return value type. Note that the `toString` method does not print anything. It simply converts an object to a string.

```
class Die{
  public static final int DEFAULT_NUMBER_OF_SIDES=6;
  private int dieValue;
  private int numberOfSides;

  public Die(){
    numberOfSides = DEFAULT_NUMBER_OF_SIDES;
    dieValue = getRandomDieValue();
  }

  public Die(int numberOfSides){
    this.numberOfSides = numberOfSides;
    dieValue = getRandomDieValue();
  }

  public void rollDie(){
    dieValue = getRandomDieValue();
  }
```

```
  private int getRandomDieValue() {
    return (int) (Math.random() * numberOfSides + 1);
  }

  public String toString(){
    return dieValue+"";
  }

  public boolean equals(Die otherDie){
    return (dieValue==otherDie.dieValue);
  }
}
```

The above class is well designed. Every method does a single operation. The methods are built around the data item `dieValue`.

6.5 Instance versus Static

Let us carefully examine the changes to the code. We introduced a variable DE-FAULT_NUMBER_OF_SIDES, which stores the default number of sides for a die. This variable is not subject to change (i.e., it is a constant) and therefore it is defined using the `final` keyword. It is safe to define a constant as `public` because its value cannot be changed. If someone wants to see the default number of sides for a die, then they can refer to the variable `Die.DEFAULT_NUMBER_OF_SIDES`. Note that the variable is defined as `static`, which means that it belongs to the class and not to a particular instance of the class. This is the reason that it is accessed by specifying the name of the class and not the name of an instance of the class. The variable is `static` because the default number of sides will be the same for every die that is created.

Figure 6.3 shows a pictorial representation of the `Die` class. In the example, three objects are created. Since the variable `dieValue` is instance, every object of type `Die` has a unique copy of this variable. As the figure suggests, we can have three different values for the variable `dieValue` – one value for every object. Conversely, we have a single variable DEFAULT_NUMBER_OF_SIDES. We could have 0 dice or 100 dice. The default number of sides will still be equal to 6.

Note that we have made the `getRandomDieValue` method an instance method by removing the `static` keyword. The reason is that it needs access to the variable `numberOfSides`. However, this new variable is an instance variable (i.e., every die can have a different value for this variable). Therefore, the method also needs to become instance (i.e., it matters which die it is invoked on). Note that as Table 6.1 suggests a static method cannot access instance variables. The new design allows us to have different dice with a different number of sides. Maybe this is stupid for the Yahtzee game. However, it will allow us to easily extend the game if we want to introduce one ten-sided die as part of the game.

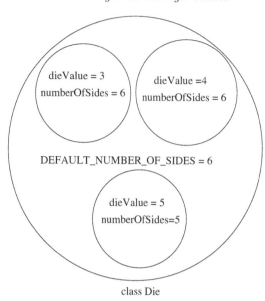

class Die

FIGURE 6.3: The Die class.

Good software practices suggest that we write code that is easily extendable. However, we should only do that when the complexity of the code is not negatively affected. For example, it may not be worth adding 1000 lines of code in order to make the code friendly toward a future feature that will probably be never implemented. However, if only 10 lines are needed to make the code new-feature-friendly, then the extra effort may be well worth it. The good programmer knows how to strike a balance between making the code expendable and keeping it simple.

Note that a static method is invoked on a class and not an object. Therefore, if the getRandomDieValue method was static, then we could not refer to the variable numberOfSides in it. The reason is that there are three objects inside the Die class and every object can have a different value for the variable numberOfSides. Another way to think about it is that every instance method has an access to a hidden parameter: the object on which the method is called. The hidden parameter will tell the getRandomDieValue method which one of the three variables numberOfSides should be used.

6.6   Non-empty Constructors and the Hidden Parameter this

Two constructors are added to the Die class: an empty constructor and a constructor that takes as input the number of sides. A default empty constructor is only created if no constructors are present in the class. In other words, if the empty constructor is missing from the Die class code, then a default empty constructor that does nothing will not be generated.

A default empty constructor is only created if no explicit constructors are created. Therefore, if you create any constructor, you should consider creating an empty constructor. If you do not do so, then existing code that relies on the default empty constructor will no longer compile.

The empty constructor contains the following code.

```
public Die(){
    numberOfSides = DEFAULT_NUMBER_OF_SIDES;
    dieValue = getRandomDieValue();
}
```

The first line sets the number of sides of the die to the default number. The second line sets the value of the die to a random value. Note that the `getRandomDieValue` method was changed to generate a random number between 1 and the value for the variable `numberOfSides`. Note as well that the constructor sets the value of both instance variables. This is not accidental.

A constructor is called when an object is being created. Initially, the value of all the instance variables of the object are undefined. Therefore, it is the job of the constructor to give value to these variables. If the value of a variable is not specified as input to the constructor, then a default value or a random value can be used to initialize the instance variable.

In our case, the empty constructor gives no information about the value of the two variables. Therefore, we set the variable `numberOfSides` to the default value and the variable `dieValue` to a random number.

The second constructor has the following code.

```
public Die(int numberOfSides){
    this.numberOfSides = numberOfSides;
    dieValue = getRandomDieValue();
}
```

The first line sets the number of sides of the die to the value of the input parameter. Note that in this method there are two variables `numberOfSides`: the input variable to the method (i.e., the formal parameter) and the instance variable of the class. When we refer to the variable `numberOfSides`, we are referring to the variable that is defined in the innermost scope, which will be the input parameter to the method. If we want to refer to the instance variable `numberOfSides`, then we need to write `this.numberOfSides`. The `this` object is the hidden parameter on which the method is called. For constructors, it is the object that is being created. Therefore, when we write: `this.numberOfSides`, we actually mean the variable `numberOfSides` of the current object. The second line of the method sets the value of the other instance variable of the `Die` class. Note that the second line of the method can also be rewritten as follows.

```
this.dieValue = getRandomDieValue();
```

However, since there is a single variable `dieValue` that is visible inside the method, the extra indirection is unnecessary.

Note that the two constructors of the `Die` class are similar to the `rollDie` method. All methods change the variable `dieValue` to a random number. Note that even if the `rollDie` method had the same code as a constructor, the two methods are not interchangeable.

Each of the constructors is used to create a new object. During this creation, the variable `dieValue` is initialized to a random value. Conversely, the `rollDie` method is called after an object is already created in order to update the existing value of the variable `dieValue` to a random number.

Sometimes, the different constructors of a class have a lot of code in common and it is tedious to write the same code multiple times. After all, the hallmark of a good program is that the same code should not repeat. Fortunately, Java provides a mechanism for one constructor to call a different constructor. In particular, the empty constructor of the `Die` class can be rewritten as follows.

```
public Die() {
    this (DEFAULT_NUMBER_OF_SIDES);
}
```

The call `this(DEFAULT_NUMBER_OF_SIDES)` means call the constructor of this class that takes as input a single integer and pass the number `DEFAULT_NUMBER_OF_SIDES` as a parameter. Having the empty constructor call other constructors with a default value is a common trick when writing constructors. Note that the empty constructor cannot directly call the other constructor by its method name and needs to use the syntax `this(...)`. The `this` keyword is used because in Java it means the current object (or the hidden parameter). The call calls the second constructor and passes the current object as a hidden parameter.

Consider next the new `equals` method of the `Die` class.

```
public boolean equals(Die otherDie){
    return (this.dieValue==otherDie.dieValue);
}
```

If `d1` and `d2` are die objects, then `d1.equals(d2)` will return `true` exactly when the values of the two dice are the same. The formal parameter `otherDie` corresponds to the actual parameter `d2`. One can think of the `this` object as being a hidden formal parameter that corresponds to the actual parameter `d1`. Therefore, the method simply checks if `d1` and `d2` have the same value for the variable `dieValue`. Of course, the reference to the `this` object is unnecessary when there is a single variable `dieValue` that is in scope and the code can be rewritten as follows.

```
public boolean equals(Die otherDie){
    return (dieValue==otherDie.dieValue);
}
```

6.7   Array of Objects and Multi-Class Solutions

Now that we are satisfied with the `Die` class, let us examine an implementation of the `DiceCup` class. In the real world, a dice cup will contain a collection of dice. We will model the real world by creating an array of die objects in the `DiceCup` class.

```
public class DiceCup {
    private Die[] dice;
    private int numberOfDice;
    public static int DEFAULT_NUMBER_OF_DICE=5;

    public DiceCup(){
        numberOfDice = DEFAULT_NUMBER_OF_DICE;
```

```
    dice = new Die[numberOfDice];
    for(int i = 0; i < numberOfDice; i++){
      dice[i] = new Die();
    }
  }

  public DiceCup(int numberOfDice, int numberOfSides){
    this.numberOfDice = numberOfDice;
    dice = new Die[numberOfDice];
    for(int i = 0; i < numberOfDice; i++){
      dice[i] = new Die(numberOfSides);
    }
  }

  public String toString(){
    String result = "Your dice are: ";
    for(Die d: dice){
      result += d+" ";
    }
    return result;
  }

  public boolean isYahtzee(){
    for(Die d: dice){
      if(! d.equals(dice[0])){
        return false;
      }
    }
    return true;
  }

  public void rollDice(int[] diceToChange){
    for(int i: diceToChange){
      dice[i-1].rollDie();
    }
  }
}
```

We have created two constructors for the class. The first constructor uses the default number of dice and the default number of sides for every die. The second constructor uses the values of the input parameters to set these values. Note that the memory for the array of dice is allocated inside the constructors. The reason is that initially we do not know the size of the array.

> When an array of objects is created, the **new** keyword needs to be used multiple times. It needs to be used once to create the array and then once for every object of the array.

The `toString`, `isYahtzee`, and `rollDice` methods from the previous chapter are now instance (i.e., non-static). This allows us to create multiple objects of type `DiceCup`, where every dice cup can have different dice inside.

The `isYahtzee` method now uses the `equals` method of the `Die` class to determine if two dice are equal. This is a very powerful approach. For example, we can define deuces to be wild. In other words, we can define the value 2 to be equal to all the other values in the `Die` class. In this case, {5,2,5,2,5} will be considered a Yahtzee.

Let us compare the old and the new versions of the `rollDice` method. The old version is shown below.

```java
public static void rollDice(int[] diceToChange) {
  for (int i: diceToChange) {
    dice[i - 1] = getRandomDieValue();
  }
}
```

The expression `dice[i-1] = getRandomDieValue()` is replaced with `dice[i-1].rollDie()`. The new expression sends the `dice[i-1]` object as a hidden parameter to the `rollDie` method of the `Die` class, which changes the value of the die.

The new version of the `Yahtzee` class is shown next.

```java
public class Yahtzee {
  public static final int NUMBER_REROLLS=2;

  public static void main(String[] args) {
    Scanner keyboard = new Scanner(System.in);
    DiceCup dc = new DiceCup();
    System.out.println(dc);
    for (int i = 0; i < NUMBER_REROLLS; i++) {
      if (dc.isYahtzee())  {
        break;
      }
      System.out.print("Which dice do you want to reroll: ");
      dc.rollDice(convert(keyboard.nextLine()));
      System.out.println(dc);
    }

    if (dc.isYahtzee()) {
      System.out.println("You got Yahtzee!");
    } else {
      System.out.println("Sorry, better luck next time!");
    }
  }

  static int[] convert(String s) {
    StringTokenizer st = new StringTokenizer(s);

    int[] a = new int[st.countTokens()];
    int i = 0;

    while (st.hasMoreTokens()) {
      a[i++] = Integer.parseInt(st.nextToken());
    }
    return a;
  }
}
```

The `diceToString` method is gone because the to-string conversion now happens in the `toString` method of the `DiceCup` class. This is a better design because the `DiceCup` class should be responsible for converting an object of type `DiceCup` to a string.

When designing methods within classes, always think about **delegation of responsibility**. A class is only responsible for manipulating its own data. If Java code manipulates data from a different class, then consider moving the code to the other class.

The **convert** method remains unchanged. The novelty is that a **DiceCup** object is created in the **main** method. The existence of the **DiceCup** class allows us to now create a game with several dice cups, if needed.

6.8 Multi-Class Solution to the Battleship Game

Next, we will examine a multi-class solution to the Battleship game, which was described in Chapter 5. We will implement a simple version of the program that supports a single board that is controlled by the computer. Here is an excerpt from an example run of the program (user input is in italic).

```
    0 1 2 3 4 5 6 7 8 9
    - - - - - - - - - -
0 | 0 0 0 0 0 0 0 0 0 0
1 | 0 0 0 0 0 0 0 0 0 0
2 | 0 0 0 0 0 0 0 0 0 0
3 | 0 0 0 0 0 0 0 0 0 0
4 | 0 0 0 0 0 0 0 0 0 0
5 | 0 0 0 0 0 0 0 0 0 0
6 | 0 0 0 0 0 0 0 0 0 0
7 | 0 0 0 0 0 0 0 0 0 0
8 | 0 0 0 0 0 0 0 0 0 0
9 | 0 0 0 0 0 0 0 0 0 0
Enter guess: 5 5
Ship Damaged!
    0 1 2 3 4 5 6 7 8 9
    - - - - - - - - - -
0 | 0 0 0 0 0 0 0 0 0 0
1 | 0 0 0 0 0 0 0 0 0 0
2 | 0 0 0 0 0 0 0 0 0 0
3 | 0 0 0 0 0 0 0 0 0 0
4 | 0 0 0 0 0 0 0 0 0 0
5 | 0 0 0 0 0 X 0 0 0 0
6 | 0 0 0 0 0 0 0 0 0 0
7 | 0 0 0 0 0 0 0 0 0 0
8 | 0 0 0 0 0 0 0 0 0 0
9 | 0 0 0 0 0 0 0 0 0 0
Enter guess: 5 6
Ship Damaged!
    0 1 2 3 4 5 6 7 8 9
    - - - - - - - - - -
0 | 0 0 0 0 0 0 0 0 0 0
```

```
1 | 0 0 0 0 0 0 0 0 0 0
2 | 0 0 0 0 0 0 0 0 0 0
3 | 0 0 0 0 0 0 0 0 0 0
4 | 0 0 0 0 0 0 0 0 0 0
5 | 0 0 0 0 0 X X 0 0 0
6 | 0 0 0 0 0 0 0 0 0 0
7 | 0 0 0 0 0 0 0 0 0 0
8 | 0 0 0 0 0 0 0 0 0 0
9 | 0 0 0 0 0 0 0 0 0 0
Enter guess: 5 7
Empty!
     0 1 2 3 4 5 6 7 8 9
     - - - - - - - - - -
0 | 0 0 0 0 0 0 0 0 0 0
1 | 0 0 0 0 0 0 0 0 0 0
2 | 0 0 0 0 0 0 0 0 0 0
3 | 0 0 0 0 0 0 0 0 0 0
4 | 0 0 0 0 0 0 0 0 0 0
5 | 0 0 0 0 0 X X   0 0
6 | 0 0 0 0 0 0 0 0 0 0
7 | 0 0 0 0 0 0 0 0 0 0
8 | 0 0 0 0 0 0 0 0 0 0
9 | 0 0 0 0 0 0 0 0 0 0
Enter guess: 5 4
Empty!
     0 1 2 3 4 5 6 7 8 9
     - - - - - - - - - -
0 | 0 0 0 0 0 0 0 0 0 0
1 | 0 0 0 0 0 0 0 0 0 0
2 | 0 0 0 0 0 0 0 0 0 0
3 | 0 0 0 0 0 0 0 0 0 0
4 | 0 0 0 0 0 0 0 0 0 0
5 | 0 0 0 0   X X   0 0
6 | 0 0 0 0 0 0 0 0 0 0
7 | 0 0 0 0 0 0 0 0 0 0
8 | 0 0 0 0 0 0 0 0 0 0
9 | 0 0 0 0 0 0 0 0 0 0
Enter guess: 6 5
Ship Destroyed!
     0 1 2 3 4 5 6 7 8 9
     - - - - - - - - - -
0 | 0 0 0 0 0 0 0 0 0 0
1 | 0 0 0 0 0 0 0 0 0 0
2 | 0 0 0 0 0 0 0 0 0 0
3 | 0 0 0 0 0 0 0 0 0 0
4 | 0 0 0 0 0 0 0 0 0 0
5 | 0 0 0 0   X X   0 0
6 | 0 0 0 0 0 X 0 0 0 0
7 | 0 0 0 0 0 0 0 0 0 0
8 | 0 0 0 0 0 0 0 0 0 0
9 | 0 0 0 0 0 0 0 0 0 0
```

```
Enter guess:
```

Note that in the above example the ship that was destroyed covered the cells (5,5) and (6,5). There was also a different ship that was going through the cell (5,6). There are different versions of the game that create different numbers and types of ships. We will assume that the array `placement` contains the type of ship that we want to build on the board. For example, if `placement = {5,4,3,2,2,1,1}`, then this means that we will create one ship of 5 cells, one ship of 4 cells, one ship of 3 cells, two ships of 2 cells, and two ships of 1 cell. The numbers in the array do not have to be ordered.

We will create a `Main` class that contains the `main` method. In addition, we will create a class for the `Board`, the `Ship`, and the `Cell` (every board consists of a 10x10 grid of cells).

Let us start with the `Cell` class. In other words, this time we will follow a *bottom-up design*. We will start with the most rudimentary class and build other classes from it. For every cell, we need to keep track of whether the cell is visited or not. As our example output suggests, we are going to display a cell differently depending on whether it is visited or not and depending on whether it is part of a ship or not. If a cell that is visited is part of a ship, then we want to inform the user whether the ship is damaged or destroyed. Therefore, for every cell we will also keep a reference to the ship that crosses through the cell. If the cell is not part of a ship, then the ship variable will be equal to `null`. This means that the value for the ship object will not be assigned.

> Consider the `C` class. Writing: `C object;` will define the variable `object` to be of type `C`. The initial value of the variable `object` will be equal to `null`. This means that it does not reference anything. Later on, we can assign a value to the variable, for example: `object = new C()`. If at any point we do not want the variable to point to the object, then we can write `object = null`. If there are no more references to the object, it will be automatically deleted by the garbage collector.

Here is an example implementation of the `Cell` class.

```java
public class Cell {
  private Ship ship;
  private boolean isVisited = false;

  public void visit() {
    isVisited = true;
  }

  public boolean isVisited() {
    return isVisited;
  }

  public boolean isPartOfShip() {
    return (ship != null);
  }

  public void putShip(Ship ship) {
    this.ship = ship;
  }

  public String toString() {
    if (!isVisited) {
      return "0";
```

```
    } else {
      if (ship != null) {
        return "X";
      } else {
        return " ";
      }
    }
  }

  public boolean isSunk() {
    return ship.isSunk();
  }
}
```

Note that the class does not have a constructor. This means that a default constructor with no formal parameters is automatically introduced. This default constructor will not do anything. The first four methods provide access to the two variables of the class. Note that there is no method to return the ship that crosses through the current cell. The reason is that a class should be designed the same way as the Central Intelligent Agency (CIA) agent. It should receive only the information it needs and it should provide information to the outside world on a need-to-know basis. For example, the outside world does not need to know which ship crosses through the current cell and therefore a `getShip` method should not be part of the interface of the class. The need-to-know basis design reduces the interaction between the class and the outside world, which simplifies the code.

The `toString` method converts an object of type `Cell` to a `String`. If the cell is not visited, then `"O"` will be returned (meaning that we do not know whether there is a ship crossing the cell). If the cell is visited and empty, then `" "` will be returned. Finally, if the cell is visited and contains part of a ship, then `"X"` will be returned. The symbol `"X"` symbolizes that this cell of the ship is hit.

Once a cell that is part of a ship is visited, we want to inform the player whether they hit or destroyed the ship. The `isSunk` method determines if the ship that crosses though the cell is destroyed or just damaged.

Next, let us concentrate on the `Ship` class. The constructor of the class will need to place the ship on the board. Of course, we have to be careful that the ship does not go outside the board and that it does not overlap with another ship. We will represent a ship by its starting coordinates, its direction (i.e., horizontal or vertical), and its size. We will also keep a reference to the board so that we know where the ship can be placed. Our algorithm tries to place the ship at a random position. However, if this position is not valid, then another position is selected at random. The code for the constructor of the `Ship` class follows.

```
public class Ship {
  private int startRow, startColumn;
  private boolean direction;
  private int size;
  private Board board;

  public Ship(int size, Board board) {
    this.board = board;
    this.size = size;
    do {
      startRow = (int) (Math.random() * Board.BOARD_SIZE);
      startColumn = (int) (Math.random() * Board.BOARD_SIZE);
      direction = (Math.random() > 0.5) ? Board.VERTICAL : Board.
        HORIZONTAL;
```

```
  } while (!board.isFree(startRow, startColumn, direction, size));
  board.populate(startRow, startColumn, direction, size, this);
}
...
}
```

The constants HORIZONTAL, VERTICAL, and BOARD_SIZE will be defined in the Board class. Remember that constants are written in all capital letters. The first two constants contain opposite Boolean values, while the third constant stores the size of the board (i.e., 10 in our case). The isFree method of the Board class tests whether the ship can be placed at the specified location. The populate method of the Board class places the ship on the board. Note that the parameters of the ship and the this reference are sent as parameters to the populate method of the Board class. The reason is that the Board class needs a reference to the ship. It will give this reference to the cells of the board.

The constructor chooses a random start row, start column, and direction. Note that we have two choices for the direction. Remember that Math.random() returns a random number between 0 and 1. If this number is greater than 0.5, then we use the vertical direction. Otherwise, we use the horizontal direction. The loop keeps executing until we are able to successfully place the ship on the board (i.e., the isFree method returns true).

Next, we will introduce one more method to the Ship class. It is named isSunk and it tests whether the ship is sunk (i.e., all its cells are visited).

```
public class Ship {
  private int startRow, startColumn;
  private boolean direction;
  private int size;
  Board board;

  ...
  public boolean isSunk() {
    if (direction == Board.VERTICAL) {
      for (int row = startRow, column = startColumn;
          row <= startRow + size - 1; row++) {
        if (!board.isVisited(row, column)) {
          return false;
        }
      }
    } else {
      for (int row = startRow, column = startColumn;
          column <= startColumn + size - 1; column++) {
        if (!board.isVisited(row, column)) {
          return false;
        }
      }
    }
    return true;
  }
}
```

The isVisited method of the Board class will check if the cell in question is visited. The above method goes through all cells of the ship. If one of the cells is not visited, then the method returns false (i.e., the ship is not sunk). Otherwise, the method returns true.

Next, let us consider the Board class. In it, we will have the following constants.

```
public static final int BOARD_SIZE = 10;
public static final boolean HORIZONTAL = true;
```

```
public static final boolean VERTICAL = false;
public static final int[] placement = {5,4,3,2,2,1,1};
```

The first constant stores the size of the board, where the program only works with a square board. The next two constants define the horizontal and vertical direction, while the last constant lists the sizes of the ships that will be placed on the board. This design is elegant because it allows us to easily change the board size or the ship sizes without modifying any other code.

For every board, we will store the ships and cells that make up the board. Here is the definition of the two variables:

```
Ship[] ships = new Ship[placement.length];
Cell[][] grid = new Cell[BOARD_SIZE][BOARD_SIZE];
```

Note that the number of ships is equal to the size of the `placement` array.

Next, we present the constructor of the `Board` class. As expected, it will simply initialize the instance variables of the class (i.e., the variables `ships` and `grid`).

```
public class Board{
    ...
    public Board() {
        populateGrid();
        populateShips();
    }

    public void populateGrid() {
        for (int row = 0; row < BOARD_SIZE; row++) {
            for (int col = 0; col < BOARD_SIZE; col++) {
                grid[row][col] = new Cell();
            }
        }
    }

    public void populateShips() {
        for (int i=0; i < placement.length; i++) {
            ships[i]= new Ship(placement[i], this);
        }
    }
}
```

The constructor is split into two methods. The `populateGrid` method creates the cells, while the `populateShips` method creates the ships and adds them to the array of ships. The `for` loop in the `populateShips` method traverses the `placement` array. For each element of the array, the method creates a ship with the required size and adds the ship to the `ships` array. Note that, as expected, the `new` keyword is called multiple times on the `ships` array. It is called once to create the array and then again for each element of the array. When we call the constructor of the `Ship` class, the second parameter is the `this` reference because the `Ship` class needs access to the board object.

Next, we show the `toString` method of the `Board` class. It traverses the cells of the grid and calls the `toString` method on each cell of the grid.

```
public String toString(){
    String result = "    0 1 2 3 4 5 6 7 8 9\n    - - - - - - - - - - ";
    int line = 0;

    for(Cell[] row: grid){
        result+="\n";
```

```
      result+= (line++)+" | ";
      for(Cell cell: row){
        result += cell+" ";
      }
    }
  return result;
}
```

The code iterates over all rows of the grid. For each row, it adds to `result` a new line and the line number. Note that the expression: `result += (line++)+" | ";` means add the current value of the variable `line` to the variable `result` and then increment the value of the variable `line` by 1. The line can be rewritten as follows.

```
result = result + (String)(line) + " | ";
line = line +1;
```

Remember that adding an integer and a string concatenated the integer to the string. This is why we did not need the explicit cast to `String` in the original expression.

Next, the code iterates over all cells of the row. The statement: `result += cell+" "` is equivalent to `result = result+ cell.toString()+" "`. In other words, the `toString` method for the `cell` object is automatically called to convert the object into a string.

The complete code for the `Board` class is presented next.

```
import java.util.*;

public class Board {
  public static final int BOARD_SIZE = 10;
  public static final boolean HORIZONTAL = true;
  public static final boolean VERTICAL = false;
  public static final int[] placement = {5,4,3,2,2,1,1};


  private Cell[][] grid = new Cell[BOARD_SIZE][BOARD_SIZE];
  private Ship[] ships = new Ship[placement.length];

  public String toString(){
    String result="    0 1 2 3 4 5 6 7 8 9\n    - - - - - - - - - - ";
    int line = 0;

    for(Cell[] row: grid){
      result+="\n";
      result+= (line++)+" | ";
      for(Cell cell: row){
        result += cell+" ";
      }
    }
    return result;
  }

  public Cell getElement(int row, int column) {
    if ((row >= 0 && row < BOARD_SIZE) &&
                      (column >= 0 && column < BOARD_SIZE)) {
      return grid[row][column];
    }
    return null;
  }
```

```java
public Board() {
  populateGrid();
  populateShips();
}

public void populateGrid() {
  for (int row = 0; row < BOARD_SIZE; row++) {
    for (int col = 0; col < BOARD_SIZE; col++) {
      grid[row][col] = new Cell();
    }
  }
}

public void populateShips() {
  for (int i=0; i < placement.length; i++) {
    ships[i]= new Ship(placement[i], this);
  }
}

public boolean isFree(int row, int column, boolean direction,
                                          int size) {
  if (direction == HORIZONTAL) {
    for (int newColumn = column; newColumn <= column + size - 1;
                                         newColumn++) {
      if (getElement(row, newColumn) != null) {
        if (grid[row][newColumn].isPartOfShip()) {
          return false;
        }
      } else {
        return false;
      }
    }
    return true;
  } else {
    for (int newRow = row; newRow <= row + size - 1; newRow++){
      if (getElement(newRow,column) != null) {
        if (grid[newRow][column].isPartOfShip()) {
          return false;
        }
      } else {
        return false;
      }
    }
    return true;
  }
}

public void populate(int row, int column, boolean direction,
                int size, Ship ship) {
  if (direction == HORIZONTAL) {
    for (int newColumn = column; newColumn <= column + size - 1;
                                         newColumn++) {
      grid[row][newColumn].putShip(ship);
    }
  } else {
```

```
    for(int newRow = row; newRow <= row + size - 1; newRow++){
      grid[newRow][column].putShip(ship);
    }
  }
}

public void visit(int row, int column){
  grid[row][column].visit();
}

public boolean isAllMarked() {
  for (Cell[] row : grid) {
    for (Cell element : row) {
      if (element.isPartOfShip() && !element.isVisited()) {
        return false;
      }
    }
  }
  return true;
}

public boolean isPartOfShip(int row, int column){
  return (grid[row][column].isPartOfShip());
}
public boolean isVisited(int row, int column){
  return grid[row][column].isVisited();
}
public boolean isSunkAt(int row, int column){
  return grid[row][column].isSunk();
}
}
```

Note that the **main** method of our program will create a single board object and interact with it. Therefore, the **Board** class provides methods to access the ships and cells of the board. Following the need-to-know principle, the **Board** class does not provide direct access to its ships and cells. As a general rule, a class should not return any of its internal objects because this will expose them to the outside world and practically nullify the information isolation principle. Remember that once someone has a reference to an object, then they will have access to all of its public methods.

The **visit** method simply marks a cell as visited. The **isAllMarked** method is responsible for checking whether all the ships are sunk. When this condition becomes **true**, the game can end. The method examines all the cells of the board. If a cell contains part of a ship that is not visited, then obviously not all ships are sunk and the method returns **false**. If all the ship cells are visited, then the method returns **true**. The **isFree** method checks to see if a ship can be placed at the specified location. Instead of directly accessing the cells of the grid, it calls the **getElement** method, which ensures that the current cell is inside the grid. This prevents an **ArrayIndexOutOfBounds** exception from occurring. The latter occurs when we try to access an element of an array that does not exist. It is the job of the **getElement** method to ensure that the coordinates of the cell are in the board. If they are not, then the method will return **null**, which means that the requested cell does not exist. The **populateShip** method simply places a ship on the board by marking the appropriate cells of the grid. The **isVisited** method checks to see if the cell is visited.

Lastly, let us examine the **main** method of the **Main** class.

```
import java.util.*;
```

```java
public class Main {
  public static void main(String[] args){
    Scanner k = new Scanner(System.in);
    Board board = new Board();
    System.out.println(board);
    while(!board.isAllMarked()){
      int row,column;
      System.out.print("Enter guess: ");
      row = k.nextInt();
      column = k.nextInt();
      board.visit(row,column);
      if(board.isPartOfShip(row,column)){
        if(board.isSunkAt(row, column)){
          System.out.println("Ship Destroyed!");
        } else{
          System.out.println("Ship Damaged!");
        }
        System.out.println(board);
      } else {
        System.out.println("Empty!");
        System.out.println(board);
      }
    }
  }
}
```

The method has a continuous loop that asks for user input and then visits the specified cell. The loop terminates when all the ships are sunk. If the user hits a ship, then the `isSunk` method of the `Ship` class checks to see whether the ship is sunk and an appropriate message is printed.

Although at first glance simple, the design of the battleship game is not rudimentary and it involves the interaction of four classes. When creating the design, we observed the following general design rules.

1. All non-constant variables of a class should be private.

2. All public methods of a class should be used to provide access to the data of the class to the outside world.

3. All methods should be simple and perform a single task.

4. Inter-class interaction should be minimized.

In order to demonstrate the last point, note that the `Main` class interacts only with the `Board` class. A design where the `Main` class interacts additionally with objects of the `Cell` and `Ship` classes is certainly possible. However, this will increase the number of inter-class interactions and will make the `Board` class partially obsolete. That is, why have a `Board` class if the `Main` class directly interacts with the cells and the ships of the game?

6.9 Summary

The chapter describes how to create classes and objects. While a class is a general template that describes the type of data that we are interested in modeling, an object is an instance of a class that has a concrete value for each data item. The pillar of every class is its data. Following the data encapsulation and abstraction principles, all non-constant variables of a class should be made `private`. This means that the outside world does not have direct access to the data and needs to interact with it through the available methods. These methods make the interface of the class. As a general rule, every method inside a class should be simple and perform a single task.

Instances of a class are created by invoking the class constructor, where a default empty constructor is provided when no constructors are defined. The job of the constructor is to initialize the local variables of the class, where they can be set to default values when the constructor method does not receive their initial values. There are two types of class members: static and instance. Static methods and variables are defined on the whole class (e.g., for every class, there is a single instance of a static variable). Conversely, instance methods and variables are associated with an object of the class (e.g., every object has its own copies of the instance variables).

The chapter also presents multi-class program solutions. Class interaction principles are demonstrated through examples. As a general rule, inter-class interaction should be minimized in order to keep the design simple and extendable.

6.10 Syntax

- `this` ⇒ Refers to the current instance of the class.

- `this(...)` ⇒ Calls a different constructor of the class.

- `toString()` ⇒ A method that converts an object to a `String`. It is automatically called in the printing methods and when we use the operator "+" to concatenate a `String` to an object.

- `equals(... other)` ⇒ Create this method when you want to check for object equality. The method should return `true` exactly when the objects `this` and `other` are equal.

- `new Foo(...)` ⇒ Creates a new instance of the `Foo` class by calling the appropriate constructor.

- `public` vs. `private` ⇒ Public members are visible everywhere, while private members are only visible from within the class.

- `static` ⇒ Static members belong to the whole class, while every object has its own set of instance variables. A variable/method is instance when it does not have the static identifier in front of it.

- `null` ⇒ The value of a reference that does not reference any object.

- `o.m()` ⇒ The `m` instance method of the `C` class is called (`C` is the class of the `o` object).

The o object is passed to the m method as a hidden parameter. The m method can refer to this hidden parameter by calling the `this` reference.

- C.m() ⇒ The m static method is called on the C class. Since the method is static, it does not have direct access to the instance variables and methods of the class. There is no hidden parameter.

6.11 Important Points

1. Classes represent abstract data types.

2. Class names should start with a capital letter. This distinguishes them from variables because variables start with a lowercase letter.

3. Objects are instances of classes.

4. Every class has `static/instance` and `public/private` variables and methods.

5. Public members of a class (variables and methods) can be accessed from outside the class. Conversely, `private` members of a class can only be accessed from within the class. Note that every method of a class can access the `private` variables of any object of the class.

6. Every object (a.k.a., instance) of a class has its own state. The state of an object is determined by the value of its instance variables.

7. Instance (i.e., non-static) methods of a class contain a hidden parameter. This is an object of the type of the class where the method appears. Therefore, instance methods have access to the instance variables of the class. Conversely, static methods have no hidden parameter and therefore have no direct access to the instance variables of the class.

8. A static method cannot directly call an instance method. The reason is that every call to an instance method requires a hidden parameter. However, a static method does not have such a parameter. Of course, the call o.m() is possible from a static method, where o is an object that the static method can reference.

9. Every class has a constructor that initializes the instance variables of the class. If a constructor is not included in a class, then a default constructor that takes no parameters and does nothing is automatically created.

10. The constructor of a class is a method that has exactly the same name as the name of the class and no return value (not even `void`).

11. All non-constant variables of a class should be defined as private.

12. The objects of classes communicate with each other by calling each other's methods.

6.12 Exercises

1. Write a class that is called `Complex` and that manipulates complex numbers.

   - The class should have the variables `realPart` and `imaginaryPart`, which should be both of type `double`.

   - The class should support the `add` method. For example, if `c1` and `c2` are objects of type `Complex`, then `c1.add(c2)` will return a `Complex` object that is the sum of the two objects. The constructed object will have a real part that is the sum of the real parts of the two objects, and an imaginary part that is the sum of the imaginary parts of the two objects.

   - Similarly, write a `subtract` method. The constructed object will have a real part that is the difference of the real parts of the two objects, and an imaginary part that is the difference of the imaginary parts of the two objects.

   - Write static versions of the `add` and `subtract` methods. For example, `Complex.add(c1,c2)` will return the result of adding two complex numbers. Note that now the hidden parameter is gone. Similarly, `Complex.subtract(c1,c2)` will return the difference of the two numbers.

   - Write an empty constructor and a constructor that takes in the real and imaginary part of the number.

   - Write a `toString` method that returns the complex number as a `String`. For example, it will return 3+2i when the real part is 3 and the imaginary part is 2.

   - Add an `equals` method that compares two objects of type `Complex` for equality.

   Create a second class with a `main` method and use it to test the methods of the `Complex` class.

2. Write a class that is called `Number`. An object of type `Number` represents an integer with up to 100 digits. Recall that the type `int` only supports integers up to roughly 2^{31}. To remove this restriction, the `Number` class will contain the following variable declaration: `short[] digits = new short[100]`. In other words, the digits of the number will be saved in an array. Create an additional Boolean variable to store the sign of the number (i.e., positive or negative). Add static and non-static methods to add and subtract numbers and the `toString` and `equals` methods as explained in Exercise 1. The adding and subtracting should be performed similar to the way you add and subtract numbers on paper. Write a `main` method that tests the class.

3. Write an `Employee` class. Every employee has `name` and `age`. Include empty and non-empty constructors. Include meaningful `equals` and `toString` methods. Add a `private static` variable that keeps track of the number of employees. Create a `public static` method that returns the number of created employees. Include a `main` method that tests all the features of your class.

4. Write the `FuelGauge` and `Odometer` classes. The `FuelGauge` class keeps track of the amount of fuel in the car in gallons. It also contains methods for putting fuel in the car and burning fuel. The `Odometer` class keeps track of the current mileage of the car. It has a method for incrementing the car's mileage by one. Every object of type `Odometer` should contain an object of type `FuelGauge`. Every time the mileage on the `Odometer` object goes up, the amount of fuel should go down by the appropriate

amount (calculated from the gallons per mile of the car). Write constructors and `toString` and `equals` methods for both classes. Create a `main` method with a menu in a third class to test the other two classes.

5. Create a `Coin` class. It should have a private variable `face` that can be equal to either `HEADS` or `TAILS`, where the last two are integer constants. It should also contain the private variable `bias`, which is the probability that you will get heads after flipping the coin in the air (for a perfect coin `bias=0.5`). Create a `flip` method that assigns a value to the variable `face` using a random number (e.g., `Math.random()`) and the value of the variable `bias`. For example, if the random number is smaller than the bias, then the coin should be heads. Also, create an `isHead` method that returns `true` when the coins is heads. Write a `main` method that creates a coin, flips it 10000 times, and then prints the number of heads. Create a `setBias` method that changes the variable `bias`. Use the method to change the bias of the coin and then run the experiment again.

6.13 Lab

Write a bank application. The application should give you the following choices.

```
What do you want to do today?
1. Open account
2. Withdraw money
3. Deposit money
4. Show balance
5. Go home
```

The first option should open a new bank account. An object of type `BankAccount` should be created and added to an array of bank accounts. Set the size of the array to 1000. When a new bank account is created, the account number should be generated automatically. Use a static variable to do so. For example, the account number can be the current value of the static variable, where the static variable should be incremented by one after the bank account is created. Choice 1 should print the account number. Choices 2–4 should ask for the account number. A `for` loop can iterate through the array of bank accounts and find the bank account with the correct account number. This is the bank account on which the operation should be performed. All operations should be defined as methods. Make sure that the `withdraw` method in the `BankAccount` class does not allow you to withdraw more money than you have. The menu should be printed by the `menu` method in the main class. Choice 5 should terminate the program. This can be done, for example, by calling `System.exit(0)`. This means terminate the program and return error code that signals normal program termination.

6.14 Project

Rewrite the project from Chapter 5 to use an object-oriented design. Create the `Die` and `DiceCup` classes.

Chapter 7

The `ArrayList` *Class and the* `enum` *Keyword*

The main goal of the chapter is to introduce the reader to the `ArrayList` class. It allows us to create an array without specifying the size of the array. Creating an array this way is much more convenient because the amount of main memory that is needed by the array is automatically managed. The chapter also covers the topic of immutable objects. These are objects that cannot be modified. Lastly, the chapter focuses on the `enum` construct. Unlike a class that can merge several primitive types, an `enum` is used to define a type that is restricted to a finite subset of a primitive type.

7.1   Introduction to the `ArrayList` Class

One limitation of arrays is that their size cannot be changed once fixed. Consider an application that stores information about employees. Suppose that initially we do not know the number of employees that we want to store. Maybe we can create an array of one thousand employees? This approach has two drawbacks. First, a lot of space is allocated that may never be used. Second, if we end up using more than one thousand employees, then the program will crash. Therefore, a more versatile approach for managing the size of an array is needed. The `ArrayList` class fulfills this task. An `ArrayList` of employees can be defined as follows.

ArrayList<Employee> emps = **new** ArrayList<Employee>();

The above definition states that the variable `emps` refers to an array of employees. However, it does not specify the size of the array. Note that an `ArrayList` is not your normal class. It is a *generic class.*

> A generic class takes as input the name of one or more classes as a parameter. These classes are specified immediately after the name of the class, they are separated by commas, and they are surrounded by angle brackets <>.

In our example, the `ArrayList` class takes as input the `Employee` class. This means that the array list can store inside it only employees. If we try to insert an object of a different type in the `ArrayList`, then an error will occur. Note that, starting with Java 7, the above syntax can be simplified as follows.

```
ArrayList<Employee> emps = new ArrayList<>();
```

The second reference to the `Employee` class is redundant, and therefore can be omitted. Note that a generic class can take as input only the name of a class and not the name of a primitive type. For example, the following code will not compile.

```
ArrayList<int> dice = new ArrayList<int>();
```

However, we can use the wrapper `Integer` class as input to the `ArrayList` class. For the most part, an `Integer` object behaves exactly like an `int`, but it is still an object. Therefore, an `ArrayList` of integers can be declared as shown below.

```
ArrayList<Integer> dice = new ArrayList<>();
```

A common mistake by novice programmers is to specify the size of the `ArrayList` as a parameter in the parentheses. However, this is the wrong approach because we do not need to specify the size of an `ArrayList` when we create it. The size of an `ArrayList` is dynamically determined by the number of objects that is stores. Therefore, a newly created `ArrayList` will always have size of zero.

7.2 Immutable Objects

Consider the following code.

```
class Test{
  public static void inc(Integer i){
    i++;
  }

  public static void main(String[] args){
    Integer i=3;
    inc(i);
    System.out.println(i);
  }
}
```

The behavior of the code is very interesting and counterintuitive. Note that the code: `Integer i = 3` is rewritten by Java to: `Integer i = new Integer(3)`. Therefore, as Figure 7.1 suggests, a new object is created inside the main method. Let the location of the new object be 2000. Next, this object is passed as a parameter to the `inc` method. Recall that only the object's address will be passed to the `inc` method. Now the variable i inside the `inc` method will be initially equal to 2000. However, if we try to display the variable, then we will see the number 3. The reason is that the `Integer` class contains a `toString` method that returns the integer that is stored inside the class.

Next, let us examine the statement `i++`. This is where all the magic happens! This code is equivalent to `i = i +1`, which in turn means change the value inside the i object to 4. However, the `Integer` class is immutable.

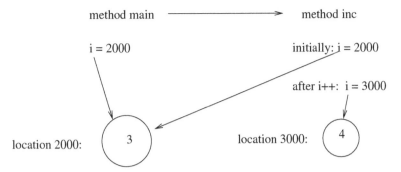

FIGURE 7.1: Passing an immutable object to a method.

You can create an object that belongs to an immutable class. However, this object cannot be modified. If you try to modify an immutable object, then a new object is automatically created. Examples of immutable Java classes include Integer, Character, Double, and String.

Since the existing object at location 2000 cannot be modified, a new object will be created, say, at location 3000. The variable i inside the inc method will now be equal to 3000. However, the variable i inside the main method will still be equal to 2000. The reason is that a Java method cannot change the content of the input parameter. When the control returns to the main method, the object at location 2000 will be displayed and therefore the number 3 will be printed. In other words, the result will be exactly the same as if we used a variable of type int. Therefore, one cannot use the class version of a primitive type in order to allow a method to modify the input. In general, any changes to a variable of a primitive type or a *wrapper class* for a primitive type (e.g., Integer, Double, etc.) by a method will not be seen by the calling method. The reason is that Java passed values to a method by value and all wrapper classes are immutable.

In order to complete the example, suppose that we created our own MyInteger class that stores an integer. Since this class will now be a regular class (and not immutable), the result of our example will be different. Here is our new program.

```java
import java.util.*;

class Test{
  public static void inc(MyInteger i){
    i.setValue(i.getValue()+1);
  }

  public static void main(String[] args){
    MyInteger i = new MyInteger(3);
    inc(i);
    System.out.println(i);
  }
}

class MyInteger{
  private int i;
  public MyInteger(int i){
    this.i = i;
```

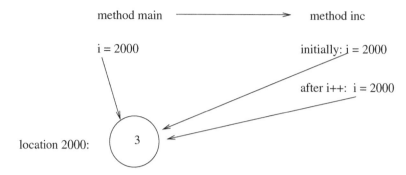

FIGURE 7.2: Passing a mutable object to a method.

```
    }
    public int getValue(){
      return i;
    }
    public void setValue(int i){
      this.i = i;
    }
    public String toString(){
      return i+"";
    }
}
```

Figure 7.2 shows the new configuration. As before, the number 2000 will be passed to the `inc` method. The difference now is in the statement: `i.setValue(i.getValue()+1)`. Since the `i` object is mutable, the variable inside the object will be changed from 3 to 4. Now, when control returns to the `main` method, the variable `i` will still be equal to 2000. However, this time the content at location 2000 has changed from 3 to 4 and therefore the program will print the number 4.

7.3 The `StringBuffer` Class

Most immutable classes do not have a mutable version. For example, there is no class in a Java library that is similar to the `MyInteger` class. This is intentional because this will break the rule: "If you pass a variable of type integer to a method, then the calling method will not see any changes to the variable". The only exception is the `String` class. Sometimes, we want to modify the characters of a `String` without creating a new `String` object. The mutable version of the `String` class is `StringBuffer`. Below is an example of how it can be used.

```
public class Example{
  public static void removeFirstCharacter(StringBuffer s){
    for(int i = 1; i < s.length(); i++){
      s.setCharAt(i-1, s.charAt(i));
    }
    s.deleteCharAt(s.length()-1);
  }
  public static void main(String[] args) {
```

```
StringBuffer s = new StringBuffer("hello");
removeFirstCharacter(s);
System.out.println(s);


    }
}
```

In the example, the removeFirstCharacter method removes the first character of the string. Note that if the method took as input a String instead of a StringBuffer, then it would be impossible for the method to modify the string and the changes to be seen inside the main method. The setCharAt method changes the character at the position that is specified as the first parameter. The setCharAt method is part of the StringBuffer class, but not the String class. The reason is that the String class is immutable and therefore cannot be modified. The charAt method is part of both classes and returns the element at the specified position.

It is worth examining the method removeFirstChracter in detail. When i=1, the method reads the character at position 1 and places it at position 0. Then it reads the character at position 2 and places at position 1 and so on. In other words, all the characters except for the first character are shifted to the left by one position. Note that if we first shifted the last character one to the left, then the whole string will contain just the last character. Therefore, it is important that we started shifting characters from left to right and not from right to left. The deleteCharAt method is used to delete the last character. If the method was not executed, then we would have two copies of the last character at the last two positions of the string (i.e., gotten the string "elloo" instead of the string "ello"). The smart reader has probably noticed that the method removeFirstCharacter can be significantly shortened.

```
public static void removeFirstCharacter(StringBuffer s){
   s.delteChraAt(0);
}
```

However, we chose the longer version in order to demonstrate how an element of a list can be deleted by moving elements.

Note that we cannot use the following syntax for the StringBuffer s.

```
s = "dog";
```

To put it differently, the String class behaves similar to a primitive type. It can be directly assigned a value and we do not need to use the new keyword to crate a new string. However, this is not the case for the StringBuffer class. A new StringBuffer can be created by passing a string to its constructor.

```
StringBuffer s = new StringBuffer("dog");
```

As we saw, once a StringBuffer is created, we cannot simply change its value. However, we can use the append method to append more characters to the StringBuffer. Consider the following code.

```
s.append("cat");
```

It will append the string cat to the StringBuffer s. In other words, the StringBuffer s will now be equal to dogcat.

7.4   The Interface of an `ArrayList`

Since `ArrayList` is a class, the interface of objects of type `ArrayList` is a lot different than the interface of arrays. For example, the interface [] to access the element of an array is not supported. An element of an `ArrayList` can be accessed using the `get(i)` method, where `i` is the index of the element. The `size` method returns the numbers of elements in the `ArrayList`. This differs from the variable `length`, which returns the size of the array and not the number of elements in it. In fact, the variable `length` is not defined for an `ArrayList` because, by definition, an `ArrayList` can store a variable number of elements and does not have preset capacity. To demonstrate how an `ArrayList` works, the following method converts an `ArrayList` of employees to an array of employees.

```java
public static Employee[] convert(ArrayList<Employee> emps){
    Employee[] result = new Employee[emps.size()];
    for(int i=0; i < emps.size(); i++){
        result[i] = emps.get(i);
    }
    return result;
}
```

The above method is for demonstration purposes only and it is not the easiest way to convert an `ArrayList` to an array. Actually, Java supports the `toArray` method that will convert any `ArrayList` into an array. The only caveat of using this method is that the result needs to be cast to the proper array of objects. For example, the following code converts an `ArrayList` of employees to an array of employees.

```java
Employee[] emps = (Employee[]) empArrayList.toArray();
```

Note that the `get` method is not identical to the [.] operator for arrays. For example, we can write:

```java
emps[0] = new Employee("John");
```

but we cannot use the following syntax.

```java
emps.get(0) = new Employee("John");
```

The `get` method simply retrieves an element from the `ArrayList` and cannot be used to modify an element of the `ArrayList`. An element of an `ArrayList` can be modified as follows.

```java
emps.set(0,new Employee("John"));
```

The first parameter of the `set` method is the index in the `ArrayList`, while the second parameter is the new value of the element. Note that the `set` method can only be used to modify an existing element of an `ArrayList`. It cannot be used to create an element at a position that does not exist. For example, the following code will generate `IndexOutOfBoundsException` exception.

```java
ArrayList<Employee> emps = new ArrayList<Employee>();
emps.set(0,new Employee("John"));
```

The reason is that the code tries to change the element at position 0, but an element at position 0 does not exist. The correct approach is to use the `add` method to insert a new element in the `ArrayList`. Here is the correct version of the above code.

```java
ArrayList<Employee> emps = new ArrayList<Employee>();
emps.add(new Employee("John"));
```

When called with one argument, the add method inserts the element at the end of the ArrayList. Conversely, consider the syntax: emps.add(0, new Employee()). This code inserts the element at position 0 and shifts the rest of the elements one position to the right. Similarly, the code emps.remove(e) will delete the first occurrence of the employee e from the ArrayList. Alternatively, the expression emps.remove(0) will delete the employee at position 0. When an element is deleted, the other elements are shifted so that there is no gap left by the deleted element.

Note that the delete method may sometimes seem ambiguous. Suppose that we have an ArrayList of integers called a and write a.delete(7). Will this delete the number at position 7 or the first occurrence of the number 7 in the ArrayList? In order to answer this important question, consider the following example.

```java
import java.util.*;
public class Test {
  public static void main(String[] args) {
    ArrayList<Integer> a = new ArrayList<Integer>();
    for(int i = 0; i < 10; i++){
      a.add(i+5);
    }
    a.remove(6);
    System.out.println(a);
  }
}
```

First, note that there is a toString method for the ArrayList class that prints the elements of the ArrayList. However, such a method does not exist for arrays. When executed, the program will display.

```
[5, 6, 7, 8, 9, 10, 12, 13, 14]
```

Therefore, the element at position 6 is removed (remember that counting starts at 0). Alternatively, if we want to remove the object 6, then we need to write the following code.

```java
import java.util.*;
public class Test {

  public static void main(String[] args) {
    ArrayList<Integer> a = new ArrayList<Integer>();

    for(int i = 0; i < 10; i++){
      a.add(i+5);
    }
    a.remove(new Integer(6));
    System.out.println(a);
  }
}
```

In other words, in this case we need to tell Java that we want to delete the object 6 and not the element at position 6. In this case, the following output will be displayed.

```
[5, 7, 8, 9, 10, 11, 12, 13, 14]
```

7.5 Introducing the enum Construct

We will next write a game that is similar to the Yahtzee game. However, we will use coins instead of dice. Every coin has two faces: heads and tails. When we flip a coin, we can get either heads or tails (depending of which face is on top). Every coin also has a value: 1, 5, 10, or 25. This is the value of the coin in cents. In the game, we will flip ten coins in the air and let them land. We will assume that the value of a coin can only be seen if the coin is tails. As Figure 7.3 suggests, the value of a coin is not visible when it is heads. Our score is the sum of the face values of all the coins that are tails. Once we get our score, we have two choices: either reroll selected coins or keep the current total. We are allowed up to two rerolls.

Our solution will be similar to the Yahtzee solution from Chapter 6 in that we will use a multi-class approach. However, this time we will use an `ArrayList` instead of an array. Let us start with the `Coin` class (i.e., we will perform a bottom-up design as we did in the Battleship game). A coin has two variables: `value` and `face`. The first value represents the value of the coin, while the second value is the face of the coin. To be even more general, we will assume that our coin does not need to be fair. We will introduce a variable `bias`, which represents the probability that the coin is heads. One of our constructors will take as input the value and the bias of the coin and flip it to determine if the coin is heads or tails. Another constructor will take as input only the value of the coin and use the default bias. We will also add a `toString` method that returns a string description of the coin. A possible implementation follows.

```java
public class Coin {
  public static final double DEFAULT_BIAS = 0.5;
  private int value;
  private boolean face;
  private double bias;

  public Coin(){
    this.bias = DEFAULT_BIAS;
    this.value = getRandomCoinValue();
    flip();
  }
  public Coin(int value){
    this.value = value;
    this.bias = DEFAULT_BIAS;
    flip();
  }
  public Coin(int value, double bias){
    this.value = value;
```

FIGURE 7.3: Heads of different coins.

```
    this.bias = bias;
    flip();
  }
  public void flip(){
    face = (Math.random()<bias) ? true : false; // true is heads
  }
  public String toString(){
    switch(value){
      case 1:
        return  "penny that is "+((face)?"heads":"tails");
      case 5:
        return  "nickel that is "+((face)?"heads":"tails");
      case 10:
        return  "dime that is "+((face)?"heads":"tails");
      case 25:
        return "quarter that is "+((face)?"heads":"tails");
      default:
        return "";
    }
  }
  private int getRandomCoinValue(){
    double randomNumber = Math.random();
    if(randomNumber < 0.25){
      return 1;
    }
    if(randomNumber < 0.5){
      return 5;
    }
    if(randomNumber < 0.75){
      return 10;
    }
    return 25;
  }
  public int getValue(){
    return value;
  }
  public boolean isHeads(){
    return face;
  }
}
```

Note that we have defined the default value of 0.5 for the bias of the coin. Note as well that the switch statement inside the toString method does not need break statements. The reason is that the return statement terminates the execution of the method. Note that the default construct inside the switch is needed for the program to compile. If it is missing, then Java will not know what to return if value does not match one of the cases that are enumerated. Finally, note that the flip method calls the Math.random method, which in turn returns a real number between 0 (inclusive) and 1 (exclusive). Suppose that the bias is 0.7. This means that there is a 70% chance that we will get heads. If our random number is smaller than 0.7, then the face of the coin will be heads. Otherwise, the face of the coin will be tails.

Although elegant, the above design can be improved. One problem with the design is that nothing prevents us from assigning an arbitrary number, for example 37, to the variable value. However, we all know that there is no coin that is 37 cents. Another shortcoming is that the toString method is a little *clunky* because it needs to go through all possible values of the variable `value`. The `enum` construct allows us to create a better solution that overcomes both shortcomings.

The `enum` construct is similar to a class in that it allows us to create a user-defined type. A class usually combines several types. For example, an `Employee` class can combine the name of the person (of type `String`) and the age of the person (of type `int`). Conversely, an `enum` focuses on a single primitive type and enumerates a finite number of allowed values. An example of how to use the `enum` construct in our program follows.

```java
enum Currency {
  PENNY(1), NICKEL(5), DIME(10), QUARTER(25);
  private int value;

  private Currency(int value) {
    this.value = value;
  }
  public int getValue(){
    return value;
  }
}

enum Face {
  HEADS(true), TAILS(false);
  private boolean value;

  private Face(boolean value) {
    this.value = value;
  }
  public boolean getValue(){
    return value;
  }
}

public class Coin {

  public static final double DEFAULT_BIAS = 0.5;
  private Currency value;
  private Face face;
  private double bias;

  public Coin() {
    this.bias = DEFAULT_BIAS;
    this.value = getRandomCoinValue();
    flip();
  }

  public Coin(Currency value) {
    this.value = value;
    this.bias = DEFAULT_BIAS;
    flip();
  }

  public Coin(Currency value, double bias) {
    this.value = value;
    this.bias = bias;
    flip();
```

```
  }

  public void flip () {
    face = (bias < Math.random()) ? Face.HEADS : Face.TAILS; // true is
        heads
  }

  private Currency getRandomCoinValue () {
    double randomNumber = Math.random();
    if (randomNumber < 0.25) {
      return Currency.PENNY;
    }
    if (randomNumber < 0.5) {
      return Currency.NICKEL;
    }
    if (randomNumber < 0.75) {
      return Currency.DIME;
    }
    return Currency.QUARTER;
  }

  public String toString () {
    return value+" that is "+face;
  }

  public int getValue () {
    return value.getValue();
  }

  public boolean isHeads () {
    return (face == Face.HEADS);
  }
}
```

If you create a penny that is heads and try to print it, the `toString` method will return "PENNY that is HEADS". As you can see, we have eliminated the switch statement. Next, let us examine in details the `enum` construct.

```
enum Currency {
  PENNY(1), NICKEL(5), DIME(10), QUARTER(25);
  private int value;

  private Currency (int value) {
    this.value = value;
  }
  public int getValue () {
    return value;
  }
}
```

The definition is similar to that of a class. The only difference is that the first line defines a set of constants. A number that each constant maps to can be specified in parentheses. If this mapping is specified, then you must define a variable of this type (in our case `int`) and a constructor that sets the value of the variable. Note that the constructor must be private. Alternatively, one can specify an `enum` type as follows.

```
enum Currency {
```

PENNY, NICKEL, DIME, QUARTER;
}

However, now the mapping that the penny is 1 cent, the nickel is 5 cents, the dime is 10 cents, and the quarter is 25 cents is missing.

Suppose that we have a reference to a variable `value` of type `Currency`. If we want to access the text that is associated with the coin (e.g., PENNY), then we can just call the `toString` method on the `value` object. Note that in our example, the `toString` method is automatically called on the variable `value`. In other words, Java actually executed the following code.

```java
public String toString() {
    return value.toString()+" that is "+face.toString();
}
```

The reason is that the `toString` method is automatically called when the concatenation operator "+" is used and an object is specified. This implies that a variable of an `enum` type is treated in Java similar to an object variable. Note that there is no actual `toString` method created for the `enum` type `Currency`. In other words, Java automatically creates this `toString` method that returns the name of the coin.

Conversely, suppose that we want our `toString` method to display the value of the coin as a number. In this case, we should rewrite the code as follows.

```java
public String toString() {
    return value.getValue()+" that is "+face;
}
```

Now the `getValue` method is executed to retrieve the value of the coin.

> Inside an `enum` block one can specify a set of constants. These are the possible values of the type. If it is required that additional information is stored for every constant, then create an additional variable of this type and appropriate constructor and `getValue` method. Note that the constructor must be defined as `private`. The reason is that one cannot create an instance of an `enum` type directly using the `new` keyword.

Let us now go back to our Coin game. We will modify the `toString` method as follows.

```java
public String toString() {
    return (face == Face.TAILS) ? value.toString() : "HEADS";
}
```

The reason for the modification is that we want the method to return the value of the coin when the coin is tails and we want the method to return the string HEADS otherwise. Note that `Face.TAILS` returns a reference to the constant `TAILS` of the `FACE` enum type. In other words, the values of an `enum` type can be accessed similarly to the static constants of a class. Note that now we need to call the `toString` method explicitly. In this scenario, Java will not automatically convert the object to a `String`.

It is also worth examining the `getRandomCoinValue` method in detail. First of all, note that it is a `private` method because we do not want anyone from outside the class to be aware of its existence. The method generates a random number between 0 and 1. Based on that value, it returns penny, nickel, dime, or quarter. In other words, it generates a random value for the coin. Note that the code can also be rewritten as follows.

```
1   private Currency getRandomCoinValue(){
2     double randomNumber = Math.random();
3     if(randomNumber < 0.25){
4       return Currency.PENNY;
5     }
6     if(randomNumber < 0.5 && randomNumber >= 0.25){
7       return Currency.NICKEL;
8     }
9     if(randomNumber < 0.75 && randomNumber >= 0.50){
10      return Currency.DIME;
11    }
12    if(randomNumber >= 0.75){
13      return Currency.QUARTER;
14    }
15  }
```

However, the extra conditions are unnecessary. For example, if Java is executing Line 6, then it must be the case that randomNumber >= 0.25. If this was not the case, then the condition at Line 3 would have fired and the return statement would have terminated the method (i.e., we would have never reached Line 6). This means that the original method returns each of the four coin values with equal probability.

Let us now present the Change class. The class can contain several coins, which we will store using an ArrayList. The class will have appropriate constructors, a method for converting the change to a string, and a method that evaluates the value of the change. The last method will return the sum of all the coins that are tails.

```
public class Change {

    ArrayList<Coin> coins = new ArrayList<Coin>();

    public Change(){}

    public Change(int count){
        for(int i = 0; i < count; i++){
            coins.add(new Coin());
        }
    }

    public Change(ArrayList<Currency> values) {
        for (Currency value : values) {
            coins.add(new Coin(value));
        }
    }

    public void flipAllCoins() {
        for (Coin c : coins) {
            c.flip();
        }
    }

    public void flipSomeCoins(ArrayList<Integer> indexes) {
        for (int i : indexes) {
            coins.get(i).flip();
        }
    }
```

```java
public int computeSum() {
  int sum = 0;
  for (Coin c : coins) {
    if (!c.isHeads()) {
      sum = sum + c.getValue();
    }
  }
  return sum;
}

public String toString() {
  String result = "";
  for (Coin c : coins) {
    result = result+c+" ";
  }
  result = result + " Total: "+ computeSum();
  return result;
}
}
```

The empty constructor is included because of the cardinal rule: "If you specify any constructors, it is always a good idea to include an empty constructor". If the empty constructor is omitted, then existing code that calls the empty default constructor will no longer compile. The first non-empty constructor generated the number of default coins that are requested. Note that the value and the face of the coin is chosen randomly inside the Coin class. The second non-empty constructor takes as input an ArrayList of currency values, creates the coins, and populates the coins ArrayList. Note that, as expected, new is called multiple times in both constructors. It is called once to create the ArrayList and then once for each element of the ArrayList. Note as well the elegancy of the for-each for statement in the second non-empty constructor. Since we only want to iterate through the ArrayList without modifying it, we can use this template.

While the flipAllCoins method flips all coins, the flipSomeCoins method only flips the input coins. Recall that if a is an ArrayList, a.get(i) will return the ith element of the list. The computeSum method sums the value of all the coins that are tails. Similarly, the toString method creates a string from all the coins and their sum. The design looks very elegant. Every method is self-explanatory.

Finally, let us consider the CoinGame class that implements the game.

```java
import java.util.*;
public class CoinGame {
  public static final int NUMBER_FLIPS=2;

  public static void main(String[] args) {
    Scanner keyboard = new Scanner(System.in);
    ArrayList<Currency> currency = new ArrayList<>();
    System.out.println(change);
    for (int i = 0; i < NUMBER_FLIPS; i++) {
      System.out.print("Which coins do you want to flip: ");
      change.flipSomeCoins(convert(keyboard.nextLine()));
      System.out.println(change);
    }
  }

  static ArrayList<Integer> convert(String s) {
    StringTokenizer st = new StringTokenizer(s);
```

```
ArrayList<Integer> result = new ArrayList<Integer>();

    while (st.hasMoreTokens()) {
        result.add(Integer.parseInt(st.nextToken())-1);
    }
    return result;
  }
}
```

The code is very similar to the Yahtzee game from the previous chapter. The only difference is that the convert method now returns an ArrayList instead of an array and that we do not have to check for a Yahtzee. Here is a possible execution of the program (user input in *italic*).

```
HEADS HEADS HEADS HEADS QUARTER HEADS PENNY HEADS QUARTER HEADS  Total: 51
Which coins do you want to flip: 1 2 3
HEADS NICKEL PENNY HEADS QUARTER HEADS PENNY HEADS QUARTER HEADS  Total: 57
Which coins do you want to flip: 1
HEADS NICKEL PENNY HEADS QUARTER HEADS PENNY HEADS QUARTER HEADS  Total: 57
```

If we want to make the game more challenging and only allow the user to flip all coins, then we can rewrite the CoinGame class as follows.

```
import java.util.*;
public class CoinGame {
  public static final int NUMBER_FLIPS=2;

  public static void main(String[] args) {
    Scanner keyboard = new Scanner(System.in);
    Change change = new Change(10);
    System.out.println(change);
    for (int i = 0; i < NUMBER_FLIPS; i++) {
      System.out.print("Flip all?: ");
      if (!keyboard.nextLine().equals("yes")){
        break;
      }
      change.flipAllCoins();
      System.out.println(change);
    }
  }
}
```

Inside the for loop we ask the user if they want to flip all coins. If they do not answer yes, then we terminate the program. If they answer yes, then we flip all the coins and show the new coins. This can repeat up to NUMBER_FLIPS times. Here is possible execution of the program

```
HEADS QUARTER QUARTER HEADS QUARTER NICKEL QUARTER PENNY DIME HEADS
    Total: 116
Flip all?: no
```

Note that following good programming practices allowed us to change the behavior of the program by changing very little code. This is the hallmark of an excellent design and this is what we should strive for when writing software.

7.6 Summary

The chapter covered `ArrayList` class and `enum` keyword topics, among others. An `ArrayList` is an alternative for an array when the size of the array is unknown. The size of an `ArrayList` is automatically expended when required. Similar to arrays, a for-each `for` loop can be used to iterate over the elements of an `ArrayList` when the `ArrayList` does not need to be modified.

The `enum` construct is similar to creating a new class. However, instead of merging several types into a new type, `enum` enumerates the valid values of an existing type. Each value can be associated with a string description.

The chapter also presented a multi-class solution of the Coin game. Every class contained only the methods that were needed to modify the data. Methods that should not be called outside the class were defined as `private`. As expected, the tasks of printing to the screen and reading from the console were not part of the methods in the classes `Coin` and `Change`, and were left to be implemented in the class that contained the `main` method.

7.7 Syntax

- `ArrayList<Employee> a = new ArrayList<>();` ⇒ Creates a new `ArrayList` of employees.

- `ArrayList<Integer> a = new ArrayList<>();` ⇒ Creates a new `ArrayList` of integers.

- `a.size()` ⇒ Returns the size of the `ArrayList`.

- `a.add(3);` ⇒ Inserts the number 3 at the end of the `ArrayList` a.

- `a.add(3,new Employee());` ⇒ Inserts a new employee at position 3. Employees must exist at positions 0, 1, and 2. The employees at position 3 and after are shifted to the right by one position.

- `a.set(2,new Employee("John"));` ⇒ Changes the element at position 2. An element at position 2 must exist.

- `Employee[] emps = (Employee[]) empArrayList.toArray();` ⇒ Converts an `ArrayList` of employees into an array of employees.

- `a.get(3)` ⇒ Returns the element at position 3.

- `a.remove(e);` ⇒ Removes the first occurrence of the e object from the `ArrayList`.

- `a.remove(new Integer(6));` ⇒ Removes the integer 6 from the `ArrayList` of integers.

- `a.remove(3);` ⇒ Removes the element at position 3 from the `ArrayList`.

- `s.charAt()` ⇒ Returns the character at position 3 (counting starts at 0) for objects of type `String` and `StringBuffer`.

- `s.setCharAt(3,'a');` ⇒ Changes the character at position 3 to 'a'. The method can only be applied to objects of type `StringBuffer`.

- `s.deleteCharAt(3);` ⇒ Removes the character at position 3. The characters after position 3 are shifted one position to the left. The method can only be applied to objects of type `StringBuffer`.

- `StringBuffer s = new StringBuffer("John");` ⇒ Creates a new `StringBuffer` object with text `John`.

- `s.append("Bob");` ⇒ Appends Bob to the `StringBuffer`.

7.8   Important Points

1. The classes `Integer`, `Character`, `Double`, and `String`, among others, are immutable. In other words, we cannot modify objects that belong to these classes. If we try to do so, then new objects are created. As a consequence, if a method tries to modify a formal parameter object that belongs to an immutable class, the changes will not be seen by the calling method.

2. If we want to modify the characters of a `String`, then we need to create a `StringBuffer` object instead.

3. An `ArrayList` takes as input a type parameter. This parameter must be the name of a class and cannot be the name of a primitive type (e.g., `int`, `double`, or `char`). To allow an `ArrayList` of primitive type, the wrapper classes `Byte`, `Short`, `Integer`, `Long`, `Float`, `Double`, `Character`, and `Boolean` are supported by Java.

4. If we want to associate a value with the constants of an `enum` type, then we need to include a `private` constructor and a getter method.

5. Do not use the `set` method to add new values to an `ArrayList`. Instead, use the `add` method. The `set` method should be used to change existing values of an `ArrayList`.

6. The `size` method for an `ArrayList` returns the number of elements in the `ArrayList`. This is different from the variable `length` for an array that returns the capacity of the array. An `ArrayList` has no capacity. We can insert in it as many elements as we want. The only restriction is the size of the available main memory.

7.9   Exercises

1. Write a method that takes in an `ArrayList` of doubles. The method should return the second largest double in the `ArrayList`. You can assume that the `ArrayList` contains at least two elements. The signature of the method should be as follows.

   public static double secondLargest (ArrayList <Double> a)

2. Write a method that takes as input a `StringBuffer` and reverses it. For example, if the input string is `abc`, then the method will change the string to `cba`. The method should have `void` return type.

3. Write a method that takes in an `ArrayList` of `Integer` and an integer and returns true if the integer is in the `ArrayList` and false otherwise.

4. Write a program that prints five random playing cards, where all cards must be different. Example output is: "queen of spades", "ten of clubs", "three of diamonds", "five of hearts", "seven of spades". Use the `enum` construct for both the value and suit of the card. The value of a card can be: "two", "three", "four", "five", "six", "seven", "eight", "nine", "ten", "Jack", "Queen", "King", or "Ace". The suit of a card can be "spades", "hearts", "diamonds", or "clubs". Store the cards in an `ArrayList`. Before inserting a new card in the `ArrayList`, ensure that the card is not already in the list.

5. Write a method that takes as input an `ArrayList` of integers. The methods should reverse the elements and have `void` return type.

6. Write a method that takes as input an `ArrayList` of integers. The methods should return an `ArrayList` of integers that contains the three consecutive integers in the input `ArrayList` with the biggest sum.

7. Write a method that takes as input an `ArrayList` of doubles. The method should return an `ArrayList` of the doubles that are at even positions (i.e., position 0, 2, 4, and so on).

8. Write a method that takes as input two `ArrayList`s of integers. The method should return `true` when the `ArrayList`s have at least one element in common and `false` otherwise.

7.10 Lab

Create a phone book program. Add capabilities for inserting a new name and phone number, deleting a person from the directory, searching for the phone number of a person, and reverse lookup (i.e., searching for a name by phone number). Create a `Person` class and an `ArrayList` of people as part of the implementation.

7.11 Project

Pig Latin is a twist of English for people who want to be silly, or for kids who do not want their parents to know what they are talking about. There are different ways in which people speak pig Latin. For this project, we are going to use the following dialect. For words that begin with a single consonant, take the consonant off the front of the word and add it to the end of the word. Then add "ay" after the consonant. Here are some examples.

```
cat = atcay
dog = ogday
simply = implysay
noise = oisenay
```

For words that begin with double or multiple consonants, take the group of consonants off the front of the word and add them to the end, adding "ay" at the very end of the word. Here are some examples.

```
scratch = atchscray
thick = ickthay
flight = ightflay
grime = imegray
```

For words that begin with a vowel, just add "yay" at the end.

```
is = isyay
apple =appleyay
under = underyay
octopus = octopusyay
```

Recall that a, e, i, o, u, and y are the vowels in the Latin alphabet.

Your program should read a sentence from the keyboard, convert it to Pig Latin, and then output it. Use a `StringTokenizer` to parse the sentence. Use an `ArrayList` of `StringBuffer` objects to store the words.

Part II

Advanced Programming Techniques

Chapter 8

Classes Revisited

This chapter covers advanced topics related to classes. Inheritance allows one class to inherit the methods and data of another class. This is often referred to as an *is-a* relationship. For example, a manager *is-a* an employee. Therefore the **Manager** class may inherit from the **Employee** class. Polymorphism allows dynamic method invocation. For example, we can create several **print** methods in classes and subclasses. Then, we can call the **print** method on an object. The appropriate **print** method will be executed based on the type of the object. Abstract classes and interfaces are special classes that cannot be used to create objects directly. Instead, they are templates from which other classes can inherit. While an abstract class can contain regular methods and data, an interface contains only methods with no bodies and constants.

8.1   Class Containment

Consider the `DiceCup` class from Chapter 6.

```
public class DiceCup {
    private Die[] dice;
    . . .
}
```

The `DiceCup` class contains an array of objects of type `Die`. Figure 8.1 shows an example of a `DiceCup` object. This is referred to as *class containment* (or *class composition*). Every object of type `DiceCup` can contain an array of die objects. In the figure, the object of type

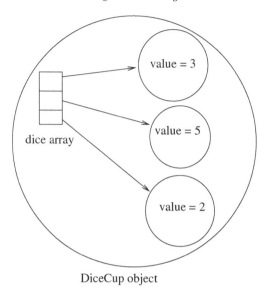

DiceCup object

FIGURE 8.1: Object composition.

`DiceCup` contains three dice with values: 3, 5, and 2. Note that it is possible that memory for the array has not been allocated, that is, a `DiceCup` object may contain no dice.

> *Class composition* is sometimes referred to as the *has* relationship. For example, a `DiceCup` has `Die` objects. Class composition is implemented by defining a variable of one type inside a class of a different type.

An object that contains other objects is sometimes referred to as a *composite object*. As we will see later in this chapter, special care needs to be taken when copying composite objects. Not only the data inside the object, but also all the objects inside it need to be copied.

8.2 Inheritance and the super Keyword

Let us consider a game of villains and superheroes. The player can create villains and superheroes. For villains, the player needs to specify the name of the villain and the strength of their evil power and narcissism. For superheroes, the player needs to specify how much they are respected and the strength of their good powers. All strengths will be represented as an integer between 1 and 10. The program will make the fictional characters fight each other and report the results. A possible design of the two classes is shown next.

```
public class Superhero {
    private String name;
    private int goodPower;
    private int respect;

    public void setName(String name){
```

```
    this.name = name;
  }
  public String getName(){
    return name;
  }
  ...
}

public class Villain {
  private String name;
  private int evilPower;
  private int narcissism;

  public void setName(String name){
    this.name = name;
  }
  public String getName(){
    return name;
  }
  ...
}
```

Note that the two classes share attributes and methods. They both have the **name** attribute and they both have the **setName** and **getName** methods. This is not a coincidence. Both superheroes and villains are fictional characters and therefore they both **inherit** attributes and methods from the **FictionalCharacter** class. A better design is shown next.

```
public class FictionalCharacter {
  private String name;
  public void setName(String name){
    this.name = name;
  }
  public String getName(){
    return name;
  }
}

public class Villain extends FictionalCharacter{
  private int evilPower;
  private int narcissism;
  ...
}

public class Superhero extends FictionalCharacter {
  private int goodPower;
  private int respect;
  ...
}
```

Now the classes **Villain** and **Superhero** inherit from the **FictionalCharacter** class. Our design is shown in Figure 8.2. Such figures are sometimes referred to as UML diagrams, where UML stands for *Unified Modeling Language*. In a UML diagram, every class is surrounded by a rectangle. The rectangle contains the class name, variables, and methods. Arrows between classes are used to represent inheritance.

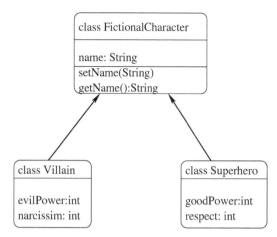

FIGURE 8.2: Class inheritance example.

The inheritance relationship is also referred to as an *is-a* relationship. For example, a superhero *is-a* fictional character. The subclass inherits all the attributes and method of the superclass.

In Java, the **extends** keywords is used to denote inheritance. Note that both `Superhero` and `Villain` extend from `FictionalCharacter`. The `FictionalCharacter` class is the *superclass*, while the `Superhero` and `Villain` classes are the *subclasses*.

The new design helped us avoid defining the variable `name` and the `setName` and `getName` methods multiple times. Note that inside the `Superhero` class we do not have direct access to the name of the superhero. The reason is that the variable `name` is `private` and therefore it is only accessible from within the `FictionalCharacter` class. However, inside the `Superhero` class we have access to the `FictionalCharacter` by using the `super` keyword. The `super` keyword is similar to the `this` keyword. However, instead of giving us access to the current object, it gives us access to the super object (i.e., the object of the superclass). For example, if we put the following code inside a method of the `Superhero` class, it will print the name of the superhero.

```
System.out.println(super.getName());
```

Class inheritance is similar to class containment. If the `Superhero` class inherits from the `FictionalCharacter` class, then every object of type `Superhero` will have an object of type `FictionalCharacter` inside it. Figure 8.3 shows an example object for Superman. As a superhero, he has values for `goodPower` and `respect`. In other words, we could have defined the `Superhero` class as follows.

```
public class Superhero{
   private int goodPower;
   private int respect;
   ...
   private FictionalCharacter superObject;
}
```

Since a `Superhero` is a type of `FictionalCharacter` and a `Superhero` does not have a `FictionalCharacter` inside it, the first design is obviously better. After all, we want our design to follow the scenario that we are modeling as closely as possible.

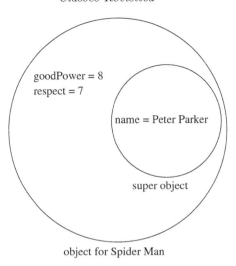

object for Spider Man

FIGURE 8.3: Class inheritance and super object.

Although similar, there are three subtle differences between inheritance and containment. First, they use very distinct syntax. Second, inheritance guarantees the presence of exactly one super object in the subclass. Conversely, the value of the contained object can be equal to `null`. Lastly, as we will see later on in this chapter, we can use polymorphism with inheritance. However, it is impossible to use polymorphism with class containment alone.

8.3   Multiple Inheritance

Java does not support multiple inheritance. In other words, a class cannot inherit from more than one superclass. This is the reason the **super** reference is not ambiguous. If a class could inherit from more than one superclasses, then we could not speak of a unique superclass and the **super** keyword will be ambiguous.

We should always use inheritance instead of containment when applicable. For example, the **Student** class should inherit from the **Person** class and not contain the **Person** class. However, sometimes it is warranted to use class containment as a substitute for class inheritance. Consider, for example, the design from Figure 8.4. Both teachers and students inherit from the **Person** class. However, a teaching assistant is both a student and a teacher and therefore multiple inheritance is needed here. However, Java does not support multiple inheritance.

One way to represent multiple inheritance in Java is by using class containment in its place. Here is one possible implementation of the above design.

```
class Person{
   ...
}

class Teacher extends Person{
```

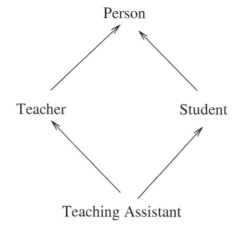

FIGURE 8.4: Example of multiple inheritance.

```
   ...
}

class Student extends Person{
   ...
}

class TeachingAssistant extends Teacher{
   Student studentSuperObject;
}
```

Of course, this design is not perfect and will prevent us from using some Java features related to inheritance, such as polymorphism. However, since Java does not support multiple inheritance, we have no choice but to simulate it using class containment.

8.4   Constructors of Subclasses

Let us go back to our superhero and villain example. If we add an empty and non-empty constructors to the `FictionalCharacter` class, then we get the following version of the class.

```
public class FictionalCharacter {
   private String name;
   public FictionalCharacter(){
   }
   public FictionalCharacter(String name){
      this.name = name;
   }

   public String getName(){
      return name;
   }
   public void setName(String name){
```

```
    this.name = name;
  }
}
```

Next, let us explore the Superhero class and its constructors. When creating a Superhero object, we also need to create a FictionalCharacter object. Therefore, in the first line of every constructor of the Superhero class, we must create a FictionalCharacter super object. If such an object is not explicitly created, then the empty constructor for the FictionalCharacter class is explicitly called. Here is one possible implementation of the non-empty constructor for the Superhero class.

```
public class Superhero extends FictionalCharacter {
  private int goodPower;
  private int respect;
  public Superhero(String name, int goodPower, int respect){
    this.goodPower = goodPower;
    this.respect = respect;
    super.setName(name);
  }
}
```

In the above code, a call that creates the super object is not present. Therefore, the empty constructor is called to create the super object. In the last line, the name for the super object is changed using the setName method. This design looks clumsy. Alternatively, we can explicitly create the super object as shown next.

```
public class Superhero extends FictionalCharacter {
  private int goodPower;
  private int respect;
  public Superhero(String name, int goodPower, int respect){
    super(name);
    this.goodPower = goodPower;
    this.respect = respect;
  }
}
```

The statement super(name) creates the super object. Note that this statement must be the first statement of the constructor. This command calls a constructor of the FictionalCharacter class (i.e., the superclass). The call to the constructor is used to create the super object.

The empty constructor for the Superhero class can be created as follows.

```
class Superhero extends FictionalCharacter{
  class Superhero(){
  }
  ...
}
```

We can add super() to the first line of the constructor. However, this is not necessary. The reason is that the empty constructor of the superclass is called if the super keyword is not used to call it in the first line of the method. If the superclass does not have an empty constructor, then a syntax error is generated. The above code is equivalent to the following code.

```
class Superhero extends FictionalCharacter{
  class Superhero(){
    super();
```

```
  }
  ...
}
```

8.5   Abstract Classes and Methods

Let us reexamine the `FictionalCharacter` class. It stores the name of the fictional character. Maybe we do not want anyone to be able to directly create fictional characters. In other words, let us suppose that the only reason the class exists is so that we can inherit from it and create the subclasses `Superhero` and `Villain`. In this case, we can make the class `abstract`.

> An abstract class is similar to a regular class. It can contain variables, methods, and even constructors. However, an object cannot be directly instantiated from it. An object of an abstract class can only be instantiated from a subclass using the **super** keyword.

Here is a rewrite of the `FictionalCharacter` class using the `abstract` keyword.

```java
public abstract class FictionalCharacter {
  private String name;
  public FictionalCharacter(){
  }
  public FictionalCharacter(String name){
    this.name = name;
  }

  public String getName(){
    return name;
  }
  public void setName(String name){
    this.name = name;
  }
}
```

We will add one more method to the `FictionalCharacter` class: `computeStrength`. The method computes the strength of a fictional character. We assume that we can compute the strength of any fictional character. However, the `FictionalCharacter` class does not store enough information to compute this value. In other words, we will have this information in every subclass of the `FictionalCharacter` class, but not in the class itself. Therefore, we want to force every class that inherits from the `FictionalCharacter` class to redefine the `computeStrength` method and include proper implementation. The `computeStrength` method inside the `FictionalCharacter` class will not have a body and the method will be defined as `abstract`.

An abstract method does not have a body. The **abstract** keyword must be used to define an abstract method. An abstract method can be only part of an abstract class. Any non-abstract class must *override* all abstract methods of the superclass and include the bodies for the methods. Overriding a method means including a method with the same signature in the subclass.

Here is the new version of the `FictionalCharacter` class.

```
public abstract class FictionalCharacter {
  private String name;
  public FictionalCharacter(){
  }
  public FictionalCharacter(String name){
    this.name = name;
  }

  public String getName(){
    return name;
  }
  public void setName(String name){
    this.name = name;
  }
  public abstract double computeStrength();
}
```

Note that an abstract class does not need to contain an abstract method. However, an abstract method can only be defined as part of an abstract class. For example, if the `FictionalCharacter` class was not abstract, then the following code will be ambiguous.

```
FictionalCharacter fc1 = new FictionalCharacter("Superman");
System.out.println(fc1.computeStrength());
```

The problem is that the implementation of the `computeStrength` method is missing inside the `FictionalCharacter` class. That is, the method can only be invoked on an object that belongs to a subclass of the `FictionalCharacter` class. By defining the `FictionalCharacter` class abstract, we can guarantee that the class will only be instantiated from subclasses of the `FictionalCharacter` classes and therefore calling the `computeStrength` method will be meaningful.

8.6 Auto-casting, Polymorphism, and Dynamic Binding

Let us now examine an implementation of the `Superhero` and `Villain` classes. In each class, the strength of the fictional character is computed differently.

```
public class Superhero extends FictionalCharacter {
  private int goodPower;
  private int respect;
  public Superhero(String name, int goodPower, int respect){
    super(name);
    this.goodPower = goodPower;
    this.respect = respect;
```

```
  }
  public double  computeStrength(){
    return goodPower*respect*Math.random();
  }
  public String toString(){
    return super.getName()+" is a superhero that has good power = "+
      goodPower+" and respect = "+respect;
  }
}

public class Villain extends FictionalCharacter {
  private int evilPower;
  private int narcissism;

  public Villain(String name, int evilPower, int narcissism){
    super(name);
    this.evilPower = evilPower;
    this.narcissism = narcissism;
  }
  public double computeStrength(){
    return evilPower*narcissism*Math.random()*0.9;
  }
  public String toString(){
    return super.getName()+" is a villain that has evil power = "+
      evilPower+" and narcissism = "+narcissism;
  }
}
```

Note that we have multiplied the power of villains by 0.9 just because we do not like them (i.e., we do not want to give them a fair shot at winning a fight with a superhero). As expected, both subclasses have an implementation of the computeStrength method. If this method was missing from one of the subclasses, then a compilation error would be produced.

We have added a toString method to both classes. We will use this method to print a fictional character. Note that since the variable name inside the FictionalCharacter class is private, we had to resort to calling a method to get the name of the fictional characters. Even subclasses do not have access to the private variables of the superclass.

We are now ready to start building our main class: we will call it FaceOff. For starters, let us create several fictional characters and just print them. We will allow the player to specify the parameters of the characters. A menu method that prints a menu and lets the user choose between entering a villain or entering a superhero will be created. We will store the fictional characters inside an ArrayList because we do not know how many fictional characters the user will want to create. The first iteration of the class follows.

```
import java.util.*;
public class FaceOff {
  public static void main(String[] args){
    ArrayList<FictionalCharacter> characters = new ArrayList<>();
    populateCharacters(characters);
    for(FictionalCharacter character: characters){
      System.out.println(character.toString());
    }
  }
  public static void populateCharacters(ArrayList<FictionalCharacter>
    characters){
```

```
  while(true){
    printMenu();
    int choice = getIntValue("Enter your choice: ");
    switch(choice){
      case 1:
        characters.add(new Superhero(getStringValue("Name: "),
            getIntValue("Good Power[1-10]: "), getIntValue("Respect
            :[1-10]: ")));
        break;
      case 2:
        characters.add(new Villain(getStringValue("Name: "),
            getIntValue("Evil Power[1-10]: "), getIntValue("
            Narcissism[1-10]: ")));
        break;
      case 3: return;
    }
  }
}

public static void printMenu(){
  System.out.println("1. Enter Superhero");
  System.out.println("2. Enter Villain");
  System.out.println("3. Finish Entering");
}
public static int getIntValue(String prompt){
  int choice;
  Scanner keyboard = new Scanner(System.in);
  System.out.print(prompt);
  choice = keyboard.nextInt();
  return choice;
}
public static String getStringValue(String prompt){
  String choice;
  Scanner keyboard = new Scanner(System.in);
  System.out.print(prompt);
  choice = keyboard.next();
  return choice;
}
}
```

We have added two auxiliary methods: `getIntValue` and `getStringValue`. They read an integer or a string from the keyboard. This is a good design because each of the methods is used multiple times. A possible output of the program follows. As usual, user input is in italic.

```
1. Enter Superhero
2. Enter Villain
3. Finish Entering
Enter your choice: 1
Name: Superman
Good Power[1-10]: 8
Respect:[1-10]: 8
1. Enter Superhero
2. Enter Villain
3. Finish Entering
```

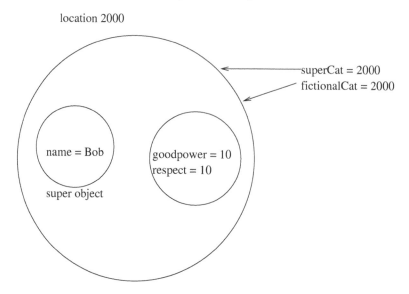

FIGURE 8.5: Autocasting.

```
Enter your choice: 2
Name: Joker
Evil Power[1-10]: 7
Narcissism[1-10]: 10
1. Enter Superhero
2. Enter Villain
3. Finish Entering
Enter your choice: 3
Superman is a superhero that has good power = 8 and respect = 8
Joker is a villain that has evil power = 7 and narcissism = 10
```

Few *magical* things happened while the program was executing. First, note that we were able to insert both superheroes and villains in the `ArrayList`. The reason is that the `ArrayList` was defined to contain objects of type `FictionalCharacter`. Since both superheroes and villains are fictional characters, Java automatically converts them to fictional characters. In other words, in an `ArrayList<FictionalCharacter>` we can store any object that is of type `FictionalCharacter` or that belongs to a subclass of the `FictionalCharacter` class.

Here is a simple example to clarify things.

```
Superhero superCat = new Superhero("Bob",10,10);
FictionalCharacter fictionalCat = superCat;
```

Figure 8.5 explains the design. We have two pointers to the same object. Note that the type of the `fictionalCat` object is `FictionalCharacter`, but it references a `Superhero`. Java automatically casts the `superCat` object to an object of type `FictionalCharacter`. Note that the code can also be rewritten as follows.

```
Superhero superCat = new Superhero("Bob",10,10);
FictionalCharacter fictionalCat = (FictionalCharacter)superCat;
```

However, the cast is not required.

Java automatically casts an object that belongs to a subclass to an object that belongs to the superclass. The reverse is not true. However, an object that belongs to the subclass can be explicitly cast to an object of type superclass. However, a `ClassCastException` will be raised if the super object variable does not actually reference an object of the subclass type.

For example, even if the `FictionalCharacter` class was not abstract, the following line will produce a compilation error.

```
Superhero s = (Superhero) new FictionalCharacter();
```

The reason is that s references an object of type `FictionalCharacter` and therefore s does not support variables such as `goodPower`. However, the syntax `Superhero s` implies that the s object must have the variables `goodPower` and `respect` associated with it.

The second *magical* feature of our program is that the correct `toString` method is executed for every fictional character of the `ArrayList`. Here is what happened. When Java sees the syntax `element.toString()`, it determines the object that `element` refers to. If `element` refers to an object of type `Superhero`, then the `toString` method from the `Superhero` class is executed. Otherwise, if `element` refers to an object of type `Villain`, then the `toString` method from the `Villain` class is executed. This magical property of always finding the right method to execute is called *polymorphism*. This term was chosen because the `toString` method takes many forms and the correct version is always executed.

When the Java compiler sees the syntax o.m(...), where o is an object variable and m is an instance method, the type of the o object is ignored. Java only considers the object which o references. Suppose that this object belongs to the C class. If the C class contains the m method with the correct parameters, then the method is executed. Otherwise, Java searches in the superclass of the C class for the m method. The search continues until Java reaches the root or inheritance hierarchy (more on this later). Note that if neither the C class nor one of its ancestors contains the m method, then the code o.m(...) will not compile. The reason is that the C class must be either the class to which the o object belongs or one of its descendants in the inheritance hierarchy.

Let us examine the following code from the `main` method.

```
for(FictionalCharacter character: characters){
    System.out.println(character.toString());
}
```

We did not need to add the call to the method `toString` (it is automatically called for the method `println`), but we did so in order to make the example clearer. The variable `characters` is an `ArrayList` of objects of type `FictionalCharacter`. The variable `character` iterates over the elements of the `ArrayList`. Even though the type of the variable `character` is `FictionalCharacter`, Java disregards this type when it tries to find the correct method to execute. If the `character` object references a superhero, then the `toString` method from the `Superhero` class is executed. Alternatively, if the `character` object references a villain, then the `toString` method from the `Villain` class is executed. Note that in order for the code to compile, the `FictionalCharacter` class or one of its superclasses (or, in general, ancestors in the inheritance heterarchy) must contain the `toString` method. However, this is not necessarily the `toString` method that will be executed.

Java implements polymorphism through *dynamic binding* (also called *late binding*). This means that the method to be executed is determined at run time during the program execution.

Note that we can call the `toString` method on any object. Here is the reason.

In Java, we can invoke the `toString` method on any object. The reason is that all classes inherit (directly or indirectly) from the `Object` class, which contains the method `toString` as part of its public interface.

The `Object` class contains a default implementation of the `toString` method that simply prints the address of the object (it actually prints a number that is associated with the object because the address of the object can change during the execution, but this detail is irrelevant to the programmer). This default behavior of the `toString` method can be overridden in any class. Note that the `computeStrength` method is not defined in the `Object` class, which is the only superclass of the `FictionalCharacter` class. Therefore, we have to define the method as an abstract method inside the `FictionalCharacter` class. If the method is not defined inside the `FictionalCharacter` class, then the following code will not compile.

```
FictionalCharacter tom;
...
System.out.println(tom.computeStrength());
```

The reason is that even though `tom` may actually point to an object that belongs to a class that has the `computeStrength` method (e.g., the `Superhero` class), Java does not know this at compile time and will not allow the program to compile.

As a last point in this section, we could have used the following code to print the `ArrayList characters`.

```
System.out.println(characters);
```

The reason is that the `ArrayList` class contains a `toString` method that prints the `ArrayList`. This method will be automatically called on the `ArrayList`. The method, in turn, will call the `toString` method on each of the elements of the `ArrayList characters`. However, we chose the previous syntax in order to explain how polymorphism works.

8.7   Interfaces and the `Comparable` Interface

Including the `computeStrength` method in the `FictionalCharacter` class is a valid approach to allow the rest of the world to compare fictional characters. However, we seem to be giving too much of our "secret sauce" away.

One rule of designing classes is that they should provide only the interface that is needed by the outside world and should not provide any implementation-related details. The reason is that these implementation-related details may change in the future, but the interface of the class should remain constant.

Suppose that we create a new methodology for computing the strength of a fictional character. Then, if the user has saved past results, this value would be meaningless and can result in the program behaving erroneously. Therefore, we will rewrite our program and only provide a public interface that allows us to compare two fictional characters.

Remember that we used the `compareTo` method to compare two strings.

$$\text{s1.compareTo(s2)} = \begin{cases} \text{positive integer} & \text{if s1>s2} \\ \text{negative integer} & \text{if s1<s2} \\ 0 & \text{if s1=s2} \end{cases} \tag{8.1}$$

For strings, $<$ and $>$ refer to the lexicographical ordering of strings. In general, we can use the `compareTo` method to compare two objects and define the meaning of an object to be smaller, equal to, or greater than another object.

In Java, there is a class that includes the `compareTo` method. It is a simple class; it only includes the method and defines it as an abstract method. We can tell the world that our class supports the `compareTo` method by inheriting from this class. This class is special because it only contains the abstract `compareTo` method. It does not contain any methods with bodies, constructors, or variables. In Java, such classes are referred to as *interfaces*.

An *interface* is a special class that contains only methods without bodies (i.e., abstract methods). The **abstract** keyword is not used when defining a method inside an interface because all the methods are abstract. An interface cannot contain regular variables, but it can contain constants (i.e., **final static** variables). An interface cannot contain constructors.

Note that an interface is similar to an abstract class because one cannot directly create an object that belongs to an interface or an abstract class. However, there is a subtle difference. Since all the methods in an interface are abstract and there are no instance variables inside, we will never need to use the **super** keyword to refer to an interface object. In other words, an object for an interface is never created. Conversely, an object for an abstract class is created as part of the super object of a subclass. Since we cannot use the **super** keyword when we inherit from an interface and a super object is not created, Java allows us to inherit from multiple interfaces.

In Java, inheriting from an interface is different than inheriting from a class. When inheriting from an interface, a super object is not created. In order to emphasize the difference, Java uses the following terminology. A class **extends** from another class, but it **implements** an interface. A class implementing an interface means that the class overrides and implements (i.e., includes the bodies of) all the methods of the interface. In Java, one can extend a single class, but implement multiple interfaces.

The interface that contains the `compareTo` method is called `Comparable`. Therefore, the `FictionalCharacter` class can implement this interface and override the `compareTo` method. Here is the new implementation.

```
public abstract class FictionalCharacter implements Comparable<
    FictionalCharacter >{
  private String name;
  public FictionalCharacter(){
  }
```

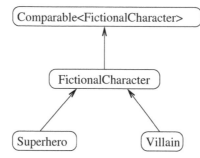

FIGURE 8.6: Inheritance hierarchy.

```
public FictionalCharacter(String name){
  this.name = name;
}

public String getName(){
  return name;
}
public void setName(String name){
  this.name = name;
}
public abstract double computeStrength();

public int compareTo(FictionalCharacter other){
  if(computeStrength() > other.computeStrength()){
    return 1;
  }
  if(computeStrength() < other.computeStrength()){
    return −1;
  }
  return 0;
}
}
```

The `implements` keyword is used to denote that objects of type `FictionalCharacter` will be comparable. Note that the interface `Comparable` is generic. The type parameter describes the input type of the `compareTo` method. In other words, since the `compareTo` method takes as input an object of type `FictionalCharacter`, we must implement `Comparable<FictionalCharacter>`. The inheritance hierarchy for our example is shown in Figure 8.6.

Let us now look at the `compareTo` method. Consider the following call.

```
if (batman.compareTo(superman) > 0){
  ...
}
```

The method call will return 1 if Batman has more strength, -1 if Superman has more strength, or 0 if they have equal strength. In this case, `batman` is the hidden parameter (or the `this` object). The `other` object formal parameter in the `compareTo` method will become equal to `superman`.

First, note that we could have tried to use this alternative syntax for the `compareTo` method.

```
public int compareTo(FictionalCharacter other){
```

```
   return (int)(computeStrength()-other.computeStrength());
}
```

However, this would have only worked if the `computeStrength` method returned an `int` instead of a `double`. For example, if the two strengths are 3.1 and 3.0, then subtracting them and converting the result to an integer will give us the number 0. However, this will indicate that the strengths are equal, which is not the case.

Second, note that calling the `computeStrength` method on an object of type `FictionalCharacter` does not result in a compilation error. The reason is that, although the method is abstract, so is the `FictionalCharacter` class. This means that the method will actually be called on an object that belongs to a subclass of the `FictionalCharacter` class where the `computeStrength` method will be implemented. Java uses dynamic binding to decide during program execution the method that needs to be called. For example, if we have an object that refers to a `Superhero`, then the `computeStrength` method from the `Superhero` class will be executed.

Note that the classes `Superhero` and `Villain` do not need to be modified. We will slightly modify the `FaceOff` class. In the new implementation, only the fictional character that is the strongest will be printed. Here is the new implementation.

```
import java.util.*;
public class FaceOff {
  public static void main(String[] args){
    ArrayList<FictionalCharacter> characters = new ArrayList<>();
    populateArray(characters);
    Collections.sort(characters);
    System.out.println(characters.get(characters.size()-1));
  }
  ...
}
```

The `Collections` class is a utility class that contains only static methods. The `sort` method of the class can take as input an `ArrayList` of objects and sort them. The last line simply prints the last element of the sorted `ArrayList`. Note that something very interesting is happening here. The reason that the `sort` method can sort the elements is because it knows that they are comparable. In other words, a compilation error will occur if the `FictionalCharacter` class did not implement the interface `Comparable`. By implementing this interface, the `FictionalCharacter` class announces to the rest of the world that its objects are `Comparable`. As a result, the `sort` method calls the `compareTo` method on objects of type `FictionalCharacter` multiple times in order to sort the objects. One can think of a call to the `compareTo` method as a fight between two fictional characters. Random numbers are used to calculate their current strength and the one with the highest strength wins. There is also a method `sort` that belongs to the utility `Arrays` class. It can be used to sort an array of objects that implement the interface `Comparable`.

8.8 Access Privileges

There is a slight problem with our previous solution. Although the program works, the design is not perfect. Remember that we introduced the `compareTo` method in order to hide from the rest of the world the value of a fictional character's strength. After all, a random number is used to determine this strength and maybe we do not want to reveal this secret

TABLE 8.1:   Access privilege modifiers.

Modifier	Accessible from
public	everywhere
protected	same package and subclasses
no modifier	only within same package
private	only from same class

to the rest of the world. However, the `computeStrength` method is still defined as `public` and anyone can call it. The astute reader may suggest that we can simply define the method as `private`. However, this is impossible in this case. The reasons are that (1) an abstract method cannot be defined as private and (2) a `private` method cannot be overridden.

Before we present the solution to the problem, let us first examine the possible modifiers for access privileges in Java. Table 8.1 shows them in tabular format. The `protected` keyword means that the data or method is accessible within the same package and within the subclasses. No modifier is when no access privileges are specified. In this case, the class member is accessible only within the package.

> When overriding a method in a subclass, Java does not allow us to assign weaker access privileges. For example, a `protected` method cannot be overridden as `private`. It can only be overridden as `protected`, no modifier, or `public`.

Note that a private method cannot be overridden. The reason is that the subclass should not know about the existence of a `private` method in the superclass. Note that we cannot define the `computeStrength` method in the `FictionalCharacter` class as `private`. The reason is that we will not be able to override it in the subclasses. Our next choice is to define it using no modifier. Here is the refactored code that shows a better design.

```java
public abstract class FictionalCharacter implements Comparable<
    FictionalCharacter >{
  private String name;
  public FictionalCharacter(){
  }
  public FictionalCharacter(String name){
    this.name = name;
  }

  public String getName(){
    return name;
  }
  public void setName(String name){
    this.name = name;
  }
  abstract double computeStrength();

  public int compareTo(FictionalCharacter other){
    if(computeStrength()-other.computeStrength()>0){
      return 1;
    }
     if(computeStrength()-other.computeStrength()<0){
      return -1;
    }
    return 0;
```

```
    }
}

public class Superhero extends FictionalCharacter {
  private int goodPower;
  private int respect;
  public Superhero(String name, int goodPower, int respect){
    super(name);
    this.goodPower = goodPower;
    this.respect = respect;
  }
  double computeStrength(){
    return goodPower*respect*Math.random();
  }
  public String toString(){
    return super.getName()+" is a superhero that has good power = "+
        goodPower+" and respect = "+respect;
  }
}

public class Villain extends FictionalCharacter {
  private int evilPower;
  private int narcissism;
  public Villain(String name, int evilPower ,int narcissism){
    super(name);
    this.evilPower = evilPower;
    this.narcissism = narcissism;
  }
  double computeStrength(){
    return evilPower*narcissism*Math.random() *0.9;
  }
  public String toString(){
    return super.getName()+" is a Villain that has evil power = "+
        evilPower+" and narcissism = "+narcissism;
  }
}
```

Note that the three classes must be created in three separate files. As a general rule, provide the weakest possible access privilege to each variable and method. In our example, since the `computeStrength` method could not be defined as `private`, we defined it using no modifier. If we put it inside a closed package, then nobody outside the package will be able to access it.

Note that, so far, we have used either `public` or no modifier when defining classes. Similar to variables and methods, a `public` class can be accessible from everywhere, while a class with no modifier can only be accessible within the package. Remember that every file must have exactly one `public` class that has the same name as the name of the file. A nested class (i.e., a class within a class) can be defined as `private`; more on this in Chapter 10.

8.9   The `final` Keyword

Sometimes, we want to create a method and disallow it to be overridden. In our example, we may want to fix the way the `computeStrength` method works. In other words, we want to make sure that someone does not create a class called `SpecialSuperhero` where the strength is calculated in a different way. Maybe this class will give unfair advantage to special superheroes. In order to prevent this, we can define the `computeStrength` method in the `Superhero` class as `final`. Here is the rewritten code.

```
public class Superhero extends FictionalCharacter {
  ...
  final double  computeStrength(){
    return goodPower*respect*Math.random();
  }
  ...
}
```

> A `final` method cannot be overridden in a subclass. Polymorphism does not apply to final methods.

Similar to methods, classes can also be defined as `final`. A `final` class cannot be inherited from. For example, consider the following code.

```
public final class Superhero extends FictionalCharacter {
  ...
}
```

This means that a `SpecialSuperhero` class that extends from the `Superhero` class cannot be created.

8.10   Static Methods and Polymorphism

Note that polymorphism does not apply to static methods. In order to demonstrate the consequences, we will add the `memberCount` static method to the `FictionalCharacter` class. The method will simply return the number of fictional characters that are created.

```
public abstract class FictionalCharacter implements Comparable<
    FictionalCharacter >{
  private String name;
  private static int memberCount = 0;
  public FictionalCharacter(){
    memberCount++;
  }
  public FictionalCharacter(String name){
    this.name = name;
    memberCount++;
  }
```

```
  public String getName(){
    return name;
  }
  public void setName(String name){
    this.name = name;
  }
  abstract double computeStrength();

  public int compareTo(FictionalCharacter other){
    if(computeStrength()-other.computeStrength()>0){
      return 1;
    }
    if(computeStrength()-other.computeStrength()<0){
      return -1;
    }
    return 0;
  }
  public static int memberCount(){
    return memberCount;
  }
}
```

The static variable `memberCount` keeps track of the number of fictional characters. The count is initially zero and is incremented by one every time a new fictional character is created. The variable is `static` because it is not associated with a particular object, but rather with the whole class. Next, imagine we also add object counting capabilities to the `Superhero` class.

```
public class Superhero extends FictionalCharacter {
  private int goodPower;
  private int respect;
  private static int memberCount = 0;
  public Superhero{
    memberCount++;
  }
  public Superhero(String name, int goodPower, int respect){
    super(name);
    this.goodPower = goodPower;
    this.respect = respect;
    memberCount++;
  }
  double  computeStrength(){
    return goodPower*respect*Math.random();
  }
  public String toString(){
    return super.getName()+" is a superhero that has good power = "+
        goodPower+" and respect = "+respect;
  }
  public static int memberCount(){
    return memberCount;
  }
}
```

Now, if we call `Superhero.memberCount()`, then we will get the number of superheroes. Conversely, the code `FictionalCharacter.memberCount()` will return the number of fictional characters. Note that if the `memberCount` method for the `Superhero` class is removed, then the call `Superhero.memberCount()` will result in error. The reason is that the `Superhero` class will now not contain the method and Java will not check the superclass. The reason is that polymorphism does not apply to methods of type `static`.

8.11   Explicit Type Checking

Let us continue our superhero and villain example. Suppose that we have created several superheroes and villains and have added them to the single `ArrayList characters`.

```
ArrayList<FictionalCharacter> characters = new ArrayList<>();
...
```

Suppose that now we want to count the number of superheroes and the number of villains in the `ArrayList`. We can call the `memberCount` method that was described in the previous section. However, this method will give us the total number of superheroes and not the number of superheroes in the `ArrayList`. Note that in the `ArrayList` we have a number of objects of type `FictionalCharacter`. However, since the `FictionalCharacter` class is abstract, these objects must belong to its subclasses. Therefore, we need a way to determine the type of an object. One way of performing this task is using the `instanceof` keyword. Here is an example.

```
int count = 0;
for(FictionalCharacter el: characters){
  if(el instanceof Superhero){
    count++;
  }
}
```

The `instanceof` keyword checks if the object belongs to the class. It returns `true` if it does and `false` otherwise. The above code iterates through all the elements of the `ArrayList`. If an element belongs to the `Superhero` class, then the counter is incremented by one. The code computes the number of superheroes in the `ArrayList`.

> The expression `o instanceof C` returns `true` exactly when the `o` object is an instance of the `C` class or one of its descendents in the inheritance hierarchy.

Note that the code: `el instance of FictionalCharacter` will be true for all the elements `el` of the `ArrayList`.

Alternatively, one can use the `getClass` method to determine the type of an object. The method returns the class of an object. Here is an example.

```
for(FictionalCharacter el: characters){
  if(el.getClass()==Superhero.class){
    count++;
  }
}
```

The `getClass` method is defined in the `Object` class. In other words, it can be called on any object. It returns the runtime type of the object.

The *runtime type* of an object is what the object references. The *compile-time type* of an object is what it is defined to be. For example, consider the following code: `FictionalCharacter c = new Superhero()`. The runtime type of the c object will be `Superhero`, while the compile-time type of the c object will be `FictionalCharacter`.

Note that polymorphism uses the runtime type of an object to decide which version of a method to call and ignores the compile-time type of the object. Alternatively, polymorphism does not apply to static methods and the compile-time type of the object is used to determine which version of the method to call.

The `getClass` method actually returns an object of type `Class`. Such an object is created for every class. One can call the `getName()` method to get the string description of an object of type `Class`. Note as well the new syntax `Superhero.class`. The code refers to the `Class` object for the `Superhero` class.

8.12 Cloning Objects

Once a fictional character is created, it may be nice to have the ability to *clone* them. After all, we may need several Batmans to fight off the evil Joker. Inside the `Object` class, a `clone` method is already defined. However, this method is defined as `protected`. Therefore, Java forces us to override it as `public` before we can use it. The reason is that the default `clone` method that is defined inside the `Object` class does not copy inner objects. Consider the following simple example.

```java
public class FictionalCharacter implements Cloneable{
  private String name;
  private Address address;
  public FictionalCharacter(){
  }
  public FictionalCharacter(String name, Address address){
    this.name = name;
    this.address = address;
  }
  public String toString(){
    return name +" lives at "+address;
  }
  protected Object clone() throws CloneNotSupportedException{
    return super.clone();
  }
}

public class Address{
  private String streetName;
  private int number;
  public Address(){}
  public Address(String streetName, int number){
    this.streetName = streetName;
    this.number = number;
  }
}
```

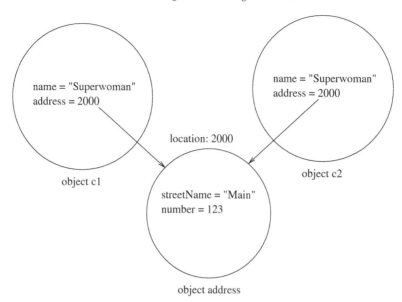

FIGURE 8.7: Cloning example.

```java
  public String toString(){
    return number+" "+streetName;
  }
  public void changeAddress(String streetName, int number){
    this.streetName = streetName;
    this.number = number;
  }
}

public class CloneTest{
  public static void main(String[] args) throws Exception{
    Address address = new Address("Main",123);
    FictionalCharacter c1 = new FictionalCharacter("Superwoman",
        address);
    FictionalCharacter c2 = (FictionalCharacter) c1.clone();
    address.changeAddress("Main", 235);
    System.out.println(c2);
  }
}
```

Figure 8.7 depicts what happens. We call `super.clone()` to perform the cloning of our fictional character object. However, the default `clone` method inside the `Object` class does not know anything about the structure of an object of type `FictionalCharacter`. It simply copies all the data. As a result, both `c1` and `c2` will contain the same object of type `Address`. Now, if this address is modified, the change will affect both objects.

> **Shallow copy** happens when we copy the data of an object, but we do not make copies of the inner objects. Shallow copy is dangerous because changes to an inner object of one class leads to changes of the same inner object of the other class. The default `clone` method inside the `Object` class performs shallow copy. If we want to perform deep copy, we need to override the method.

In our example, the program will print **Superwoman lives at 235 Main**. This is not the desired behavior. After all, we only changed the address of the **c1** object. Why should the address of **c2** be affected? The Java creators knew about the dangers of shallow copy. Therefore, they designed the language in a way that requires the programmer to jump through several hoops before they can use the **clone** method.

1. Override the **clone** method as public.

2. Inherit from the interface **Cloneable**.

3. Catch an exception.

The interface **Cloneable** happens to be empty. Implementing it simply tells Java: "I know cloning is tricky and that the default cloning only provides shallow copy. I am either satisfied with shallow copy, or I have rewritten the **clone** method to implement deep copy."

> **Deep copy** happens when we copy the data of an object, but we also copy all inner objects by making new instances of them. Deep copy is only possible when there are no recursive references. For example, if an object can contain a reference to itself, then the deep copy method may never terminate.

Java requires that all subclasses that override the **clone** method implement the **Cloneable** interface. For example, if this interface is not implemented, then the **CloneNotSupportedException** exception is raised. Therefore, we need to add exception-handling code when dealing with the **clone** method. In the above code, **throws Exception** means that the method can generate an exception and the exception is not handled.

Next, let us rewrite our code. This time we will use deep copy.

```java
class FictionalCharacter implements Cloneable {
  private String name;
  private Address address;

  public FictionalCharacter() {
  }

  public FictionalCharacter(String name, Address address) {
    this.name = name;
    this.address = address;
  }

  public String toString() {
    return name + " lives at " + address;
  }

  protected Object clone() throws CloneNotSupportedException {
    FictionalCharacter result = (FictionalCharacter) super.clone();
    result.address = (Address) address.clone();
    return result;
  }
}

class Address implements Cloneable {
  private String streetName;
  private int number;
```

```java
  public Address() {
  }

  public Address(String streetName, int number) {
    this.streetName = streetName;
    this.number = number;
  }

  public String toString() {
    return number + " " + streetName;
  }

  public void changeAddress(String streetName, int number) {
    this.streetName = streetName;
    this.number = number;
  }

  public Object clone() throws CloneNotSupportedException {
    Address result = (Address) super.clone();
    result.streetName = new String(streetName);
    return result;
  }
}
```

When we execute the program, we get: **Superwoman lives at 123 Main**. This is more desirable behavior. The address of the fictional character **c1** is changed, but this does not lead to the change of the address of fictional character **c2**. After all, the clone of Superwoman may live down the street from the original Superwoman. The **clone** method inside the **FictionalCharacter** class uses the **clone** method of the **Object** class. The latter method just copies the data. Since the returned object must be of type **Object**, it needs to be explicitly cast to a **FictionalCharacter**. In addition, we make a copy of the address object by calling the **clone** method on the address object. Note that the **Address** class is now rewritten to support the **clone** method.

8.13   Comparing Objects for Equality

Now that we know how to clone fictional characters, it is reasonable to ask ourselves when two fictional characters are equal. In Java, the following code will compile.

```java
Superhero s1 = new Superhero("Superman",5,5);
Superhero s2 = new Superhero("Superman",5,5);
if(s1 == s2){
  ...
}
```

One might anticipate that the condition inside the **if** statement will be true because the two superheroes have the same **name**, **goodPower**, and **respect**. However, when "==" is used to compare two objects, only their addresses are compared. In the above case, we clearly have two distinct objects, and therefore the condition inside the **if** statement will be false. If we need access to a more meaningful way of comparing two objects for equality, then we need to override the **equals** method of the **Object** class. Since the **equals** method is defined in the `Object` class, it can be used to compare any two objects. However, the default implementation in the `Object` class is equivalent to the "==" operator: it just checks if the two objects are identical. Consider the following rewrite.

```
Superhero s1 = new Superhero("Superman",5,5);
Superhero s2 = new Superhero("Superman",5,5);
if(s1.equals(s2)){
  ...
}
```

If the `Superhero` does not override the `equals` method, then the condition in the `if` statement will be false again because the two objects are distinct. In order for the condition to be true, we need to override the `equals` method in the `Superman` class by defining what does it mean for two Supermans to be equal. Let us start with the `FictionalCharacter` class.

```
public class FictionalCharacter{
  private String name;
  ...
  public boolean equals(Object other){
    if(other.getClass()!= getClass()){
      return false;
    }
    return name.equals(((FictionalCharacter)other).name);
  }
}
```

The `equals` method compares the input object to the `this` object. If they have different runtime types, then the objects cannot be the same. If they have the same runtime type, then the input object must be of type `FictionalCharacter`. It therefore must have the attribute `name` and we can simply compare the names of the two objects. Remember that strings should always be compared using the `equals` method. The reason is that the creators of the `String` class created a meaningful `equals` method for objects of type `String`. Remember as well that the input to the `equals` method in the class `Object` is of type `Object`. Therefore, when we override the `equals` method, we must perform the following tasks.

1. Determine the type of the input object.

2. Cast the input object to the appropriate type.

3. Compare the variables of the two objects.

Extra care should be taken when creating classes that have both the `equals` and `compareTo` methods. Although not required, it is good programming practice that `o1.equals(o2)` is true exactly when `o1.compareTo(o2)==0`.

Next, let us focus on the `Superhero` class and its equal methods.

```
public class Superhero extends FictionalCharacter {
  private int goodPower;
  private int respect;
  ...
  public boolean equals(Object other){
    if(! super.equals(other)){
      return false;
```

```
          }
     return  (goodPower == ((Superhero)other).goodPower && respect == ((
          Superhero)other).respect);
     }
}
```

The method first calls `super.equals`. This calls the `equals` method for the
`FictionalCharacter` class. It checks if the two objects have the same type and the same
name. Only if we know that this is true should we compare them for the values of `goodPower`
and `respect`. When we know that the input object is of the same runtime type as the `this`
object, that is, it is of type `Superhero`, we can cast the input object to an object of type
`Superhero` and compare the variables `goodPower` and `respect` of the two objects.

8.14   Summary

The chapter covered issues related to inheritance and the `Object` class. We showed
that inheritance is similar to class composition. However, there are some subtle differences.
While a class can contain a null pointer to an object of a different class, the super object
can never be null. To guarantee this, Java creates the super object as the first operation in
the constructor of the subclass. Inheritance also allows for polymorphic method calls, while
this feature is not supported when class composition is used.

Polymorphism means that one of several methods may be executed using the same
syntax. Every object has a runtime and a compile-time type. The compile-time type of an
object is the type that is declared in the program. However, during program execution, the
object may reference an object that belongs to one of the subclasses, which becomes the
runtime type of the object. When calling a non-private instance method on an object, the
runtime type of the object is used to determine the method that will be executed.

The chapter also explains how abstract classes and interfaces work. An abstract class
is a class that cannot be instantiated. An abstract class may contain an abstract method
with no bodies, but it does not need to. All abstract methods need to be overridden in the
subclasses. Alternatively, an interface contains only abstract methods and constants. Java
allows a class to implement multiple interfaces.

Lastly, the chapter covered some of the methods of the `Object` class, including the `clone`
and `equals` methods. The chapter also covered the interface `Cloneable` and the `compareTo`
method. These are all methods that are part of Java and are usually overridden by the
programmer.

8.15   Syntax

- `class C extends A{...}` $\Rightarrow$ The `C` class inherits from the `A` class.

- `class C implements A{...}` $\Rightarrow$ The `C` class implements the `A` interface.

- `super` $\Rightarrow$ Reference to the super object.

- `o1.equals(o2)` $\Rightarrow$ Returns true if the two objects are equal.

- `o1.compareTo(o2)` ⇒ Returns a positive integer if `o1` is bigger, 0 if they are equal, and a negative number if `o1` is smaller.

- `o1.class` ⇒ Returns the runtime type of `o1`.

- `o1 instanceof C` ⇒ Returns true if the runtime type of `o1` is the `C` class or one of its direct or indirect subclasses.

- `o1 = o2.clone();` ⇒ The `o1` object becomes a copy of the `o2` object.

- `class C implements Comparable<C>{...}` ⇒ The `C` class contains a `compareTo` method that can be used to compare objects of type `C`.

- `Collections.sort(a);` ⇒ Sorts an `ArrayList` of `Comparable` objects. The `compareTo` method is used to compare the objects.

- `Arrays.sort(a);` ⇒ Sorts an array of `Comparable` objects. The `compareTo` method is used to compare the objects.

- `public int m(){...}` ⇒ The `m` method is accessible everywhere.

- `int m(){...}` ⇒ The `m` method is accessible only within the package.

- `protected int m(){...}` ⇒ The `m` method is accessible within the package and in subclasses (direct or indirect).

- `private int a;` ⇒ The variable `a` is only accessible within the class. As a general rule, define all non constant variables as `private`.

- `private int m(){...}` ⇒ The `m` method is accessible within the class.

- `public class C{...}` ⇒ The `C` class is accessible from everywhere. Every Java file must have exactly one `public` class that has exactly the same name as the name of the file.

- `class C{...}` ⇒ The `C` class is only accessible within the package.

- `final int m(){...}` ⇒ The `m` method cannot be overridden.

- `abstract void m();` ⇒ Defines the `m` method as abstract. The method must be overridden in the subclasses.

8.16   Important Points

1. Class composition and class inheritance are similar. However, there are few differences.

   (a) They use different syntax.

   (b) Every object in a subclass contains a reference to exactly one object of the superclass that is not `null`. Conversely, an object can contain inside it 0 or more non-null references to objects.

   (c) Class composition does not support dynamic binding.

2. Use `extends` when inheriting from a class and `implements` when inheriting from an interface.

3. An abstract method is a method without a body. This method must be overridden in any non-abstract subclasses with full body.

4. An abstract class is similar to a regular class, but it cannot be instantiated. Conversely, an interface has no variables other than constants and only abstract methods.

5. Java allows us to inherit from one class and from multiple interfaces.

6. The `Object` class is the superclass of all classes.

7. `o1.m()` results in calling exactly one of potentially several methods. The runtime type of the `o1` object is determined. Then Java searches for the `m` method in this type and its ancestors in the inheritance hierarchy and executes the first method that it finds.

8. An object can be automatically cast to an object of type of the superclass of the object. However, one needs an explicit cast to convert an object to an object of one of the subclasses.

9. We need to implement the `Cloneable` interface and override the `clone` method as `public` in order to use it. The `clone` method should also be designed to handle an exception of type `CloneNotSupportedException`. When overriding the `clone` method, we need to make sure that the inner objects are properly cloned using deep copy. The default `clone` method in the `Object` class only copies the addresses of the inner objects, that is, it performs shallow copy.

10. It is a good programming practice for the `equals` and `compareTo` methods to work in noncontradictory fashion. In other words, `o1.equals(o2)` should be true exactly when `o1.compareTo(o2)==0`.

11. We cannot assign weaker access privileges when overriding a method. For example, a method that overrides a `public` method must be of type `public`.

12. All non-constant variables should be defined as `private`. Methods can be defined as `private`, no modifier, `protected`, or `public`.

13. Polymorphism does not apply for `static`, `final`, or `private` methods.

8.17 Exercises

1. Can a subclass inherit the private members of the superclass as private members of the subclass?

2. Consider the `Person` class.

```java
class Person{
  private String name;
  public Person(String name){
    this.name=name;
  }
}
```

Complete the missing code.

```
class Student extends Person{
  char grade;
  public Student(String name, char grade){
    ...


  }
}
```

3. Give an example of a protected method. Explain how protected methods can be accessed and when methods should be defined as protected.

4. Give an example of polymorphism. Explain what dynamic binding is and why polymorphism requires dynamic binding.

5. Write the code to print the income of all objects in the **a** array, where **a** contains objects of type **Employee** that have the **getSalary** method and objects of type **Student** that have the **getStudentLoan** method. Employees and students inherit from the **Person** class. Use the **instanceof** keyword to determine the type of the objects in the array.

6. Write the body of a **PrintedLiterature** class that contains the variables:

   - **String name**
   - **String author**

   and a constructor that initializes them. Then write the body of a **Book** class that inherits from the **PrintedLiterature** class. The **Book** class should have in addition the variable:

   - **int isbn**

   and a constructor that initializes all the variables.

7. Consider the following code.

```
Person p = new Person(....);
Object o = p;
System.out.println(o.toString());
```

   What will be printed if the **Person** class has the appropriate **toString** method? What will be printed if the **Person** class does not have the appropriate **toString** method? If the **Person** class has a **toString** method, then which **toString** method will be executed, the one for the **Person** class or the one for the **Object** class? Explain why.

8. Consider a **HockeyPlayer** class that inherits from the Player **class**. Write a **getSalary** method that returns 10 plus the value of calling **getSalary** for the superclass (i.e., calling **getSalary** for the corresponding **Player** object).

```
public class HockeyPlayer extends Player{

  public double getSalary(){
    ...


  }

  ...
}
```

9. What are the differences between an abstract class and an interface?

8.18 Lab

Create a program that keeps track of students and their advisors. Your program will have a **Test** class, a **Student** class, an **Advisor** class, and a **Person** class. The **Student** and **Advisor** classes should inherit from the abstract **Person** class. The **Person** class should implement the interface **Comparable** in order to allow the use of **Collections.sort** to sort its elements. Remember that an interface is similar to a class, but it contains only method definitions and no method bodies. A class **implements** rather than **extends** an interface. Implementing an interface means that the subclass will implement all the methods in the interface. The interface **Comparable** contains the single **compareTo** method. The objects of every class that implements the interface **Comparable** can be sorted because the **compareTo** method can be called on them. People should be compared based on their names. Here are the variables and methods of each class.

```
public abstract class Person implements Comparable<Person>:
private String name
public Person(String name)
public String toString()
public int compareTo(Person other)
public String getName()

public class Advisor extends Person:
private ArrayList<Student> students
public Advisor(String name)
public String listStudents() //returns the advisor's
            // students sorted by name
public void addStudent(Student s)
public String toString()

public class Student extends Person
private Advisor advisor
public Student(String name, Advisor advisor)
public String listAdvisor() //returns the student's advisor
```

Note that the constructor of the **Student** class needs to add the new student to the list of students for the specified advisor. Create an **ArrayList<Person>** in the main method of the **Test** class to store the current list of people. You can populate the **ArrayList** with example values (i.e., you do not have to read them from the keyboard). When students are printed, their name and the name of their advisor should appear. When advisors are printed, their name and the names of their students (in sorted order) should appear. Sort the elements in the **ArrayList** of people and print them.

8.19 Project

In this project, you are going to create simple bank software. You program will contain the Test class, which contains the main method, and the Customer, BankAccount, and Employee classes, the abstract Person class, and the Transaction class. The Customer and Employee classes will both inherit from the Person class.

The Person class will be abstract and will contain the name, address, and telephone number of the person. Each object of the Customer class will store, in addition, an ArrayList of the bank accounts for that person. Each object of the Employee class will store, in addition, the salary of the employee. Each object of the BankAccount class will have a variable corresponding to the account number (of type integer) and an ArrayList of the transactions for that account. Each object of type Transaction will contain the date of the transaction (of type Date), the type of transaction (deposit or withdraw), the employee who performed the transaction, the bank account on which the transaction was performed, and the dollar amount of the transaction (to be stored in a double). Note that the current day and time can be saved in a variable of type Date as follows: Date d = new Date(). Note that all instance variables should be declared private.

As you have probably guessed by now, you will need to create an ArrayList of People in the Test class. Your main method should print a menu that allows the user to insert a new employee or a customer, create a new account for a person, or withdraw/deposit money from/to a bank account. Operations, such as changing the address and phone number of a person or the salary of an employee should also be supported. Your program should not allow negative balances for bank accounts and should print an appropriate message, for example, "Insufficient funds to perform transaction" when a withdraw transaction tries to withdraw too much money. For simplicity, you can assume that people and bank accounts are never deleted. Use an automatically generated ID for people, transactions, and bank accounts. The ID can be generated from a static variable that is initially set to 0.

Chapter 9

Fun with Swing

If you have ever used a graphical Java application, you may have noticed that Java has its own way of displaying windows, menus, buttons, and toolbars. In fact, Java has its own library for displaying graphical components called *Swing*. Swing allows Java to provide the same look and feel under different operating systems. In this chapter we will explore basic Swing primitives, including drawing formatted text, shapes, and images inside a window.

9.1   Introduction to Swing

A *graphical user interface (GUI)* allows a program to provide a graphical interface to the user. Unlike a text interface that involves writing text to the console and reading text from the keyboard, a GUI allows the user to see graphics and interact with the system not only using the keyboard, but also using the mouse and/or other pointing devices. The advantage of using a GUI is that it is more intuitive and easier to learn. A GUI program is usually written on top of a graphical operating system, such as Microsoft Windows, X Windows, or Apple Mac OS X. Windows are typically the basic component of current graphical operating systems, where every application displays one or more windows. All components are usually displayed inside the windows.

In Java, there are two distinct ways to display a window and the graphical components inside it: using Swing and using the *Abstract Window Toolkit (AWT)*. While AWT uses the primitives (that is, the application programming interface (API)) of the operating system, Swing relies on the Java native implementation to draw the components inside the windows.

Menus, scroll bars, and text fields will look and behave differently under different operating systems under AWT. This implies that an application needs to be tested under different operating systems before it can be released, which complicates the application development process. In contrast, a Swing application will look exactly the same under any operating system. The downside is that Swing is a little slower because the windows are painted by the Java virtual machine rather than by the operating system. However, with today's fast computers, the difference in speed is negligible.

This chapter teaches us how to use Swing to write GUI programs. There is a perception among some programmers that writing GUI code is not hard work. In fact, you do not even need to write actual code. You can just use the mouse to drag and drop buttons, resize windows, and so on. There are several GUI building tools that allow us to do so (e.g., the ones available with the NetBeans and Eclipse integrated development environments). However, these tools are not covered in this textbook. Rather, the book shows us how to create robust GUI components from scratch by writing our own Java code. Many of the components that we will create will have the added advantage that their size and placement will not be fixed and will be determined automatically.

9.2 Creating Windows

The basic component of any GUI program is the window. In Java, there is a class called `Frame` that creates a window. The `Frame` class is part of the AWT library, while the `JFrame` class is part of the Swing library. In fact, all classes in the Swing library start with the letter J.

As usual, we will introduce the different ways to create JAVA GUI using a game. *Breakout* is a game that was developed by Atari in 1976. A layer of bricks covers the top third of the screen. A ball travels across the screen, bouncing off the top and the side walls of the screen. When a brick is hit, the ball bounces away and the brick is destroyed. The player loses a turn when the ball touches the bottom of the screen. To prevent this from happening, the player has a movable paddle to bounce the ball upward, keeping it in play.

This chapter describes how to display the different components of the Breakout game (Figure 9.1). The actual Breakout game is finished in Chapter 11, where the ball movement and mouse and keyboard interactions are addressed.

The first order of business is to create the window where all the action happens. A typical design is to create a class that extends the `JFrame` class (i.e., a Swing window). Here is a possible implementation of the `main` method of the Breakout game.

```java
public class Breakout {
  public static void main(String [] args){
    BreakoutFrame frame = new BreakoutFrame();
    frame.setVisible(true);
  }
}
```

The first line in the `main` method creates a `BreakoutFrame` object (i.e., the window for the Breakout game). The constructor of the `BreakoutFrame` class will create the window and place the paddle, the ball, and the bricks in the window. By default, every Java window is created to be initially invisible. This is done in order to allow the developer to populate the window before it is displayed. The second line of the `main` method displays the window.

Note that unlike console programs, GUI programs do not terminate immediately after all the code is executed. If a window is open, then the program will wait for the window to be closed before it finishes execution, unless a command, such as `System.exit(0)`, forces the program to terminate. The last command simply quits the program with exit code 0, which means normal program termination. Note that even putting the command `return` inside the main method will not terminate the program if a window is already created. Usually, using the `exit` method to terminate a program is considered bad programming practice. It is much better to wait for the user to close all the windows before the program terminates. An exception to this rule is when something bad happens and the program does not know how to proceed and the only alternative is to terminate the program.

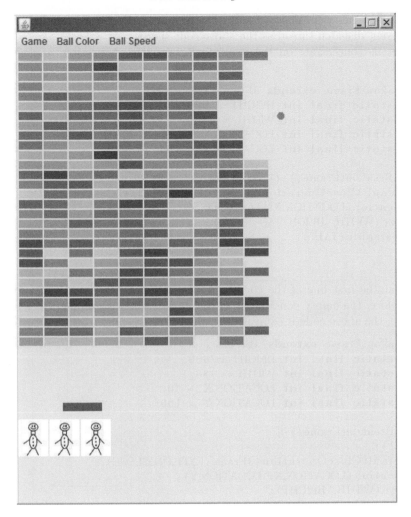

FIGURE 9.1: The Breakout game.

On a side note, our initial code does not follow best practices. The Java manual recommends that the code be rewritten as follows.

```java
public class Breakout {
  public static void main(String[] args){
    EventQueue.invokeLater(new Runnable(){
      public void run(){
        BreakoutFrame frame = new BreakoutFrame();
        frame.setVisible(true);
      }
    });
  }
}
```

The new code moves the creation of the window into the event dispatch thread. This guarantees that the program will not stall because a component is slow to be displayed. Although this code is recommended when writing commercial applications, it brings unnecessary complications for the novice programmer. For this reason, we will stick to the first way of creating windows in this textbook. The reader, however, can easily modify the code to use the event dispatch thread as the above code shows.

Next, let us concentrate on the `BreakoutFrame` class. A possible implementation is shown next.

```
class BreakoutFrame extends JFrame {
    public static final int HEIGHT = 600;
    public static final int WIDTH = 488;
    public static final int LOCATION_X = 50;
    public static final int LOCATION_Y = 100;

    public BreakoutFrame() {
        setDefaultCloseOperation(JFrame.EXIT_ON_CLOSE);
        setLocation(LOCATION_X, LOCATION_Y);
        setSize(WIDTH, HEIGHT);
        setResizable(false);
    }
}
```

Note that the first line of the constructor does not call the constructor of the super class. Therefore, the empty constructor of the `JFrame` class is automatically called. As a consequence, the above code is equivalent to the following code.

```
class BreakoutFrame extends JFrame {
    public static final int HEIGHT = 600;
    public static final int WIDTH = 488;
    public static final int LOCATION_X = 50;
    public static final int LOCATION_Y = 100;

    public BreakoutFrame() {
        super();
        setDefaultCloseOperation(JFrame.EXIT_ON_CLOSE);
        setLocation(LOCATION_X, LOCATION_Y);
        setSize(WIDTH, HEIGHT);
        setResizable(false);
    }
}
```

The actual window is created by the call `super()`. All the methods that are invoked in the constructor (i.e., `setDefaultCloseOperation`, `setLocation`, `setSize`, and `setResizable`) belong to the `JFrame` class (or its superclasses). Since the `BreakoutFrame` class does not contain these methods, Java automatically searches for the methods in the `JFrame` superclass.

The `setDefaultCloseOperation` method defines the behavior of the close button of the window. There are four possible actions, which are specified by constants in the `JFrame` class. The constant `EXIT_ON_CLOSE` means that the program will terminate when the window is closed. The constant `HIDE_ON_CLOSE` means that the window will be hidden, but the program will not terminate. If we want to display the window later, then we need to call the `setVisible` method again. The constant `DISPOSE_ON_CLOSE` describes the behavior where the window is destroyed, but the program is not terminated. Lastly, the constant `DO_NOTHING_ON_CLOSE` means that pressing the button that closes the window will have no effect.

Before we explain how the `setLocation` and `setSize` methods work, let us first describe the architecture of a computer screen. The screen of a computer is divided into pixels. The actual resolution of the screen can be changed, where, for example, 1366 by 768 pixels is a

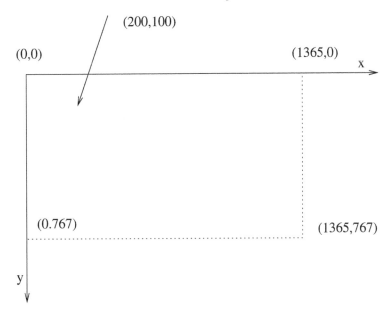

FIGURE 9.2: Pixels in a screen.

typical resolution for a 15" monitor. A pixel is just a dot on the screen. In other words, the screen is comprised of a rectangular grid of pixels.

Figure 9.2 shows the coordinates of the different pixels of the screen. This is similar to the standard x/y axes from geometry, where the only difference is that the y axis goes down instead of up. The top left corner of the screen is pixel (0,0). Assuming we have 1366 by 768 pixel screen, the bottom right corner will have coordinates (1365, 767) (remember that counting starts at 0). The pixel that is shown in the figure has coordinates (200,100). Of course, no program should assume a specific screen resolution. Instead, a well-designed program should dynamically determine the current resolution. Here is an example code that prints the number of vertical and horizontal pixels of the current resolution.

```
Dimension scrnsize = Toolkit.getDefaultToolkit().getScreenSize();
System.out.println("The height in pixels is: "+scrnsize.height);
System.out.println("The width in pixels is: "+scrnsize.width);
```

We are now ready to explain how the `setLocation` and `setSize` methods work. The `setLocation` method specifies the top left location of the window. The x value is specified first and the y value is specified second. The statement:

```
setLocation(50,100)
```

means that the window will be placed 50 pixels to the right of the top left corner of the screen and 100 pixels down from it. The statement:

```
setSize(488, 600)
```

defines the size of the window. The width of the window will be 488 pixels, while the height of the window will be 600 pixels. Note that in the initial code, the numbers were defined as constants in order to make the code more versatile.

The last line of the constructor, `setResizable(false)`, makes the window non-resizable. By default, a window is resizable. We decided to make the window non-resizable in order to restrict the movement of the ball to the specified window size.

9.3   Panels and Drawing

Our program, as written so far, will display an empty window. Our next task is to display the bricks, ball, paddle, and player icons inside the window (we will display a player icon for each life remaining). Java does not allow us to directly draw inside a window. Instead, it requires that first a canvas (called a panel) be created. The content of the panel may have to be repainted many times during the execution of a program. For example, every time a window is restored after being minimized and every time a window is resized, its content is repainted.

> Java calls the `paintComponent` method of the panel to do the painting. This method is unique because it cannot be directly called by your Java program. Alternatively, you should call the `repaint` method in order to force the refreshing of the content of the panel. The `repaint` method forces the `paintComponent` method to be called sometime in the future.

The behavior of the `paintComponent` method is not trivial and is tricky to understand by novice programmers. Here is an important principle to remember.

> The programmer has no control of when the `paintComponent` method will be called. Therefore, it is important that the behavior of the method be consistent with previous executions of the method. For example, never generate data inside the method. The method should be used to **only to display the data**, where the data can be created in the constructor of the panel or as the result of events occurring. If the programmer generates and displays data inside the method, then the behavior of the application will be strange. For example, the drawing inside the window can change just because the screen is resized.

We will add to end of the constructor of the `BreakoutFrame` class the following code.

```
BreakoutPanel panel = new BreakoutPanel();
add(panel);
```

This creates the panel and adds it to the windows. Let us now examine the code for the `BreakoutPanel` class.

```
class BreakoutPanel extends JPanel {
    public static final int NUM_BRICK_ROWS = 10;
    public static final int NUM_BRICK_COLUMNS = 30;
    private Ball ball = new Ball(Color.red);
    private ArrayList<Brick> bricks = new ArrayList<>();
    private Paddle paddle = new Paddle(Color.BLUE);
    private Player player = new Player();

    public BreakoutPanel() {
        for (int row = 0; row < NUM_BRICK_ROWS; row++) {
            for (int col = 0; col < NUM_BRICK_COLUMNS; col++) {
                bricks.add(new Brick(row, col, getRandomColor()));
            }
        }
    }
```

```
}

public Color getRandomColor() {
  Color color = new Color((int) (Math.random() * 256),
    (int) (Math.random() * 256), (int) (Math.random() * 256));
  if (getBackground().equals(color)) {
    return Color.RED;
  }
  return color;
}

public void showMessage(String s, Graphics2D g2) {
  Font myFont = new Font("SansSerif", Font.BOLD+Font.ITALIC,40);
  g2.setFont(myFont);
  g2.setColor(Color.RED);
  Rectangle2D textBox = myFont.getStringBounds(s,
                                  g2.getFontRenderContext());
  g2.drawString(s, (int)(getWidth()/2 - textBox.getWidth() / 2),
                (int) (getHeight() / 2 - textBox.getHeight()));
}

public void paintComponent(Graphics g) {
  super.paintComponent(g);
  Graphics2D g2 = (Graphics2D) g;

  if (bricks.size() == 0) {
    showMessage("YOU WIN!", g2);
  } else if (!player.isAlive()) {
    showMessage("GAME OVER!", g2);
  } else {
    ball.draw(g2);
    paddle.draw(g2);
    for (Brick brick : bricks) {
      brick.draw(g2);
    }
  }
  player.draw(g2);
}
}
```

The `BreakoutPanel` class creates the ball, paddle, and bricks. In addition, an object of `Player` class is created. The `Player` class displays icons corresponding to the number of lives that the player has.

Let us next carefully examine the `paintComponent` method, which is usually the heart of the panel class. Since this method can be executed multiple times (i.e., every time the window needs to be repainted), no variable initialization should occur in the method. The method simply displays the information that is already stored in the instance variables of the `BreakoutPanel` class. The method takes as input an object of type `Graphics`. This object is the brush that is needed to paint. Without a handle to this brush, we cannot display anything in the panel. The first line of the method is `super.paintComponent(g)`. This line calls the `paintComponent` method of the superclass of the `BreakoutPanel` class, that is, the `paintComponent` method for the `JPanel` class. The latter method simply clears the panel (a.k.a. the drawing canvas) so that the new drawings are not displayed on top of the old drawings. Next, the line `Graphics2D g2 = (Graphics2D) g` converts our brush

TABLE 9.1:   Font masks.

Mask	Result
Font.BOLD	bold font
Font.ITALIC	italic font
Font.PLAIN	plain font
Font.BOLD+Font.Italic	bold and italic font

to a two-dimensional brush. In this book, we will only cover how to draw different shapes (e.g., rectangles, circles, and ellipses) using a brush of type `Graphics2D`.

The variable `bricks` stores an `ArrayList` of bricks. Every time the ball hits a brick, we will remove the brick that is hit from the `ArrayList`. When the `ArrayList` becomes empty, we need to print "You Win". This is done by the `showMessage` method. Note that the brush is passed as a parameter to the method. The reason is that there must be access to the brush before anything can be displayed in the panel. If the player is no longer alive, then we will display the message "GAME OVER". Otherwise, if the game continues, we will display the ball, the paddle, and the bricks. Since there are multiple bricks, we need a `for` statement to iterate over all the bricks. Finally, we will display the number of lives on the screen. Note that all the drawing methods take as input the brush. It is needed in order to do the painting.

Next, let us examine the `showMessage` method. Before we can display text inside the panel, we need to set the font for the text. Since everything in Java is object oriented, we will first create an object of type `Font`. The constructor of the `Font` class takes as input three parameters: the name of the font, the mask of the font (used to determine whether the text should be bold, italic, or both), and the point size of the font. A problem arises when the font that we want to use is not supported by the operating system. There are two ways to deal with this problem. One way is to use one of the predefined five fonts.

- `SansSerif`

- `Serif`

- `Monospaced`

- `Dialog`

- `DialogInput`

Java guarantees that these fonts can be used under any configuration of any operating system. If the operating system does not support one of the fonts, then Java will use the closest available font instead. The second option is to check the available fonts before committing to a font. The following expression will return an array of strings that contains all the fonts that are currently installed.

```
String [] fontNames =GraphicsEnvironment.getLocalGraphicsEnvironment().
getAvailableFontFamilyNames();
```

The first parameter of the constructor of the `Font` class is the name of the font. The second parameter is a combination of font masks. Table 9.1 shows popular choices. Note that `BOLD`, `ITALIC`, and `PLAIN` are defined as constants (i.e., `static final` variables) in the `Font` class. The constant `PLAIN` has all bits set to 0 (0000 0000 in binary notation). All other constants have exactly one bit set. For example, `BOLD` can be defined as 0000 0001 in binary notation and `ITALIC` can be defined as 0000 0010 in binary notation. Then the expression BOLD+ITALIC will be equal to 0000 0011, that is, the bits for both bold and italic will be set. This prompts Java to make the text both bold and italic. Of course, your program should never rely on knowing the value for these constants because they can change in future Java implementations. The third parameter of the constructor of the `Font` class is the height of the font in pixels. This is also sometimes referred to as the *point size* of the font.

The expression `g2.setColor(Color.RED)` changes the color of the brush to red. Any drawings that will be done after the command will be in red until the color of the brush is changed again. The `Color` class defines the following constants: `BLACK`, `BLUE`, `CYAN`, `DARK_GRAY`, `GRAY`, `GREEN`, `LIGHT_GRAY`, `MAGENTA`, `ORANGE`, `PINK`, `RED`, `WHITE`, and `YELLOW`. Java also allows us to use a custom color. Note that the color of each pixel on the screen has three components: red, green, and blue. Any imaginable color can be created as a combination of these three colors. Java allows the specification of true colors, which means that a value between 0 and 255 can be assigned for the strength of each of the three primitive colors. This results in $2^{8*3} = 16,777,216$ colors. Since the human eye is popularly believed to be capable of discriminating among as many as ten million colors, this seems like a good match. Here is an example of how the color of the brush can be changed to a new color.

```
g2.setColor(new Color(20,30,40));
```

The value 20 defines the strength of red, the value 30 defines the strength of green, and the value 40 defines the strength of blue. Since red, green, and blue are the primary colors, this approach is commonly referred to as the RGB model. Note that if the current display settings of the monitor do not support true colors, then the closest available color will be selected.

Next, consider the last two lines of the `showMessage` method.

```
Rectangle2D textBox = myFont.getStringBounds(s,
g2.getFontRenderContext());
g2.drawString(s, (int) (getWidth() / 2 - textBox.getWidth() / 2),
  (int) (getHeight() / 2 - textBox.getHeight()));
```

The first line returns a rectangle (i.e., an object of type `Rectangle2D`) that corresponds to the virtual rectangle that will surround the string s when displayed. This line will give us information about the size of the string box. The `getStringBounds` method will take into account the current font and point size that are associated with the `myFont` object. The expression `textBox.getWidth()` will return the width of the rectangle in pixels, while `textBox.getHeight()` will return the height of the rectangle in pixels. Conversely, the `getWidth` and `getHeight` methods of the `JPanel` class will return the width and height of the current drawing panel, respectively. Note that the size of the panel is smaller than the size of the window. For example, the window has border and title bar, which are not part of the panel. Once we know the size of the current panel and the size of the virtual rectangle that surrounds the string, we can display the string in the center of the panel. The integer conversion in the last line is needed because the coordinates of the `textBox` rectangle are doubles. Note that the `drawString` method takes as input the string and the coordinates of where the bottom left corner of the text should be positioned.

Let us next examine the constructor of the `BreakoutPanel` class. It simply creates a grid of bricks with random colors. The `getRandomColor` method chooses a random number between 0 and 255 for the intensity of red, blue, and green, respectively. If the chosen color happens to coincide with the background color or the panel, then the red color is chosen. This prevents the creation of "invisible" bricks that have the same color as the panel background color. The `getBackgound` method in the `JPanel` class returns the background color of the panel. Note that the color of the bricks should be set outside the `paintComponent` method. If the random color is chosen inside the `paintComponent` method, then the color of the

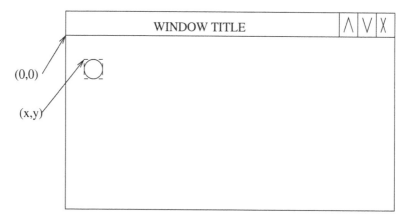

FIGURE 9.3: Coordinates of a ball.

bricks will change every time the panel is resized. This is, certainly, undesirable behavior of the program.

Next, let us consider the `Ball` class and how it displays the game ball.

```java
class Ball {
    public static final int SIZE = 10;
    public static final int START_X = 200;
    public static final int START_Y = 400;
    private Color color;
    private int x, y;

    public Ball(Color color) {
        this.color = color;
        x = START_X;
        y = START_Y;
    }

    public void draw(Graphics2D g2) {
        g2.setPaint(color);
        Ellipse2D e = new Ellipse2D.Double(x, y, SIZE, SIZE);
        g2.fill(e);
    }
}
```

A ball is characterized by its location in the panel and its color. Note that creating a `Ball` class allows us to easily extend the game and add multiple balls if needed. The x and y coordinates of the ball correspond to the top left corner of the virtual rectangle that surrounds the ball. The coordinates are relative to the top left corner of the panel; see Figure 9.3.

The constructor of the `Ball` class sets the color and starting (x,y) coordinates of the ball. The `draw` method displays the ball. In order to be able to draw inside a panel, an access to the 2-D drawing brush is needed. It is passed as a parameter to the method. The method first sets the color of the brush. All consecutive drawing operations will use this color until the color of the brush is changed. Next, an ellipse object is created and drawn. An ellipse is created because Java does not have a class for a circle (an ellipse is a special case of a circle).

Let us now carefully examine the `Ellipse2D.Double` class. It inherits from the `Ellipse2D` class. It is unusual to have a class name that contains a dot in the middle.

The reason is that the `Double` class is actually defined inside the `Ellipse` class, where more information about static nested classes is provided in the next chapter.

The `Ellipse2D` class has two subclasses: `Ellipse2D.Double` and `Ellipse2D.Float`. The constructor of the first class takes, as parameters, doubles, while the constructor of the second class takes, as parameters, floats. The four parameters of the constructor are the coordinates of the top left corner of the surrounding rectangle followed by the width and height of the surround rectangle.

The astute reader may be wondering why the constructors of the classes `Ellipse2D.Double` and `Ellipse2D.Float` take as input numbers of type `double` and `float`, respectively, when the computer can only set the color of pixels that have integer coordinates. After all, it is impossible to set the color of a pixel with coordinates (2.4, 3.1) because such a pixel simply does not exist. The answer is that although the pixel does not exist, the color of this pixel can be set or at least appear as though it is set. The color of a virtual pixel that has non-integer coordinates is set by setting the colors of its four neighboring pixels that do have integer coordinates. In this way, an optical illusion that a pixel that does not exist is set is created.

The statement `g2.fill(e)` draws the ellipse `e` using the brush `g2` and fills it. Alternatively, the expression `g2.draw(e)` just draws the ellipse without filling it.

Next, let us examine the `Paddle` class. It is similar to the `Ball` class with the only exception that a rectangle instead of a circle is drawn.

```java
class Paddle {
  public static final int WIDTH = 50;
  public static final int HEIGHT = 10;
  public static final int START_X = 200;
  public static final int START_Y = 430;
  private Color color;
  private int x, y;

  public Paddle(Color color) {
    this.color = color;
    x = START_X;
    y = START_Y;
  }

  public void draw(Graphics2D g2) {
    g2.setPaint(color);
    Rectangle2D r = new Rectangle2D.Double(x, y, WIDTH, HEIGHT);
    g2.fill(r);
  }
}
```

The constructor sets the color of the paddle and its initial (x,y) coordinates (i.e., the coordinates of its top left corner). The `draw` method takes as input the drawing brush. It first sets the color of the drawing bush. It then creates a rectangle and draws it with its interior filled.

Note that the `Rectangle2D.Double` class inherits from the `Rectangle2D` class. The `Rectangle2D` class has two subclasses: `Rectangle2D.Double` and `Rectangle2D.Float`. In the first class, the coordinates of the rectangle are specified as doubles, while in the second class they are specified as floats. Note that the first two numbers in the constructor of the `Rectangle2D.Double` class specify the x and y coordinates, respectively, of the top left corner of the rectangle, while the next two numbers specify the width and height of the rectangle, respectively.

Let us next examine the `Brick` class.

```
class Brick{
  public static final int HEIGHT = 10;
  public static final int WIDTH = 30;
  public static final int BRICK_H_GAP = 2;
  public static final int BRICK_V_GAP = 2;
  private int x, y;
  private Color   color;

  public Brick(int row, int col, Color color) {
    this.color = color;
    x = BRICK_H_GAP + row * (BRICK_H_GAP + Brick.WIDTH);
    y = BRICK_V_GAP + col * (BRICK_V_GAP + Brick.HEIGHT);
  }

  public void draw(Graphics2D g2) {
    g2.setPaint(color);
    Rectangle2D r = new Rectangle2D.Double(x, y, WIDTH, HEIGHT);
    g2.fill(r);
  }
}
```

The constants BRICK_H_GAP and BRICK_V_GAP store the horizontal and vertical gap between the bricks in pixels. The constructor sets the color and computes the top left corner of the brick. The draw method simply displays the brick, where the top left corner of the brick and the brick's color are assigned during the construction of the brick.

In addition to ellipses and rectangles, one can display points and lines in Java. A point in Java is created using the following syntax.

```
Point2D  p = new Point2D.Double(x,y);
```

The coordinates (x,y) are relative to the top left corner of the panel that contains the point. Similarly, one can create a line in Java as follows.

```
Line2D l = new Line2D.Double(x1,y1,x2,y2);
```

Note that (x1,y1) is the starting coordinate of the line and (x2,y2) is the ending coordinate. This differs from the way that rectangles are ellipses are created. For rectangles and ellipses, the width and length of the rectangle (or surrounding rectangle) are specified as the last two parameters.

> When drawing a line, one specifies the starting and ending coordinates of the line. Alternatively, when drawing a rectangle or ellipse, one needs to specify the coordinates of the top left corner and the width and height of the rectangle (or surrounding rectangle).

Let us next examine the Player class. It will initially display three player pictures, which symbolizes that the player initially has three lives. Every time the player loses a life, the number of pictures will be decremented by one.

```
class Player {
  public static int INITIAL_NUM_LIVES = 3;
  public static int IMAGE_DISTANCE = 40;
  public static int IMAGE_Y = 450;
  private int numLives;
```

```
public Player() {
  this.numLives = INITIAL_NUM_LIVES;
}

public void killPlayer() {
  numLives--;
}

public boolean isAlive() {
  return (numLives > 0);
}

public void draw(Graphics2D g2) {
  try {
    Image image = ImageIO.read(new File("player.gif"));
    for (int x = 0; x < numLives; x++) {
      g2.drawImage(image, x * IMAGE_DISTANCE, IMAGE_Y, null);
    }
  } catch (Exception myException) {}
}
}
```

The `killPlayer` method reduces the number of lives by one. The `isAlive` method checks if there are any lives left. The `draw` method draws the specified number of stickmen on the panel. The image for the stickman is read from a file. The command:

```
Image image = ImageIO.read(new File("player.gif"));
```

reads an image from the file `player.gif` and associates the image with the object image. The file `player.gif` must be in the root project directory. Alternatively, a path where the file is stored can be specified as follows: `c:/pictures/player.gif`. Note that a forward slash should be used regardless of the operating system. The reason is that a backward slash has a special meaning in Java. Note that an exception can occur if the specified file does not exist on the hard disc. Unlike most languages, Java forces us to handle such exceptions. The `try-catch` block handles the exception. The catch part is empty, which means that we will do nothing when an exception occurs. The code where the exception can occur is put in the `try` block. More information about exceptions will be provided in Chapter 13. Note that the `draw` method cannot throw an exception because it overrides the `draw` method in the `JPanel` class that does not throw an exception. In other words, the following version of the `draw` method will not compile.

```
public void draw(Graphics2D g2) throws Exception {
  Image image = ImageIO.read(new File("player.gif"));
  for (int x = 0; x < numLives; x++) {
    g2.drawImage(image, x * IMAGE_DISTANCE, IMAGE_Y, null);
  }
}
```

The above code means that the `draw` method will not handle the exception and it will simply require the calling method to deal with it. This is a handy way of handling exceptions when it is possible to implement.

The command:

```
g2.drawImage(image, x * IMAGE_DISTANCE, IMAGE_Y, null);
```

draws the image, where (x,y) is the top left corner of the image. The last parameter is an image observer that is notified as more of the image becomes available. For the purposes of this book, the last parameter of the `drawImage` method will always be equal to null.

Below is a listing of all our code so far for the game Breakout. It displays the ball, bricks, and paddle, but there is no code to move them. However, the different components are separated into different classes, which makes adding the ball motion and keyboard and mouse interaction easier. We will complete the game in Chapter 11.

```java
import java.util.*;
import javax.swing.*;
import java.awt.*;
import java.awt.geom.*;
import java.io.*;
import javax.imageio.*;

public class Test {
  public static void main(String[] args) {
    BreakoutFrame frame = new BreakoutFrame();
    frame.setVisible(true);
  }
}


class BreakoutFrame extends JFrame {
  public static final int HEIGHT = 600;
  public static final int WIDTH = 488;
  public static final int LOCATION_X = 50;
  public static final int LOCATION_Y = 100;

  public BreakoutFrame() {
    setDefaultCloseOperation(JFrame.EXIT_ON_CLOSE);
    setLocation(LOCATION_X, LOCATION_Y);
    setSize(WIDTH, HEIGHT);
    setResizable(false);
    BreakoutPanel panel = new BreakoutPanel();
    add(panel);
  }
}


class BreakoutPanel extends JPanel {
  public static final int NUM_BRICK_ROWS = 10;
  public static final int NUM_BRICK_COLUMNS = 30;
  private Ball ball = new Ball(Color.red);
  private ArrayList<Brick> bricks = new ArrayList<>();
  private Paddle paddle = new Paddle(Color.BLUE);
  private Player player = new Player();

  public BreakoutPanel() {
    for (int row = 0; row < NUM_BRICK_ROWS; row++) {
      for (int col = 0; col < NUM_BRICK_COLUMNS; col++) {
        bricks.add(new Brick(row, col, getRandomColor()));
      }
    }
  }

  public Color getRandomColor() {
    Color color = new Color((int) (Math.random() * 256),
```

```
        (int) (Math.random() * 256), (int) (Math.random() * 256));
        if (getBackground().equals(color)) {
            return Color.RED;
        }
        return color;
    }

    public void showMessage(String s, Graphics2D g2) {
        Font myFont = new Font("SansSerif", Font.BOLD + Font.ITALIC, 40);
        g2.setFont(myFont);
        g2.setColor(Color.RED);
        Rectangle2D textBox = myFont.getStringBounds(s,
                    g2.getFontRenderContext());
        g2.drawString(s, (int) (getWidth() / 2 - textBox.getWidth()/ 2),
                    (int) (getHeight() / 2 - textBox.getHeight()));
    }

    public void paintComponent(Graphics g) {
        super.paintComponent(g);
        Graphics2D g2 = (Graphics2D) g;

        if (bricks.size() == 0) {
            showMessage("YOU WIN!", g2);
        } else if (!player.isAlive()) {
            showMessage("GAME OVER!", g2);
        } else {
            ball.draw(g2);
            paddle.draw(g2);
            for (Brick brick : bricks) {
                brick.draw(g2);
            }
        }
        player.draw(g2);
    }
}

class Ball {
    public static final int SIZE = 10;
    public static final int START_X = 200;
    public static final int START_Y = 400;
    private Color color;
    private int x, y;

    public Ball(Color color) {
        this.color = color;
        x = START_X;
        y = START_Y;
    }

    public void draw(Graphics2D g2) {
        g2.setPaint(color);
        Ellipse2D e = new Ellipse2D.Double(x, y, SIZE, SIZE);
        g2.fill(e);
    }
}
```

```java
class Paddle {
  public static final int WIDTH = 50;
  public static final int HEIGHT = 10;
  public static final int START_X = 200;
  public static final int START_Y = 430;
  private Color color;
  private int x, y;

  public Paddle(Color color) {
    this.color = color;
    x = START_X;
    y = START_Y;
  }

  public void draw(Graphics2D g2) {
    g2.setPaint(color);
    Rectangle2D r = new Rectangle2D.Double(x, y, WIDTH, HEIGHT);
    g2.fill(r);
  }
}

class Brick  {
  public static final int HEIGHT = 10;
  public static final int WIDTH = 30;
  public static final int BRICK_H_GAP = 2;
  public static final int BRICK_V_GAP = 2;
  private int x, y;
  private Color   color;

  public Brick(int row, int col, Color color) {
    this.color = color;
    x = BRICK_H_GAP + row * (BRICK_H_GAP + Brick.WIDTH);
    y = BRICK_V_GAP + col * (BRICK_V_GAP + Brick.HEIGHT);
  }

  public void draw(Graphics2D g2) {
    g2.setPaint(color);
    Rectangle2D r = new Rectangle2D.Double(x, y, WIDTH, HEIGHT);
    g2.fill(r);
  }
}

class Player {
  public static int INITIAL_NUM_LIVES = 3;
  public static int IMAGE_DISTANCE = 40;
  public static int IMAGE_Y = 450;
  private int numLives;

  public Player() {
    this.numLives = INITIAL_NUM_LIVES;
  }

  public void killPlayer() {
    numLives--;
```

```
  }

  public boolean isAlive() {
    return (numLives > 0);
  }

  public void draw(Graphics2D g2) {
    try {
      Image image = ImageIO.read(new File("player.gif"));
      for (int x = 0; x < numLives; x++) {
        g2.drawImage(image, x * IMAGE_DISTANCE, IMAGE_Y, null);
      }
    } catch (Exception my) {}
  }
}
```

9.4 Summary

This chapter introduced the Swing framework in Java. We showed how to create windows and panels. We also showed how to display text, shapes, and images inside a panel and how to change the color of drawings. The next chapter shows how the drawings that are inside a window can react to different events, such as elapsed time period, mouse movement, and keyboard keys being pressed.

9.5 Syntax

- `JFrame` ⇒ The window class (we usually inherit from it).

- `JPanel` ⇒ The panel class (we usually inherit from it).

- `panel.repaint();` ⇒ Repaints the panel.

- `frame.setLocation(10,10);` ⇒ Sets the location (top left corner) of the frame to position (10,10).

- `frame.setSize(200,200);` ⇒ Makes the frame 200 by 200.

- `frame.setResizable(false);` ⇒ Makes the frame non-resizable. It is resizable by default.

- `frame.setVisible(true);` ⇒ Makes the frame visible. By default, it is invisible.

- `frame.setDefaultCloseOperation(...);` ⇒ The parameter can be `EXIT_ON_CLOSE`, `IDE_ON_CLOSE`, `DISPOSE_ON_CLOSE`, and `DO_NOTHING_ON_CLOSE`. All parameters are defined as constants in the class `JFrame`. The method specifies the action that will be performed when the user tries to close the frame.

- `Toolkit.getDefaultToolkit().getScreenSize()` $\Rightarrow$ Returns the dimension of the display in pixels.

- `Color` $\Rightarrow$ The class for colors.

- `Color c = Color.RED;` $\Rightarrow$ Creates an object for the red color.

- `Color c = new Color(2,3,4);` $\Rightarrow$ Creates a new color with red=3, green=4, and blue=5.

- `panel.getBackround()` $\Rightarrow$ Returns the background color of the panel.

- `panel.setBackground(Color.RED);` $\Rightarrow$ Changes the background color of the panel to red.

- `Graphics` $\Rightarrow$ The drawing brush class.

- `Graphics2D` $\Rightarrow$ The 2D drawing brush class, which inherits from the `Graphics` class.

- `Font f = new Font("SansSerif",Font.Bold+Font.Italic,20);` $\Rightarrow$ Creates a new font object with font: SansSerif, bold and italic, and 20-point size.

- `GraphicsEnvironment.getLocalGraphicsEnvironment().getAvailableFontFamilyNames()` $\Rightarrow$ Returns an array of the names of all available fonts that are currently installed in the operating system.

- `g2.setColor(Color.red);` $\Rightarrow$ Changes the color of the brush to red, where g2 is an object of type `Graphics2D`.

- `g2.setFont(f);` $\Rightarrow$ Changes the font of the brush.

- `g2.drawString(s,10,20);` $\Rightarrow$ Draws the string s with bottom left position of (10,20).

- `g2.draw(new Rectangle2D.Double(2,2,10,20));` $\Rightarrow$ Draws a rectangle starting with top left corner of (2,2) of width 10 and height 20.

- `g2.fill(new Rectangle2D.Double(2,2,10,20));` $\Rightarrow$ Fills a rectangle starting with top left corner of (2,2) of width 10 and height 20.

- `g2.draw(new Ellipse2D.Double(2,2,10,20));` $\Rightarrow$ Draws an ellipse with surrounding rectangle with top left corner of (2,2) of width 10 and height 20.

- `g2.draw(new Line2D.Double(2,2,10,20));` $\Rightarrow$ Draws a line between the pixels (2,2) and (10,20).

- `g2.draw(new Point2D.Double(2,2));` $\Rightarrow$ Displays the point (2,2).

- `Image image = ImageIO.red(new File("player.gif"));` $\Rightarrow$ Creates an image objet from gif file.

- `g2.drawImage(image,10,10);` $\Rightarrow$ Draws the image at position (10,10).

- `System.exit(0);` $\Rightarrow$ Terminates the program.

9.6 Important Points

1. In order to create a window in Java, create a class that inherits from the `JFrame` class and instantiate it.

2. Call the `setVisible` method on a window in order to make it visible.

3. Initialize the content of the window inside the constructor of the class that inherits from the `JFrame` class.

4. The `paintComponent` method does the drawing inside a `JPanel`. It will be called multiple times (i.e., every time the window needs to be repainted). The `paintComponent` method takes as input an object of type `Graphics`, which is used to do the drawing. Always call the super class at the beginning of the `paintComponent` method, which guarantees that you will start painting on a blank canvas.

5. The `paintComponent` method only displays the data. It should never generate new data.

6. Never call the `paintComponent` method directly. Instead, call the `repaint` method in order to refresh a panel.

9.7 Exercises

1. Write code that displays the picture from Figure 9.4, that is, a circle and a horizontal and vertical line segment through its center.

2. Write code that displays the window from Figure 9.5. The ball is displayed as an image (search the Internet for a blue ball to get a similar image). Set the initial size of the window appropriately and make the window non-resizable.

3. Write a program that displays GAME OVER in the middle of a window. The text color should be white, while the background color should be red.

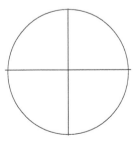

FIGURE 9.4: Picture for Exercise 1.

FIGURE 9.5: Picture for Exercise 2.

9.8   Lab

Create an application that displays a number of shapes (including lines, rectangles, circles, and ellipses) in a window. The type of shape to be displayed should be chosen at random. The color of the shape and whether or not to fill the shape (if it can be filled) should also be chosen at random. Make sure that the content of the window does not change as you resize or restore the window. For this purpose, you can create a class called MyShape that can draw each of the shapes (should store the type of shape, color of the shape, coordinates of shape, etc.). Also, save an ArrayList of shapes in the MyPanel class. The paintComponent method in the MyPanel class should simply draw all the shapes from the ArrayList. The paintComponent method should not generate any of the data.

Chapter 10

Nested Classes and Event Handling

The chapter teaches how to write Java code that responds to events. We will show how to write code that responds to keyboard strokes, mouse movement, window closing, and so on. Since Java is an object-oriented language, we cannot directly tell Java to execute a method when an event occurs. Instead, we need to create an object that supports the method that needs to be executed when the event occurs and pass this object as a parameter. In other words, event handling is supported in Java by creating new classes and objects that belong to them. However, creating too many new classes can be burdensome. To simplify the code, Java allows us to create a class within a class and even within a method. The chapter describes the different ways of creating such nested classes in the context of event handling.

10.1 The Timer Class

We will start this chapter with the *Typing Game*. The objective of the game is to type characters faster than they appear on the screen. We will create an `ArrayList` of characters, where the `ArrayList` will be initially empty. Every 200 milliseconds (or 1/5 of a second) we will add a new character to the list and display it. If the user types in a character that is in the list, then we will remove the character from the list and redisplay the list. The player wins if they are able to stay alive for more than 30 seconds. They lose if the list becomes longer than 10 characters. We will allow duplicate characters in the list.

When implementing the game, we want to tell Java to execute a method that adds a character to the list every 200 milliseconds. However, Java does not allow us to send a method name as a parameter to another method. Instead, we need to create a new class that implements the method and pass as input an instance of that class. For example, Java contains a `Timer` class that can be used to call a method periodically. Consider the following program.

```java
import java.awt.event.*;
import javax.swing.Timer;
import java.util.*;
public class TypingGame {
  public static void main(String[] args){
    Timer t = new Timer(200,new TimerListener());
    t.start();
    JFrame frame = new JFrame();
    frame.setVisible(true);
  }
}

class TimerListener implements ActionListener{
  ArrayList<Character> charList = new ArrayList<>();
  public void actionPerformed(ActionEvent e){
    charList.add((char)('a'+(int)((Math.random()*26))));
    System.out.println(charList);
  }
}
```

First, note that in the Java standard libraries there are several classes that are named `Timer`. Here, we want to use the class that is defined in `javax.swing.Timer`. Note that we cannot simply import `javax.swing.*`. The reason is that there is another `Timer` class in the package `java.util.*` and Java will not know which one to use. Next, note that the above code needs to be written in the file `TypingGame.java`. Remember that inside every Java file we can have several classes, where exactly one of them can be `public`. The class that is `public` must have exactly the same name as the name of the Java file.

The first parameter of the constructor of the `Timer` class determines the delay between method calls in milliseconds. The second parameter of the constructor is an object that belongs to a class that implements the `ActionListener` interface. Here is the code that defines the interface (it is part of `java.util.*`).

```java
interface ActionListener{
  public void actionPerformed(ActionEvent e);
}
```

After the timer is started, the `actionPerformed` method will be repeatedly invoked. The `Timer` class knows that it can call the `actionPerformed` method on the input object because the object must belong to a class that implements the interface `ActionListener`. The `start` method is used to start the timer. If we want to stop it, we can use the `stop` method.

The last two lines of the `main` method create a window and make it visible. This prevents the program from immediately terminating. The `actionPerformed` method creates a random character, adds it to the `ArrayList`, and prints the list. Note that the cast `(char)` can convert an integer to the character that has that ASCII code. The code also explicitly references 'a', which is converted to the ASCII code of 'a': 97. Note that hard-coding the number 97 in the program would be an inferior choice because the ASCII table can potentially change. The code in the `actionPerformed` method generates a new random character, adds it to the `ArrayList`, and then the `ArrayList` is printed. Every 200 milliseconds, the `actionPerformed` method is called.

Method callback is when a method is passed as a parameter. When an event occurs, the method will be called back. Java does not directly support method callbacks. The reason is that methods themselves cannot be passed as arguments to methods. Alternatively, one needs to create a class that supports the required methods and pass an object of that class as a parameter. Java uses interfaces to guarantee that the object supports the required methods.

10.2 Nested Classes

It seems burdensome to create a brand new class every time we want to implement a method callback. To simplify the process, Java allows us to create a class within another class. Such classes are referred to as *nested classes*.

10.2.1 Static Nested Classes

Let us now explore how nested classes apply to our typing program. First, consider the following rewrite of our typing game.

```java
public class TypingGame {
    public static void   main(String[] args) {
        Timer t = new Timer(1000, new TimerListener());
        t.start();
        JFrame frame = new JFrame();
        frame.setVisible(true);
    }

    public static class TimerListener implements ActionListener {
        ArrayList<Character> charList = new ArrayList<>();

        public void actionPerformed(ActionEvent e) {
            charList.add((char) ('a' + (int) ((Math.random() * 26))));
            System.out.println(charList);
        }
    }
}
```

Now the `TimerListener` class is defined inside the `TypingGame` class. The class is defined as `static` because it is not connected to a particular instance of the outer `TypingGame` class. In other words, objects that belong to the `TimerListener` class will not be associated with an object of the `TypingGame` class. Note that defining the `TimerListener` class without using the `static` keyword will result in an error. The reason is that this will imply that the class is associated with an instance of the `TypingGame` class. However, the `TypingGame` class is never instantiated.

The nested class is defined as `public`, which means that everyone can create an instance of it. For example, the following code is valid outside the `TypingGame` class.

```java
TypingGame.TimerListener listener = new TypingGame.TimerListener();
```

Nested static classes that are `public` can be accessed from everywhere by specifying the name of the outer class followed by a dot and then the name of the nested classes. Within the outer class, nested static classes can be accessed directly by specifying only the name of the class.

Note that nested classes can be defined without an access privilege modifier. Then they will be accessible only within the package. Alternatively, they can be defined using the `private` keyword. Such classes will only be visible within the outer class. Although uncommon, nested classes can also be defined as `protected`. Then they will be accessible within the package and within the subclasses of the outer class.

The new code for the typing game seems a little more compact. We did not have to create a new outer class. Probably, we do not want anyone outside the `TypingGame` class to be aware of our nested class and we can define it as `private`.

The classes `Double` and `Float` inside the class `Rectangle2D` are examples of nested static classes.

10.2.2 Inner Classes

Nested classes in Java that are not static are called **inner**. In order to show an example of an inner class, let us refactor our program and create a separate class that handles populating the `ArrayList` with random characters.

```java
public class TypingGame{
  public static void main(String[] args) throws Exception {
    new PopulateChars();
    JFrame frame = new JFrame();
    frame.setVisible(true);
  }
}
public class PopulateChars {
  ArrayList<Character> charList;
  public PopulateChars(){
    charList = new ArrayList<Character>();
    Timer timer = new Timer(200,new TimerListener());
    timer.start();
  }

  private class TimerListener implements ActionListener {
    public void actionPerformed(ActionEvent e) {
      charList.add((char) ('a' + (int) ((Math.random() * 26))));
      System.out.println(charList);
    }
  }
}
```

Now the `TimerListener` class is an inner class for the `PopulateChars` class. A nice feature of inner classes is that they have access to the variables of the outer class. For example, the `actionPerformed` method has access to the variable `charList` in the outer class. However, note that there can be multiple instances of the `PopulateChars` class. Therefore, every object of the `TimerListener` class must be associated with exactly one object that belongs to the `PopulateChars` class. If this is not the case, then the reference to the variable `charList` can be ambiguous. Figure 10.1 shows how the object that belongs to the `TimerListener` class must be related to an object of the outer class.

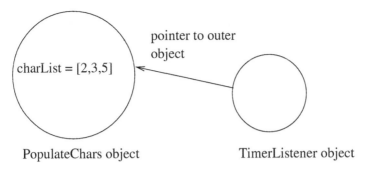

FIGURE 10.1: Example of inner class.

In our example, a `TimerListener` object is created within the constructor of the `PopulateChars` class. The outer object for the new object of type `TimerListener` is the object that created the `TimerListener` object. An inner object can also be created from outside the outer class. However, the syntax is more involved because the outer object needs to be explicitly identified. Here is an example.

```
public class  TypingGame{
  public static void main(String[] args) throws Exception {
    PopulateChars populateChars = new PopulateChars();
    Timer timer = new Timer(200,populateChars.new TimerListener());
    timer.start();
    JFrame frame = new JFrame();
    frame.setVisible(true);
  }
}

public class PopulateChars {
  ArrayList<Character> charList;
  public PopulateChars(){
    charList = new ArrayList<Character>();
  }

  public class TimerListener implements ActionListener {
    public void actionPerformed(ActionEvent e) {
      charList.add((char) ('a' + (int) ((Math.random() * 26))));
      System.out.println(charList);
    }
  }
}
```

Examine the code `populateChars.new TimerListener()`. This means create a new object of type `TimerListener`. However, instead of specifying the outer `PopulateChars` class, we need to specify the outer object: `populateChars`. The reason is that every inner object needs to have a reference to an outer object. This is similar to class inheritance because every object that belongs to a subclass needs to have a reference to an object that belongs to the superclass.

> Objects of nested static classes have a reference to the outer class. Conversely, objects of inner classes have a reference to an object of the outer class.

Note that sometimes a method with the same name and parameters can exist in the inner class and the outer class. Here is an example of how such a method can be called.

```java
public class PopulateChars {
  ArrayList<Character> charList;
  public PopulateChars(){
    charList = new ArrayList<Character>();
  }
  public void printChars(){
    System.out.println(charList);
  }
  public class TimerListener implements ActionListener {
    public void actionPerformed(ActionEvent e) {
      charList.add((char) ('a' + (int) ((Math.random() * 26))));
      PopulateChars.this.printChars();
    }
    public void printChars(){
    }
  }
}
```

The syntax is `PopulateChars.this.printChars()`. This means go to the outer object that belongs to the `PopulateChars` class, get its `this` reference (i.e., the reference to the outer object), and call the `printChars` method on it. Conversely, the syntax `PopulateChars.printChars()` can be used to call a static method of the outer class when a method with the same name exists in the nested class.

10.2.3 Local Classes

Declaring a class inside a class is useful when we want to quickly define a class without creating a new outer class. As we saw, nested classes are particularly useful for event handling. Sometimes, however, one needs to create an object that belongs to a class inside a method. Such a class is called a *local class* and can have a name, but it is usually anonymous. For example, when we need to create a callback method, we can just create an object that supports this method. The object can belong to a new class that is created on the fly. Note, however, that if the class is not given a name, then it cannot be reused to create more objects of the class. Here is how our typing program can be rewritten to use anonymous local classes.

```java
public class TypingGame{
  public static void main(String[] args) {
    final ArrayList<Character> charList = new ArrayList<Character>();
    Timer t = new Timer(200, new ActionListener() {
      public void actionPerformed(ActionEvent e) {
        charList.add((char) ('a' + (int) ((Math.random() * 26))));
        System.out.println(charList);
      }
    });
    t.start();
    JFrame frame = new JFrame();
    frame.setVisible(true);
  }
}
```

We will use anonymous local classes only when we want to create an object from a class and we will never need to refer to the class again.

Note the unusual syntax for creating anonymous local classes. We write **new** `ActionListener()`. However, this does not mean that we are creating a new object of type `ActionListener`. After all, `ActionListener` is an interface and it is illegal to instantiate an object from an interface. We are actually creating a new object that belongs to a class with name X, where we are not naming the X class. What we require is that the X class inherits from the `ActionListener` class. In other words, the above code is equivalent to the following code.

```java
public class TypingGame {
    public static void main(String[] args) {
        final ArrayList<Character> charList = new ArrayList<>();
        class X implements ActionListener{
            public void actionPerformed(ActionEvent e) {
                charList.add((char) ('a' + (int) ((Math.random() * 26))));
                System.out.println(charList);
            }
        }
        Timer t = new Timer(1000, new X());
        t.start();
        JFrame frame = new JFrame();
        frame.setVisible(true);
    }
}
```

The only difference between the above and the original rewrite is that the X class is given a name. However, since the X class will be referenced only once, the first version of the code is preferred. It is shorter and more intuitive. Consider again the anonymous local class creation.

```java
Timer t = new Timer(200, new ActionListener() {
    public void actionPerformed(ActionEvent e) {
        charList.add((char) ('a' + (int) ((Math.random() * 26))));
        System.out.println(charList);
    }
});
```

The code creates a timer that will be executed every 200 milliseconds. Every 200 milliseconds, the `actionPerformed` method will be executed. The rest of the code is simply syntax that circumvents the fact that Java allows only an object, and not a method, to be a method parameter.

The observant reader may have noticed that the variable `charList` was changed to `final`. This is not a coincidence.

A local class can access only the constant (i.e., `final`) variables of the method in which it is defined. The reason is that an object that belongs to a local class can continue to exist after the method terminates. Local variables that are defined as `final` are preserved so that they can be accessed long after the method has terminated. The reason they are preserved is because they are defined as `final` and will therefore not change.

Note that the `ArrayList` of characters can be defined as `final` because the location of the `ArrayList` does not change. The only data that could change is the content of the `ArrayList`.

10.3 Event Listeners

One can associate an event listener with an event source. When an event occurs, a method of the event listener is called and the event object is passed as a parameter. Examples of events include window movement, keystroke, mouse movement, button being pressed, and so on. Examples of event sources include windows, panels, buttons, menus, and other graphical user interface components. The event listener is an object that is created by the programmer to listen for an event. The event listener should inherit the interface that is responsible for the particular type of event.

10.3.1 Key Listeners

In order to complete our typing game, we need to be able to capture keystrokes. Note that the `Scanner` class does not suffice. For example, consider the following code.

```
Scanner keyboard = new Scanner(System.in);
String s = keyboard.next();
```

This will require the user to enter a character and then press `Enter`. The `Scanner` class only processes user input after the `Enter` key is pressed on the keyboard. In order to capture keystrokes, we need to create a listener that listens for key strokes.

When creating event handling code, one needs to always identify the *event source*, the *event*, and the *event listener*, where all three will be objects. The event listener and the event source are objects that need to be created by the programmer. The event object is automatically created by Java. After creating the event source and the event listener, one needs to *register* the event listener with the event source. When the event occurs, the event source calls a method of the event listener and sends the event object as a parameter.

In our example, we can create a window (i.e., `JFrame`) to be the event source. Note that only graphical components can capture keystrokes and a window is the simplest example. Next, we need to create a keystroke listener. Our listener will inherit from the interface `KeyListener`. Here is what the interface looks like, where the interface is defined in `java.awt.*`.

```
interface KeyListener{
    void keyPressed(KeyEvent e);
    void keyReleased(KeyEvent e);
    void keyTyped(KeyEvent e);
}
```

In order to listen for keystrokes, one needs to perform the following tasks.

1. Create a class that overrides the three methods of the `KeyListener` interface.

2. Instantiate an object of that class. This will be the event listener.

3. Register the event listener with the event source (e.g., a window or a panel).

Note that if a keyboard key is pressed and then released, then the **keyPressed**, **keyReleased**, and **keyTyped** methods of the event listener will be called in that order. Here is an example of creating a key listener object.

```
1   class MyKeyListener implements KeyListener {
2     public void keyPressed (KeyEvent e) {
3       char c = e.getKeyChar ();
4       if (charList.contains(c)) {
5         charList.remove((Character) c);
6       }
7       System.out.println(charList);
8     }
9     public void keyReleased (KeyEvent e){}
10    public void keyTyped (KeyEvent e){}
11  }
12  ...
13  MyKeyListener keyListener = new MyKeyListener ();
```

Note that all three methods take as input an event. When the event occurs, the corresponding method is called and the event is passed as a parameter. For key events, the event class is **KeyEvent**. The **getKeyChar** method for the event object returns the key on which the event occurred. Note that the cast at Line 5 of the code is required. If it is not present, Java will take the ASCII code of the character and remove from the **ArrayList** the element with that index. The **keyPressed** method finds the key that is pressed and removes it from the **ArrayList** if present. At the end, the **ArrayList** is redisplayed. Note that the **contains** method of the **ArrayList** class checks to see if the element belongs to the **ArrayList**.

Often, when writing event listeners, one does not want to override all the methods of the interface that we are inheriting. For example, the interface for a mouse listener has five methods and one rarely needs to override all of them. To help the programmer, abstract classes were added to the Java library that contain empty implementation of the methods for most interfaces. For example, there is a **KeyAdapter** class that contains empty implementation of the three methods of the **KeyListener** interface. Here is an example of how the class can be used.

```
class MyKeyListener implements KeyAdapter {
  public void keyPressed (KeyEvent e) {
    char c = e.getKeyChar ();
    if (charList.contains(c)) {
      charList.remove((Character) c);
    }
    System.out.println(charList);
  }
}
...
MyKeyListener keyListener = new MyKeyListener ();
```

This rewrite saves some space because we can choose which methods to override. After the key listener is created, we need to *register* it with the event source (in our case this will be a **JFrame** object). Here is an example of how one can do that.

```
JFrame frame = new JFrame ();
frame.addKeyListener (keyListener);
```

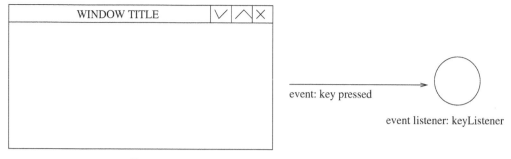

event source

FIGURE 10.2: Example of key listener.

Note that a key listener can also be added to a panel. However, before doing so, call the `setFocusable(true)` method inside the panel constructor. By default, a panel cannot get the focus and only the component that has the focus is notified about key events. Figure 10.2 shows an example of how everything works. The window must have the focus because only components that have the focus can listen for key strokes. A key listener is registered with the window. Once a key is pressed, the window calls the `keyPressed` method of the key listener and sends the event as a parameter. The key listener can extract the key that is being pressed from the event and take appropriate action.

Here is the new version of the typing program, where we have made use of anonymous local classes in order to shorten the code.

```java
import java.awt.event.*;
import java.util.*;
import javax.swing.*;
import javax.swing.Timer;

public class TypingGame {
  public static final int MAX_COUNTER = 150;
  public static final int MAX_SIZE = 10;
  public static final int INTERVAL = 200;
  public static void main(String[] args) {
    JFrame frame = new JFrame();
    final ArrayList<Character> charList = new ArrayList<>();
    frame.addKeyListener(new KeyAdapter() {
      public void keyPressed(KeyEvent e) {
        char c = e.getKeyChar();
        if (charList.contains(c)) {
          charList.remove((Character) c);
        }
        System.out.println(charList);
      }
    });
    Timer t = new Timer(INTERVAL, new ActionListener() {
      int counter = 0;
      public void actionPerformed(ActionEvent e) {
        charList.add((char) ('a' + (int) ((Math.random() * 26))));
        System.out.println(charList);
        counter++;
        if (counter == MAX_COUNTER) {
          System.out.println("You win!");
```

```
        System.exit(0);
      }
      if(charList.size()>MAX_SIZE){
        System.out.println("You lose!");
        System.exit(0);
      }
    }
  });
  t.start();
  frame.setSize(200, 200);
  frame.setVisible(true);
  }
}
```

Note that we have also added code to determine when the player wins or loses. Every time interval the counter is incremented by one. If the user is able to survive till the counter reaches 150, then they win. Alternatively, if the `ArrayList` becomes more than 10 characters, then the player loses. After running the program, we may find that it is difficult to win if the timer is set at 200 milliseconds. Accordingly, we can adjust the game by changing the three constants at the beginning of the code. This is a good design because one can change the parameters of the game just by changing the values of the constants.

10.3.2 Mouse Listeners

We will next create a simple drawing program. In the previous chapter, we showed how different shapes can be displayed inside a panel. Here, we will describe how the user can draw any arbitrary collection of freehand shapes. When the user presses the left mouse button, the program will start drawing the shape. It will keep drawing the shape until the user releases the mouse button. In order to implement the program, we need to be aware of two types of Java interfaces that can be used to capture mouse events: `MouseListener` and `MouseMotionListener`. Information about the two interfaces is shown below.

```
interface MouseListener{
  void mouseClicked(MouseEvent e);
  void mouseEntered(MouseEvent e);
  void mouseExited(MouseEvent e);
  void mousePressed(MouseEvent e);
  void mouseReleased(MouseEvent e);
}

interface MouseMotionListener{
  mouseDragged(MouseEvent e);
  mouseMoved(MouseEvent e);
}
```

Note that while a `MouseListener` is notified when the buttons of the mouse are clicked, a `MouseMotionListener` is notified when the mouse is moved. In our drawing game, we will use both listeners. Of course, we will inherit from the abstract classes `MouseAdapter` and `MouseMotionAdapter` in order to avoid the need to override all methods. These classes contain empty implantations of all the methods of the interfaces. One can register a mouse listener with a panel by writing the following code.

```
MouseAdapter mouseAdapter = ...
panel.addMouseListener(mouseAdapter);
```

Looking at the code for the key listeners and the mouse listeners, a pattern has emerged.

In order to handle an event of type X, one needs to create an event listener and register it with the event source. The event listener belongs to the *X*Listener class, where *X* should be substituted with the type of the event (e.g., MouseListener, KeyListener, etc.). The event, which will be of type *X*Event (e.g., MouseEvent, KeyEvent, etc.), will be passed as a parameter to the method of the event listener. Call the add*X*Listener method on the event source to register the event listener with it.

With every rule, there are exceptions. Here the exception is that there is a MouseEvent, but there is no MouseMotionEvent.

Going back to our drawing program, we will first create a MyShape class. A freehand object will be represented by an object of type MyShape.

```java
class MyShape {
    private ArrayList<Point2D> points = new ArrayList <>();

    public MyShape(Point2D point){
        points.add(point);
    }

    public MyShape(){}

    public void addPoint(Point2D point){
        points.add(point);
    }

    public void drawShape(Graphics2D g){
        g.setPaint(Color.RED);
        if(points.size()==0){
            return;
        }
        Point2D start=points.get(0);
        for(Point2D end: points){
            g.draw(new Line2D.Double(start,end));
            start=end;
        }
    }
}
```

A shape is stored as an ArrayList of points. The drawShape method takes as input a drawing brush. It sets the paint color to red and then draws the shape by connecting the dots of the shape with lines. Note that we have added an empty constructor. Although we will not use it in our code, good programming practices suggest that an empty constructor be added to a class that contains constructors. The reason is that adding a constructor to a class removes the default empty constructor and can invalidate code that previously compiled.

In our program, we will create a window and a panel inside it. We will do the drawing inside the panel and we will register our mouse listeners with the panel. In general, a mouse listener can be registered with both the window and the panel. However, registering it with the panel is usually more convenient because the drawing happens inside the panel and the mouse listener usually updates the data for the drawing. When the user presses the left key of the mouse, we will start drawing a new shape. Here is the code that handles this event.

```java
class MyPanel extends JPanel{
    ArrayList<MyShape> shapes = new ArrayList <>();
```

```
  public MyPanel(){
    addMouseListener(new MouseAdapter (){
      public void mousePressed(MouseEvent e){
        if(e.getButton()==1){
          shapes.add(new MyShape(e.getPoint()));
          repaint();
        }
    }});
    ...
  }
  public void paintComponent(Graphics g){
    super.paintComponent(g);
    Graphics2D g2 = (Graphics2D) g;
    for(MyShape s: shapes){
      s.drawShape(g2);
    }
  }
}
```

Note that we can use the input event to determine the mouse key that is being pressed. By calling the `getButton` method, we can determine which mouse button is pressed. The method can return 1, 2, or 3, which corresponds to the left, middle, and right buttons of the mouse being pressed, respectively. If the left mouse button is pressed, then we will create a new object of type `MyShape` and add it to the `ArrayList` of shapes. Note that we can use the code `e.getPoint()` to determine the coordinates of the mouse cursor when the mouse event was generated. Since the event is registered within the panel, the coordinates will be relative to the top left corner of the panel (and not the computer screen). We pass this point to the constructor of the `MyShape` class in order to create a new shape with a single point.

At the end of the `mousePressed` method, we call the `repaint` method. This will redisplay the picture. We need the picture redisplayed because we have added a new shape to it. The `repaint` method leads to the eventual call of the `paintComponent` method (note that the `paintComponent` method should not be called directly). In the `paintComponent` method, the first line clears the drawing area. Next, a brush is created and the shapes in the `ArrayList` are drawn.

In a GUI application, most listeners usually change the data to be displayed. After this data is changed, the `repaint` method needs to be called. It in turn calls the `paintComponent` method when possible and the picture is redisplayed. Recall that the `paintComponent` method does not generate data, it simply displays it. The actual data is usually generated in the listeners or the constructor methods.

Next, we need to register a mouse listener that will change the current shape when the mouse is dragged. Here is the code.

```
class MyPanel extends JPanel{
  ArrayList<MyShape> shapes = new ArrayList<>();
  addMouseMotionListener(new MouseMotionAdapter () {
    public void mouseDragged(MouseEvent e){
      if((e.getModifiersEx() & MouseEvent.BUTTON1_DOWN_MASK)!=0){
        shapes.get(shapes.size()-1).addPoint(e.getPoint());
        repaint();
```

```
}}});
    ...
}
```

The `mouseMoved` method is called when the mouse is moved without a mouse button being pressed. The `mouseDragged` method is called when the mouse is moved while one or more buttons are being pressed. Note that we should not use the code `e.getButton()` in this case because more than one mouse button could potentially be pressed. Instead, when writing code for the `mouseDragged` method, we should always call the `getModifiersEx` method. It will return code that shows us which mouse buttons are pressed.

Note that the behavior of the `getModifiersEx` method is a little tricky to understand. If we do an experiment, we will see that method returns 1024 when the left mouse button is pressed, 2048 when the middle mouse button is pressed, 4096 when the right mouse button is pressed, 3072 when both the left and middle button are pressed and so on. In other words, Java will return a unique integer for every mouse–button combination. We may be tempted to just enumerate all combinations when the left mouse button is pressed. However, this is the wrong approach because there is no guarantee that the `getModifiersEx` method will not return different values in the next Java version.

Let us look in greater detail at the codes that are returned by the `getModifiersEx` method. If the left mouse button is pressed, then the number 1024 is returned, which is the binary number 0000 0100 0000 0000. If the middle button is pressed, then the binary number 0000 1000 0000 0000 is returned. If both the left and middle button are pressed, then the number 0000 1100 0000 0000 is returned. In other words, there is a bitmap mask for each mouse button. If more than one button is pressed, then the combination of the bitmap masks of the buttons is returned. If we try to print the constant `MouseEvent.BUTTON1_DOWN_MASK`, then we will get the binary number 0000 0100 0000 0000. This corresponds to just the left mouse button being pressed. The operation "&" is the bitwise *and* operator. It performs the operation *and* on each pair of bits. The result is 1 only when both bits are one. In other words, we can think of 1 as `true` and of 0 as `false`. Suppose that we want to evaluate the result of the expression `e.getModifiersEx() & MouseEvent.BUTTON1_DOWN_MASK`. If `e.getModifiersEx()` returns 0000 1100 0000 0000 and `MouseEvent.BUTTON1_DOWN_MASK` is equal to 0000 0100 0000 0000, then we will get the following result.

```
    0000  1100  0000  0000
    0000  0100  0000  0000
----------------------------------  (result of &)
    0000  0100  0000  0000
```

In other words, the result is different from 0, which means that the left mouse button is pressed. Alternatively, if we want to check if the left or right mouse button is pressed, then we can write the following code.

```
e.getModifiersEx() & (MouseEvent.BUTTON1_DOWN_MASK | MouseEvent.
    BUTTON2_DOWN_MASK)
```

Note that the operator "|" is the bitwise *or* operator. The resulting bit is 1 if one of the input bits is 1. In the above expression, the right-hand side of the operator & will create a number that has two 1s in its binary representation. If the left-hand side has one of these 1s set (i.e., the left or middle mouse button is pressed), then the whole expression will evaluate to a number that is different from 0.

On a side note, one might be tempted to use & instead of && and | instead of ||. This is certainly possible. However, the operations are not equivalent. For example, the && operation will not evaluate the second argument if the first argument is `false`. Conversely, the & operation always evaluates both arguments.

Going back to our drawing code, the mouse motion listener checks if the left mouse button is pressed. If it is, it gets the current coordinates of the cursor and adds the point to the current shape. The last line redraws the panel so that we can see the new shape. When we draw too much on a sheet of paper, it may become cluttered and we may want to clear it. We will fix this problem by allowing the panel to be cleared when the right mouse button is pressed. Here is our complete code.

```java
import java.awt.*;
import java.awt.event.*;
import java.awt.geom.*;
import java.util.*;
import javax.swing.*;

public class DrawingGame {
  public static void main(String[] args) {
    MyFrame f = new MyFrame();
    f.setVisible(true);
  }
}

class MyFrame extends JFrame {
  public MyFrame() {
    setSize(300, 300);
    MyPanel p = new MyPanel();
    add(p);
  }
}

class MyPanel extends JPanel {
  ArrayList<MyShape> shapes = new ArrayList<>();
  public MyPanel() {
    addMouseListener(new MouseAdapter() {
      public void mousePressed(MouseEvent e) {
        if (e.getButton() == 1) { // left mouse button
          shapes.add(new MyShape(e.getPoint()));
          repaint();
        }
        if(e.getButton() == 3){ // right mouse button
          shapes = new ArrayList<>();
          repaint();
        }
      }
    });

    addMouseMotionListener(new MouseMotionAdapter() {
      public void mouseDragged(MouseEvent e) {
        if ((e.getModifiersEx() & MouseEvent.BUTTON1_DOWN_MASK) != 0) {
          shapes.get(shapes.size() - 1).addPoint(e.getPoint());
          repaint();
        }
      }
    });
  }

  public void paintComponent(Graphics g) {
```

```
    super.paintComponent(g);
    Graphics2D g2 = (Graphics2D) g;
    for (MyShape s : shapes) {
      s.drawShape(g2);
    }
  }
}

class MyShape {
  private ArrayList<Point2D> points = new ArrayList<>();

  public MyShape(){
  }
  public MyShape(Point2D point) {
    points.add(point);
  }

  public void addPoint(Point2D point) {
    points.add(point);
  }

  public void drawShape(Graphics2D g) {
    g.setPaint(Color.RED);
    if (points.size() == 0) {
      return;
    }

    Point2D start = points.get(0);
    for (Point2D end : points) {
      g.draw(new Line2D.Double(start, end));
      start = end;
    }
  }
}
```

Of course, this program must be put in a file with the name `DrawingGame.java`. Remember that we must have a single class of type `public` in every Java file that matches the name of the file.

10.3.3 Menu Listeners

Drawing using the red color is nice. However, what if we want to create a multi-colored drawing? We will show how to do this next. We will allow the user to select the color of his or her drawing using a menu.

Every window can have at most one menu bar. The menu bar can have one or more menus. Every menu can have several menu items. An event listener of type `ActionListener` can be registered with every menu item. The method `actionPerformed` of the listener will be called when the menu item is selected.

Creating a menu is pretty straightforward. Here is the code to add a menu to the drawing game.

```
class MyFrame extends JFrame {
```

```
public MyFrame() {
    ...
    JMenuBar bar = new JMenuBar();
    setJMenuBar(bar);
    JMenu color = new JMenu("Color");
    bar.add(color);
    JMenuItem green = new JMenuItem("Green");
    JMenuItem red = new JMenuItem("Red");
    JMenuItem blue = new JMenuItem("Blue");
    color.add(green);
    color.add(red);
    color.add(blue);
}
}
```

Since the menu is part of Swing, we need to use J in front of all the class names. Note that since a window can have at most one `JMenuBar`, we need to use the `setJMenuBar` method to add the menu bar to the window. Every menu and menu item has a name, which is specified in the constructor of the class. The menus are added to the menu bar and the menu items are added to the menus.

The life of a menu item is relatively simple. The only thing that can happen is that it is pressed. Therefore, it only needs to notify the `actionPerformed` method that belongs to the interface `ActionListener`. We will add a variable `color` to the `MyPanel` class. Since the variable will be private, we will also add a setter method for it. We will then add action listeners to the three menu items that simply call this setter method in order to change the drawing color for the panel. Here is the rewritten code.

```
import java.awt.*;
import java.awt.event.*;
import java.awt.geom.*;
import java.util.*;
import javax.swing.*;

public class DrawingGame {
    public static void main(String[] args) {
        MyFrame f = new MyFrame();
        f.setVisible(true);
    }
}

class MyFrame extends JFrame {
    MyPanel p;
    public MyFrame() {
        setSize(300, 300);
        p = new MyPanel();
        add(p);
        JMenuBar bar = new JMenuBar();
        setJMenuBar(bar);
        JMenu color = new JMenu("Color");
        bar.add(color);
        JMenuItem green = new JMenuItem("Green");
        JMenuItem red = new JMenuItem("Red");
        JMenuItem blue = new JMenuItem("Blue");
        color.add(green);
        color.add(red);
        color.add(blue);
```

```java
      green.addActionListener(new ColorListener(Color.GREEN));
      red.addActionListener(new ColorListener(Color.RED));
      blue.addActionListener(new ColorListener(Color.BLUE));
    }
  class ColorListener implements ActionListener{
    private Color color;
    public ColorListener(){
      color = Color.RED;
    }
    public ColorListener(Color color){
      this.color = color;
    }
    public void actionPerformed(ActionEvent e){
      p.changeColor(color);
    }

  }
}

class MyPanel extends JPanel {
  ArrayList<MyShape> shapes = new ArrayList<MyShape>();
  private Color currentColor;
  public void changeColor(Color newColor){
    currentColor = newColor;
  }
  public MyPanel() {
    addMouseListener(new MouseAdapter() {
      public void mousePressed(MouseEvent e) {
        if (e.getButton() == 1) {
          shapes.add(new MyShape(e.getPoint(),currentColor));
          repaint();
        }
        if(e.getButton() == 3){
          shapes = new ArrayList<MyShape>();
          repaint();
        }
      }
    });

    addMouseMotionListener(new MouseMotionAdapter() {
      public void mouseDragged(MouseEvent e) {
        System.out.println(e.getModifiersEx());
        if ((e.getModifiersEx() & MouseEvent.BUTTON1_DOWN_MASK) != 0) {
          shapes.get(shapes.size() - 1).addPoint(e.getPoint());
          repaint();
        }
      }
    });
  }

  public void paintComponent(Graphics g) {
    super.paintComponent(g);
    Graphics2D g2 = (Graphics2D) g;
    for (MyShape s : shapes) {
      s.drawShape(g2);
```

```
        }
      }
    }

class MyShape {
  private ArrayList<Point2D> points = new ArrayList<Point2D>();
  private Color color;
  public MyShape(){
    color = Color.RED;
  }
  public MyShape(Point2D point, Color color) {
    this.color = color;
    points.add(point);
  }

  public void addPoint(Point2D point) {
    points.add(point);
  }

  public void drawShape(Graphics2D g) {
    g.setPaint(color);
    if (points.size() == 0) {
      return;
    }
    Point2D start = points.get(0);
    for (Point2D end : points) {
      g.draw(new Line2D.Double(start, end));
      start = end;
    }
  }
}
```

Note that the `ColorListener` class is an inner class for the `MyFrame` class. Using anonymous local classes is not the best solution here because the class is referenced three times to create the three color listeners. The constructor of the `ColorListener` class simply saves the color. When the user selects that they want to use the color, the `actionPerformed` method is executed, which in turn changes the current drawing color in the `MyPanel` class. When a new shape is created, the current color is passed as a parameter to the shape. When a shape is drawn, the brush is first set to this color. To accomplish this, we have added the variable `color` to the `MyShape` class. The constructor of the `MyShape` class is also updated to set the initial value for the color of the shape.

10.4   Multicasting

In our drawing game, we created three event listeners and associated them with the three menu items. It turns out that one can associate multiple event listeners with the same event source. When the event occurs, the event source will multicast the event to all the event listeners that are registered with the event source. Note that Java provides no guarantees on the order in which the event listeners will be contacted. In order to demonstrate the multicasting mechanism, we will create a simple application that creates and destroys windows using a menu. We will have a single main window with two menu items. The first menu item will create a new window, while the second menu item will destroy all windows. The beauty of the design is that a single event source, the menu item for close all windows, will have multiple event listeners that are associated with it. When the close all menu item is selected, all windows will be closed. Here is the implementation.

```java
import java.awt.*;
import java.awt.event.*;
import java.util.*;
import javax.swing.*;

public class RandomWindows {
  public static void main(String[] args) {
    MainFrame f = new MainFrame();
    f.setVisible(true);
  }
}

class MainFrame extends JFrame{
  private static int counter = 0;
  public MainFrame(){
    setSize(200,200);
    JMenuBar bar = new JMenuBar();
    setJMenuBar(bar);
    JMenu windowMenu = new JMenu("Window");
    bar.add(windowMenu);
    final JMenuItem newWindow = new JMenuItem("New Window");
    final JMenuItem closeAll = new JMenuItem("Close All");
    windowMenu.add(newWindow);
    windowMenu.add(closeAll);
    newWindow.addActionListener( new ActionListener(){
      public void actionPerformed(ActionEvent e){
        MyFrame f = new MyFrame(closeAll);
        f.setLocation((int)(Math.random()*500), (int)(Math.random()
          *500));
        f.setSize(200,200);
        f.setVisible(true);
      }
    });
  }
}

class MyFrame extends JFrame{
  public MyFrame(final JMenuItem closeAll){
    closeAll.addActionListener( new ActionListener(){
      public void actionPerformed(ActionEvent e){
        dispose();
      }
    });
  }
}
```

Note that the position of every new window is chosen randomly. Figure 10.3 shows how the three event listeners are registered with the same event source. When the `Close All` menu item is chosen, all three windows will be closed. Note that the menu item `closeAll` is part of the window constructor. Every time a window is created, an `ActionListener` is registered with the menu item `closeAll`. Therefore, if there are three windows, then

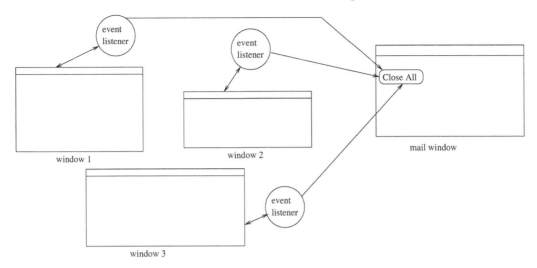

FIGURE 10.3: Example of multicasting.

there will be three objects of type `ActionListener` that are registered with the menu item `closeAll`, one for each window. The `actionPerformed` method for every window simply closes the window.

Note that the variable `closeAll` inside the `MyFrame` constructor had to be defined as `final`. The reason is that it is accessed from an anonymous local class. The `final` keyword means that the variable will not be assigned a new value in the method.

10.5   Summary

The chapter describes how to use the `Timer` class. It allows us to execute a method periodically. This method is executed in parallel with the rest of the program. A timer is implemented by creating a separate thread, but multithreading is an advanced subject that is not covered in this book.

The chapter also describes how to create nested classes. There are four types of nested classes: static, inner, local, and anonymous local. The first two types allow us to create a class within a class, while the last two types allow us to create a class within a method. A local class that is not anonymous is rarely useful and not covered in detail in the chapter. Static classes are associated only with the outer class, while inner classes are associated with an instance of the outer class. In this regard, there is a similarity between inner classes and subclasses. In both cases, there is a hidden reference to an outside object.

Nested classes are useful to create method callbacks. Note that an event listener object must be created every time we want to handle an event. The reason is that we cannot directly tell Java to execute a method every time an event occurs. Instead, we need to create an object (called an event listener) and register it with the source of the event. Every time the event occurs, the event listener is notified by calling one of its methods. The event is passed as a parameter when calling the method.

The chapter also covers multicasting. Multicasting occurs when several event listeners are registered with the same event source. This is a powerful mechanism for handling events because a single event can trigger multiple methods.

10.6 Syntax

- `Timer t = new Timer(20, o);` ⇒ A new timer is created. The o object must belong to a class that implements the interface `ActionListener`. The statement `o.actionPerformed()` will be executed every 20 milliseconds.

- `t.start();` ⇒ Starts the timer.

- `t.stop();` ⇒ Stops the timer.

- `C1.C2 o = new C1.C2();` ⇒ Creates a new o object that belongs to the static nested C2 class, which is inside the C1 class.

- `o.new C2()` ⇒ Creates a new object that belongs to the inner C2 class inside the C1 class. The o object must belong to the C1 class and is the outer object for the newly created object.

- `C1.this.m();` ⇒ Calls the m method that belongs to the outer C1 class. The call is only valid from an inner class (i.e., non-static nested class).

- `o = new ActionListener(){public void actionPerformed(ActionEvent e){...` `} };` ⇒ Creates a new object that belongs to an anonymous X class. The X class must implement the interface `ActionListener` and therefore override the `actionPerformed` method. The body of the X class is specified between the inner pair of braces.

- `panel.addKeyListener(new KeyAdapter(){ ... });` ⇒ Creates and registers a new key listener. The `KeyAdapter` class implements the interface `KeyListener` with empty body for the `keyPressed`, `keyReleased`, and `keyTyped` methods.

- `panel.addMouseListener(new MouseAdapter(){ ... });` ⇒ Creates and registers a new mouse listener. The `MouseAdapter` class implements the `MouseListener` interface with empty body for the `mouseClicked`, `mouseEntered`, `mouseExited`, `mousePressed`, and `mouseReleased` methods.

- `panel.addMouseMotionListener(new MouseMotionAdapter(){ ... });` ⇒ Creates and registers a new mouse motion listener. The `MouseMotionAdapter` class implements the `MouseMotionListener` interface with empty body for the `mouseMoved` and `mouseDragged` methods.

- `e.getX()` ⇒ Gets the x coordinate. Can be called inside any mouse listener or mouse motion listener method. The coordinate is relative to the top left corner of the event source (e.g., window or panel).

- `e.getY()` ⇒ Gets the y coordinate. Can be called inside any mouse listener or mouse motion listener method. The coordinate is relative to the top left corner of the event source (window or panel).

- `e.getPoint()` ⇒ Returns the point of where the cursor is currently. Can be called inside any mouse listener or mouse motion listener method. The coordinates are relative to the top left corner of the event source (e.g., window or panel).

- `e.getButton()` ⇒ Returns the mouse button on which the event e occurred (1 is the left button, 2 is the middle, 3 is the right button). Can be called in the following mouse listener methods: `mouseClicked`, `mousePressed`, and `mouseReleased`.

- `e.getModifiersEx()` $\Rightarrow$ Returns a button mask showing the mouse buttons that are pressed when the event `e` occurred. Should be called only in the `mouseDragged` method of a mouse motion listener.

- `(e.getModifiersEx() & MouseEvent.BUTTON1_DOWN_MASK)!=0)` $\Rightarrow$ True if the left mouse button is pressed, where `e` is the event. Should appear only inside the `mouseDragged` method of a mouse motion listener. Note that button 1 is the left mouse button, button 2 is the middle, while button 3 is the right mouse button.

- `JMenuBar bar= new JMenuBar();` $\Rightarrow$ Creates a menu bar object using Swing.

- `frame.setJMenuBar(bar);` $\Rightarrow$ Adds the menu bar to the frame. Since every window can have at most one menu bar, the `setJMenuBar` method is used instead of the `add` method.

- `Menu m = new Menu("File");` $\Rightarrow$ Creates a new `File` menu.

- `bar.add(m);` $\Rightarrow$ Adds the menu `m` to the menu bar. One can add multiple menus to the same menu bar.

- `MenuItem mi = new MenuItem("Open...");` $\Rightarrow$ Creates the menu item "Open...".

- `m.add(mi);` $\Rightarrow$ Adds the menu item to the menu.

- `a.contains(b)` $\Rightarrow$. Returns `true` if the element `b` belongs to the `ArrayList a`.

10.7 Important Points

1. There are four types of nested classes: nested static, inner, local, and local anonymous. A nested static class is a static class within a class. The name of the outer class must be used when creating an instance of the class outside the outer classes. Nested static classes have access to only the static variables of the outer class. Inner classes are classes within classes, where an inner class always has a reference to the outer object and can therefore access the variables of the outer class. A local class is a class within a method. It only has access to the `final` variables of the method.

2. Create an anonymous inner class only when the class will not be reused. That is, an object is created from a class and no other objects will need to be created from this class again.

3. When handling an event, one needs to be always aware of the event source, the event listener, and the event object. While the event object is created by Java, the event source and the event listener must be created by the programmer. The event listener must belong to a class that implements the appropriate interface so that the event source can call the correct methods.

4. After creating the event source, do not forget to register the event source with the event listeners. Write `eventSoure.addXListener(eventListener)`, where `X` should be substituted with the type of event (e.g., Key, Mouse, etc.).

5. Nested classes can be `public`, `private`, or no modifier. Classes with no modifiers can be accessed within the package. Public classes can be accessed from everywhere. Private classes can be accessed only from within the outer class.

6. When inheriting from an interface that has multiple methods and we do not want to override all of them, we can use the adapter class when present. The adapter class has empty implementation of all the methods. For example, if we only care about the `mousePressed` method, then our listener should inherit from the `MouseAdapter` class instead of the `MouseListener` interface.

7. Every window can have at most one menu bar. Therefore, use the `setJMenuBar` method to add the menu bar to the window.

8. Every menu bar can have multiple menus. Every menu can have multiple menu items. Menu items are similar to buttons and an `ActionListener` can be registered with them.

9. It is possible to register multiple event listeners with the same event source. When the event occurs, the event listeners will be notified in some random order.

10. Call `setFocusable(true)` inside the constructor of a panel in order to make the panel focusable and allow key events to be registered with it.

10.8　Exercises

1. Write a program that prints `Howdy!` to the screen every 10 seconds. The program should have only a single outer class with a main method that contains an anonymous local class.

2. What is the difference between a `KeyListener` and a `KeyAdapter`?

3. What is the difference between a `MouseListener` and a `MouseMotionListener`?

4. Given a `MouseEvent`, Java has the `getButton` and `getModifiersEx` methods for determining which mouse buttons are pressed. Are both methods really needed, that is, do they differ in any way?

5. White a program that creates a window with a menu bar. The menu bar should have a single menu that has 10 menu items with text: 0, 1, ... , 9, respectively. When a user selects a number from the menu bar, the corresponding number should be displayed inside the panel of the window. Once finished, add a key listener. When a user types a digit between 0 and 9, the digit should be displayed in the window. Create an array to store the menu items.

6. Create a game that displays a filled circle. Add a mouse motion listener that keeps track of the mouse movement. When the mouse cursor gets close to the circle, move the circle to a new random location within the panel.

7. Write an application that has two menus. The first menu is used to choose a color: red, green, or blue. The second menu contains the exit menu item. The user can use the first menu to change the background panel color (use the `setBackground` method).

You should also display the current chosen color as a text somewhere inside the panel, where the initial background color is blue. The `getHeight` and `getWidth` methods can be called on a panel object to determine its height and width in pixels. The user should also be able to change the background color to red, green, or blue by pressing the r, g, and b keys on the keyboard (the color should be changed to red, green, or blue, respectively). Remember to call the `setFocusable` method on the panel.

8. Write an application that draws ellipses. The ellipse should start drawing when the left mouse button is pressed. The ellipse is completed when the left mouse button is released. Create an `ArrayList` to store the ellipses. The `paintComponent` method should display the `ArrayList` of ellipses and the current ellipse (i.e., the ellipse that is currently being drawn). The content on the window should not change when the window is resized. Pressing the right mouse button should clear the window.

10.9   Lab

Find a pretty image from the Internet and use an image editor to break it down into 9 pieces (for example, you can use the application `Paint` in Windows). Display the 9 images in a 3x3 grid in a random order. Add a mouse listener. Allow the user to swap two images by clicking on them. The goal of the game is to re-create the original image. Display an appropriate message when the user wins.

10.10   Project

For this project, you will need to implement the Reversi game. The game is played on an 8 by 8 board. The starting position of the game is shown in Figure 10.4. The game is played by two players. At every turn, a player can place at most 1 disk. When a disk is placed, all disks of the opponent's color that are in a straight line and bounded by the disk just placed and another disk of the current player's color are turned over to the current player's color. A move is valid only if it turns over some disks. If a player does not have a valid move, then they pass and the other player plays again. The objective of the game is to have the most disks at the end of the game. One of the players is the computer and the other player is a human. Choose randomly who starts first. During a human's move, if a cell on the grid is valid, then turn it to green when the user hovers over it with the mouse. This will signal to the human player that this is a valid square to play. Alternate moves between the computer and the human, unless one needs to pass. Display an appropriate message when the game ends. The game ends when the board is filled. The player with the most disks at the end wins. Note that it is possible that the game is a draw.

The Artificial Intelligence (AI) of this game is tricky. To simplify it, follow these basic rules in this order.

1. If the computer can go in one of the four corners, it should always do so.

2. The computer should avoid going in the squares that are adjacent to a corner when the corner is free.

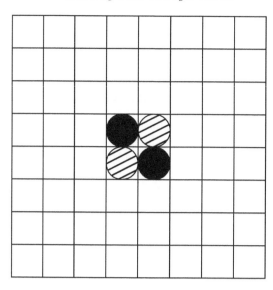

FIGURE 10.4: Start of the Reversi game.

3. Select the valid move that removes the fewest opponent's disks.

Chapter 11

The Breakout Game (Complete Version)

Implementing the Breakout game is relatively challenging. We will use a **for** statement to display the blocks. We will use a combination of **if** statements to determine if the ball intersects one of the other objects in the game. We will remind ourselves how to use the **enum** construct by defining a new type that contains the constants **FAST**, **NORMAL**, and **SLOW**, that is, the possible ball speeds. We will use a mouse listener and a keyboard listener to move the paddle. We will override methods and rely on dynamic binding to simplify the code. In summary, we will cover most of the material that is presented so far in the book. Needless to say, our solution will be a multi-class solution that utilizes a lot of nested classes. Most importantly, this chapter will show an example of the whole process of designing and writing non-trivial software. Our code will contain eight classes, two **enum** types, and approximately 700 lines of code. Although there are infinitely many choices of how to implement the game, we will strive to create a design that is elegant, easy to understand, easy to modify, and that conforms to good software practices.

11.1   Overview of the Game

Our game will have a menu bar with three menus: **Game**, **Ball Color**, and **Ball Speed**. From the game menu, the player can start and pause the game or entirely quit the game. From the ball color menu, the player can select the color of the ball. We will allow the ball to be red, blue, or green. From the speed menu, the player can select the speed of the ball: **FAST**, **NORMAL**, or **SLOW**. A blue paddle will appear at the bottom of the screen and it can be moved left or right with the mouse or keyboard. The ball will jump left if it hits the left part of the paddle and right if it hits the right part of the paddle. The ball will also change direction when it hits one of the walls or one of the bricks. The bricks are arranged in a rectangular grid. When a brick is hit, it should be removed from the screen. We will use a random generator to select the color of every brick. At the bottom left part of the screen, we will display stickman icons. A life is lost when the user is unable to use the paddle to

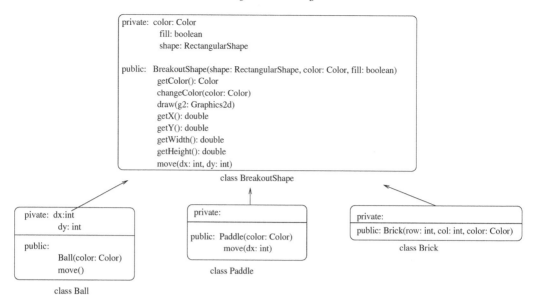

FIGURE 11.1: UML Diagram of the game Breakout.

stop the ball from escaping. When the player loses a life, a stickman should be removed from the screen. The game ends when all lives are exhausted.

11.2 Game Design

First, we need to decide on the classes and the data and methods in them. We will demonstrate an approach that was first proposed by Abbott in 1983. The approach states to identify the classes from the textual description of the problem. Looking at the description, we will create the `Breakout` class where the `main` method is written. We will also include classes for the main participants of the game: `Ball`, `Brick`, `Paddle`, and `Player`. We will create two enumeration types: `BallColor` and `Speed`. There, we will store the possibilities for the ball color and ball speed. We will need to create two additional classes that relate to Java: `BreakoutFrame` and `BreakoutPanel`. These will be the window and the drawing panel for our application, respectively. Lastly, we will create a `BreakoutShape` class that will be the superclass of all the shapes that will be displayed. Since drawing the paddle, ball, and brick are similar, it is reasonable to create a single superclass. Part of our initial design is shown in Figure 11.1.

The `BreakoutShape` class is used to represent a shape that is bounded by a rectangle, that is, a ball, a paddle, or a brick. A breakout shape can have a color and can be filled or not filled. In our case, all breakout shapes are filled. However, the field `fill` is added just in case we want to create a breakout shape that is not filled in the future. Writing a class that is versatile and that supports features that may not be currently needed is a common programming approach. However, one should not go overboard implementing features that are not presently required.

11.3 Moving the Ball

The initial code for the BreakoutShape class is shown next.

```java
import java.awt.*;
import java.awt.geom.*;
public class BreakoutShape {
  private Color color;
  private boolean fill;
  private RectangularShape shape;

  public BreakoutShape(RectangularShape shape, Color color, boolean
      fill) {
    this.shape = shape;
    this.color = color;
    this.fill = fill;
  }

  public Color getColor() {
    return color;
  }

  public void changeColor(Color color) {
    this.color = color;
  }

  public void draw(Graphics2D g2) {
    g2.setPaint(color);
    g2.draw(shape);
    if (fill) {
      g2.fill(shape);
    }
  }

  public double getX() {
    return shape.getX();
  }

  public double getY() {
    return shape.getY();
  }

  public double getHeight() {
    return shape.getHeight();
  }

  public double getWidth() {
    return shape.getWidth();
  }

  public void move(int dx, int dy) {
    shape.setFrame(getX() + dx, getY() + dy, getWidth(), getHeight());
  }
}
```

The RectangularShape abstract class is part of the Java library. Shapes that are determined by a surrounding rectangle, such as Rectangle and Ellipse inherit from this class. It supports methods for getting the x and y coordinates of the top left corner of the rectangle and the width and height of the rectangle. The class supports the intersects method that checks if the rectangular shape intersects a rectangle. The class also supports the setFrame method that can be used to change the coordinates of the rectangular shape and the getBounds method that returns the coordinates of the shape as an object of type Rectangle.

Note that the BreakoutShape class contains an object of type RectangularShape. This is a superclass for the classes Rectangle2D.Double and Ellipse2D.Double, and therefore can be used to store either a reference to an ellipse or rectangle. In both cases, we store the top left corner and the width and height of the surrounding rectangle. The draw method is straightforward. It uses the input brush to draw the shape. If we need to fill the shape, then we call the fill method to do so. Note that the Player class is not a subclass of the BreakoutShape class because an image is drawn differently and an image is not a subclass of the RectangularShape class.

The BreakoutShape class has a getter and setter method for the color of the shape. For convenience, we have also included methods that show the current coordinates of the surrounding rectangle. The move method allows us to move the breakout shape in the X direction by dx and in the Y direction by dy. For example, the ball and the paddle will be moved using this method.

Next, let us focus our attention on the Ball class, which inherits from the BreakoutShape class. The code for the class is shown below.

```java
import java.awt.*;
import java.awt.geom.*;

public class Ball extends BreakoutShape {
  private static final int SIZE = 10;
  private static final int START_X = 200;
  private static final int START_Y = 400;

  private int dx = 1;
  private int dy = -1;
  private BreakoutPanel panel;

  public Ball(Color color, BreakoutPanel panel) {
    super(new Ellipse2D.Double(START_X, START_Y, SIZE, SIZE), color,
        true);
    this.panel = panel;
  }

  public void move() {
    if (getX() + dx < 0) {
      dx = 1;
    }
    if (getX() + getWidth() + dx > panel.getWidth()) {
      dx = -1;
    }
    if (getY() + dy < 0) {
      dy = 1;
```

```
        }
        if (getY()+getHeight()+dy > panel.getHeight()){
            dy = -1;
        }
        super.move(dx, dy);
    }
}
```

The size of the ball and its initial coordinates are defined as constants. The constructor of the ball creates a ball by calling the constructor of the `BreakoutShape` class. A ball will be moved by changing its `x` and `y` coordinates. The ball should move with constant speed. Therefore, we will move the ball by adding `dx` and `dy` to its `x` and `y` coordinates, respectively. Therefore, $(x+dx,y+dy)$ are the new coordinates of the ball. Note that the constructor of the `Ball` class takes as input the panel in which the ball will move. The ball needs to know about the panel so that it can bounce off the panel's walls.

Let us examine the `move` method in greater detail. Before the ball is moved, the value of the variables `dx` of `dy` may need to be changed. For example, if `x+dx <0`, this means that the new value of `x` will be smaller than 0 and the value of `dx` needs to be made positive. Similarly, if `x+ballWidh+dx > panelWidth`, then the new value of `x` will make the ball go over the right corner of the screen and the value of `dx` needs to be made -1. The value of `dy` is computed similarly.

Let us see how our code works so far. Here is the main class.

```
public class Breakout {
    public static void main(String[] args) {
        BreakoutFrame frame = new BreakoutFrame();
        frame.setVisible(true);
    }
}
```

The class simply creates the game window and makes it visible. Here is the code for the game window.

```
import javax.swing.*;
import java.awt.event.*;

public class BreakoutFrame extends JFrame {
    private static final int HEIGHT = 600;
    private static final int WIDTH = 488;

    private BreakoutPanel panel = new BreakoutPanel();

    public BreakoutFrame() {
        setDefaultCloseOperation(JFrame.DISPOSE_ON_CLOSE);
        setLocation(100,100);
        setSize(WIDTH, HEIGHT);
        add(panel);
        setResizable(false);
    }
}
```

The `setDefaultCloseOperation` method assures that the window will be disposed of when the close button is pressed. The width and the height of the window are set, where the two numbers are defined as constants so that the dimensions of the window can be easily changed. Finally, the panel is added to the window and the window is made non-resizable. Let us next examine the code for the panel.

```java
import javax.swing.*;
import java.awt.*;
import java.awt.event.*;

public class BreakoutPanel extends JPanel {
    private javax.swing.Timer timer;
    private Ball ball;

    public BreakoutPanel() {
        ball = new Ball(Color.red, this);
        timer = new javax.swing.Timer(10, new ActionListener() {
            public void actionPerformed(ActionEvent e) {
                ball.move();
                repaint();
            }
        });
        timer.start();
    }

    public void paintComponent(Graphics g) {
        super.paintComponent(g);
        Graphics2D g2 = (Graphics2D) g;
        ball.draw(g2);
    }
}
```

Note that we have used `javax.swing.Timer` as the timer class. The reason is that there is more than one class that is called `Timer`. Alternatively, we could have imported `javax.swing.Timer` and only referred to the `Timer` class in the code.

The constructor of the class creates the ball and the timer and starts the timer. When the 10 milliseconds expire, the coordinates of the ball are updated and the panel is repainted. The `paintComponent` method creates the two-dimensional brush and uses it to draw the ball. If we run the program so far, we will see the ball bouncing off the walls.

When working on a non-trivial software, it is always a good idea to start with a small feature and test it. Next, build the program from there. Adding small features one at a time and testing them has the advantage that it is easier to isolate any errors. If one writes a big program (e.g., more than 1000 lines) without testing it, then it will be difficult to isolate the errors. Note that errors are not the product of bad programming. Every time non-trivial code is written, errors will emerge. The hallmark of good software practices is to identify and correct errors as early as possible in the process.

11.4   Adding the Paddle

Next, let us add the paddle to the game. The `Paddle` class will be similar to the `Ball` class. However, the main difference is that it can only move horizontally. Here is the code for the `Paddle` class.

```
public class Paddle extends BreakoutShape {
  private static final int START_X = 200;
  private static final int START_Y = 430;
  private static final int WIDTH = 50;
  private static final int HEIGHT = 10;
  private static final int SPEED = 10;

  private BreakoutPanel panel;

  public Paddle(Color color, BreakoutPanel panel) {
    super(new Rectangle2D.Double(START_X, Paddle.START_Y, Paddle.WIDTH,
        Paddle.HEIGHT), color, true);
    this.panel = panel;
  }

  public void move(int dx) {
    if ((getX() + dx >= 0) && (getX() + dx + WIDTH <= panel.getWidth())
        ) {
      move(dx, 0);
    }
  }

  public void moveRight() {
    move(SPEED);
  }

  public void moveLeft() {
    move(-SPEED);
  }
}
```

Note that we need a reference to the bounding panel in order to ensure that the paddle does not move outside the panel. We have two sets of move methods. The `moveLeft` and `moveRight` methods will be used to move the paddle in response to the key listener. For example, when the left button is pressed, the paddle will move to the left by 10 pixels. The *speed* of the paddle is declared as a private constant and can be easily modified. The `move` method will be used by the mouse listener and it needs finer granularity. For example, moving the mouse slightly to the left can move the paddle by one pixel. The paddle is moved by calling the `move` method of the `BreakoutShape` superclass. Note that the second parameter of the call is 0, which means that the paddle will not move vertically.

Our design does not allow someone from outside the `Paddle` class to move the paddle outside the panel or even move the paddle in non-horizontal direction. Restricting the paddle movement in this way is a good design because it helps us easily isolate buggy code. For example, if the paddle was moving diagonally instead of horizontally, we know that the error must be somewhere in the `Paddle` class.

Next, let us examine how to modify the `BreakoutPanel` class to support the paddle. In the constructor of the class we need to create a paddle object. In the `paintComponent` method we need to call the `draw` method on the paddle object in order to display it. We also need to add a key listener and a mouse listener to the panel that move the paddle. This can be done, for example, in the constructor of the panel. Here is the updated version of the `BreakoutPanel` class.

```
import javax.swing.*;
import java.awt.*;
import java.awt.event.*;
```

```java
public class BreakoutPanel extends JPanel {
  private javax.swing.Timer timer;
  private Ball ball;
  private Paddle paddle;

  public BreakoutPanel() {
    ball = new Ball(Color.RED, this);
    paddle = new Paddle(Color.BLUE, this);
    timer = new javax.swing.Timer(10, new ActionListener() {
      public void actionPerformed(ActionEvent e) {
        ball.move();
        repaint();
      }
    });
    timer.start();
    addKeyListener(new KeyAdapter() {
      public void keyPressed(KeyEvent e) {
        if(e.getKeyCode()==KeyEvent.VK_LEFT){
          paddle.moveLeft();
        }
        if (e.getKeyCode()==KeyEvent.VK_RIGHT) {
          paddle.moveRight();
        }
        repaint();
      }
    });

    addMouseMotionListener(new MouseMotionAdapter() {
      boolean firstTime = true;
      int oldX;

      public void mouseMoved(MouseEvent e) {
        if (firstTime) {
          oldX = e.getX();
          firstTime = false;
        }
        paddle.move(e.getX() - oldX);
        oldX = e.getX();
        repaint();
      }
    });
    setFocusable(true);

  }

  public void paintComponent(Graphics g) {
    super.paintComponent(g);
    Graphics2D g2 = (Graphics2D) g;

    ball.draw(g2);
    paddle.draw(g2);
  }
}
```

Let us first examine the key listener. The `getKeyCode` method returns an integer that is associated with the pressed key. We could not use the `getKeyChar` method because there are no characters that are associated with the arrow keys (and even if there were, we do not know how to refer to them). The `KeyEvent` class stores the code of most virtual keys as constants. For example, `KeyEvent.VK_LEFT` is the left arrow. The code changes the coordinates of the paddle by calling the `moveLeft` or `moveRight` method and then it refreshes the panel.

Note that we could have also rewritten the code as follows.

```
String s= KeyEvent.getKeyText(e.getKeyCode());
if(s.equals("Left")){
...
}
```

The `getKeyText` method converts the key code to text. However, this is an inferior solution because it assumes that the string `Left` will be returned. For example, nothing stops Java from returning the string `LEFT` in future implementations.

Note that the panel needs to be made focusable in order for the key listener to work. Only components that have the focus can receive key events and by default the panel is not focusable. The call `setFocusable(true)` makes the panel focusable.

The mouse listener is a little more interesting than the key listener. It saves the old position of the mouse cursor and it compares it with the new position of the mouse cursor. The paddle is moved by the value of the difference of the two numbers. This means that if we move the mouse fast, then the paddle will be moved fast as well. Of course, we do not know the old value of the cursor the first time we move the mouse. Therefore, we need an extra variable and an `if` statement to address this special case. Finally, note that we can use the mouse to move the paddle only when the cursor is inside the panel. The reason is that mouse events are reported to a component only while the mouse cursor is over that component.

If we run the program that we have so far, we will note that everything works except that the ball goes right though the paddle. The reason is that we have not added code that bounces the ball off the paddle. We will add this code in the time listener inside the `BreakoutPanel` class. Our code will create a *virtual ball* that predicts were the ball will go next without actually moving the ball. We will then check to see if the virtual ball intersects the paddle. The reason a virtual ball is created is because we want to change the trajectory of the ball before it overlaps with the paddle. If the virtual ball intersects the paddle, then we will check if it intersects the left or right part of the paddle. If it intersects the left part of the paddle, then the ball will bounce to the left. Alternatively, if it intersects the right part of the paddle, then the ball will bounce to the right. Here is the new version of the `Ball` class that supports the extended interface.

```
public class Ball extends BreakoutShape {
    private static final int SIZE = 10;
    private static final int START_X = 200;
    private static final int START_Y = 400;

    private BreakoutPanel panel;
    private int dx = 1;
    private int dy = -1;

    public Ball(Color color, BreakoutPanel panel) {
        super(new Ellipse2D.Double(Ball.START_X, Ball.START_Y, Ball.SIZE,
            Ball.SIZE), color, true);
        this.panel = panel;
    }
```

```java
private Ball(Color color, Ellipse2D.Double ellipse){
  super(ellipse,color,true);
}

public Ball getVirtualBall(){
  return new Ball( super.getColor() ,new Ellipse2D.Double(getX()+dx,
    getY()+dy,SIZE,SIZE));
}

public void move() {
  if (getX() + dx < 0) {
    dx = 1;
  }
  if (getX() + getWidth() + dx > panel.getWidth()) {
    dx = -1;
  }
  if (getY() + dy < 0) {
    dy = 1;
  }
  if (getY()+getHeight() +dy > panel.getHeight()){
    dy = -1;
  }
  super.move(dx, dy);
}
public void goUp(){
  dy = -1;
}

public void goDown(){
  dy = 1;
}

public void goLeft(){
  dx = -1;
}

public void goRight(){
  dx = 1;
}
}
```

The `getVirtualBall` method creates a new ball that corresponds to the next position of the ball. It uses a new private constructor that creates a new ball object from the given color and elliptical shape. We have also included the `goDown()`, `goUp()`, `goLeft()`, and `goRight()` methods. They can be used to change the trajectory of the ball.

We also need to modify the `BreakoutShape` class and add the following method.

```java
class BreakoutShape{
  ...
  public boolean intersects(BreakoutShape other) {
    return shape.intersects(other.shape.getBounds());
  }
  ...
}
```

The method checks to see if the two shapes intersect. The `RectangularShape` class has an `intersects` method that takes as input an object of type `Rectangle2D` and checks if the two shapes intersect. The `getBounds` method returns the bounds of a `RectangularShape` as an object of type `Rectangle2D`.

The updated code for the `BreakoutPanel` class is shown next.

```
public BreakoutPanel() {
  ...
  public BreakoutPanel(){
    ...
    timer = new javax.swing.Timer(10, new TimeListener());
    ...
  }
  class TimeListener implements ActionListener {
    public void actionPerformed(ActionEvent e) {
      Ball newBall = ball.getVirtualBall();
      if (newBall.intersects(paddle)) {
        ball.goUp();
        if (newBall.getX() + newBall.getWidth() / 2 < paddle.getX() +
          paddle.getWidth() / 2) {
          ball.goLeft();
        } else {
          ball.goRight();
        }
      } else if (ball.getY() > paddle.getY() - paddle.getHeight()) {
        System.exit(0);
      }
      ball.move();
      repaint();
    }
  }
}
```

Note that the `TimeListener` class is now an inner class instead of a local anonymous class. The reason is that the class is becoming large and we decided to give it a name. Creating a large local anonymous class can put extra burden on someone who tries to understand how the program works. The `actionPerformed` method creates a virtual ball and checks to see if the virtual ball intersects the paddle. If it does, it first changes the ball direction to up. Since the ball has hit the panel, it should not continue going down. Next, the program checks to see if the ball intersects the left or right part of the paddle. The expression `newBall.getX() + newBall.getWidth()/2` gives the X value of the middle of the ball, while the expression `paddle.getX() + paddle.getWidth() / 2` returns the X coordinate of the middle of the paddle. If the virtual ball is predominantly in the left part of the paddle, then the ball goes next to the left. Conversely, if the virtual ball touches the right part of the paddle, then the ball bounces to the right. We have also added a simple code that checks if the ball is below the paddle. For now, this code simply exits the program.

If we run and compile the program, we will see that the ball now bounces off the paddle. If we are unable to catch the ball, then the game ends. In order to prevent the game from ending, we will need to keep track of the number of lives.

11.5   Drawing the Stickmen

Next, we will add code that keeps track of the number of lives. Let us first start with the `Player` class that keeps track of the number of available lives and draws stickmen for them.

```java
import java.awt.*;
import java.io.File;
import javax.imageio.ImageIO;

public class Player {
  private static int INITIAL_NUM_LIVES = 3;
  private static int IMAGE_Y_POSITION = 450;
  private static int IMAGE_H_GAP = 5;
  private int numLives;

  public Player() {
    this.numLives = INITIAL_NUM_LIVES;
  }

  public void killPlayer() {
    numLives--;
  }

  public boolean isAlive() {
    return (numLives > 0);
  }

  public void draw(Graphics2D g2) {
    try {
      Image image = ImageIO.read(new File("player.gif"));
      for (int x = 0; x < numLives; x++) {
        g2.drawImage(image, x * (image.getWidth(null) + IMAGE_H_GAP),
            IMAGE_Y_POSITION, null);
      }
    } catch (Exception newException) {
    }
  }
}
```

The code starts with 3 lives, where this number is saved in a constant and can be changed. The `killPlayer` method removes a life, while the `isAlive` method reports on whether there are lives left. Note that this is an excellent example of data encapsulation because the world outside the class does not know how many lives are left. It does not know because it does not need to know. As is the case in the CIA, information between classes should be shared only on a need-to-know basis. The less information that is shared, the easier it is to identify erroneous code.

The `draw` method draws a stickman for each available life. In our code, the image of a stickman is saved in `player.gif`. Feel free to create your own image. Depending on the size of the image, the variable `IMAGE_Y_POSITION` may have to be modified. Note that the method has a `try-catch` block, which is formally explained in Chapter 13. The reason is that the code can raise an exception if the file `player.gif` does not exist. The code does nothing to handle the exception.

To draw the stickmen, we need to modify the `paintComponent` method in the BreakoutPanel class. Of course, we also need to check that there are any lives left before we draw anything in the method. Here is the rewritten code.

```
class BreakoutPanel{
  private Player player = new Player();
  ...
  public void paintComponent(Graphics g) {
    super.paintComponent(g);
    Graphics2D g2 = (Graphics2D) g;
    if (!player.isAlive()) {
      showMessage("GAME OVER!", g2);
      return;
    }
    player.draw(g2);
    ball.draw(g2);
    paddle.draw(g2);
  }
  public void showMessage(String s, Graphics2D g2) {
    Font myFont = new Font("SansSerif", Font.BOLD + Font.ITALIC, 40);
    g2.setFont(myFont);
    g2.setColor(Color.RED);
    Rectangle2D textBox = myFont.getStringBounds(s, g2.
        getFontRenderContext());
    g2.drawString(s, (int) (getWidth() / 2 - textBox.getWidth() / 2), (
        int) (getHeight() / 2 - textBox.getHeight()));
  }
}
```

We also need to modify the code when the ball goes under the paddle. Instead of exiting the program, we will start moving the ball upward and kill the player (i.e., remove one life).

```
class TimeListener implements ActionListener {
    public void actionPerformed(ActionEvent e) {

      Ball newBall = ball.getVirtualBall();
      if (newBall.intersects(paddle)) {
        ball.goUp();
        if (newBall.getX() + newBall.getWidth() / 2 < paddle.getX() +
            paddle.getWidth() / 2) {
          ball.goLeft();
        } else {
          ball.goRight();
        }
      } else if (ball.getY() > paddle.getY() - paddle.getHeight()) {
        ball.goUp();
        player.killPlayer();
      }
      ball.move();
      repaint();
    }
  }
}
```

If you run the game now, three stickmen will appear. Every time we are unable to catch the ball with the paddle, a stickman will be lost. When we lose all three stickmen, the message GAME OVER will appear.

11.6   Adding the Menus

Next, we will add menus for our program. We will add menus for starting/stopping the game and for changing the color and speed of the ball. We will create the following two **enum** types: for the possible value of the ball speed and ball color.

```java
public enum BallColor {
  Red( Color .RED) ,
  Blue ( Color .BLUE) ,
  Green ( Color .GREEN) ;
  private Color color;

  BallColor (Color color) {
    this.color = color;
  }

  Color color () {
    return color;
  }
}

public enum BallSpeed {
  FAST(1) ,
  NORMAL(10) ,
  SLOW(20) ;
  private int speed;

  BallSpeed(int speed) {
    this.speed = speed;
  }
  int speed (){
    return speed;
  }
}
```

We set the ball color to red, blue, and green and the speed to fast, normal, or slow. Let us first examine the new version of the `BreakoutFrame` class that shows the menus.

```java
import javax.swing.*;
import java.awt.event.*;

public class BreakoutFrame extends JFrame {
  private static final int HEIGHT = 600;
  private static final int WIDTH = 488;
  private BreakoutPanel panel = new BreakoutPanel();

  public BreakoutFrame() {
    setDefaultCloseOperation(JFrame.DISPOSE_ON_CLOSE);
    displayMenu();
    setLocation(100, 100);
    setSize(WIDTH, HEIGHT);
    add(panel);
    setResizable(false);
  }
```

```java
public void displayMenu() {
  JMenuBar menuBar = new JMenuBar();
  menuBar.add(new GameMenu());
  menuBar.add(new ColorMenu());
  menuBar.add(new SpeedMenu());
  setJMenuBar(menuBar);
}

private class GameMenu extends JMenu {

  public GameMenu() {
    super("Game");
    JMenuItem startGameMI = new JMenuItem("Start",'S');
    startGameMI.setAccelerator(KeyStroke.getKeyStroke(KeyEvent.VK_S,
        InputEvent.CTRL_MASK));
    JMenuItem pauseMI = new JMenuItem("Pause", 'P');
    pauseMI.setAccelerator(KeyStroke.getKeyStroke(KeyEvent.VK_P,
        InputEvent.CTRL_MASK));
    JMenuItem quitMI = new JMenuItem("Quit");
    startGameMI.addActionListener(new ActionListener() {
      public void actionPerformed(ActionEvent e) {
        panel.start();
      }
    });
    pauseMI.addActionListener(new ActionListener() {
      public void actionPerformed(ActionEvent e) {
        panel.pause();
      }
    });
    quitMI.addActionListener(new ActionListener() {
      public void actionPerformed(ActionEvent e) {
        System.exit(0);
      }
    });

    add(startGameMI);
    add(pauseMI);
    add(quitMI);
  }
}

private class ColorMenu extends JMenu {
  public ColorMenu() {
    super("Ball Color");
    for (BallColor color : BallColor.values()) {
      JMenuItem menuItem = new JMenuItem(color.name() + " Ball");
      menuItem.addActionListener(new BallColorListener(color));
      add(menuItem);
    }
  }
}

private class BallColorListener implements ActionListener {
  private BallColor color;
```

```java
    public void actionPerformed(ActionEvent e) {
      panel.changeBallColor(color);
    }
    public BallColorListener(BallColor color) {
      this.color = color;
    }
  }

  private class SpeedMenu extends JMenu {
    public SpeedMenu() {
      super("Ball Speed");
      for (BallSpeed s : BallSpeed.values()) {
        JMenuItem menuItem = new JMenuItem(s.name());
        menuItem.addActionListener(new BallSpeedListener(s.speed()));
        add(menuItem);
      }
    }
  }

  private class BallSpeedListener implements ActionListener {
    private int speed;
    public void actionPerformed(ActionEvent e) {
      panel.changeBallSpeed(speed);
    }
    public BallSpeedListener(int speed) {
      this.speed = speed;
    }
  }
}
```

The constructor of the `BreakoutFrame` class calls the `displayMenu` method to display the menu. Let us first examine the constructor of the `GameMenu` class. The call `super("Game")` calls the constructor of the `JMenu` class to set the title of the menu. When the user clicks the `Start` or `Pause` menu item, we will call the `start` and `pause` methods of the `BreakoutPanel` class, respectively. If the user selects the `Quit` menu item, then the code executes `System.exit(0)` to terminate the program. Note that the `Timer` object interacts with the ball and other shapes of the panel class, and therefore it is defined inside the panel class. In the frame class we do not have direct access to the timer, but we can call methods of the panel class to start and stop the timer.

Note that the code `JMenuItem startGameMI = new JMenuItem("Start",'S')` creates a menu item and underlines the character S. The following code creates a key accelerator. It allows us to start the game by pressing `Ctrl+S` from the keyboard.

```java
startGameMI.setAccelerator(KeyStroke.getKeyStroke(KeyEvent.VK_S,
    InputEvent.CTRL_MASK))
```

Next, let us examine the `ColorMenu` class. Since `BallColor` is an `enum` type, we can use the syntax `BallColor.values()` to get all the possible values of the type. The code `color.name()` gives us the name that is associated with the color in the `enum` type. In our case, we will have the menu items: `Red Ball`, `Blue Ball`, and `Green Ball`. The constructor of the color listener simply saves the color. When one of the color menu items is selected, then the `changeBallColor` method is called for the panel. Since the ball is inside the panel class, we cannot directly change the color of the ball.

Lastly, the `SpeedMenu` class takes care of the speed menu. Again, since the ball is declared inside the panel, a method from the panel class needs to be called to change the speed of the ball.

Next, we will present the new code for the `BreakoutPanel` class. Note that now the ball does not start automatically. Therefore, the timer will be started in the `start` method and stopped in the `pause` method. We will also stop the timer when all lives are exhausted. However, we need to allow the option for the user to restart the game after the game finishes. For that reason, we introduce the Boolean variable `gameStarted`, which keeps track of whether or not the game is started.

```java
public class BreakoutPanel extends JPanel {
    private javax.swing.Timer timer;
    private Ball ball;
    private Paddle paddle;
    private Player player;
    private boolean gameStarted = false;

    ...

    public void start() {
        gameStarted = true;
        if (timer != null) {
            timer.stop();
        }
        if (!player.isAlive()) {
            player = new Player(); //restart the game
            ball = new Ball(Color.RED, this);
        }
        timer = new javax.swing.Timer(BallSpeed.NORMAL.speed(), new
            BreakoutPanel.TimeListener());
        timer.start();
        repaint();
    }

    public void pause() {
        if (timer == null) {
            return;
        }
        timer.stop();
    }

    public void changeBallColor(BallColor color) {
        ball.changeColor(color.color());
        repaint();
    }

    public void paintComponent(Graphics g) {
        super.paintComponent(g);
        Graphics2D g2 = (Graphics2D) g;

        if (!player.isAlive()) {
            showMessage("GAME OVER!", g2);
            gameStarted = false;
        } else {
            ball.draw(g2);
```

```
      paddle.draw(g2);
    }
    if (gameStarted) {
      player.draw(g2);
    }
  }

  public void changeBallSpeed(int speed) {
    timer.setDelay(speed);
  }
  ...
}
```

The setDelay method of the Timer class changes the delay of the timer. The color of the ball is changed by calling the changeColor method on the Ball class. Note that the Ball class actually does not have a changeColor method, and therefore the changeColor method of the BreakoutShape superclass is called. The stickmen are drawn only when the game has started.

Note that the start and stop methods are careful about the value of the variable timer. For example, the variable is initially equal to null when the program started. Therefore, the pause method needs to check that the variable is not equal to null before it stops the timer. Conversely, the start method needs to make sure that there is no timer that is currently running. If there is such a timer, then it is stopped before creating and starting the new timer.

If we run the program so far, we can use the menu to change the color of the ball, the speed of the ball, and to start and stop the game. The only thing that is left to do is add the bricks.

11.7 Adding the Bricks

As a last step, let us add the bricks to the game. Every time before we move the ball, we will now check that the virtual ball will not intersect one or more of the bricks. If it does, then the ball needs to bounce off the bricks. Note that in the current setup, the virtual ball can intersect at most two of the bricks. First, let us consider the new Brick class.

```
public class Brick extends BreakoutShape {
  private static final int HEIGHT = 10;
  private static final int WIDTH = 30;
  private static final int BRICK_H_GAP = 2;
  private static final int BRICK_V_GAP = 2;

  public Brick(int row, int col, Color color) {
    super(new Rectangle2D.Double(BRICK_H_GAP + row * (BRICK_H_GAP +
        Brick.WIDTH), BRICK_V_GAP + col * (BRICK_V_GAP + Brick.HEIGHT),
        WIDTH, HEIGHT), color, true);
  }

  private Brick(Rectangle2D rectangle, Color color){
    super(rectangle, color, true);
  }
```

```
public Brick add(Brick other){
  Rectangle2D rectangle1 = super.getBounds();
  Rectangle2D rectangle2 = other.getBounds();
  rectangle1.add(rectangle2);
  return new Brick(rectangle1,super.getColor());
}
}
```

The **add** method is used to *add* two bricks. Each of the bricks is first converted into a rectangle using the **getBounds()** method. Next, the **add** method for the **Rectangle** class is used to add the two rectangles. Finally, a brick is created from the new rectangle. Note that the constructor that creates a brick out of a rectangle is private because we only want to use it from within the **Brick** class. The **add** method is used when the virtual ball intersects two bricks. In this case, we will merge the bricks and bounce the ball off the new big brick. In practice, this only happens when there are two bricks that are adjacent horizontally or vertically.

Next, we will modify the **BreakoutShape** class. When the virtual ball intersects one or more bricks, we want to determine the relative location of the ball to the brick. That is, is the ball to the left, right, above, or below the brick. The trajectory of the ball will change accordingly.

```
public class BreakoutShape {
  private Color color;
  private boolean fill;
  private RectangularShape shape;

  public BreakoutShape(RectangularShape shape, Color color, boolean
      fill) {
    this.shape = shape;
    this.color = color;
    this.fill = fill;
  }
  public Color getColor() {
    return color;
  }

  protected Rectangle getBounds(){
    return shape.getBounds();
  }
  public void changeColor(Color color) {
    this.color = color;
  }

  public void draw(Graphics2D g2) {
    g2.setPaint(color);
    g2.draw(shape);
    if (fill) {
      g2.fill(shape);
    }
  }

  public double getX() {
    return shape.getX();
  }
```

```java
public double getY() {
    return shape.getY();
}

public double getHeight() {
    return shape.getHeight();
}

public double getWidth() {
    return shape.getWidth();
}

public boolean intersects(BreakoutShape other) {
    return shape.intersects(other.shape.getBounds());
}

public boolean below(BreakoutShape other) {
    return getY() >= other.getY() + other.getHeight();
}

public boolean above(BreakoutShape other) {
    return getY() + getHeight() <= other.getY();
}

public boolean leftOf(BreakoutShape other) {
    return getX() + getWidth() <= other.getX();
}

public boolean rightOf(BreakoutShape other) {
    return getX() >= other.getX() + other.getWidth();
}

public void move(int dx, int dy) {
    shape.setFrame(getX() + dx, getY() + dy, getWidth(), getHeight());
}
}
```

Let us examine the **below** method in greater detail, where the **above**, **leftOf**, and **rightOf** methods work in a similar way; see Figure 11.2. Assume that the ball is the object on which the method is called and the **other** object is a brick. The method adds **other.getY()** and **other.getHeight()**. This will give us the Y coordinate of the bottom side of the brick. If this number is smaller than or equal to the y coordinate of the ball (i.e., the top of the ball), then the method will return **true** (i.e., that ball is below the brick). Otherwise, the method will return **false**.

Lastly, let us examine the new version of the **BreakoutPanel** class, which is also the final version. Now an **ArrayList** of bricks will be created. Before the ball is moved, we will check to see if the virtual ball intersects with one of the bricks. If it does, then the trajectory of the ball is changed accordingly and the brick is removed from the **ArrayList**.

```java
public class BreakoutPanel extends JPanel {
    private static final int NUM_BRICK_ROWS = 10;
    private static final int NUM_BRICK_COLUMNS = 30;
    private javax.swing.Timer timer;
    private Ball ball;
    private ArrayList<Brick> bricks;
    private Paddle paddle;
```

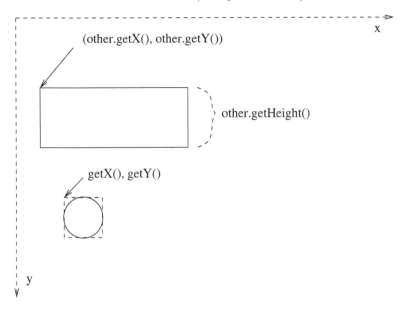

FIGURE 11.2: Explanation of the `below` method.

```java
private Player player;
private boolean gameStarted = false;

public BreakoutPanel() {
  ball = new Ball(BallColor.Red, this);
  paddle = new Paddle(Color.BLUE, this);
  bricks = new ArrayList<>();
  player = new Player();
  createBricks();
  addKeyListener(new KeyAdapter() {
    public void keyPressed(KeyEvent e) {
      String s = KeyEvent.getKeyText(e.getKeyCode());
      if (e.getKeyCode() == KeyEvent.VK_LEFT) {
        paddle.moveLeft();
      }
      if (s.equals("Right")) {
        paddle.moveRight();
      }
      repaint();
    }
  });
  setFocusable(true);
  addMouseMotionListener(new MouseMotionAdapter() {
    boolean firstTime = true;
    int oldX;

    public void mouseMoved(MouseEvent e) {
      if (firstTime) {
        oldX = e.getX();
        firstTime = false;
      }
      paddle.move(e.getX() - oldX);
```

```java
            oldX = e.getX();
            repaint();
        }
    });
}

private Color getRandomColor() {
    Color color = new Color((int) (Math.random() * 256), (int) (Math.
        random() * 256), (int) (Math.random() * 256));
    if (getBackground().equals(color)) {
        return Color.RED;
    }
    return color;
}

private void createBricks() {
    for (int row = 0; row < NUM_BRICK_ROWS; row++) {
        for (int col = 0; col < NUM_BRICK_COLUMNS; col++) {
            bricks.add(new Brick(row, col, getRandomColor()));
        }
    }
}

public void start() {
    gameStarted = true;
    if (timer != null) {
        timer.stop();
    }
    if (!player.isAlive()) {
        player = new Player();
        ball = new Ball(BallColor.Red, this);
        createBricks();
    }
    timer = new javax.swing.Timer(BallSpeed.NORMAL.speed(), new
        TimeListener());
    timer.start();
    repaint();
}

public void pause() {
    if (timer == null) {
        return;
    }
    timer.stop();
}

public void changeBallColor(BallColor color) {
    ball.changeColor(color);
    repaint();
}

public void showMessage(String s, Graphics2D g2) {
    Font myFont = new Font("SansSerif", Font.BOLD + Font.ITALIC, 40);
    g2.setFont(myFont);
    g2.setColor(Color.RED);
```

```
    Rectangle2D textBox = myFont.getStringBounds(s, g2.
        getFontRenderContext());
    g2.drawString(s, (int) (getWidth() / 2 - textBox.getWidth() / 2), (
        int) (getHeight() / 2 - textBox.getHeight()));
}

public void paintComponent(Graphics g) {
    super.paintComponent(g);
    Graphics2D g2 = (Graphics2D) g;

    if (bricks.size() == 0 && !gameStarted) {
        showMessage("YOU WIN!", g2);
        gameStarted = false;
    } else if (!player.isAlive()) {
        showMessage("GAME OVER!", g2);
        gameStarted = false;
    } else {
        ball.draw(g2);
        paddle.draw(g2);
        for (Brick brick : bricks) {
            brick.draw(g2);
        }
    }
    if (gameStarted) {
        player.draw(g2);
    }
}

public void changeBallSpeed(int speed) {
    timer.setDelay(speed);
}

class TimeListener implements ActionListener {
    public void bounceBall(Ball ball, Brick brick) {
        if (ball.below(brick)) {
            ball.goDown();
        }
        if (ball.above(brick)) {
            ball.goUp();
        }
        if (ball.leftOf(brick)) {
            ball.goLeft();
        }
        if (ball.rightOf(brick)) {
            ball.goRight();
        }
    }

    public void bounceBall(Ball ball, ArrayList<Brick> bricks) {
        if (bricks.size() == 0) {
            return;
        }
        if (bricks.size() == 1) {
            bounceBall(ball, bricks.get(0));
            return;
```

```
    }

    Brick combinedBrick = bricks.get(0).add(bricks.get(1));
    bounceBall(ball, combinedBrick);
  }

  public void actionPerformed(ActionEvent e) {
    Ball newBall = ball.getVirtualBall();
    ArrayList<Brick> bricksToBeDeleted = new ArrayList<Brick>();
    for (Brick brick : bricks) {
      if (brick.intersects(newBall)) {
        bricksToBeDeleted.add(brick);
      }
    }
    bounceBall(ball, bricksToBeDeleted);
    for (Brick brick : bricksToBeDeleted) {
      bricks.remove(brick);
    }
    if (newBall.intersects(paddle)) {
      ball.goUp();
      if (newBall.getX() + newBall.getWidth() / 2 < paddle.getX() +
          paddle.getWidth() / 2) {
        ball.goLeft();
      } else {
        ball.goRight();
      }
    } else if (ball.getY() > paddle.getY() - paddle.getHeight()) {
      player.killPlayer();
      ball.goUp();
    }
    ball.move();
    repaint();
  }
 }
}
```

In the `actionPerformed` method, we first collect the bricks that intersect the virtual ball and bounce the ball off the bricks by calling the `bounceBall` method. Note that we cannot delete a brick inside the loop that iterates over the bricks. If we try to do so, an exception of type `ConcurrentModificationException` will be generated. The reason is that an array or an `ArrayList` cannot be modified while it is traversed using a for-each `for` loop. An iterator is created while the elements are traversed and removing an element will make the method that gets the next element in the list ambiguous.

If the virtual ball intersects a single brick, then we simply check the location of the ball relative to the brick and change the trajectory of the ball accordingly. This is done in the first `bounceBall` method. If there are two bricks that intersect the virtual ball, then we merge the bricks and call the first `bounceBall` method again. This case only happens when the bricks are adjacent horizontally or vertically. Note that it is possible that a ball is both above and to the right of a brick. In this case, both the horizontal and vertical direction of the ball will be changed. The class also introduced the `createBricks` and `getRandomColor` methods, which were described in detail in Chapter 9.

We have also changed the `paintComponent` method. Now it checks if the game has started and the number of bricks is equal to zero. If this is the case, then this means that all the bricks have been destroyed and we have won the game. An appropriate message is displayed and the game is stopped. If he or she chooses to do so, the player can restart the game from the menu.

Compile and run the code. See if you can win!

11.8 Summary

The chapter presented the case study of creating a full working game. Many Java features were reviewed: creating subclasses, drawing shapes, different kinds of `if` and `for` statements, `enum` types, inheritance, event handling, and so on. Most importantly, the chapter demonstrated how to create the design and implement a non-trivial program. Here is a summary of the most important principles that were followed.

1. `Delegation` ⇒ Delegate responsibilities to classes and methods. For example, the `Ball` class should be responsible for the movement of the ball.

2. `Avoid long methods` ⇒ Every methods is simple and performs just one task. If a method becomes long, then it is broken down into several methods. For example, the `BreakoutPanel` constructor calls the `createBricks` method to create the bricks.

3. `Limit interaction between classes` ⇒ All data is declared `private`. Methods that should be not be accessed outside the class are also declared `private`. For example, the new constructors in the `Ball` and `Brick` class were defined private.

4. `Test often` ⇒ Do not write the whole program in one breath. Create a simple feature, test it, and make sure it works before proceeding to the next feature.

11.9 Syntax

- `t.setDelay(20);` ⇒ Changes the delay of the timer `t` to 20 milliseconds.

- `startGameMI.setAccelerator(KeyStroke.getKeyStroke(KeyEvent.VK_S,` `InputEvent.CTRL_MASK));` ⇒ When Ctrl+S is pressed, an `ActionEvent` will be generated by the menu item `startGameMI`.

- `shape.setFrame(getX() + dx, getY() + dy, getWidth(), getHeight());` ⇒ Change the surrounding frame of the `shape` object of type `RectangularShape`.

- `shape.getBounds()` ⇒ Returns the bounds of a shape as an object of type `Rectangle`.

- `String s = KeyEvent.getKeyText(e.getKeyCode());` ⇒ Computes a textual description of the key that is pressed. For example, the value of `s` can be "F1", "Space", "Esc", etc.

- `Rectangle r3 = r1.add(r2);` ⇒ Code that adds two rectangles. The result is the smallest rectangle that encompasses rectangles `r1` and `r2`.

- for(int el: a){ ... a.remove(...) ... } ⇒ Will generate ConcurrentModificationException because it is illegal to modify an array or an ArrayList while there is an iterator (i.e., a for-each `for` loop) active on it.

11.10   Important Points

1. Before starting to write a big software system, we should always create a preliminary design of our classes.

2. This design will change with time. New features will be added and existing features will change. This is part of the development process.

3. Start by creating a small program and test it. Next, add new features incrementally and always make sure that the current code is working before extending it.

4. When creating a class, start with the data. Build the methods around the data. Remember that every class has the responsibility to provide public interface to its data. The methods in every class should be simple and provide a single function. Break down long methods by creating private methods that perform part of the required work. Creating private constructors can be part of this process.

11.11   Exercises

1. The JColorChooser class can be used to get a color from the user. Change the game Breakout and add a menu item option that allows the user to enter his or her own color. Read the JavaDoc for the class to find more information on how to use it.

2. Create a simple program with a menu that can be used to change the background color of the panel. Use the setBackground method to change the color of the panel. Allow the color of the panel to also be changed using accelerator keys. For example, Ctrl+B should change the color to blue.

3. Modify the game so that the ball changes trajectory more randomly after hitting an object. You can achieve this by allowing the variables dx and dy of the Ball class to take values other than 1 and −1. You may even define them as doubles and use a function of the value that is returned by Math.random to set their new values.

4. Modify the game so the bricks fill the whole top of the window and the small gap in the right part of the window is removed.

5. Add code that allows the player to start/pause the game by pressing the right mouse button.

FIGURE 11.3: Pieces of the Tetris game.

11.12   Lab

Modify the game `Breakout` by allowing the user to fire bullets. A bullet can be fired by pressing the `Space` key on the keyboard. When a bullet hits a brick, the brick and the bullet should both be destroyed. The bullet should be destroyed if it reaches the top of the panel without hitting a brick. If the bullet hits the ball, then a life should be lost.

11.13   Project

Create a version of the Tetris game. Different shapes can fall from the top of the screen. Allow the player to move the shapes using the arrow keys. Each shape should consist of four blocks, where the possible shapes are shown in Figure 11.3. Pressing the key `Space` should rotate the shape. Pressing the down key should move the shape down to its place. The playing area should be 10 blocks wide and 40 blocks high. When a horizontal line becomes full, the line should be removed from the screen. Feel free to create levels. For example, the user can move to the next level after removing 10 lines. As the levels increase, the bricks should drop faster. Create a way to score the performance of the player and display the score in the top right corner of the screen outside the playing area. The game ends when the playing area is full and a shape cannot drop from the top of the screen.

Chapter 12

Layout Management and GUI Components

So far, we have seen how to create menus and how to draw graphics and pictures on a panel. In this chapter, we will see how to display different graphic user interface (GUI) components inside a window. These include buttons, labels, text fields, text areas, combo boxes, check boxes, radio buttons, and so on. However, the goal of this chapter is not to list all GUI components that are available in Swing. Rather, we will list the main GUI components and we will show how to use them as part of building working software. We will also show how the components can be arranged inside a window and we will explore the *flow layout*, *border layout*, and *grid layout*. As part of presenting the material, working code for simple programs, such as converting Celsius to Fahrenheit, a calculator program, and a poor man's version of Notepad, will be presented.

12.1   Creating Buttons

The simplest type of a GUI component is a button. A button has text that is displayed on it. We will start with a very simple application that displays a button. Initially, the button will have the text **Press me please**. Once the button is pressed, its text will change to **Thank you!**.

```
import java.awt.event.*;
import javax.swing.*;

public class ButtonGame {
  public static void main(String[] args) {
    MyFrame f = new MyFrame();
```

```
      f.setVisible(true);
   }
}

class MyFrame extends JFrame {
   public MyFrame() {
      final JButton button = new JButton("Press me please");
      button.addActionListener(new ActionListener() {
         public void actionPerformed(ActionEvent e) {
            button.setText("Thank You!");
         }
      });
      add(button);
      pack();
   }
}
```

First, note that no panel is created. The button is added directly to the window. It turns out that every window has a default canvas to which one can add GUI components. However, if we want to use the `paintComponent()` method to draw something, then we need to create a `JPanel`. A button belongs to the `JButton` class (we have the letter J because we are using Swing). As the example shows, the constructor of the `JButton` class takes as input the text of the button. An empty constructor that creates a button with no text is also available. A button is a very simple component. The only thing that can happen in the life of a button is that it is pressed. Therefore, a button generates action events when it is being pressed. One can register an event listener with a button by calling the `addActionListener` method. When the button is pressed, the `actionPerformed` method of the event listener is called. The `setText` method changes the text of the button. Note that most of the GUI components that we will examine in this chapter belong to Swing. Remember that all classes in Swing start with the letter J.

The `pack` method is used to automatically set the size of the window. The method evaluates the size of the components inside the window and sets the window size accordingly. Note that the method should be called after all the components are added to the window. Go ahead and run the application. Note that when the window is resized, the button continues to take the whole window.

12.2   Flow Layout

The flow layout is the simplest layout and it is the default layout for panels. The idea of the flow layout is that the GUI components fill the container starting from the top left corner and filling it line by line. To see how this works, let us create a very simple application that displays three buttons that do nothing.

```
import java.awt.*;
import javax.swing.*;

public class Test{
   public static void main(String[] args){
      MyFrame f = new MyFrame();
      f.setVisible(true);
   }
```

```
}

class MyFrame extends JFrame {
    public MyFrame() {
        JButton button1 = new JButton("First Button");
        JButton button2 = new JButton("Second Button");
        JButton button3 = new JButton("Third Button");
        setLayout(new FlowLayout());
        add(button1);
        add(button2);
        add(button3);
        pack();
    }
}
```

Initially, all three buttons are displayed on the same line. However, if the window is resized and made narrower, then the buttons are rearranged on several lines. The idea is that the first line is filled with components. When the first line becomes full, the second line is filled with components and so on.

Note that the `setLayout` method takes as input a layout object. There are several versions of the constructor of the `FlowLayout` class. For example, the call `setLayout(new FlowLayout(FlowLayout.LEFT))` will make the components left justified, where 5 pixels are left between components by default. Alternatively, the call `setLayout(new FlowLayout(FlowLayout.LEFT,2,10))` will leave a 2-pixel horizontal gap and a 10-pixel vertical gap between components, where the components will be left justified again. We can also use the constant `FlowLayout.RIGHT` to make the layout right justified. By default, the components are placed in the center.

Usually, several panels are inserted inside a window and the flow layout is used to place the components in each panel. This is the reason that the flow layout is the default layout for panels.

12.3 Border Layout

The border layout is the default layout for an object of type `JFrame`. As Figure 12.1 suggests, one can place a component in one of five locations. When a component is added to the window, we can specify the area in which to place the component. By default, a component is placed in the center. Note that only one component can be placed in each area. If a second component is placed in the same area, then it will be placed on top of the first component. In our example with one button, the button was placed in the center using the border layout. Note that the center region takes all unused space – in this case the whole window. When the window is resized, the center area is the only area that changes size.

In order to better understand how the border layout works, we will create an example application that simply adds five panels with different colors in the five areas of the border layout.

```
import java.awt.*;
import javax.swing.*;

public class Test{
```

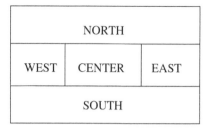

FIGURE 12.1: The border layout.

```
public static void main(String[] args){
  MyFrame f = new MyFrame();
  f.setVisible(true);
  }
}

class MyFrame extends JFrame {
  public MyFrame() {
    JPanel p1 = new JPanel();
    p1.setBackground(Color.RED);
    JPanel p2 = new JPanel();
    p2.setBackground(Color.GREEN);
    JPanel p3 = new JPanel();
    p3.setBackground(Color.ORANGE);
    JPanel p4 = new JPanel();
    p4.setBackground(Color.WHITE);
    JPanel p5 = new JPanel();
    p5.setBackground(Color.BLACK);
    add(p1, BorderLayout.NORTH);
    add(p2, BorderLayout.WEST);
    add(p3, BorderLayout.CENTER);
    add(p4, BorderLayout.EAST);
    add(p5, BorderLayout.SOUTH);
    pack();
  }
}
```

Note that the non-center areas are small. The reason is that their size is automatically determined by the components in them. Since in this case they are empty panels, the default minimal size is used. As the window is resized, only the center panel changes size. One can specify that a panel is to use the border layout. For example, the code `p1.setLayout(new BorderLayout())` will make panel `p1` use the border layout.

12.4   Text Fields and Labels

Next, we will write a program that converts between degrees Celsius and degrees Fahrenheit. The program will have the design that is shown in Figure 12.2. We will create three panels: in the north, center, and south. We will make the frame non-resizable so that the

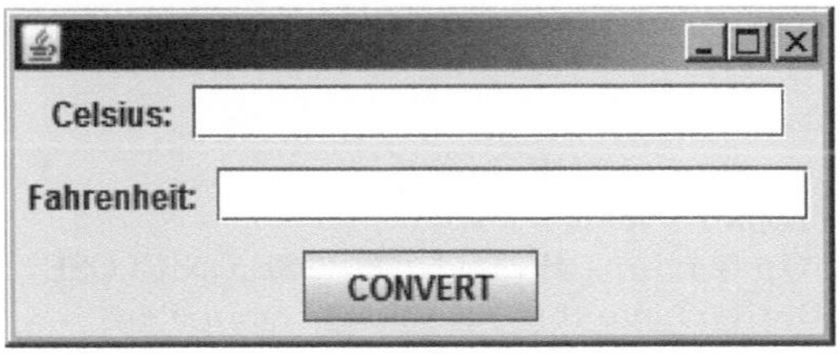

FIGURE 12.2: Degree converter program.

user cannot see our design. The north panel consists of two components: a label and a text field.

A label can be created by instantiating an object from the `JLabel` class. The text of the label goes in the constructor of the class. The label is usually added to a frame or a panel using the `add` method.

A text field can be created by instantiating in an object from the `JTextField` class. Constructors of the object take as input the approximate size of the text field (in characters) and/or the initial text of the text field. The text field is usually added to a frame or panel using the `add` method.

For example, the north panel can be created as follows.

```
JPanel cPanel = new JPanel();
cPanel.add(new JLabel("Celsius: "));
JTextField cField = new JTextField(20);
cPanel.add(cField);
```

The number 20 in the constructor of the `JTextField` class represents the approximate size of the text field in characters. Since every character can have a different width, this is an approximate number. Since the default layout for a panel is the flow layout with center placement, the label and the text field will be centered in the middle of the panel. The panel can be added to the window as follows.

```
add(cPanel, BorderLayout.NORTH);
```

This means that the panel will be added at the north part of the window. This syntax is allowed because the default layout for the window is the border layout.

Below is the complete code for the degree converter program. Note that the `getText` method can be used to retrieve the text from a text field, while the `setText` method can be used to set it. The `trim` method removes leading and trailing spaces. It is always a good idea to call it after reading a string from a text field.

```
import java.awt.*;
import java.awt.event.*;
import javax.swing.*;

public class DegreeConverter{
  public static void main(String[] args){
    ConverterFrame f = new ConverterFrame();
    f.setVisible(true);
```

```
      }
}

class ConverterFrame extends JFrame {
  public ConverterFrame() {
    setDefaultCloseOperation(JFrame.DISPOSE_ON_CLOSE);
    setLayout(new BorderLayout()); //not required
    JPanel cPanel = new JPanel();
    JPanel fPanel = new JPanel();
    JPanel buttonPanel = new JPanel();
    final JTextField cField = new JTextField(20);
    final JTextField fField = new JTextField(20);
    cPanel.add(new JLabel("Celsius: "));
    cPanel.add(cField);
    fPanel.add(new JLabel("Fahrenheit: "));
    fPanel.add(fField);
    JButton convertButton = new JButton("CONVERT");
    buttonPanel.add(convertButton);
    add(cPanel, BorderLayout.NORTH);
    add(fPanel, BorderLayout.CENTER);
    add(buttonPanel, BorderLayout.SOUTH);
    convertButton.addActionListener(new ActionListener() {
      public void actionPerformed(ActionEvent e) {
        if (cField.getText().trim().equals("") && fField.getText().trim
            ().equals("")) {
          return;
        }
        if (cField.getText().trim().equals("")) {
          String result = fField.getText().trim();
          double number = Double.parseDouble(result);
          number = (number-32)*(5/9.0);
          cField.setText("" + number);
        }
        if (fField.getText().trim().equals("")) {
          String result = cField.getText().trim();
          double number = Double.parseDouble(result);
          number = number * (9 / 5.0) + 32;
          fField.setText("" + number);
        }
      }
    });
    pack();
  }
}
```

The code creates three panels: in the north, center, and south. In each panel, several components are added. Since the default layout for a panel is the flow layout, the components are added in the panel using the flow layout (i.e., they are placed from left to right inside the panel). The `actionPerformed` method is associated with the `CONVERT` button. The method first checks if both the Celsius and Fahrenheit text fields are empty. If this is the case, then there is nothing to do. If only one of them is empty, then its value is calculated based on the value of the other field. The `parseDouble` static method of the `Double` class is used to convert a `String` to a `double`. There is also a `parseInt` static method in the class `Integer` that converts a string to an integer. If the conversion fails, that is, the input is not a number, then an exception is raised. The `setText` method is used to set the new value of the text fields. Note the two text fields need to be declared as `final`. If they were not `final`, then they could not be accessed from the anonymous local class that inherits from the class `ActionListener`.

12.5 Grid Layout

We will next build a simple calculator. Figure 12.3 shows what our calculator will look like. We will create three panels in the window: in the north, south, and center. The panel in the middle will use the *grid layout*.

> Whenever components need to be placed in a grid, one can use the grid layout. When adding the components to a grid layout, the rows are filled from left to right and from top to bottom. In other words, the first row is filled first and so on. The call to the constructor `new GridLayout(3,5)` will create a 3x5 grid (3 rows and 5 columns). Alternatively, the call `new GridLayout(2,4,3,6)` will generate a grid with 2 rows, 4 columns, a 3-pixel horizontal gap, and a 6-pixel vertical gap between the components.

For the calculator application, we will create a 4x4 grid in the center. Our calculator will have very simple behavior. When the `CLEAR` button is pressed, the text field in the top will be cleared. Alternatively, when the `EVALUATE` button is pressed, the expression in the text field will be evaluated and its value will be displayed in the text field. Since computing arithmetic expressions is beyond the scope of this book, we will use the JavaScript function `eval` to evaluate an expression. Note that `JavaScript` is a programming language that is different from Java. However, there is a mechanism for calling `JavaScript` functions from Java. The complete code for the calculator program follows.

```
import java.awt.*;
import java.awt.event.*;
import javax.swing.*;
import javax.script.*;

public class Calculator{
```

FIGURE 12.3: Calculator program.

```java
  public static void main(String[] args) throws Exception{
    CalculatorFrame f = new CalculatorFrame();
    f.setVisible(true);
  }
}


class CalculatorFrame extends JFrame {
  JTextField text = new JTextField(20);

  public CalculatorFrame() throws Exception {
    setDefaultCloseOperation(JFrame.DISPOSE_ON_CLOSE);
    JPanel displayPanel = new JPanel();
    JPanel buttonPanel = new JPanel();
    JPanel bottomPanel = new JPanel();

    displayPanel.add(text);
    String[] buttonNames = {"7", "8", "9", "+", "4", "5", "6", "-", "1"
        , "2", "3", "*", "0", "(", ")", "/"};
    buttonPanel.setLayout(new GridLayout(4, 4, 5, 5));
    for (String el : buttonNames) {
      buttonPanel.add(new CalculatorButton(el));
    }
    JButton evaluateButton = new JButton("EVALUATE");
    JButton clearButton = new JButton("CLEAR");
    clearButton.addActionListener(new ActionListener() {
      public void actionPerformed(ActionEvent e) {
        text.setText("");
      }
    });
    evaluateButton.addActionListener(new ActionListener() {
      public void actionPerformed(ActionEvent e) {
        try {
          String s = (new ScriptEngineManager().getEngineByName("
              JavaScript").eval(text.getText().trim())).toString();
          text.setText(s);
        } catch (Exception exc) {
          text.setText("");
        }
      }
    });
    bottomPanel.add(new CalculatorButton("."));
    bottomPanel.add(clearButton);
    bottomPanel.add(evaluateButton);

    add(displayPanel, BorderLayout.NORTH);
    add(buttonPanel, BorderLayout.CENTER);
    add(bottomPanel, BorderLayout.SOUTH);
    setResizable(false);
    pack();
  }

  private class CalculatorButton extends JButton {
    public CalculatorButton(String name) {
      super(name);
```

```
     addActionListener(new ActionListener() {
       public void actionPerformed(ActionEvent e) {
         text.setText(text.getText().trim() + CalculatorButton.super.
           getText());
       }
     });
   }
 }
}
```

Note that all the number and operation buttons act similarly and therefore they belong to same `CalculatorButton` class. Examine the body of the constructor of the `CalculatorButton` class. The `super(name)` call creates the button. The action listener is notified when the button is pressed. It responds by appending the text from the button to the text field in the north. Note the strange syntax: `CalculatorButton.super.getText()`. The expression `CalculatorButton.super` refers to the super class of the outer object (i.e., the JButton). On the button object, the `getText` method is called. Note that we could have also used the simpler syntax `text.setText(text.getText().trim() + getText())`. Since there is no `getText` method in the local anonymous class, a method with name `getText` is searched for in the outer object and its super objects.

Next, let us examine the action listener for the button `EVALUATE`. The `eval` method from JavaScript is used to evaluate the value of the expression in the text field. Once the expression is evaluated, it is placed in the top text field. Note that the call may create an exception if the expression is not mathematically sound. In this case, we simply change the text field to display the empty string.

12.6 Creating Text Areas with Scroll Bars

We will next create a poor man's Notepad. For starters, we need an area where the user can type text. Such an area can be created by instantiating an object of type `JTextArea`.

The `JTextArea` class has an empty constructor that creates the text area and the size is automatically set. An object of type text area can also be created as follows: `new JTextArea(20,30)`. This creates a text area that has 30 lines. The number 20 represents the approximate width of the text area in characters (i.e., one can fit approximately 20 characters per line).

We will start by adding a text area to the center of the window. We will want this area to display scroll bars when needed. In order to do so, we will create an instance of the `JScrollPane` class and add it to the window. The constructor of the class takes as input the text area where the scroll bars should be added. Here is our initial version of the program.

```
import java.awt.*;
import javax.swing.*;

public class Notepad{
  public static void main(String[] args) {
    NotepadFrame f = new NotepadFrame();
    f.setVisible(true);
```

```
    }
}

class NotepadFrame extends JFrame{
  private static int WIDTH = 600;
  private static int HEIGHT = 600;
  public NotepadFrame(){
    setSize(WIDTH,HEIGHT);
    setDefaultCloseOperation(JFrame.DISPOSE_ON_CLOSE);
    JTextArea textArea = new JTextArea();
    add(new JScrollPane(textArea),BorderLayout.CENTER);
  }
}
```

If you run the application, you will see a text area where one can enter text. Scroll bars appear only when the text is too big to be displayed in the window. Note that the code `BorderyLayout.CENTER` is optional because by default a component is added in the center when the border layout is used and border layout is the default layout for frames. Similar to the `JTextField` class, the `JTextArea` class supports the `getText` and `setText` methods for getting and setting the text. Note that both methods work with strings, where a string can contain multiple lines that are separated by the character '\n'. In addition, the `JTextArea` class supports the `append` method for appending text to the `JTextArea` class.

12.7   The Combo Box

Our Notepad application looks pretty basic even for a poor man's version. To make the program more interesting, we will next add a feature for changing the font of the text; see Figure 12.4. As the figure suggests, we will add a panel to the north part of the window. In the panel, we will add a combo box that displays all the fonts that are supported by the operating system.

First, we need to determine the fonts that are available from the operating system. The following expression will give us this set as an array of strings.

```
String[] fontNames = GraphicsEnvironment.getLocalGraphicsEnvironment().
    getAvailableFontFamilyNames();
```

Next, we will create a combo box, which is also known as a drop-down list. We can use the empty constructor of the `JComboBox` class to create a combo box and then add the elements using the `addItem` method. Alternatively, an array of objects can be specified in the constructor. The `getSelectedItem` method can be used on a combo box to find the item that is selected, where the method returns an object of type `Object`.

Next, let us examine the `Font` class, which is used to create a new font.

The most common constructor of the `Font` class takes as input three parameters: the name of the font, the style of the text (e.g., bold), and the point size of the font. Possible values for the style of the text include `Font.PLAIN`, `Font.BOLD`, `Font.Italic`, where values can be combined by adding them. For example, `Font.Bold+Font.Italic` creates style that is both bold and italic.

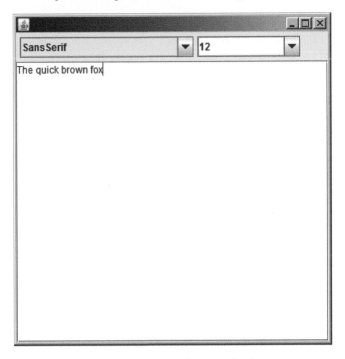

FIGURE 12.4: A font combo box.

Sometimes, we just want to create a font object without examining the fonts that are available in the operating system. This is why Java always supports to following five basic fonts: `SansSerif`, `Serif`, `Monospaced`, `Dialog`, and `DialogInput`. In our example, we can create the font combo box as follows.

```
JComboBox fontComboBox = new JComboBox(fontNames);
```

We will also create a combo box for the size.

```
JComboBox sizeComboBox = new JComboBox();
for(int i = 8; i<=72; i++){
   sizeComboBox.addItem(i);
}
```

The `addItem` method adds the specified object to the combo box. In our example, the integers are automatically converted to objects of type `Integer`.

Here is the rewritten version of the `NotepadFrame` class that supports a font and size chooser.

```
import java.awt.*;
import java.awt.event.*;
import javax.swing.*;


public class Notepad{
   public static void main(String[] args) {
      NotepadFrame f = new NotepadFrame();
      f.setVisible(true);
   }
}
```

```
class NotepadFrame extends JFrame{
  private static int WIDTH = 600;
  private static int HEIGHT = 600;
  public NotepadFrame(){
    setDefaultCloseOperation(JFrame.DISPOSE_ON_CLOSE);
    setSize(WIDTH,HEIGHT);
    final JTextArea textArea = new JTextArea();
    add(new JScrollPane(textArea),BorderLayout.CENTER);
    JPanel controlPanel = new JPanel();
    controlPanel.setLayout(new FlowLayout(FlowLayout.LEFT));
    String[] fontNames = GraphicsEnvironment.
                      getLocalGraphicsEnvironment().
                        getAvailableFontFamilyNames();
    final JComboBox fontComboBox = new JComboBox(fontNames);
    fontComboBox.setSelectedItem("SansSerif");
    final JComboBox sizeComboBox = new JComboBox();
    for(int i = 8; i <= 72; i++){
      sizeComboBox.addItem(i);
    }
    sizeComboBox.setSelectedItem(12);
    sizeComboBox.setEditable(true);
    ActionListener changeListener = new ActionListener(){
      public void actionPerformed(ActionEvent e){
          textArea.setFont(new Font((String)fontComboBox.
                  getSelectedItem(),Font.PLAIN,(Integer)sizeComboBox.
                  getSelectedItem()));
      }
    };
    fontComboBox.addActionListener(changeListener);
    sizeComboBox.addActionListener(changeListener);
    controlPanel.add(fontComboBox);
    controlPanel.add(sizeComboBox);
    add(controlPanel,BorderLayout.NORTH);
  }
}
```

The font of the text area is set by calling the `setFont` method. Note that the variable `textArea` is defined as final because it is referenced in a local anonymous class. Note that the `setSelectedItem` method is used to set a default font and default size for the text. The method takes as input an object and selects that object in the combo box. Note as well that there is a `getSelectedItem` method that returns the selected element of the combo box. Since the method returns an object, a cast to the appropriate type is needed (in our case, to `String` and to `Integer`). The `setEditable` method can make the combo box editable or not editable. If the combo box is editable, then the user can type text in the combo box. Otherwise, they can just selected one of the available menu options. By default, a combo box is not editable. By making the `size` combo box editable, we have allowed the user to type in the size of the font.

Note that inside the `actionPerformed` method we directly referred to the combo box. If we did not have access to the combo box, then we could have used the call `e.getSource()` to get the source of the action listener event.

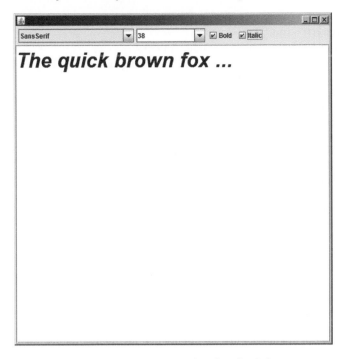

FIGURE 12.5: Example of a check box.

12.8 Check Boxes

Next, we will examine how to add check boxes to our Notepad application. A check box can be either checked on unchecked. In our example, we will add check boxes to selected whether the font should be bold and whether it should be italic; see Figure 12.5.

A check box can be created by calling the constructor for the `JCheckBox` class. One possible input to the constructor is the text that is to be displayed next to the check box. A check box is similar to a button and an action listener can be associated with it. The `isSelected` method can be used to examine if the check box is selected. The modified version of the code is shown next.

```java
import java.awt.*;
import java.awt.event.*;
import javax.swing.*;

public class Test{
  public static void main(String[] args) {
    NotepadFrame f = new NotepadFrame();
    f.setVisible(true);
  }
}

class NotepadFrame extends JFrame {
  private static int WIDTH = 600;
  private static int HEIGHT = 600;

  public NotepadFrame() {
```

```
setDefaultCloseOperation(JFrame.DISPOSE_ON_CLOSE);
setSize(WIDTH, HEIGHT);
final JTextArea textArea = new JTextArea();
add(new JScrollPane(textArea), BorderLayout.CENTER);
JPanel controlPanel = new JPanel();
controlPanel.setLayout(new FlowLayout(FlowLayout.LEFT));
String[] fontNames = GraphicsEnvironment.
    getLocalGraphicsEnvironment().
        getAvailableFontFamilyNames();
final JComboBox fontComboBox = new JComboBox(fontNames);
fontComboBox.setSelectedItem("SansSerif");
final JComboBox sizeComboBox = new JComboBox();
final JCheckBox boldCheckBox = new JCheckBox("Bold");
final JCheckBox italicCheckBox = new JCheckBox("Italic");
for (int i = 8; i <= 72; i++) {
  sizeComboBox.addItem(i);
}
sizeComboBox.setSelectedItem(12);
sizeComboBox.setEditable(true);
ActionListener changeListener = new ActionListener() {
  public void actionPerformed(ActionEvent e) {
    int mask = Font.PLAIN;
    if (boldCheckBox.isSelected()) {
      mask += Font.BOLD;
    }
    if (italicCheckBox.isSelected()) {
      mask += Font.ITALIC;
    }
    textArea.setFont(new Font((String) fontComboBox.getSelectedItem
        (), mask, (Integer) sizeComboBox.getSelectedItem()));
  }
};
fontComboBox.addActionListener(changeListener);
sizeComboBox.addActionListener(changeListener);
boldCheckBox.addActionListener(changeListener);
italicCheckBox.addActionListener(changeListener);
controlPanel.add(fontComboBox);
controlPanel.add(sizeComboBox);
controlPanel.add(boldCheckBox);
controlPanel.add(italicCheckBox);
add(controlPanel, BorderLayout.NORTH);
  }
}
```

Note that the mask of the font is set based on the state of the bold and italic check boxes. Note as well that a single action listener is associated with the two combo boxes and the two check boxes. The reason is that a single event handler is responsible for changing the font. The `actionPerformed` method sets the font, the size of the font, and its style.

12.9 Radio Buttons

Radio buttons are similar to check boxes because they can be either checked or unchecked. However, there are two major differences. First, unlike check boxes, radio buttons are round. Second, radio buttons are usually logically placed inside the same button group. Only one radio button can be selected at any time inside a button group. When a radio button is pressed, the last radio button in the button group that was selected is deselected. To see how radio buttons work, here is a very simple program.

```java
import java.awt.*;
import javax.swing.*;


public class Test{
  public static void main(String[] args) {
    NumbersFrame f = new NumbersFrame();
    f.setVisible(true);
  }
}

class NumbersFrame extends JFrame{
  public NumbersFrame(){
    setSize(400,100);
    JPanel p = new JPanel();
    add(p,BorderLayout.NORTH);
    JRadioButton upButton = new JRadioButton("Increment",true);
    JRadioButton downButton = new JRadioButton("Decrement",false);
    p.add(upButton);
    p.add(downButton);
    ButtonGroup group = new ButtonGroup();
    group.add(upButton);
    group.add(downButton);
  }
}
```

The program's window is shown in Figure 12.6. Note that the text field in the figure will be added in the next section. The constructor of the `JRadioButton` class takes as input the name of the button and a Boolean variable that specifies if the button is initially selected. Note that at most one radio button in the group can be initially selected.

There is no J before the name of the `ButtonGroup` class. The reason is that this is a logical class and is not part of the Swing library. The `add` method is used to add radio buttons to a button group. In every button group, at most one radio button can be selected. Note that if the button group was not created and the radio buttons added to it, then both the `Increment` and `Decrement` radio buttons could be selected at the same time. If you run the program, you will see that only one radio button in the group can be selected at any given time.

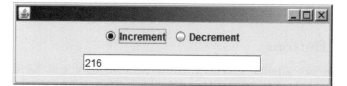

FIGURE 12.6: Example of radio buttons.

12.10   Document Listeners

The following interface is part of the library `javax.swing.event.*`.

```
interface DocumentListener{
    public void insertUpdate(DocumentEvent e);
    public void removeUpdate(DocumentEvent e);
    public void changedUpdate(DocumentEvent e);
}
```

This interface can be used to create a listener that can be added to a document. The `insertUpdate` method is called when a new character is inserted in the text. The `removeUpdate` method is called when text is deleted. The `changeUpdate` method is called every time the text is modified. Given a text field or a text area, the `getDocument` method returns the document that is associated with the field (i.e., an object of type `Document`). The `addDocumentListener` method can be used to register an event listener with the document.

Next, let us extend the application from the last section by adding a text field. The text field will contain a number that increases by one every second. If the radio button `Decrement` is selected, then the value in the text field will start decrementing by one every second. Conversely, if the radio button `Increment` is selected, then the value in the text field will increment by one every second. At the same time, we will add a listener to the text field that allows the user to enter a new value for the text field. Here is the complete code.

```java
import java.awt.*;
import java.awt.event.*;
import javax.swing.*;
import javax.swing.event.*;

public class Test{
    public static void main(String[] args) {
        NumbersFrame f = new NumbersFrame();
        f.setVisible(true);
    }
}

class NumbersFrame extends JFrame {
    JRadioButton upButton;
    JRadioButton downButton;
    public NumbersFrame() {
        setSize(400,100);
        JPanel p = new JPanel();
        add(p, BorderLayout.NORTH);
        upButton = new JRadioButton("Increment", true);
```

```
    downButton = new JRadioButton("Decrement", true);
    p.add(upButton);
    p.add(downButton);
    ButtonGroup group = new ButtonGroup();
    group.add(upButton);
    group.add(downButton);
    CenterPanel centerPanel = new CenterPanel();
    add(centerPanel, BorderLayout.CENTER);
  }

  class CenterPanel extends JPanel {
    JTextField textField = new JTextField("0", 20);
    int x = 0;

    public CenterPanel() {
      add(textField);
      Timer t = new Timer(1000, new ActionListener() {
        public void actionPerformed(ActionEvent e) {
          if (upButton.isSelected()) x++;
          if(downButton.isSelected()) x--;
          textField.setText("" + x);
        }
      });
      t.start();
      textField.getDocument().addDocumentListener(new DocumentListener
          () {
        public void insertUpdate(DocumentEvent e) {
          try {
            x = Integer.parseInt(textField.getText().trim());
          } catch (Exception es) {
          }
        }
        public void removeUpdate(DocumentEvent e) {
          try {
            x = Integer.parseInt(textField.getText().trim());
          } catch (Exception es) {
          }
        }
        public void changedUpdate(DocumentEvent e) {
        }
      });
    }
  }
}
```

The program stores a variable x, which is displayed in the text field. A timer that changes the value of x every second is created. The `isSlected` method checks which radio button is selected. Depending on the outcome, the value of x is incremented or decremented by one. The user can also manually change the value of x. Every time something is inserted in or deleted from the text field, a method is called. In both cases, the variable x is updated to the new value of the text field. Note that the `parseInt` method is used to convert a string to an integer. If the user does not type in an integer, then an exception is raised. The `try-catch` blocks guarantee that in this situation the program simply continues to increment or decrement the value x and disregards the user input.

FIGURE 12.7: Example of a dialog box.

12.11   Creating Dialog Boxes

A dialog box is similar to a window (i.e., a `JFrame`). However, it cannot be minimized or restored. It has a single close button in the top right-hand corner of the window. For example, when you create a game, you may want to add an `About` dialog box; see Figure 12.7. This can include your name, when the game was developed, copyright considerations, and so on. A dialog box has a key property that distinguishes it from a regular window. It can be either *modal* or *modeless*.

> A *modal* dialog box prevents interaction with all other windows of the application. A *modeless* dialog box allows us to interact with it and other windows of the application at the same time.

A dialog box is created by creating an object of type `JDialog`. The constructor takes as input a reference to the parent window, the title of the dialog box, and a Boolean value. If the Boolean value is `true`, then the dialog is modal. Otherwise, the dialog is modeless. Note that a reference to the parent window is needed in order to disable interaction with the parent window when the dialog box is modal.

Below is a simple example of how to create an about dialog window. The `AboutFrame` class creates a menu bar that has a single menu and a single menu item. When the menu item is selected, an about dialog box is created and displayed.

```java
import java.awt.event.*;
import javax.swing.*;


public class AboutProgram{
    public static void main(String[] args) {
        AboutFrame f = new AboutFrame();
```

```
      f.setVisible(true);
  }
}

class AboutFrame extends JFrame {
  public AboutFrame() {
    setSize(300, 300);
    JMenuBar menuBar = new JMenuBar();
    setJMenuBar(menuBar);
    JMenu helpMenu = new JMenu("Help");
    menuBar.add(helpMenu);
    JMenuItem aboutMI = new JMenuItem("About");
    helpMenu.add(aboutMI);
    aboutMI.addActionListener(new ActionListener() {
      public void actionPerformed(ActionEvent e) {
        AboutDialog dialog = new AboutDialog(AboutFrame.this);
        dialog.setSize(100, 100);
        dialog.setVisible(true);
      }
    });
  }
}

class AboutDialog extends JDialog {
  public AboutDialog(JFrame owner) {
    super(owner, "About", true);
    JLabel label = new JLabel("It's all about me!");
    add(label);
  }
}
```

Examine the constructor of the `AboutDialog` class. The first line simply creates a `JDialog` with the title `About`. A reference to the parent window is needed in order to create the dialog. The third parameter simply makes the panel modal. Next, examine the `actionPerformed` method that is called when the menu item is selected. The `AboutFrame.this` reference refers to the current object of the outer class. We need this syntax because the `actionPerformed` method is inside a local anonymous class and the `this` reference will return a reference to the event listener. Lastly, note that an object of type `JDialog` is similar to an object of type `JFrame`. Methods, such as `setVisible` and `setSize` are still applicable. The first method sets the size of the dialog box, while the second method makes the dialog box visible.

Run the application. You will see that the about dialog box is really all about itself. Nothing can be done until it is closed. Alternatively, change the third parameter of the constructor of the `JDialog` class to `false`. Now a new dialog can be open while the current one exists, which is probably not the desired behavior.

12.12   Working with Password Fields

The final topic in this chapter will be how to create password fields. This can be done by instantiating an object from the `JPasswordField` class. Unlike a text field, a password

FIGURE 12.8: Example of a password field.

field shows only stars when text is entered into it. In all other aspects, the two classes work similarly.

We will create a very simple application; see Figure 12.8. The program starts by displaying a window. The window, in turn, displays a modal dialog box. Users can return to the window only after they enter the correct login and password in the dialog box.

```java
import javax.swing.*;
import java.awt.*;
import java.awt.event.*;
import java.util.Arrays;


public class PasswordGame {
  public static void main(String[] args){
    LoginFrame frame = new LoginFrame();
  }
}

class LoginFrame extends JFrame {
  public LoginFrame() {
    setVisible(true);
    setSize(300, 300);
    LoginDialog dialog = new LoginDialog(this);
    dialog.setSize(200, 100);
    dialog.setVisible(true);
  }

  class LoginDialog extends JDialog {
    public LoginDialog(JFrame owner) {
      super(owner, "Authentication", true);
      setResizable(false);
      setDefaultCloseOperation(JDialog.DO_NOTHING_ON_CLOSE);
      JPanel centerPanel = new JPanel();
```

```
centerPanel.setLayout(new GridLayout(2, 2));
JLabel label1 = new JLabel("login: ");
centerPanel.add(label1);
final JTextField loginField = new JTextField("", 10);
centerPanel.add(loginField);
JLabel label2 = new JLabel("passowrd: ");
centerPanel.add(label2);
final JPasswordField passwordField = new JPasswordField("", 10);
centerPanel.add(passwordField);
add(centerPanel, BorderLayout.CENTER);
JPanel southPanel = new JPanel();
add(southPanel, BorderLayout.SOUTH);
JButton okButton = new JButton("OK");
southPanel.add(okButton);
okButton.addActionListener(new ActionListener() {
  public void actionPerformed(ActionEvent e) {
    char[] correctPassword = {'f','u','n'};
    if (loginField.getText().trim().equals("java")){
      char[] password = passwordField.getPassword();
      if(Arrays.equals(password,correctPassword)){
        LoginDialog.this.dispose();
      }
    }
    Arrays.fill(correctPassword, '0');
  }
});
        }
    }
}
```

Note that the constructor of the `LoginFrame` class first makes the window visible. We need to display the window early because the call to create the dialog window is *blocking*. In other words, if we do not display the window initially, it will be displayed only after the dialog window is closed.

The code in the constructor of the `LoginDialog` class creates two panels. The top panel has a two-by-two grid layout and is in the center part of the dialog. It displays two labels and two text fields that store the login and the password. An OK button is displayed in a panel at the south. When the OK button is pressed, the code checks if the correct login and password is entered. Only when this is the case will dialog window close. The line `LoginDialog.this.dispose()` means execute the `dispose` method for the outer object. Of course, since the local anonymous class does not contain a `dispose` method, we could have rewritten the line as just `dispose()`. In order to prevent the dialog from closing any other way, we have made it modal and added the line `setDefaultCloseOperation(JDialog.DO_NOTHING_ON_CLOSE)`. The last statement simply means that the dialog window will not close when the user presses the X in the top right corner.

Note that there is a `getText` method for the `JPasswordField` class, which retrieves the password as a string. However, for security reasons, the method is *deprecated*. It was replaced by the `getPassword` method, which retrieves the password as an array of characters. For security reasons, Java decided that the second method is recommended. The `Arrays.equals` method compares two arrays using deep comparison. In other words, it checks if the arrays have the same content. Lastly, the line `Arrays.fill(correctPassword, '0' )` fills the `correctPassword` array with zeros. This is done so that no one can examine the main memory and see the correct password. Of course, the presented code is not bulletproof. An even better solution is to apply some function to the password and compare the result with a number that is stored somewhere. In this way, even if someone obtains the Java code, they would not be able to read the password. In order for this approach to work, it must be the case that the encoding function cannot be easily reversed. In other words, one cannot easily determine what is the input to the function from the output of the function.

12.13 Summary

The chapter describes three component layouts: flow, grid, and border. The flow layout is used when we want to place components sequentially in a window. When the top line becomes full, the components are placed on the second line and so on. The grid layout can be used to place components in a grid. The border layout allows us to place components in the south, east, west, north, or the center of the window. All three layouts can also be applied to either windows or panels. Multiple panels can be added to a window and each panel can have its own layout scheme. Note that this overview of layouts is not exhaustive. Rather, it gives the reader the basics to arrange GUI components in a window.

The chapter also covers basic GUI components, such as buttons, labels, text fields, text areas, scroll areas, combo boxes, radio buttons, and password fields. For every GUI component, a short example of how the component works is presented. Again, the overview is by no means complete. It covers only the most basic GUI components and it is a good starting point for creating GUI applications. The chapter also covers dialog boxes. They are similar to windows, but they cannot be minimized or maximized. A dialog box can also be modal, which means that it must be closed before the user can interact with the rest of the windows of the application.

12.14 Syntax

- `JButton b = new JButton("Press me");` ⇒ Creates a new button with text "Press me".

- `b.setText("new text");` ⇒ Change the label of a button.

- `b.addActionListener(a);` ⇒ Registers the action listener with the button. When the button is pressed, the `actionPerformed` method of the `a` object will be executed.

- `String s = b.getText();` ⇒ Gets the label of a button.

- `p.setLayout(new FlowLayout(FlowLayout.LEFT,2,10));` ⇒ Changes the layout of the panel `p` to flow layout. The method can also be applied on objects of type `JFrame`. The virtual lines where the components are displayed will be left justified. There will be a 2-pixel horizontal gap and a 10-pixel vertical gap.

- `p.setLayout(new BorderLayout());` ⇒ Changes the layout of the panel `p` to border layout. The method can also be applied on objects of type `JFrame`.

- `p.add(b, BorderLayout.WEST);` ⇒ Adds the button `b` to the west side of the panel

p. It must be the case that the border layout is selected as the layout for the panel. The method can also be applied on objects of type `JFrame`. Note that only one component can be added to each of the five areas. For example, if a second button is added to the west part of the window, it will be placed on top of the first button.

- `p.setLayout(new GridLayout(3,5,2,1));` $\Rightarrow$ Creates a new grid layout. The layout will have 3 rows, 5 columns, a 2-pixel horizontal gap, and 1-pixel vertical gap.

- `String s = new ScriptEngineManager().getEngineByName("JavaScript").eval(e);` $\Rightarrow$ Computes the value of the expression e. For example, if e is the string "2+2", then the value of s will become the string "4".

- `JLabel l = new JLabel("This is a label");` $\Rightarrow$ Creates a new label with text "This is a label".

- `JTextField f = new JTextField("",20);` $\Rightarrow$ Creates a text field of size 20 characters. The first parameter is the initial text in the text field.

- `String s = f.getText();` $\Rightarrow$ Gets the text in the text field.

- `f.setText("new text");` $\Rightarrow$ Sets the text of the text field.

- `f.setFont(new Font("SansSerif", Font.BOLD,10));` $\Rightarrow$ Changes the font of the text field `f`. The method also applies to text areas. The new font will be Sans Serif, bold, and point size 10.

- `f.getDocument().addDocumentListener(a);` $\Rightarrow$ Adds a document listener to the text field. The document listener interface is called `DocumentListener` and contains the `insertUpdate`, `removeUpdate`, and `changeUpdate` methods.

- `s = s.trim();` $\Rightarrow$ Removes leading and trailing spaces from the string `s`.

- `JTextArea a = new JTextArea(20,30);` $\Rightarrow$ Creates a text area with 30 lines. Every line has 20 characters.

- `String s = a.getText();` $\Rightarrow$ Gets the text from the text area.

- `a.setText("new text");` $\Rightarrow$ Sets the text of the text area.

- `p.add(new JScrollPane(textArea));` $\Rightarrow$ Adds the text area to the panel. Scroll bars will appear around the text area when the text becomes too big to fit inside.

- `JComboBox fontComboBox = new JComboBox(fontNames);` $\Rightarrow$ Creates a new combo box. The variable `fontNames` is the area of strings that will be displayed in the combo box.

- `String s = (String)fontComboBox.getSelectedItem();` $\Rightarrow$ Retrieves the selected item from the combo box as `String`.

- `fontComboBox.setEditable(false);` $\Rightarrow$ Makes the combo box not editable.

- `fontComboBox.addActionListener(a);` $\Rightarrow$ Adds an action listener to the combo box. When the value of the combo box is changed, the `actionPerformed` method of the `a` object will be called.

- `JCheckBox jb = new JCheckBox("Bold");` $\Rightarrow$ Creates a check box with label `Bold`.

- `jb.isSelected()` $\Rightarrow$ Returns `true` if the check box is selected.

- JRadioButton rb = new JRadioButton("Increment",true); ⇒ Creates a new radio button that is selected and has label Increment.

- rb.isSelected() ⇒ True if the radio button is selected.

- rb.addActionListener(a); ⇒ Adds an action listener to the radio button. When the radio button is changed, the actionPerformed method of the a object will be called.

- ButtonGroup b = new ButtonGroup(); ⇒ Creates a button group. At most one radio button in a button group can be pressed at any time.

- b.add(rb); ⇒ Add the radio button rb to the button group b.

- JDialog db = new JDialog(owner, "About", true); ⇒ Creates a new dialog box. The variable owner refers to the owner window of the dialog box. The text About is the title of the dialog box. The last parameter means that the dialog box is modal.

- JPasswordField pf = new JPasswordField("", 10); ⇒ Creates a password field of size 10 characters.

- char[] password = pf.getPassword(); ⇒ Returns the password that is typed in the password field.

- int i = Double.parseDouble(s); ⇒ Converts the string s to a double. If the conversion fails, then an exception is raised.

- int i = Integer.parseInt(s); ⇒ Converts the string s to an integer. If the conversion fails, then an exception is raised.

- e.getSource ⇒ Returns the source of the e event.

12.15   Important Points

1. A window can contain multiple panels. Every panel, in turn, can contain multiple panels.

2. In a flow layout, the components are arranged in rows from top to bottom in the surrounding container.

3. In a border layout, the components are placed in the south, east, north, west, and center of the container. One can place only one component in each of the five areas.

4. In a grid layout, the components are placed in a grid. When adding components, they fill the grid from top to bottom. The first row is filled from left to right as are the successive rows.

5. The JTextField and JTextArea classes are similar. However, the first class should be used to display a single user input line, while the second class should be used to display an area that contains multiple user input lines.

6. An event listener of type `ActionListener` can be registered with buttons, text fields, text areas, radio buttons, combo boxes, check boxes, password fields, etc. The `actionPerformed` method is executed whenever the data is modified.

7. A document listener (i.e., an object of type `DocumentListener`) can be associated with a document. The `getDocument` method can be called to extract a document from a text field, text area, or a password field. A document listener can be used to monitor for changes in the text.

8. A password field is very similar to a text field. However, there are two main differences. First, asterisks appear to hide the text that is typed by the user. Second, for added security, the `getPassword` method should be called to retrieve the password from the password field. The method returns an array of characters.

9. There are three main differences between a dialog box (i.e., an object of type `JDialog`) and a window (i.e., an object of type `JFrame`). First, a dialog box does not have minimize or restore buttons. Second, a dialog box must have a parent window. Thirdly, a dialog box can be modal. This means that all the other windows of the application will be inactive until the dialog box is closed.

12.16   Exercises

1. Create an application that calculates the fuel economy of a car. The application should display a window. In the window, the user should type in the size of the gas tank and how many miles he or she can travel with a full tank of gas. Both values should be entered in text fields. When the user presses the `Calculate` button, the fuel economy of the car should be displayed in a text field that is not editable.

2. Add a menu to the Notepad application. Add a menu item to count the number of words in the text. The result should appear as a modal dialog box that contains the result and a single `OK` button.

3. Add a menu item to the Notepad application that can wrap the text. Use the `setLineWrap` method of the `JTextArea` class to achieve the wrapping.

4. Modify the freehand drawing application from Chapter 10. Add a panel that contains three radio buttons: red, green, and blue. Add the panel to the south of the window. Allow the user to choose the painting color using the radio buttons. Do not forget to add the radio buttons to the same button group.

5. Modify the application from the previous question. This time, create a combo box from which the user can choose the drawing color.

6. Create a simple sandwich-making program. Create a window that has multiple panels with multiple components. For example, the user can select the toppings from a set of check boxes (e.g., tomato, onion, pickles, mustard, ketchup, etc.). Using a combo box here is a bad idea because several toppings can be selected. However, the main ingredient of the sandwich can be selected from a combo box (e.g., chicken, tuna fish, steak, etc.). Also, create a combo box for selecting the type of bread to use (e.g., white, whole grain, wheat, etc.). You should also add a check box that can be used to specify

if the order is to go. When the user finishes describing the order, they should press the order button. As a result, a modal dialog box should appear. A textual description of the order should appear in the dialog box.

12.17   Lab

Modify the Yahtzee game from Chapter 5 to use a GUI. Five dice should be displayed in a window. The user should use check boxes to select which dice to reroll. The actual rolling should happen by pressing the `Roll` button. The user should be allowed two rerolls. After that, a modal dialog box should appear that informs the user whether he or she got Yahtzee or not. Search images from the Internet for the 6 values of the dice (i.e., 1 through 6). That is, display a picture of a die with 3 on top instead of displaying the number 3. Try to make the game as intuitive as possible by adding labels where needed.

12.18   Project

Modify the banking software from the Chapter 8 project to use GUI components. The new program should support all the functionality of the old program. In addition, add user authentication. For example, the bank employee should log into the system. They can select from a menu item that they want to perform a withdraw. The bank employee should then type in the ID of the customer (or the name) and press search. If the customer has multiple accounts, then a combo box should list all the accounts. The bank employee should select the account on which to perform the transaction from the combo box. Next, the teller should use a radio button to select if the transaction is withdraw or deposit. In addition, the system should support adding a new employee, adding a new customer, a new bank account, and so on. Use dialog boxes where appropriate. Try to use most GUI components that were described in this chapter. Most operations in the system can be initiated through menu items.

Chapter 13

Exception Handling and Files

This chapter covers two important topics: files and exception handling. The topics are covered together because every time we are working with a file, an exception can occur. This exception can be that the file does not exist, we do not have permission to open it, the hard disk is full and we are trying to save the file, and so on. We will cover two types of files: text and data. For text files, we will read and write regular text to a file. When it comes to data files, we will read and write objects to a file. We will cover *checked* and *unchecked* exceptions. While Java forces us to handle checked exceptions, such as opening a file, Java does not require that one handles unchecked exceptions, such as division by zero.

In the spirit of the textbook, we will describe all new Java primitives in the context of applications. We will first extend the Notepad software and add features to read and write to a file. Next, we will examine how the data from a bank application can be stored on the hard disk. The latter is an interesting example because it demonstrates how to store on the hard disk interlinked objects that belong to a multiple classes.

13.1 Handling Exceptions

Consider an application that wants to read a positive integer from the keyboard. However, the application should be bullet-proofed. In particular, the application should not crash if the user enters a string, for example. Below is one possible way to implement such an application.

```
import java.util.*;

public class Test{
  public static void main(String args[]) {
    int i = -1;
    while (i <= 0) {
      i = getNumber();
    }
```

```
      System.out.println(i);

   }

   public static int getNumber() {
      try {
         Scanner console = new Scanner(System.in);
         System.out.print("Enter a positive integer: ");
         return console.nextInt();
      } catch (InputMismatchException exception) {
         return -1;
      }
   }
}
```

The **getNumber** method asks the user to enter an integer and reads the integer. However, the **nextInt** method will raise an exception if the user does not enter an integer. An exception is an object that is automatically generated by Java. Every exception belongs to an exception class. For example, **InputMismatchException** is an exception class. An exception of type **InputMismatchException** is generated when Java expects an input of one type (e.g., an integer), but receives an input of a different type (e.g., a string). All exception classes inherit from the **Exception** class. In the above code, the exception object is passed as a parameter in the **catch** statement, but not used.

> To handle an exception, create a **try** block. The **try** block must be followed by either one or more **catch** blocks, a **finally** block, or both. The **finally** block, when present, must be the last block in the statement.

An **InputMismatchException** is generated by the call to the **nextInt** method when the user does not enter an integer. This exception is handled in the **catch** part of the statement. As a result, the **getNumber** method returns −1 when the user does not enter an integer. This signals to the **main** method that something went wrong and the user is required to enter the integer again. In order for this approach to work, we assume that the user must enter a positive integer.

Next, suppose that we require that the user enters an arbitrary integer, not just a positive integer. In this case, the **getNumber** method should return two pieces of data: the integer that is entered (assuming it is an integer) and a Boolean value that tells us if the user entered an integer. Of course, as we already know, a method cannot return two pieces of data. The only way to circumvent this restriction is to give the method an address where to write the result. Here is the new implementation.

```
import java.util.*;

public class Test {
   public static void main(String args[]) {
      int a[] = new int[1];
      int i;
      while( !getNumber(a));
      i = a[0];
      System.out.println(i);
   }

   public static boolean getNumber(int[] a) {
```

```
    try {
      Scanner console = new Scanner(System.in);
      System.out.print("Enter an integer: ");
      a[0] = console.nextInt();
      return true;
    } catch (InputMismatchException exception) {
      return false;
    }
  }
}
```

This time, the `getNumber` method takes as input the address of the array where the result should be stored. The method returns `true` when it is successful in reading a integer. If the call to the `nextInt` method raises an `InputMismatchException`, that is, the user did not enter an integer, then `false` is returned. In the `main` method, the `while` loop has no body. It keeps asking the user to enter an integer until the `getNumber` method returns `true`, that is, an integer is entered.

There are two types of exceptions in Java: *checked* and *unchecked*. Java forces us to handle checked exceptions in some way. For example, `FileNotFoundException` is an example of a checked exception. Every time we open a file, we need to handle the case when the file could not be found, that is, when a `FileNotFoundException` is raised. Conversely, `InputMismatchException` is an example of an unchecked exception. Java does not force us to handle the exception in any way. However, we handled the exception in order to address the case when the user enters a string instead of an integer. `ArithmeticException` and `ArrayIndexOutOfBoundsException` are two other examples of unchecked exceptions. The first exception can be raised when we divide by 0, while the second exception can be raised when we access an index of an array that is out of bounds.

Sometimes, when we handle an exception, we want to report to the user that something went wrong. When the `printStackTrace` method is called on the exception object, information about the exception will be generated and printed. For example, if we add the line `exception.printStackTrace()` to the `catch` part of our rewritten code, we will see the following printout if the user did not enter an integer.

```
java.util.InputMismatchException
    at java.util.Scanner.throwFor(Scanner.java:909)
    at java.util.Scanner.next(Scanner.java:1530)
    at java.util.Scanner.nextInt(Scanner.java:2160)
    at java.util.Scanner.nextInt(Scanner.java:2119)
    at Test.getNumber(Test.java:18)
    at Test.main(Test.java:9)
```

This gives us detailed information about which line of which method was called when the exception occurred. For example, the above code tells us that first Line 9 of the `main` method was executed. This called the `getNumber` method. Line 18 of the `getNumber` method called the `nextInt` method. In the `nextInt` method, an input mismatch exception has occurred.

There are three main ways to handle exceptions. The most obvious is to print the stack trace and terminate the program. By the way, this is the default behavior for unchecked exceptions that are not handled. A different alternative is to fix the error. In our example, we repeatedly asked for input until input of the correct typed was given. A third option is to log the error in a log file and continue program execution. After the program terminates, the log file can be checked for possible errors during the execution of the program.

Note that sometimes when an exception occurs we do not want to print the stack trace to the screen. Instead, we want to print an informative error message and continue executing the program. Java supports the `System.err.print` and `System.err.println` methods, which are similar to the `System.out.print` and `System.out.println` methods, respectively. The only difference is that output is written to an error stream instead of to the standard output stream. Consider the following code.

```java
import java.util.*;

public class Test {
  public static void main(String args[]) {
    int i;
    try{
      Scanner console = new Scanner(System.in);
      System.out.print("Enter an integer: ");
      i = console.nextInt();
    }
    catch(Exception e){
      System.err.println("You did not enter an integer");
    }
  }
}
```

If you run the program and do not enter an integer, then you will see the error in red. It is also possible to redirect the error stream to a log file when running a program, but doing so is beyond the scope of this textbook.

Next, let us consider a third rewrite of our program.

```java
import java.util.*;

public class Test {
  public static void main(String args[]) {
    boolean repeat = true;
    int i=0;
    while (repeat) {
      try{
        i = getNumber();
        repeat = false;
      }
      catch(Exception e){
      }
    }
    System.out.println(i);
  }

  public static int getNumber() throws Exception{
    Scanner console = new Scanner(System.in);
    System.out.print("Enter an integer: ");
    return console.nextInt();
  }
}
```

This time the `getNumber` method does not handle the exception. Instead, it passes the exception back to the calling `main` method.

A method can use the syntax **throws**. This means that instead of handling the exception, the method passes the exception to the calling method. As a result, it will be the job of the calling method to handle the exception.

The third rewrite is very clever. The `getNumber` method only returns a single piece of data. However, when the `getNumber` method does not raise an exception, the line `repeat = false` is executed and the `while` loop is terminated. Now there is no need to send an array to the `getNumber` method. If the user does not enter an integer, then the `catch` block does nothing and the block of the `while` loop needs to be repeated.

Note that we can rewrite the code for the `getNumber` method as follows.

public static int getNumber () **throws** InputMismatchException {

However, since the `InputMismatchException` class inherits from the `Exception` class, both versions are fine. If we write `throws Exception`, this means that the `getNumber` method will now handle any type of exception and will throw it back to the originating method. Alternatively, the code `throws InputMismatchException` means that the method will only throw back to the calling method an exceptions of type `InputMismatchException`. If the method generates an unchecked exception of a different type, for example as a result of dividing by 0, then the program will crash. If we want to specify that a method handles exceptions of several types, then we can separate the exception classes by commas.

We need to be careful when we write code that can raise exceptions. If a method in your program raises an unchecked exception and the exception is not handled, then the program will crash and the stack trace will be printed. Alternatively, code that generates a checked exception that is not handled will simply not compile.

Although similar to an `if-else` statement, a `try-catch-finally` block acts in a much different fashion. Let us consider the following example method.

```
public static int f(int n){
   int r = 0;
   try{
      r= n*n;
      return r;
   }
   finally{
      if(n==2) return r+1;
   }
}
```

The obvious question is what will be returned by the method when **n** = 2. The secret to answering the question is knowing that the `finally` block is always executed. Therefore, the code has two **return** statements! The return statement in the `try` block will return 4, while the return statement in the `finally` block will return 5. It turns out that the method will return 5 because the second **return** statement is the last one to be executed.

The code in the `finally` block will always be executed. If there is a **return** statement in the `finally` block, then the method will rely on this statement to compute the return value. The only way to skip executing the `finally` block is to directly exit the program before that by writing `System.exit(0)`. The last command terminates the program with exit code 0.

The `finally` block is used when we want to execute something at the end regardless of whether an exception occurred or not. This can include, for example, closing a file or freeing resources.

Next, we will present an example code that can raise multiple exceptions.

```java
import java.util.*;

public class Test {
  public static void main(String args[]) {
    while (true) {
      try {
        Scanner console = new Scanner(System.in);
        System.out.print("Enter a number: ");
        int i = console.nextInt();
        if (i % 2 == 0) {
          throw new EvenException();
        }
        break;
      } catch (InputMismatchException e) {
        System.out.println("Not a number! Try again!");
      } catch (EvenException e) {
        System.out.println("Number is even! Try again!");
      } catch (Exception e) {
        System.out.println("Something went wrong! Try again!");
      }
    }
  }
}

class EvenException extends Exception {
  public EvenException() {
    super("Even number exception");
  }
}
```

First, note that we created our own exception class. As expected, our exception class inherits from the `Exception` class. The constructor passes the name of the exception to the `Exception` superclass. Next, let us examine the `main` method. An `InputMismatchException` will be generated if an integer is not entered. Similarly, an `EvenException` will be generated when an even integer is entered. The `throw` keyword is used to generate a new exception. Our code has three `catch` statements: if the user enters something that is not an integer, if the user enters an even number, and if something else goes wrong.

> Extra care should be taken in the ordering of the `catch` blocks. We should always order them from the most specific exception to the most general exception.

If `catch(Exception e)` was the first exception, then there is no chance that another `catch` block will be executed. When an exception object is generated, Java checks the first `catch` statement. If the exception object does not belong to the exception class in the first `catch` statement, then Java proceeds to the next `catch` statement and so on. On a side note, if the `check` blocks are not ordered correctly from the most specific one to the most general one, the program will simply not compile.

Finally, note the **break** at the end of the **try** statement. If an exception is generated, then the **try** block will stop executing and the point of control will be transferred to one of the **catch** blocks. After the **catch** block finishes executing, the infinite **while** loop will bring us back to the beginning of the loop. Alternatively, if the code goes through the whole **try** block without an exception being raised, then the **break** statement will transfer control to the line immediately after the **while** statement.

An obvious question is when to use the **try** statement and when to use the **throws** keyword. Undoubtedly, using the **throws** keyword is more convenient. We do not have to handle the exception. The calling method will take care of it. However, in certain situations it is impossible to use the **throws** keyword. For example, consider the **paintComponent** method inside a class that inherits from the **JPanel** class. Since the original **paintComponent** method of the **JPanel** class does not throw an exception, neither can our method that overrides the original method. In different situations, we do not want a method to throw an exception because it is extra work for the calling method. For example, if the calling method does not handle the exception, a compile-time error will be generated.

Lastly, let us consider *checked exceptions*. These are exceptions that Java forces us to handle. Opening a file is an example of a task that can potentially generate a checked exception. Therefore, we must use a **try-catch** block or add the **throws** keyword to the method in order to handle the opening of the file. Alternatively, starting with Java 7, the following syntax is also allowed.

```
try (statement that opens file){
  // do something with file
} catch (IOException exception) {
  // handle I/O problems.
}
```

If the file is not opened successfully, then one of the catch blocks is executed. Note that this syntax also closes the file automatically, which saves us some code writing. The above syntax is referred to as **try-with-resources**. The **try** statement tries to allocate some resource. If the resource is successfully allocated, it is automatically freed at the end. Otherwise, one of the **catch** blocks and/or the **finally** block is executed.

13.2 Text Files

Our poor man's Notepad program from the last chapter seems pretty limited. We cannot even save our text! Let us go ahead and see how we can extend our program to allow for saving the text in a text file and reading the text from a text file.

13.2.1 The File Chooser Dialog

There is a class called **JFileChooser** that displays the usual open file dialog; see Figure 13.1. It allows the user to select the file that they want opened.

In order to use this class, one first needs to create an object from it.

```
JFileChooser fileChooser = new JFileChooser();
```

Next, one needs to call the **showDialog** method on the file chooser. This creates a file chooser dialog. The method takes as input a reference to the parent window and the text that will be displayed on the select button. This is the button that needs to

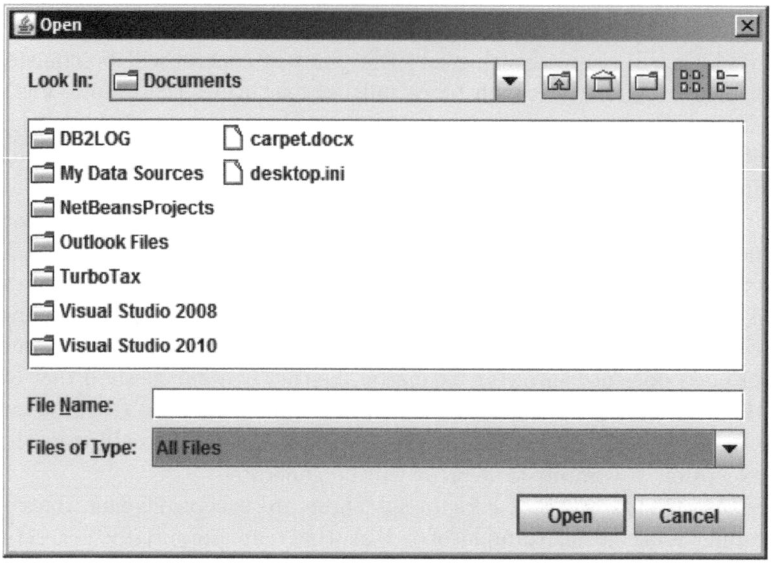

FIGURE 13.1: The file chooser dialog box.

be pressed in order to select a file. A cancel button also appears. The method returns an integer that is either `JFileChooser.APPROVE_OPTION`, `JFileChooser.CANEL_OPTION`, or `JFileChooser.ERROR_OPTION`. Next, we can use the `getSelectedFile` method to get the file that is selected by the user. Here is an example piece of code that selects a file using the file chooser dialog.

```
JFileChooser fileChooser = new JFileChooser();
if (fileChooser.showDialog(..., "Open") == JFileChooser.APPROVE_OPTION)
    {
    File newFile = fileChooser.getSelectedFile();
    ...
}
```

Note that, for now, we have left the parent window parameter unspecified because we do not know its value.

13.2.2 Reading from Text Files

Our next job is to open the text file and read the information from it. Reading from a text file is similar to reading from the keyboard. A `Scanner` object needs to be created and different methods, such as `nextInt`, `next`, and `nextLine`, can be called on it. When creating the `Scanner` object, a file object needs to be specified as input (instead of `Systems.in` for keyboard input). Here is an example code.

```
Scanner fileHandler = new Scanner(newFile);
String nextLine = fineHandler.nextLine();
```

Note that in our case the file chooser returns an object of type `File`. If we want to find the file name (as a string) that corresponds to the object, we can write `newFile.getPath()`. This will return the file name together with the directory path to the file. Alternatively, if we want to open a file with a given name, we can use the following syntax.

```
Scanner keyboard = new Scanner(System.in);
```

```
System.out.println("Please enter file to be open: ");
String fileName = keyboard.next();
File newFile = new File(fileName);
Scanner fileHandler = new Scanner(newFile);
String nextLine = fineHandler.nextLine();
```

The above code asks the user to input the file name and saves it as a string. Then it uses the file name to create a file object. Lastly, the code reads a line from the file.

When we manually specify the location of a file, we have three options.

1. No directory is specified.

```
File newFile = new File("myFile.txt");
```

In this case, Java searches for the file in the root directory of the project, which is usually different from the source directory.

2. The file directory is specified using a forward slash.

```
File newFile = new File("c:/documents/myFile.txt");
```

This is the easiest case. Note that this syntax can be used regardless of whether the operating system expects a forward or backward slash.

3. File directory is specified using a backward slash.

```
File newFile = new File("c:\\documents\\myFile.txt");
```

This is the more complicated case. In a string, a backward slash means that a special character follows. For example, \n represents a new line. The character \\ represents a single backward slash. Note that this syntax can be used regardless of whether the operating system expects a forward or backward slash.

Although similar, reading text from a file and from the keyboard is not identical. One can potentially keep reading from the keyboard forever. However, one can read from a file only until the file is exhausted. This is why one can call the hasNext, hasNextInt, or hasNextDouble methods on a file scanner. Once you open a file, an invisible cursor is created in the file. When you call the nextInt method, for example, the next integer is read from the file and the cursor skips over the integer; see Figure 13.2. The hasNext methods can be used to check if the virtual cursor has reached the end of the file and therefore there is no more information to read.

In our case, we can just keep reading lines from the file until we reach the end of the file. Here is the example code.

```
while (fileHandler.hasNext()) {
    String line = fileHandler.nextLine();
    System.out.println(line);
}
```

This code will simply read the file and print it to the screen line by line. The while statement continues until the file is exhausted.

Next, let us examine the new version of the Notepad application. We have added a menu item that can be used to open a file. When a file is opened, the content of the file is appended to the text area using the append method.

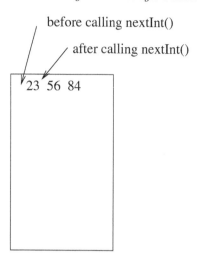

FIGURE 13.2: Moving the file cursor.

```java
import java.io.*;
import java.util.*;

public class NotepadFrame extends JFrame {
  private static int WIDTH = 600;
  private static int HEIGHT = 600;

  public NotepadFrame() {
    setDefaultCloseOperation(JFrame.DISPOSE_ON_CLOSE);
    setSize(WIDTH, HEIGHT);
    final JTextArea textArea = new JTextArea();

    JMenuBar menuBar = new JMenuBar();
    setJMenuBar(menuBar);
    JMenu fileMenu = new JMenu("File");
    menuBar.add(fileMenu);
    JMenuItem openMenuItem = new JMenuItem("Open...");
    fileMenu.add(openMenuItem);
    openMenuItem.addActionListener(new ActionListener() {
      public void actionPerformed(ActionEvent e) {
        JFileChooser fileChooser = new JFileChooser();
        if (fileChooser.showDialog(NotepadFrame.this, "Open") ==
            JFileChooser.APPROVE_OPTION) {
          File newFile = fileChooser.getSelectedFile();
          try (Scanner fileHandler = new Scanner(newFile)){
            textArea.setText("");
            while (fileHandler.hasNext()) {
              String line = fileHandler.nextLine();
              textArea.append(line + "\n");
            }
          } catch (Exception exception) {
          }
        }
      }
    });
```

```
add(new JScrollPane(textArea), BorderLayout.CENTER);
    ...
  }
}
```

Note that, for simplicity, we have removed the code for the control bar that can be used to change the font style and size. The `showDialog` method takes as input `NotepadFrame.this`. This is the reference to the outer object, that is, the window from which the file dialog should be displayed. The line `textArea.append(line + "\n")` simply appends the line that is read from the file to the text area followed by a new line.

> When reading and writing to a file, something can always go wrong. For example, we may try to open a file that does not exist or we do not have permission to access it. This is why an exception can be generated. Java forces us to always handle this type of exception because all exceptions that relate to files are checked exceptions.

In the above code, we used a `try`-with-resources block. If we are unable to open the file, control jumps over to the `catch` block. Here, we chose not to do anything in the `catch` block. The advantage of using a `try`-with-resources statement is that we did not have to close the file. If we used the regular `try-catch` block, then we had to add the line `fileHandler.close()` to the end of the `try` block or in a new `finally` block.

13.2.3 Writing to Text Files

Next, let us consider how we can write to a text file. One way to do this is by creating an object of type `PrintWriter`. The parameter of the constructor can be either the name of a file or a file object. After the print writer is created, we can call the same methods we called on the `System.out` object to print output. Here is example code that creates a file and writes two lines to it.

```
try (PrintWriter fileWritter = new PrintWriter("myFile.txt")){
    fileWritter.println("Hello");
    fileWritter.println("Do you like Java?");
} catch (Exception exception) {
}
```

Note that opening a file for writing is similar to opening a file for reading: something can go wrong. Therefore, Java requires that we always handle a possible exception. In the above syntax, we do not have to worry about closing the file. Since the file is opened inside the `try` parentheses, it will be automatically closed. If we used the regular `try-catch` block, then we had to include the statement `fileWritter.close()` at the end of the `try` block or inside a newly introduced `finally` block.

Below is the new code that needs to be added in order to allow file saving in our Notepad application.

```
import java.io.*;

public class NotepadFrame extends JFrame {
    ...
    JMenuItem saveMenuItem = new JMenuItem("Save...");
    fileMenu.add(saveMenuItem);
    saveMenuItem.addActionListener(new ActionListener() {
        public void actionPerformed(ActionEvent e) {
```

```
                JFileChooser fileChooser = new JFileChooser();
                  if (fileChooser.showDialog(NotepadFrame.this, "Save") ==
                     JFileChooser.APPROVE_OPTION) {
                     File newFile = fileChooser.getSelectedFile();
                     try (PrintWriter fileWritter = new PrintWriter(newFile)){
                        fileWritter.print(textArea.getText());
                     } catch (Exception exception) {
                     }
                  }
               }
         });
         ...
   }
```

In the above example, the code `textArea.getText()` gets the whole text from the text area. Even though this text can be multiple lines, it can be stored as a single string. Next, we call the `print` method to write the text to the file.

The full version of the Notepad program is shown next.

```
import javax.swing.*;
import java.awt.*;
import java.awt.event.*;
import java.io.*;
import java.util.*;

public class Notepad {
   public static void main(String[] args){
      NotepadFrame notepadFrame = new NotepadFrame();
      notepadFrame.setVisible(true);
   }
}

class NotepadFrame extends JFrame {

   private static int WIDTH = 600;
   private static int HEIGHT = 600;

   public NotepadFrame() {
      setDefaultCloseOperation(JFrame.DISPOSE_ON_CLOSE);
      setSize(WIDTH, HEIGHT);
      final JTextArea textArea = new JTextArea();

      JMenuBar menuBar = new JMenuBar();
      setJMenuBar(menuBar);
      JMenu fileMenu = new JMenu("File");
      menuBar.add(fileMenu);
      JMenuItem openMenuItem = new JMenuItem("Open...");
      fileMenu.add(openMenuItem);
      add(new JScrollPane(textArea), BorderLayout.CENTER);
      JPanel controlPanel = new JPanel();
      controlPanel.setLayout(new FlowLayout(FlowLayout.LEFT));

      String[] fontNames = GraphicsEnvironment.
            getLocalGraphicsEnvironment().
               getAvailableFontFamilyNames();
      final JComboBox fontComboBox = new JComboBox(fontNames);
```

```java
fontComboBox.setSelectedItem("SansSerif");
final JComboBox sizeComboBox = new JComboBox();
final JCheckBox boldCheckBox = new JCheckBox("Bold");
final JCheckBox italicCheckBox = new JCheckBox("Italic");

for (int i = 8; i <= 72; i++) {
  sizeComboBox.addItem(i);
}
sizeComboBox.setSelectedItem(12);
sizeComboBox.setEditable(true);
ActionListener changeListener = new ActionListener() {
  public void actionPerformed(ActionEvent e) {
    int mask = Font.PLAIN;
    if (boldCheckBox.isSelected()) {
      mask += Font.BOLD;
    }
    if (italicCheckBox.isSelected()) {
      mask += Font.ITALIC;
    }
    textArea.setFont(new Font((String) fontComboBox.getSelectedItem
        (), mask, (Integer) sizeComboBox.getSelectedItem()));
  }
};
controlPanel.add(fontComboBox);
controlPanel.add(sizeComboBox);
controlPanel.add(boldCheckBox);
controlPanel.add(italicCheckBox);
add(controlPanel, BorderLayout.NORTH);
boldCheckBox.addActionListener(changeListener);
italicCheckBox.addActionListener(changeListener);
sizeComboBox.addActionListener(changeListener);
fontComboBox.addActionListener(changeListener);
openMenuItem.addActionListener(new ActionListener() {
  public void actionPerformed(ActionEvent e) {
    JFileChooser fileChooser = new JFileChooser();
    if (fileChooser.showDialog(NotepadFrame.this, "Open") ==
      JFileChooser.APPROVE_OPTION) {
      File newFile = fileChooser.getSelectedFile();
      try (Scanner fileHandler = new Scanner(newFile)){
        textArea.setText("");
        while (fileHandler.hasNext()) {
          String line = fileHandler.nextLine();
          textArea.append(line + "\n");
        }
      } catch (Exception exception) {
      }
    }
  }
});
JMenuItem saveMenuItem = new JMenuItem("Save...");
fileMenu.add(saveMenuItem);
saveMenuItem.addActionListener(new ActionListener() {
  public void actionPerformed(ActionEvent e) {
    JFileChooser fileChooser = new JFileChooser();
```

```
        if (fileChooser.showDialog(NotepadFrame.this, "Save") ==
            JFileChooser.APPROVE_OPTION) {
          File newFile = fileChooser.getSelectedFile();
          try (PrintWriter fileWritter = new PrintWriter(newFile)){
            fileWritter.print(textArea.getText());
          } catch (Exception exception) {
          }
        }
      }
    });
  }
}
```

13.3   Data Files

We will next give an example of how to read and write binary data to and from a file. We will create a simple bank application. The application will be by no means complete. Rather, it will be a toy example that shows how objects can be read and written to a file. The main **BankApp** class is shown next. It creates two customers and an employee and tests how deposits and withdraws can be made and how binary data can be written to and from a file. Note that the **main** method throws an exception. This is the reason we do not need a **try-catch** block inside the method.

```
import java.io.*;
import java.util.*;

public class BankApp {
  public static void main(String[] args) throws Exception {
    ArrayList<Person> people = new ArrayList<>();
    Customer bob = new Customer("Bob", new Person.Address(123, "Main",
        "Chicago", "IL", 60641), 5555555555L);
    Customer ann = new Customer("Ann", new Person.Address(444, "King",
        "New York", "NY", 10466), 666666666L);
    Employee suzan = new Employee("Susan", new Person.Address(444, "
        King", "New York", "NY", 10466), 777777777L, 80000);
    people.add(bob);
    people.add(ann);
    people.add(suzan);
    BankAccount account1 = new BankAccount(1000, bob);
    bob.addBankAccount(account1);
    account1.deposit(100000, suzan);
    BankAccount account2 = new BankAccount(50000, ann);
    ann.addBankAccount(account2);
    account2.withdraw(200, suzan);

    FileOutputStream fileOut = new FileOutputStream("bank.ser");
    ObjectOutputStream out = new ObjectOutputStream(fileOut);
    out.writeObject(people);
    out.close();
    fileOut.close();
    people = null;
```

```
FileInputStream fileIn = new FileInputStream("bank.ser");
ObjectInputStream in = new ObjectInputStream(fileIn);
people = (ArrayList<Person>) in.readObject();
in.close();
fileIn.close();
for(Person p: people){
  System.out.println(p);
}
  }
}
```

The code first creates two customers and one employee and adds them to an `ArrayList` of people. Of course, both the `Customer` and `Employee` classes inherit from the `Person` class. The constructor of the `Person` class takes as input the name, address, and phone number of the person. The constructor of the `Employee` class takes, in addition, the salary of the employee. Note that since the phone number of a person is saved as a `long`, the letter L is used at the end of the number. The `Address` class is a static nested class of the `Person` class. We defined it as a static nested class because the `Address` class relates to the `Person` class. It is not an inner class because there can be multiple people associated with the same address. The constructor of the `Address` class takes as input the street number, street name, city name, state, and zip code. Next, the code creates two bank accounts: one for Bob and one for Ann. Note that a customer can have multiple accounts. The constructor of the `BankAccount` class takes as input the amount of initial deposit and a reference to the customer.

The reading and writing to/from a file happens in the second part of the code. In order to write binary data to a file, an instance of the `FileOutputStream` class needs to be created. The constructor of the class takes as input the name of the file where the data is to be written. If the file could not be opened, then an exception is raised. The `FileOutputStream` class allows only binary data (i.e., an array of bytes) to be written to the file. If we want to write objects to the file, then we need to create an object of type `ObjectOutputStream` from the `FileOutputStream` object. The `writeObject` method can be used to write objects to a file. The above code creates the file `bank.ser`. We used the `ser` file extension because this is a common extension for serialized data.

The `writeObject` method can only write objects that belong to a class that implements the interface `Serializable`. The interface contains no methods. The `writeObject` method is very powerful because it serializes not only the specified object, but also its internal objects that implement the interface `Serializable`. The serialization works even in the presence of cyclic references.

In our example, we only store the `ArrayList` of people. Since a customer is a person and a customer can have several bank accounts, all objects of type `BankAccount` are also stored. A bank account can contain several transactions and every transaction references a bank account. In other words, there is a circular reference between the `BankAccount` and `Transaction` classes. However, every object of each of the two classes is stored only once. The `writeObject` method is smart enough to determine that an object is already stored and it does not need to be stored again. However, all objects that are stored must implement the interface `Serializable`.

In order to make sure that we have written the data correctly, our application opens the file a second time and prints to the screen all the data in the file. Reading objects from a file is similar to writing objects to a file. The only difference is that a `FileInputStream` and an `ObjectInputStream` are used instead of `FileOutputStream` and `ObjectOutputStream`. Objects should be read from the file in the order in which they are written. The `readObject` method can be used to read an object from the file.

Note that there are also methods for working with primitive types, such as `writeDouble/readDouble`, `writeBoolean/readBoolean`, and so on. For example, the `writeChars` method can be used to store a `String` in the binary file.

Below is the code for the `Person` class. Note that the class implements the interface `Serializable`. This means that an object that belongs to the `Person` class can be saved (or serialized) on the hard disk.

```java
public class Person implements Serializable {
    private long id;
    private String name;
    private static long idCounter = 0;
    private Address address;
    private long phoneNumber;

    public Person(String name, Address address, long phoneNumber) {
        id = idCounter;
        idCounter++;
        this.name = name;
        this.phoneNumber = phoneNumber;
        this.address = address;
    }

    public String toString() {
        return "name = " + name + " " + address + " Phone number: " +
            phoneNumber;
    }

    public long getID() {
        return id;
    }

    public static class Address implements Serializable {
        private int streetNumber;
        private String streetName;
        private String cityName;
        private String state;
        private int zipCode;

        public Address(int streetNumber, String streetName, String cityName
            , String state, int zipCode) {
            this.streetNumber = streetNumber;
            this.streetName = streetName;
            this.cityName = cityName;
            this.state = state;
            this.zipCode = zipCode;
        }

        public String toString() {
            return "Address: " + streetNumber + " " + streetName + " " +
                cityName + " " + zipCode + " " + state;
        }
    }
}
```

```
}
```

Note that the `Address` class is a nested static class inside the `Person` class. The reason is that the address field applies only to people. We use a standard trick to generate the IDs of the people. We created a `static` variable that holds the next available ID. This variable is initially zero. Every time a new person is created, the current value of the variable is assigned for the ID and then the static variable is incremented by one.

Below is the code for the `Customer` class.

```java
public class Customer extends Person{
    private ArrayList<BankAccount> accounts = new ArrayList<>();
    public Customer(String name, Person.Address address, long phoneNumber
        ){
      super(name, address, phoneNumber);
    }
    public void addBankAccount(BankAccount account){
      accounts.add(account);
    }
    public String toString(){
      return "Customer: "+super.toString()+ " Accounts: "+accounts;
    }
}
```

A customer can have multiple bank accounts. Therefore, we associated an `ArrayList` of bank accounts with every customer. Note that the `Person` class inherits from the interface `Serializable` because it inherits from the `Person` class and the `Person` class inherits from the interface `Serializable`. Next, we show the code for the `Employee` class.

```java
public class Employee extends Person{
    private double salary;
    public Employee(String name, Person.Address address, long phoneNumber
        , double salary){
      super(name, address, phoneNumber);
      this.salary = salary;
    }
    public String toString(){
      return "Employee: "+super.toString()+" salary: "+salary;
    }
}
```

Similar to the `Customer` class, the `Employee` class inherits from the interface `Serializable` because inheritance is transitive. It remains to show the code for the `BankAccount` and `Transaction` classes.

```java
public class BankAccount implements Serializable {
    private static long accountCounter = 0;
    private long accountNumber;
    private double balance;
    private ArrayList<Transaction> transactions = new ArrayList<>();
    private Customer customer;

    public BankAccount(Customer customer){
      this.customer = customer;
      accountNumber = accountCounter;
      accountCounter++;
    }
    public BankAccount(double initialDeposit, Customer customer){
```

```java
      this.customer = customer;
      accountNumber = accountCounter;
      accountCounter++;
      balance = initialDeposit;
    }
    public boolean withdraw(double amount, Employee employee){
      if(balance > amount){
        balance -= amount;
        Transaction newTransaction = new Transaction(this, employee,
            TransactionType.withdraw, amount);
        transactions.add(newTransaction);
        return true;
      }
      return false;
    }
    public void deposit(double amount, Employee employee){
      Transaction newTransaction = new Transaction(this, employee,
          TransactionType.deposit, amount);
      transactions.add(newTransaction);
      balance += amount;
    }
    public String toString(){
      return "Bank account number: "+accountNumber+" balance: "+balance;
    }
    public long getAccountNumber(){
      return accountNumber;
    }
}

enum TransactionType {
  withdraw, deposit
}

public class Transaction implements Serializable {
  private static long idCounter = 0;
  private Date date;
  private long accountNumber;
  private Employee employee;
  private TransactionType type;
  private double amount;
  private long transactionID;

  public Transaction(BankAccount bankAccount, Employee employee,
      TransactionType type, double amount) {
    date = new Date();
    this.accountNumber = accountNumber;
    this.employee = employee;
    this.type = type;
    this.amount = amount;
    this.transactionID = idCounter;
    idCounter++;
  }
  public String toString(){
    return "Transaction id: "+transactionID+" amount: "+amount+"type: "
        + type.name()+" employeeID: "+employee+ " Date: "+date;
```

```
    }
}
```

Note the circular reference between the two classes. There is an `ArrayList` of transactions associated with every bank account. Conversely, every transaction is associated with a bank account. Since both the classes `Transaction` and `BankAccount` are `Serializable`, Java will correctly handle storing objects of both types and every object will be stored just once in the file.

As a second example of how binary files work, let us revisit our poor man's Notepad application. This time, however, we will store the font, the point size, and the value of the bold and italic check boxes in the file together with the text. This way, we will preserve the formatting of the file. Below is the complete code for the program.

```java
import java.awt.*;
import java.awt.event.*;
import java.io.*;
import javax.swing.*;

public class Notepad{
  public static void main(String[] args){
    NotepadFrame f = new NotepadFrame();
    f.setVisible(true);
  }
}

class NotepadFrame extends JFrame {
  private static int WIDTH = 600;
  private static int HEIGHT = 600;

  public NotepadFrame() {
    setDefaultCloseOperation(JFrame.DISPOSE_ON_CLOSE);
    setSize(WIDTH, HEIGHT);
    final JTextArea textArea = new JTextArea();

    JMenuBar menuBar = new JMenuBar();
    setJMenuBar(menuBar);
    JMenu fileMenu = new JMenu("File");
    menuBar.add(fileMenu);
    JMenuItem openMenuItem = new JMenuItem("Open...");
    fileMenu.add(openMenuItem);
    add(new JScrollPane(textArea), BorderLayout.CENTER);
    JPanel controlPanel = new JPanel();
    controlPanel.setLayout(new FlowLayout(FlowLayout.LEFT));

    String[] fontNames = GraphicsEnvironment.
        getLocalGraphicsEnvironment().
            getAvailableFontFamilyNames();
    final JComboBox fontComboBox = new JComboBox(fontNames);
    fontComboBox.setSelectedItem("SansSerif");
    final JComboBox sizeComboBox = new JComboBox();
    final JCheckBox boldCheckBox = new JCheckBox("Bold");
    final JCheckBox italicCheckBox = new JCheckBox("Italic");

    for (int i = 8; i <= 72; i++) {
      sizeComboBox.addItem(i);
    }
```

```java
sizeComboBox.setSelectedItem(12);
sizeComboBox.setEditable(true);
ActionListener changeListener = new ActionListener() {
  public void actionPerformed(ActionEvent e) {
    int mask = Font.PLAIN;
    if (boldCheckBox.isSelected()) {
      mask += Font.BOLD;
    }
    if (italicCheckBox.isSelected()) {
      mask += Font.ITALIC;
    }
    textArea.setFont(new Font((String) fontComboBox.getSelectedItem
        (), mask, (Integer) sizeComboBox.getSelectedItem()));
  }
};
controlPanel.add(fontComboBox);
controlPanel.add(sizeComboBox);
controlPanel.add(boldCheckBox);
controlPanel.add(italicCheckBox);
add(controlPanel, BorderLayout.NORTH);
boldCheckBox.addActionListener(changeListener);
italicCheckBox.addActionListener(changeListener);
sizeComboBox.addActionListener(changeListener);
fontComboBox.addActionListener(changeListener);
openMenuItem.addActionListener(new ActionListener() {
  public void actionPerformed(ActionEvent e) {
    JFileChooser fileChooser = new JFileChooser();
    if (fileChooser.showDialog(NotepadFrame.this, "Open") ==
        JFileChooser.APPROVE_OPTION) {
      File newFile = fileChooser.getSelectedFile();
      try (FileInputStream fileIn = new FileInputStream(newFile)) {
        ObjectInputStream in = new ObjectInputStream(fileIn);
        boldCheckBox.setSelected(in.readBoolean());
        italicCheckBox.setSelected(in.readBoolean());
        sizeComboBox.setSelectedItem(in.readObject());
        fontComboBox.setSelectedItem(in.readObject());
        textArea.setText((String)in.readObject());
      } catch (Exception exception) {
      }
    }
  }
});
JMenuItem saveMenuItem = new JMenuItem("Save...");
fileMenu.add(saveMenuItem);
saveMenuItem.addActionListener(new ActionListener() {
  public void actionPerformed(ActionEvent e) {
    JFileChooser fileChooser = new JFileChooser();
    if (fileChooser.showDialog(NotepadFrame.this, "Save") ==
        JFileChooser.APPROVE_OPTION) {
      File newFile = fileChooser.getSelectedFile();
      try (FileOutputStream fileOut = new FileOutputStream(newFile)
          ) {
        ObjectOutputStream out = new ObjectOutputStream(fileOut);
        out.writeBoolean(boldCheckBox.isSelected());
        out.writeBoolean(italicCheckBox.isSelected());
```

```
            out.writeObject(sizeComboBox.getSelectedItem());
            out.writeObject(fontComboBox.getSelectedItem());
            out.writeObject(textArea.getText());
        } catch (Exception exception) {
        }
      }
    }
  });
  }
}
```

Note that we stored the values for the bold and italic check boxes as `boolean`, that is, we used the `writeBoolean` method to write them to the file. We stored the values for the combo boxes and the text as objects, that is, we used the `writeObject` method to store them. When reading from the file, we used the `readBoolean` method to read the two Boolean values. Similarly, we used the `readObject` method multiple times to read the objects from the file. Note that the method `readObject` returns an object. This object may have to be cast to the appropriate type. For example, the statement `(String)in.readObject()` reads an object from the file and converts it to a string. If the object is not of type `String`, then a `ClassCastException` will be generated.

Note that the information must be read from the file in the same order that it was written to the file. Go ahead and run the program. You will see that the formatting is now preserved. If we open a file that is created by the program using a text editor, we will see that the file is no longer text and it now contains strange symbols that represent binary data.

13.4   Summary

The chapter shows how to create both text and binary files. It also discusses the topic of checked and unchecked exceptions. While Java forces us to handle checked exceptions, unchecked exceptions do not need to be handled. For example, code can access an element of an array without worrying about an `ArrayIndexOutOfBounds` exception. Conversely, every time we open a file for reading or writing, we need to add code that checks for exceptions. The reason is that something can go wrong (i.e., the file cannot be written) and Java forces us to handle this exception case.

13.5   Syntax

- `void m() throws Exception` $\Rightarrow$ If an exception is generated in the `m` method and the exception is not handled, then the exception is forwarded to the method that called the `m` method. This syntax is used primarily when there is a checked exception that needs to be addressed. If an unhandled exception is generated from the `main` method, then the program crashes.

- `System.err.print("error ...");` $\Rightarrow$ Prints the error on the screen in red.

- `try{ ... } catch(Exception e) { ... }` ⇒ If an exception occurs in the `try` block, then control transfers immediately to the `catch` block and the code in the `catch` block is executed.

- `try {...} finally { ... }` ⇒ The code in the `finally` block is always executed.

- `InputMismatchException` ⇒ Exception that occurs when the user enters the wrong type. For example, the program expects an integer and the user enters a double.

- `ArrayIndexOutOfBoundsException` ⇒ Exception that occurs when the user accesses an index of an array that is outside the elements of the array.

- `ArithmeticException` ⇒ An exception that occurs as a result of arithmetic operations, for example, division by 0.

- `FileNotFoundException` ⇒ An exception that occurs when the program tries to open a file that does not exist.

- `Exception` ⇒ The main exception class. All other exception classes inherit from it.

- `throw new Exception("...")` ⇒ Creates and throws a new exception.

- `e.printStackTrace();` ⇒ Prints the stack trace when the e exception occurs, that is, the order of methods that were called.

- `try(open a file){ ... } catch(Exception e) { ... }` ⇒ Opens a file. If an exception occurs, then control jumps over to the `catch` block. The file is closed automatically at the end.

- `if (fileChooser.showDialog(..., "Open") == JFileChooser.APPROVE_OPTION) {...}` ⇒ Shows a file chooser dialog. The missing parameter is a reference to the parent window.

- `File newFile = fileChooser.getSelectedFile();` ⇒ Gets a file object from a file chooser.

- `Scanner inFile = new Scanner(file);` ⇒ Creates a `Scanner` object from a file.

- `String s = inFile.nextLine();` ⇒ Reads a line from a file.

- `String n = inFile.nextInt();` ⇒ Reads an integer from a file.

- `inFile.hasNextLine()` ⇒ True if there is a next line in the file.

- `inFile.hasNextInt()` ⇒ True if there is a next integer in the file.

- `inFile.close()` ⇒ Closes the file.

- `File newFile = new File("myFile.txt");` ⇒ Creates an object of type `File` by opening the file `myFile.txt`.

- `PrintWriter fileWriter = new PrintWriter("myFile.txt");` ⇒ Creates an object of type `PrintWriter`.

- `fileWriter.print("hello");` ⇒ Prints hello to the file.

- `fileWriter.close();` ⇒ Closes the file.

- `FileOutputStream fileOut = new FileOutputStream("bank.ser");` ⇒ Creates a file output stream from a file.

- `ObjectOutputStream out = new ObjectOutputStream(fileOut);` ⇒ Creates an object output stream for the file.

- `out.writeObject(people);` ⇒ Writes the `people` object to the file.

- `out.writeDouble(d);` ⇒ Writes the double `d` to the binary file.

- `out.writeInt(n);` ⇒ Writes the integer `n` to the binary file.

- `out.writeChars(s);` ⇒ Writes the string `s` to the binary file.

- `out.writeBoolean(b);` ⇒ Writes the Boolean value `b` to the binary file.

- `out.close();` ⇒ Closes the object output stream.

- `fileOut.close();` ⇒ Closes the file.

- `FileInputStream fileIn = new FileInputStream("bank.ser");` ⇒ Creates a file input stream from a file.

- `ObjectInputStream in = new ObjectInputStream(fileIn);` ⇒ Creates an object input stream from a file.

- `person = (Person) in.readObject();` ⇒ Reads an object of type `Person` from the file.

- `double d=in.readDouble();` ⇒ Reads a double from a binary file.

- `int n=in.readInt();` ⇒ Reads an integer from a binary file.

- `String s=in.readChars();` ⇒ Reads a string from a binary file.

- `boolean b=in.readBoolean();` ⇒ Reads a Boolean value from a binary file.

- `in.close();` ⇒ Closes the object output stream.

- `fileOut.close();` ⇒ Closes the file output stream.

13.6 Important Points

1. There are two types of exceptions: *checked* and *unchecked*. Java forces us to handle checked exceptions. Conversely, unchecked exceptions do not have to be handled, but can be. If an exception is generated but not handled, then the program crashes.

2. When handling an exception in the `catch` blocks, always start with the most specific exceptions and then continue with the more general exceptions. If this rule is not followed, then the later `catch` blocks could never be executed and a syntax error will be generated.

3. A `finally` block is always executed. Use a `finally` block to close files and free resources.

4. Write a method that **throws** an exception when you do not want to handle the exception. It becomes the responsibility of the calling method to handle the exception.

5. A method that overrides a method that does not throw an exception cannot throw an exception. The only alternative is to use a **try-catch** statement.

6. Use **try**-with-resources when opening a file. This will close the file automatically and will simplify the code.

7. There are three ways to handle an exception: (1) print an error and terminate the program, (2) print an error message or write to a log file and continue executing the program, or (3) fix the error (e.g., ask for valid input again). It is up to the programmer to choose which way to handle exceptions.

8. Every time we write code that opens a file, we need to add exception-handling code. The reason is that opening a file generates a checked exception that needs to be handled. Using a **try**-with-resources block is the easiest way to handle a possible exception.

9. All classes that will have objects serialized (i.e., objects written to the hard disk) need to implement the **Serializable** interface.

10. Java allows objects with cyclic references to be serialized. The programmer does not need to do anything special. Java will make sure that every object is serialized just once.

11. When an aggregate object is serialized, all its inner objects that implement the **Serializable** interface are also serialized.

13.7   Exercises

1. Create a program that reads a text file, where the name of the file is specified by the user. The program should print the smallest number in the file. You can assume that the file contains only integers.

2. Create a program that asks the user to specify an input and output file. The program should open the input file and copy all the integers from the file into an **ArrayList**. It should then use **Collections.sort** to sort the **ArrayList**. As a final step, the program should output the sorted **ArrayList** into the output file.

3. Create a program that takes as input the name of a file. The program should print the content of the file.

4. Create a program that takes as input the name of a file that contains integers. The program should print the number of integers in the file. You can assume that the file contains only integers.

5. Create a program that takes as input the name of a file. The file does not need to contain only integers. The program should print the average of the integers as a **double**. Use exception handling to skip over elements of the file that are not integers.

13.8 Lab

Create a poor man's drawing program. The program should allow the user to free-draw shapes. The drawing should be represented as an `ArrayList` of shapes, where every shape should be represented as an `ArrayList` of points. Allow the user to open and save drawings through appropriate menus. A drawing should be saved in a file as a binary stream.

13.9 Project

Extend the Hangman game from Chapter 3 by allowing the words to be read from a file. To start off, you will need to create a file that contains a bunch of difficult words (use the Internet to find such a file). Next, you will select a random word from this file and ask the player to guess it by guessing letters. The player is allowed 6 wrong letter guesses, where 6, of course, will be defined as a constant at the beginning of the program. After the sixth wrong guess, the player should see the message: "You lose, the word was ...!". If the user is able to guess all the letters before there are six wrong guesses, then they should see the message "You win".

Here is an example run of the program. User input is in italic.

```
Try to guess my word!
Enter a letter:  Hi
Sorry, that's not a letter.
Enter a letter:  a
Try again
Enter a letter:  b
Try again
Enter a letter:  c
Try again
Enter a letter:  m
M _ _ _ _ _ _ _ _ _
Enter a letter:  i
M I _ _ I _ _ I _ _ I
Enter a letter:  q
Try again
Enter a letter:  p
M I _ _ I _ _ I P P I
Enter a letter:  t
Try again
Enter a letter:  w
Sorry, that's wrong.
You lose, the word was Mississippi!
```

Use a `StringBuffer` to store the current word that contains underscores.

Chapter 14

Recursion

This chapter introduces the reader to the advanced topic of recursion. Recursion is when a method calls itself. Recursive algorithms try to break a complex problem into smaller versions of the same problem, where the smaller versions are solved in the same way (i.e., by breaking them further into smaller problems). Of course, this process should not continue infinitely and at some point the problem should become simple enough so that it can be solved directly (we will refer to this as the *base case* of the recursive program).

Although a powerful tool, a recursive algorithm is not always the best option. It requires allocating extra main memory and it is often inefficient. The chapter gives examples of when recursion should be applied and when alternative approaches perform better. The chapter shows many examples of recursive programs. These include the famous Tower of Hanoi game, binary search, and popular sorting algorithms.

14.1   Base Case and General Case

In a land far far way, there lived a king that liked to play chess. He was also single and wanted to find his queen. One day, a peasant approached the king and made him the following proposal. They would play a game of chess. If the king won, then he could marry the peasant's daughter, who happened to be the fairest of them all. However, if the peasant won, then the king had to give him some grain. The peasant asked for one grain of wheat for the first day and one grain of wheat on the second day. For each day after, the peasant requested to be given the total of the previous two days. Since there are 64 squares on the chessboard, the peasant suggested that he receive grain for "only" 64 days. Before agreeing to the deal, the king decided to write a short program that calculated how many grains of wheat he may need to part with in the unlikely event that he lost the chess match. Here is the program that he wrote.

```
public class Test {
  public static void main(String args[]) {
    long sum = 0L;
    for(int i = 1; i <= 64; i++){
      sum = sum + f(i);
    }
    System.out.println(sum);
  }

  public static long f(int day){
    if( day == 1)
      return 1L;
    if( day == 2)
      return 1L;
    return f(day-1)+f(day-2);
  }
}
```

The f method calculates how much grain the king owes for that day. The main method calculates and prints the total amount of grain that the king will owe if he happens to lose.

Let us closely examine the f method. The first two if statements are the *base cases*. If it is day one or day two, then the king knows exactly how much he needs to pay. Otherwise, he needs to pay the sum of the grain for the previous two days. The recursive formula: f(x) = f(x-1)+f(x-2) is our *general case*.

> When writing a recursive method (i.e., a method that calls itself), always start with the base case or the base cases. These are the simple cases where you know the solution. Next, write the general case. This is where you break a complex problem into simpler problems. The general case is where the recursive call is made.

In the above code, the king has no idea what the exact value of f(30) is. However, he knows that, if by some kind of magic, he finds the value of f(29) and f(28), then the value of f(30) will be simply the sum of the two numbers. This is the general idea of a recursive method. We do not know how to directly solve the general problem. However, we know how to break it down into smaller problems. A recursive program must always start with the base cases. If it does not, then we will always simplify the problem into simpler problems and the process will never terminate. The base cases insure that when the problem is simple enough, we can provide a direct solution and stop the recursion.

Accidentally, the f method computes the Fibonacci number. Figure 14.1 shows how the method computes the fifth Fibonacci number. The value of f(5) is computed as f(4)+f(3). The value of f(4) is recursively computed as f(3)+f(2) and so on.

When a base case is reached, that is f(2) or f(1), our program provides a direct solution to the problem. Note that from Figure 14.1 we can determine that the algorithm is not very efficient. The reason is that, for example, the value of f(3) is computed twice.

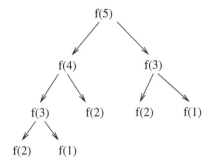

FIGURE 14.1: Example of computing the fifth Fibonacci number recursively.

14.2 Dynamic Programming

The king liked the program and tried to run it on his brand-new supercomputer. To his amazement, the program never gave him an answer. He waited and waited, but the program never terminated. The king became worried. Had he failed to add a base case and inadvertently made the program run forever? Careful consideration shows that this is not the case. The problem is that the program is too slow and runs in exponential time. It performs the same computations multiple times and is not feasible for larger input.

Having seen Figure 14.1, the king decided that a different approach was in order. How can the program avoid making the same computations over and over again? The easiest way is to save the result once it is computed. The program can save the result for f(0), f(1), f(2), and so on. In other words, a bottom-up approach may be called for (instead of the top-down approach of recursion). Here is the new program that the king wrote.

```java
public class Test {
    public static void main(String args[]) {
        long sum = 0L;
        for (int i = 1; i <= 64; i++) {
            sum = sum + f(i);
        }
        System.out.println(sum);
    }

    public static long f(int day) {
        if (day == 1) {
            return 1L;
        }
        if (day == 2) {
            return 1L;
        }
        long a[] = new long[day + 1];
        a[1] = 1L;
        a[2] = 1L;
        for (int i = 3; i <= day; i++) {
            a[i] = a[i - 1] + a[i - 2];
        }
        return a[day];
    }
}
```

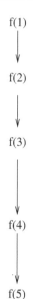

f(1)

f(2)

f(3)

f(4)

f(5)

FIGURE 14.2: Example of computing the 5th Fibonacci number using dynamic programming.

When executed, the program returns 44,945,570,212,850. If there are an average of one million grains of wheat in a bushel and a bushel of wheat costs US\$300, then the king needs to give to the peasant grain that is worth a total of roughly US\$13.5 billion. The king decided that this was a small price to risk for the fairest maiden of them all. The peasant liked that the king was prudent enough to do all the calculations and he let him win. The king married the peasant's daughter and they lived happily ever after.

Let us examine in greater detail why the second solution to the problem is better. Since the computations are performed bottom up, every Fibonacci number is calculated exactly once; see Figure 14.2. The approach in which we start by calculating the answers to the simplest problem and then we calculate the answers to more complicated problems as a function of existing results is called *dynamic programming*.

In most cases, a dynamic programming solution is faster than a recursive solution. Whenever possible, we should avoid using a recursive solution. However, in many cases a dynamic programming solution is not obvious and even nonexistent, while a recursive solution is straightforward to find and implement.

Next, let us examine a problem that is naturally suited for recursion. While a non-recursive solution is certainly possible, it cannot be easily programmed. Consider the Tower of Hanoi problem; see Figure 14.3. In the picture, there are 8 rings on the first needle. The problem is to move them to the third needle. Only one ring can be moved at a time and a ring can be placed only on top of a bigger ring.

Moving all eight rings in the right order seems a challenging task. However, if by magic, someone can show us how to move seven rings, then the problem becomes significantly easier. We just need to move seven rings from the first to the middle needle, the last ring from the first to the last needle, and then the seven rings from the second to the last needle. In this case, a recursive solution just comes naturally. On the other hand, it is not obvious

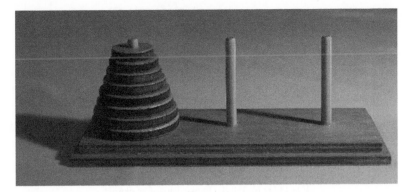

FIGURE 14.3: Towers of Hanoi. Picture taken from Wikipedia Commons.

how a non-recursive solution can be developed. Our recursive code that solves the Tower of Hanoi problem is shown next.

```
public class Test {
  public static void main(String args[]) {
    move(8, "needle 1","needle 3","needle 2");
  }

  public static void move(int count, String sourceNeedle, String
      destinationNeedle, String intermediateNeedle){
    if(count == 0) return;
    move(count-1, sourceNeedle, intermediateNeedle, destinationNeedle);
    System.out.println("Move a ring from: "+sourceNeedle+ " to "+
        destinationNeedle);
    move(count-1, intermediateNeedle, destinationNeedle, sourceNeedle);

  }
}
```

In the main method, we ask the **move** method to move 8 rings from Needle 1 to Needle 3. This can be done by moving 7 rings from Needle 1 to Needle 2, 1 ring from Needle 1 to Needle 3, and then 7 rings from Needle 2 to Needle 3. The seven rings are moved in the same way using the same method. Note that, as expected, the **move** method starts with the base case. If the variable **count** is equal to 0, then there are no rings to move and we are done.

14.3   Internal Details of a Recursive Call

In order to understand how recursion works, we first need to understand one of the most primitive data structures: the *stack*. You can think of a stack as being a stack of dishes. You have two operations: you can *push* a dish on top of the stack, or you can *pop* the dish from the top of the stack. Only the top of the stack can be accessed.

For example, consider Figure 14.4. First, we push 3 on the stack. Then, we push the number 5. At this point, only the top of the stack is accessible. If we execute the command

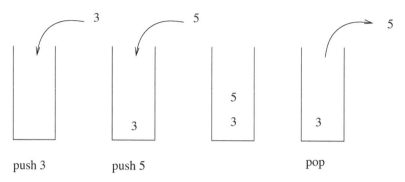

FIGURE 14.4: Example of a stack.

pop, we will get the number 5. If we execute the command **pop** again, we will get the number 3 and the stack will become empty.

During a program execution, Java creates a stack that is used to store system information.

> Every time a method is called (recursive or not), the value of all local variables and the return address are stored in a frame and pushed on top of the stack. When a method executes a **return** statement, the program pops the top frame of the stack. It transitions to the return address and it loads the value for all the local variables of the method from the frame.

Note that the same method can be executing multiple times at any given point, and for every execution the value of the local variables can be different. Therefore, when we return to a method, we need to know the value of all the local variables. We also need to know the return point in the program when the **return** statement is reached. This is the information that is saved in the stack.

Let us consider the following recursive method that computes the factorial of a number.

```
public static int f(int n){
  if(n == 0){
    return 1;
  }
  return f(n-1)*n;
}
```

Consider Figure 14.5 (for simplicity, the return address is not shown in the figure). The method first checks the base case. We know that $0! = 1$. It then uses the recursive formula $n! = (n - 1)! * n$ to create the general case. In other words, the problem is reduced to a smaller version of itself. Suppose the method is called with $n = 2$. Then the return value will be **f(1)*2**. Before the **f** method can be called again, the value of **n** and the return point are saved on the stack. Next, the method is called with $n = 1$. Since $1 \neq 0$, the method is called again with $n = 0$. However, before this call can be made, the current value of **n**, which is 1, together with the return point are stored on the stack. Now the method is executed with $n = 0$ and the value 1 is returned. The **return** statement pops a frame from the stack. The value of 1 is loaded into the variable n and the program jumps to the return address that is stored on the stack. Now the method will return $1 * 1 = 1$. The **return** statement forces another frame to be popped from the stack. This time the value of 2 is loaded into

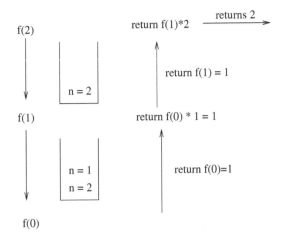

FIGURE 14.5: Example of computing 2! recursively.

the variable n and the program jumps to the new return address. Now the return value will be $2 * 1 = 2$. Therefore, the method will return the value 2.

Note that, of course, we can write an iterative method to compute $n!$.

```
public static int f(int n){
  int result = 1;
  while(true){
    if(n == 0){
      return result;
    }
    result = result * n;
    n--;
  }
}
```

The reason this non-recursive rewrite is possible and so simple is because there is a single recursive call at the end of the original method. In literature, this case is sometimes referred to as *tail recursion*. It can be shown that if a method contains a single recursive call at the end of every execution branch, then we can easily rewrite our code and substitute the recursive call with an infinite `while` loop. However, if there is a recursive call that is not at the end of an execution branch, then this approach cannot be directly applied.

Our example of computing $n!$ recursively showed us that there is extra overhead that is needed in order to make a recursive program work. Therefore, when possible, one should try to develop non-recursive solutions. However, in some cases, a recursive solution is the only option that is available short of implementing our own stack and recursive calls.

14.4 Array Algorithms

Next, we show five sorting algorithms and one algorithm that finds a number in a sorted array. Many of the problems can be easily solved without using recursion. However, in order to demonstrate how to use recursion on algorithms with arrays, we will present a recursive solution for each of the problems. Where applicable, we will also show the non-recursive solution.

14.4.1 Binary Search

It is time to write another game. We will ask the player to think of a number between 1 and 1000. Then our program will be able to guess the number in 10 tries or less. Every time the user just needs to tell the program if their number is higher, lower, or equal to the computer guess. At every step, the computer is given an interval (originally [1,1000]). The computer's guess is always in the middle of the interval. Based on the user response, the computer will keep shrinking the interval. For example, the computer will first guess 500. If the user says higher, then the computer will examine the interval [501,1000] and apply the same algorithm. The base case is when the interval consists of a single number (it must be the user's number) or when the user admits that we have guessed the number. Here is a possible implementation.

```java
import java.util.*;

public class GuessingGame {
    public static void main(String[] args){
        System.out.println("Please think of a number between 1 and 1000");
        guess(1,1000, 500);
    }
    public static void guess(int low, int high, int guess){
        if(low == high){
            System.out.println("Your number must be: "+low);
            System.exit(0);
        }
        System.out.print("Is your number higher(h), lower(l), or equal(e) to: "+guess+": ");
        Scanner keyboard = new Scanner(System.in);
        String result = keyboard.next();
        switch(result.charAt(0)){
            case 'h':
                guess(guess+1,high, (guess+high+1)/2); break;
            case 'l':
                guess(low, guess-1, (low+guess-1)/2); break;
            case 'e':
                System.out.println("I win again!");
                System.exit(0);
        }
    }
}
```

Here is one possible run of the program (user input in italic):

```
Please think of a number between 1 and 1000
Is your number higher(h), lower(l), or equal(e) to: 500:h
```

```
Is your number higher(h), lower(l), or equal(e) to: 750:l
Is your number higher(h), lower(l), or equal(e) to: 625:h
Is your number higher(h), lower(l), or equal(e) to: 687:l
Is your number higher(h), lower(l), or equal(e) to: 656:h
Is your number higher(h), lower(l), or equal(e) to: 671:l
Is your number higher(h), lower(l), or equal(e) to: 663:h
Is your number higher(h), lower(l), or equal(e) to: 667:l
Is your number higher(h), lower(l), or equal(e) to: 665:h
Your number must be: 666
```

Let us examine the **guess** method. The interval and the guess are passed as parameters. Every time there is a recursive call, the interval is reduced by half and the guess is placed in the middle of the interval. The code `System.exit(0)` guarantees that the code will exit after the solution is found. Therefore, we keep calling the **guess** method and the **guess** method never returns to the calling method. Note that in this program we cannot replace `System.exit(0)` with `return`. The reason is that we do not want to return to the calling method. This program is a case where a recursive solution is not needed because all the recursive calls are at the end of execution paths. Applying our knowledge of tail recursion, we can rewrite the code as follows.

```java
public static void guess(int low, int high, int guess) {
  while (true) {
    if (low == high) {
      System.out.println("Your number must be: " + low);
      System.exit(0);
    }
    System.out.print("Is your number higher(h), lower(l), or equal(e)
        to: " + guess + ": ");
    Scanner keyboard = new Scanner(System.in);
    String result = keyboard.next();
    switch (result.charAt(0)) {
      case 'h':
        low=guess + 1;
        guess = (guess + high + 1) / 2;
        break;
      case 'l':
        high = guess - 1;
        guess = (low + guess - 1) / 2;
        break;
      case 'e':
        System.out.println("I win again!");
        System.exit(0);
    }
  }
}
```

Note that the original recursive call had several execution paths. Since each path led to a single recursive call and this call was the last call for that branch, we were able to rewrite the code using the tail recursion principle.

We solved the problem using the 'divide-and-concur approach. We kept reducing the size of the original array until there was a single number in it. Let us next see if we can apply the same approach to a slightly different application. Suppose that we are given a sorted array of distinct numbers and we want to find the index of a specific number in the array. For example, consider the following sorted array of integers.

1 3 5 8 20 50 100

If we are searching for the integer 5, we can apply the same approach as the guessing game. We can first examine the element in the middle: 8. Since 5 is smaller than 8 and the array is sorted, then it must be the case that the number 5 is in the first part of the array. We can then shrink the search interval to the first half of the array and apply the algorithm recursively. The base case will be when we have an array of a single element. Then we can immediately tell if the number is in the array or not. If the number is not in the array, then we will return −1. Otherwise, we will return the index of the number we are searching for in the array. A possible implementation follows.

```java
class BinarySearch{
  public static void main(String[] args) {
    int[] a = {1,3,5,8,20,50,100};
    System.out.println(binarySearch(0, a.length−1, 5, a));
  }

  public static int binarySearch(int start, int end, int number, int[] a) {
    int mid = (start + end) / 2;
    if (start == end) {
      if (a[end] == number) {
        return end;
      } else {
        return −1;
      }
    }
    if (a[mid] >= number) {
      return binarySearch(start, mid, number, a);
    }
    return binarySearch(mid + 1, end, number, a);
  }
}
```

Note that every time the **binarySearch** method is called, a different part of the array needs to be passed as a parameter. Since creating a new array from an existing array is not a trivial task, we have chosen to pass the start and end index of the new array as parameters. Note that the array is also passed as a parameter. Since the value of the array reference is not changed, we can think of it as a constant that the **binarySearch** method needs to access, but never change. Such constants are common in recursive methods. As an alternative, the **a** array could have been defined as a global variable. However, this is an inferior solution because the array will now be accessible by all the methods in the class.

The base case is when the array has a single element. If it is our integer, then we return the index of the element. Otherwise, the method returns −1. In the general case, we recursively search in the first or the second half of the array depending on whether the search number is smaller or bigger than the middle of the array, respectively. It is interesting to note that the running time of the method is logarithmic. For example, we can find the element that we are looking for in an array of one million elements using at most 20 recursive calls.

Note that the binary search code uses tail recursion. Recursive calls are always at the end of the execution paths and there is at most one recursive call at the end of every path. Therefore, the code can be rewritten to use an infinite **while** loop as follows.

```java
public static int binarySearch(int start, int end,
        int number, int[] a) {
```

```
      while (true) {
        int mid = (start + end) / 2;
        if (start == end) {
          if (a[end] == number) {
            return end;
          } else {
            return -1;
          }
        }
        if (a[mid] >= number) {
          end = mid;
        } else {
          start = mid + 1;
        }
      }
    }
```

Note that the new code is missing the recursive return statements in the second part of the code. Therefore, an `if-else` structure is now needed. Alternatively, the `return` statement could have been substituted with a `continue` statement that goes back to the beginning of the infinite `while` loop as shown below.

```
public static int binarySearch(int start, int end,
          int number, int[] a) {
  while (true) {
    int mid = (start + end) / 2;
    if (start == end) {
      if (a[end] == number) {
        return end;
      } else {
        return -1;
      }
    }
    if (a[mid] >= number) {
      end = mid;
      continue;
    }
    start = mid + 1;
  }
}
```

14.4.2 Bubble Sort

Bubble sort is the easiest type of sort. You can think of boiling water. As the water boils, the lighter particles bubble to the top, while the heavier ones sink to the bottom. The algorithm uses the same principle. Let us examine one pass of the algorithm. Consider the following array.

10 5 20 2

The first pass of the algorithm goes left to right. It compares a pair of numbers. If they are in the wrong order, then the algorithm swaps them. For example, the algorithm will first look at 10 and 5. They are in the wrong order and it will swap them.

5 10 20 2

Next, the algorithm will compare the numbers 10 and 20. They are in the correct order, so nothing to do. Lastly, the algorithm will compare the numbers 20 and 2. They are in the wrong order and therefore the algorithm will swap them.

5 10 2 20

After the first pass finishes executing, the biggest number will be at the end of the array (in our case, this is the number 20). The second pass applies the same algorithm, but it is not applied on the last number, which we already know is the biggest. If the algorithm is implemented recursively, then the base case is when the array consists of a single element. In this case, nothing needs to be done because an array of a single element is already sorted. The recursive implementation follows.

```java
public class Test {
  public static void main(String args[]) {
    int[] a = {10,5,20,2};
    bubbleSort(a,a.length-1);
    for(int el: a){
      System.out.print(el+" ");
    }
  }

  public static void bubbleSort(int []a, int end){
    if(end==0) return;
    for(int i = 0; i < end; i++){
      if(a[i]>a[i+1]){
        int temp = a[i];
        a[i] = a[i+1];
        a[i+1] = temp;
      }
    }
    bubbleSort(a,end-1);
  }
}
```

Note that only the index of the last element of the array to be processed changes. The index of the first element to be processed is always 0. This is the reason why only the end of the array is passed as a parameter. Note as well that the algorithm combines a recursive call with a `for` statement. There is nothing that says that a recursive solution cannot be embedded with loops.

Since the recursive call is at the end, this is again a case of tail recursion. The `bubbleSort` method can be rewritten not to use a recursion as follows.

```java
public static void bubbleSort(int[] a, int end) {
  while (true) {
    if (end == 0) {
      return;
    }
    for (int i = 0; i < end; i++) {
      if (a[i] > a[i + 1]) {
        int temp = a[i];
        a[i] = a[i + 1];
        a[i + 1] = temp;
      }
    }
    end--;
  }
}
```

}

A possible optimization of the method is to keep track of how many times the swap was performed. If the swap was not performed at all during an iteration of the algorithm, then we know that the list is already sorted. Here is how this optimization can be added to the code.

```java
public static void bubbleSort(int[] a, int end) {
  while (true) {
    if (end == 0) {
      return;
    }
    boolean modified = false;
    for (int i = 0; i < end; i++) {
      if (a[i] > a[i + 1]) {
        int temp = a[i];
        a[i] = a[i + 1];
        a[i + 1] = temp;
        modified = true;
      }
    }
    if (!modified) return; //array not modified
    end--;
  }
}
```

Note that the algorithm runs in roughly $n * n$ time. This means that it may take one trillion operations to sort an array of one million integers. As we will see later, there are more efficient ways to sort an array.

14.4.3 Selection Sort

Selection sort works similar to the bubble sort. However, instead of moving the biggest elements to the end of the array, the algorithm moves the smallest elements to the beginning of the array. Consider the same array of integers as before.

10 5 20 2

The algorithm goes through the whole array and finds the smallest number: 2. Next, it swaps the smallest number with the first element of the array.

2 5 20 10

At this point, the smallest number of the array is the first element. The algorithm continues recursively by sorting the rest of the array (i.e., all the numbers except for the 2, which is already in the right place). The base case is when the size of the array becomes one. An array of one element is already sorted. A recursive implementation of the algorithm follows.

```java
public class SelectionSort {
  public static void main(String args[]) {
    int[] a = {10, 5, 20, 2};
    selectionSort(0, a);
    for (int el : a) {
      System.out.print(el + " ");
    }
  }
}
```

```java
public static int findMin(int a[], int start) {
  int minIndex = start;
  for (int i = start; i < a.length; i++) {
    if (a[i] < a[minIndex]) {
      minIndex = i;
    }
  }
  return minIndex;
}

public static void swap(int a[], int i, int j) {
  int temp = a[i];
  a[i] = a[j];
  a[j] = temp;
}

public static void selectionSort(int start, int[] a) {
  if (start == a.length - 1) {
    return;
  }
  int j = findMin(a, start);
  swap(a, start, j);
  selectionSort(start + 1, a);
}
}
```

The `selectionSort` method takes as input the start index. The end index does not change and therefore there is no need to pass it as a parameter to the method. The base case is when the start and the end indexes are the same, that is, the array has a single element. If we do not have the base case, then our code finds the index of the smallest element and swaps this element with the first element in the current array. Then the algorithm is recursively applied to the rest of the array. Note that we have added a method that swaps two elements in an array and a method that finds the index of the smallest number in an array. The method for swapping two elements in an array can be quite useful in a sorting algorithm. If we had created this method during the coding of the bubble sort algorithm, then we would not have to write the code again.

We again have a case of tail recursion. A non-recursive solution of the problem is shown next.

```java
public static void selectionSort(int start, int[] a) {
  while (true) {
    if (start == a.length - 1) {
      return;
    }
    int j = findMin(a, start);
    swap(a, start, j);
    start++;
  }
}
```

The method runs roughly as efficiently as the bubble sort. The main difference is that instead of moving the biggest element to the end, the method moves the smallest element to the front.

14.4.4 Insertion Sort

The *insertion sort* method works by keeping two lists. At the beginning, the first list will be empty, while the second list will contain the unsorted elements. At every iteration, the first element of the second list is removed from the second list and inserted in its proper place in the first list (i.e., the first list is always sorted). When the second list becomes empty, the first list will contain all the elements sorted. Here is an example run of insertion sort.

```
initial list :  {23,2,4,65,3}
l1:{}   l2={23,2,4,65,3}
after 1 iteration: l1: {23}      l2={2,4,65,3}
after 2 iteration: l1={2,23}, l2={4,65,3}
after 3 iterations: l1={2,4,23}, l2={65,3}
after 4 iterations: l1={2,4,23,65}, l2={3}
after 5 iterations: l1={2,3,4,23,65}, l2={}
```

Let us look at a real-world example of how to apply insertion sort. Suppose that we are given a deck of cards and we want to sort them. We can take the first card and put it in the resulting list. Next, we will take the next card and put it again in the resulting list in the right order and so on. At the end, all the cards will be sorted.

Since this algorithm involves adding and removing elements from lists, it can be more easily implemented by using **ArrayLists** instead of arrays. If we want to solve the problem recursively, we can create a method that moves the first number from the l2 list to the correct position in the l1 list and then applies the algorithm recursively. The base case will be when the l2 list becomes empty.

```java
import java.util.*;
public class InsertionSort{
  public static void main(String args[]) {
    int[] a = {23,2,4,65,3};
    ArrayList<Integer> l1 = new ArrayList<>();
    ArrayList<Integer> l2 = new ArrayList<>();
    for(int el:a) {
      l2.add(el);
    }
    insertionSort(l1, l2);
    System.out.println(l1);
  }
  public static void insertionSort(ArrayList<Integer> l1, ArrayList<
      Integer> l2){
    if(l2.size()==0){
      return;
    }
    int newElement = l2.get(0);
    l2.remove(0);
    for(int i=0;i < l1.size(); i++){
      if(newElement< l1.get(i)){
        l1.add(i,newElement);
        insertionSort(l1,l2);
        return;
      }
    }
    l1.add(newElement);
    insertionSort(l1,l2);
  }
```

}

The `insertionSort` method moves the elements from the 12 list into the 11 list. Every time an element is inserted into the 11 list, it is inserted in the right place so that the elements of the 11 list are sorted. The base case is when the 12 list becomes empty. The method iterates through all the elements of the 11 list and finds the correct place to insert the first element of the 12 list. If such a place is not found, then the element is inserted at the end. At the same time, this first element is removed from the 12 list. Note that once the insertion point is found, the recursive call is made. When we return from the recursive call, we simply exit the method by calling the `return` statement.

Once again, this is an example of tail recursion. The recursive calls are made at the end of the two execution paths of the method. The code can be rewritten to use an infinite `while` loop as follows.

```java
public static void insertionSort(ArrayList<Integer> l1, ArrayList<
    Integer> l2) {
  while (true) {
    if (l2.size() == 0) {
      return;
    }
    int newElement = l2.get(0);
    l2.remove(0);
    int i;
    for (i = 0; i < l1.size(); i++) {
      if (newElement < l1.get(i)) {
        l1.add(i, newElement);
        break;
      }
    }
    if(i == l1.size()){
      l1.add(newElement);
    }
  }
}
```

Note that there is a non-cosmetic change to the code. Since we want our algorithm to go to the next iteration when we discover the insertion point, we moved the variable i outside the `for` statement. In this way, we can check if the element was already inserted into the 12 list or if it needs to be inserted at the end of the list. Recall that the `add` method for an `ArrayList` inserts the element at the end of the list if the insert location is not specified. Similar to the bubble and selection sort, the insertion sort takes roughly $n * n$ time for an array of n elements.

14.4.5 Quick Sort

Quick sort starts by making the first element the pivot. Then it finds all the elements that are smaller than the pivot and puts them before the pivot. All the elements that are larger than the pivot are put after the pivot. The elements before and after the pivot are sorted recursively. Since there are two recursive calls at the end, the tail recursion principle does not apply and a non-recursive solution to the problem cannot be easily found.

Consider the following array of numbers.

20 3 30 5 8 40 7

Quick sort will select the first element as the pivot: the number 20. The numbers that are smaller than 20 are: 3, 5, 8, and 7. When we recursively sort them, we will get the numbers {3,5,7,8}. The numbers that are greater than 20 are {30,40}, which happen to be sorted. Therefore, the sorted array will be {3,5,7,8}, 20, {30,40}. One possible implementation is shown next. For convenience, the implementation uses an `ArrayList`.

```java
import java.util.*;
public class QuickSort {
  public static void main(String args[]) {
    int[] a = {20, 3, 30, 5, 8, 40, 7};
    ArrayList<Integer> list = new ArrayList<>();
    for (int el : a) {
      list.add(el);
    }
    list = quickSort(list);
    System.out.println(list);
  }
  public static ArrayList<Integer> quickSort(ArrayList<Integer> a){
    if(a.size()<=1) return a;
    int pivot = a.get(0);
    ArrayList<Integer> smaller = new ArrayList<>();
    ArrayList<Integer> greater = new ArrayList<>();
    for(int i=1; i < a.size(); i++){
      if(a.get(i)<= pivot){
        smaller.add(a.get(i));
      } else {
        greater.add(a.get(i));
      }
    }
    ArrayList<Integer> result = quickSort(smaller);
    result.add(pivot);
    result.addAll(quickSort(greater));
    return result;
  }
}
```

The recursive method first checks to see if the input array has 1 or 0 elements. If this is the case, then nothing needs to be done because the list is already sorted. Otherwise, the pivot element is set to the first element in the list and two empty `ArrayLists` are created. All the elements that are smaller or equal to the pivot are added to the first list (this allows sorting an array with duplicates), while all the elements that are bigger than the pivot are added to the second list. Finally, the two lists are sorted and the pivot is inserted between them to create the resulting list. The `addAll` method of the `ArrayList` class is used to merge two `ArrayLists`.

The quick sort behaves well when the `smaller` and `greater` lists are roughly of equal size at every iteration. Ironically, the quick sort performs the worst when the array is already sorted. In this case, one of the lists will contain all the elements, while the other list will be empty at every single iteration. In this case, the performance will be comparable to that of the previous sorting algorithms. When the two lists are roughly of the same size at every iteration, the performance of the algorithm is roughly $n * log(n)$ for an array of size n. This means that an array of one million elements can be processed in roughly twenty million operations, which is relatively fast. However, when the original list is close to being sorted, the method can take roughly one trillion operations.

14.4.6 Merge Sort

The main shortcoming of the quick sort algorithm is that its running time is unpredictable. For some sequences, the algorithm can perform really fast. However, if the original numbers are close to being sorted, then the algorithm will not perform that well. The main problem with quick sort is that it does not guarantee that the two lists are of roughly equal size. The *merge sort* algorithm is similar to the quick sort algorithm. However, at each step it splits the array into two lists that are of roughly equal size. The certainty that the lists are of roughly equal size comes with a price: the algorithm needs to perform an additional merge step at every iteration.

Let us consider the following list of elements.

20 3 6 11 45 2

The merge sort algorithm will first split the array into two roughly equal halves: {20,3,6} and {11,45,2}. Next, each of the halves will be sorted recursively. The result will be the halves: {3,6,20} and {2,11,45}. As a final step, the two halves will be merged. At every step of the merge, the front of each of the lists will be examined and the smallest of the two numbers will be moved to the result. When one of the lists is exhausted, then the elements of the other list will be moved to the result. An example implementation follows.

```java
import java.util.*;

public class MergeSort {
  public static void main(String args[]) {
    int[] a = {20, 3, 6, 11, 45, 2};
    ArrayList<Integer> list = new ArrayList<>();
    for (int el : a) {
      list.add(el);
    }
    list = mergeSort(list);
    System.out.println(list);
  }

  public static ArrayList<Integer> mergeSort(ArrayList<Integer> a) {
    if (a.size() <= 1) {
      return a;
    }
    ArrayList<Integer> firstHalf = new ArrayList<>();
    ArrayList<Integer> secondHalf = new ArrayList<>();
    for (int i = 0; i < a.size() / 2; i++) {
      firstHalf.add(a.get(i));
    }
    for (int i = a.size() / 2; i < a.size(); i++) {
      secondHalf.add(a.get(i));
    }
    return merge(mergeSort(firstHalf), mergeSort(secondHalf));
  }

  public static ArrayList<Integer> merge(ArrayList<Integer> l1,
      ArrayList<Integer> l2) {
    ArrayList<Integer> result = new ArrayList<>();
    while (true) {
      if (l1.size() == 0) {
        result.addAll(l2);
        return result;
```

```
    }
    if (12.size() == 0) {
      result.addAll(11);
      return result;
    }
    if (11.get(0) > 12.get(0)) {
      int nextElement = 12.get(0);
      result.add(nextElement);
      12.remove(0);
    } else {
      int nextElement = 11.get(0);
      result.add(nextElement);
      11.remove(0);
    }
  }
 }
}
```

The `mergeSort` method it relatively straightforward. The base case is when the list has one or zero elements. In this case, we can just return the list. Otherwise, we split the list into two parts: `firstHalf` and `secondHalf`. We sort each half recursively and then we merge the halves. Note that the tail recursion principle does not apply here because there are multiple recursive calls that are not at the end of an execution path.

The `merge` method can also be implemented recursively as follows.

```
public static ArrayList<Integer> merge(ArrayList<Integer> 11, ArrayList
    <Integer> 12) {
  if (11.size() == 0) {
    return 12;
  }
  if (12.size() == 0) {
    return 11;
  }
  ArrayList<Integer> result = new ArrayList<>();
  int nextElement;
  if (11.get(0) > 12.get(0)) {
    nextElement = 12.get(0);
    12.remove(0);
  } else {
    nextElement = 11.get(0);
    11.remove(0);
  }
  result.add(nextElement);
  result.addAll(merge(11,12));
  return result;
}
```

If one of the lists is exhausted, then the method returns the other list. This is the base case. Alternatively, if there are elements in both lists, then we examine the first element of each list. The smallest of the two values is saved in the variable `nextElement` and removed from the list. As a final step, the method returns an `ArrayList` that contains the value of the variable `nextElement` followed by recursively merging the rest of the lists. Note that this is a case of tail recursion because there is a single recursive call that appears at the end. Therefore, the code can be rewritten to use an infinite `while` loop as shown in the original code.

Merge sort is the only algorithm in this book that gives us good running time in the worst case. It takes roughly $n * log(n)$ operations to sort the array, which is a significant improvement over the previous algorithms. For an array of size one million elements, it will take roughly twenty million operations to sort the array.

Note that it is possible to combine several of the proposed sorting algorithms. For example, insertion sort can be used on small arrays (e.g., less than 10 elements). For a big array, merge sort can be applied until the array becomes smaller than 10 elements, at which point insertion sort can be used again. Using merge sort guarantees us good worst-case running time. Conversely, applying insertion sort to small arrays will limit the number of recursive calls and make the program more efficient. In other words, the bubble sort, insertion sort, and selection sort are good for sorting small arrays. The quick and merge sort perform better on bigger arrays. Creating an algorithm that is a combination of two sorting algorithms can give us the best of both worlds. For example, this is the approach that is used in implementing the `Arrays.sort` and `Collections.sort` Java methods.

14.5 Summary

The chapter describes the mechanisms behind recursive calls. It gives examples of using recursion and shows how recursion can be used to implement binary search and different sorting algorithms. Recursion is described in this book because it is an important programming technique. For example, it is not obvious how to solve the Tower of Hanoi or implement merge sort without using recursion. On the other hand, one should not go overboard writing recursive methods and the iterative approach is preferred when possible because it has less overhead.

The chapter also briefly describes dynamic programming. This is a bottom-up approach that calculates the result by starting with small problems and then merging the results. It is an alternative to a recursive algorithm in some cases and it is the preferred choice when applicable. The chapter also covered the topic of tail recursion. This is a scenario where all the recursive calls are at the end of the execution paths of the method. The chapter shows how tail recursion can be easily rewritten into an iterative solution that uses an infinite `while` loop.

14.6 Syntax

- `a.addAll(b);` ⇒. The `ArrayList` b is added to the end of the `ArrayList` a.

14.7 Important Points

1. A recursive solution breaks a big problem into smaller problems. The smaller problems are solved by applying exactly the same breakup algorithm. When the problem becomes simple enough, the solution can be directly identified using the base cases.

2. Always start a recursive method with the base cases. Add the recursive calls after that. If this rule is not followed, then the method may not terminate, that is, the method may run forever (a.k.a., infinite recursion).

3. Avoid using recursion when possible. An iterative solution is usually faster and takes less main memory.

4. There is a limitation to using a recursive method. Since the size of the stack grows with every recursive call, it is easy to get a stack overflow error if there are too many recursive calls.

5. Tail recursion is when there is a single recursive call that appears at the end of every execution path. A recursive method that uses tail recursion can be easily rewritten into a non-recursive method that uses an infinite `while` loop.

6. Dynamic programming creates a bottom-up solution. In contract, a recursion algorithm represents the top-down approach. When applicable, dynamic programming can be useful to avoid performing the same computations multiple times.

7. Bubble sort, insertion sort, and selection sort are easy to implement. However, they are not very fast for big arrays. Quick sort can be fast in some cases, but it performs poorly when the input array is close to being sorted. Conversely, merge sort has good worst-case running time. Quick sort and merge sort cannot be easily implemented without using recursion.

8. Binary search is very fast and it is a useful tool for locating an element in an array. However, binary search only works when the array is sorted.

14.8 Exercises

1. Write a recursive method that computes the sum of the first 100 positive integers.

2. Write a recursive method takes as input an array and returns the smallest number in the array. Add additional parameters to the method as needed.

3. Write a recursive method that takes as input an array. The method should reverse the array. Add additional parameters to the method as needed.

4. Write a recursive method that computes the number of primes between the integers a and b. The method can call the `isPrime` method, which checks if a number is prime. Identify if the original method uses tail recursion. If it does, then rewrite it as an iterative method using an infinite `while` loop.

5. A palindrome is a string that reads the same forward and backward. Write a recursive method that determines if the input string is a palindrome. Feel free to introduce additional parameters to the method.

6. Write a recursive method that takes as input an integer and returns the binary representation of the integer as a string. Feel free to introduce additional parameters to the method and/or create more methods.

14.9   Lab

Create an application that reads an odd positive integer as a parameter. The application should then print a diamond. For example, for input 5, the following diamond should be printed.

```
  *
 ***
*****
 ***
  *
```

The solution should be purely recursive, that is, no loops are allowed. The following recursive methods may be useful.

- void printTopPart(int n, int stars, int spaces)

- void printBottomPart(int n, int stars, int spaces)

- void printChars(char c, int frequency)

The printTopPart method should print the top part of the diamond. The variable n is the user input, which is 5 in the above picture. This number will not change through the recursive calls. The variables stars and spaces define the number of stars and spaces. Both variables will change at each recursive call. Since their value changes differently in the top and bottom part of the diamond, the task can be separated into two methods. The printChars method prints the character c several times (i.e., frequency number of times).

14.10   Project

In this project you will find the longest increasing sequence in a two-dimensional area of positive integers that is stored in a file. For example, the following numbers may be stored in the file matrix.dat.

```
97 47 56 36 60 31 57 54 12 55
35 57 41 13 82 80 71 93 31 62
89 36 98 75 91 46 95 53 37 99
25 45 26 17 15 82 80 73 96 17
75 22 63 96 96 36 64 31 99 86
12 80 42 74 54 14 93 17 14 55
14 15 20 71 34 50 22 60 32 41
90 69 44 52 54 73 20 12 55 52
39 33 25 31 76 45 44 84 90 52
```

Your first task is to read the integers from the file in a two-dimensional array. Since you do not know how many numbers are stored in each line, you will need to use the nextLine method to read a whole line and then use the StringTokenizer class to find the number of integers per line. Assuming s is a line that is read from the file, the following code finds the number of integers in the line and stores the result in the variable length.

```
StringTokenizer st = new StringTokenizer(s);
int length=0;
while (st.hasMoreTokens()) {
  st.nextToken();
  length++;
}
```

Your next task is to find the longest increasing sequence, where a sequence starts at an integer and moves right or down to the next integer (you are not allowed to go left or up). The output of the program consists of a list of (row, column) items. For the numbers in the example array, this is the output for the longest increasing sequence. Each cell is represented as (row, column), where counting starts at 0.

(5,0) (6,0) (6,1) (6,2) (7,2) (7,3) (7,4) (8,4)

This sequence represents the numbers {12,14,15,20,44,52,54,76}. Note that there can be several longest sequences, where the program is required to print just one of them. A simple way to solve the problem is to find the longest sequence starting from each number and then return the longest of all the sequences. The longest sequence starting at an integer can be defined recursively as a function of the longest sequences that starts from the integer to the right and the longest sequence that starts from the integer below. For extra credit, try to find a more efficient non-recursive solution. Think dynamic programming.

Chapter 15

Java Applets

The last game of this book is the popular Tic-Tac-Toe game. In order for the player to be able to play the game from more places, we will show how to place the game inside an applet. This means that the user can play the game from their favorite web browser without worrying about where to find the game and how to install it.

15.1   HTML and the Java Applet Architecture

Consider Figure 15.1. The file `TicTacToe.java` contains the code of our program. When we compile it, the `TicTacToe.class` file is created. This file contains Java binary code that can be executed by the *Java Virtual Machine (JVM)*. If we want to run a Java Applet, we first need to download a `.html` file from the server. Here is part of an example `.html` file that was automatically generated by NetBeans.

```
<HTML>
<HEAD>
   <TITLE>Applet HTML Page</TITLE>
</HEAD>

<BODY>
<H3><HR WIDTH="100%">Applet HTML Page<HR WIDTH="100%"></H3>
<P>
<APPLET codebase="classes" code="TicTacToe.class" width=350 height
   =200></APPLET>
</P>
</BODY>
</HTML>
```

HTML stands for *hypertext markup language*. It is one of the simplest kind of web pages that a web browser can display. An HTML file contains the text to be displayed together with markup information (i.e., directions of how to display the text). An HTML file must start with the <HTML> tag and then end with an </HTML> tag. The symbol / means end of the section. An HTML file usually has two sections: head and body. The title is

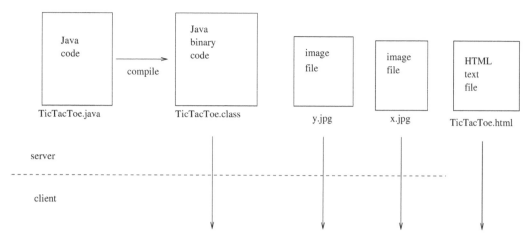

FIGURE 15.1: Java Applet architecture.

specified inside the head section. This is the title that will be displayed as the title of the web browser window when the page is opened. Inside the body of an HTML file, one cannot specify the point size of the text. Instead, one can specify headers of different size (e.g., H1, H2, and so on, where H1 is the biggest size). The <P> and </P> can be used to create a new paragraph that is surrounded by horizontal lines.

Examine the code: `<APPLET codebase="classes" code="TicTacToe.class" width = 350 height=200></APPLET>`. This means display an applet at this place on the HTML web page. The `codebase` parameter specifies the directory (relative to the directory where the `.html` file is located) where the `.class` file can be found. As suggested in Figure 15.1, both the `.html` and `.class` files need to be sent to the client.

> An applet is similar to a Java application, but it has limited capabilities. It cannot execute any program other than the applet on the client side. It cannot access any files on the client's computer, except for the files that come with the applet. The applet can communicate with the server from which the applet came and with no other computers.

15.2   Principles of Java Applets

In order to create a Java Applet from a regular Java application, follow the following general steps.

1. Remove the `main` method.

2. Create a class that extends `JApplet`. This will be the applet's window (i.e., substitutes the class that inherits from `JFrame`).

3. Add to this class the `init` method. The `init` method will be the first method to be executed (similar to the `main` method).

4. The `setVisible` method should not be called on the `JApplet` window because it is always visible.

5. The `setTitle` and `setSize` methods should not be called on the `JApplet` window because the title and the size of the applet are determined by the HTML file that opens the applet.

6. Remove any code that exits the program. An applet does not have a close button. Similarly, remove any reference to the `setDefaultCloseOperation` method for the applet window.

7. An applet can create additional `JFrame` objects (i.e., windows), but the applet window itself is not a `JFrame` object.

Following these principles, consider the following simple Java Applet code.

```java
import java.awt.*;
import javax.swing.*;

public class MyApplet extends JApplet {
  MyPanel p = new MyPanel();

  public void init() {
    p.setS("Initializing ...");
    p.repaint();
    add(p);
  }

  public void start() {
    p.setS("Starting ...");
    p.repaint();
  }

  public void stop() {
    p.setS("Stopping ...");
    p.repaint();
  }

  public void destroy() {
    p.setS("Destroying ...");
    p.repaint();
  }
}

class MyPanel extends JPanel {
  String s;
  int i = 0;

  public void setS(String s) {
    this.s = s;
    i++;
  }

  public void paintComponent(Graphics g) {
    super.paintComponent(g);
    g.drawString(s + " " + i, 10, 10);
```

```
    }
}
```

Note that there are four methods in the `MyApplet` class. All four methods override methods from the `JApplet` class. The `init` method is the first method that is called. Its job is to initialize the local variables, get data from the user, and display different GUI components.

The same applet can be started and stopped multiple times. Every time the applet starts, the `start` method is called. The `start` method is initially called immediately after the `init` method. The `start` method will also be called if the web browser decides to restart the applet. For example, consider a resource-intensive applet that displays 3D animation. If the user navigates away from the applet's web page, then the web browser will stop the applet. At this point, the `stop` method will be called. If the user navigates back to the web page, then the `start` method will be called. In this case, the job of the `start` method will be to resume the animation, while the job of the `stop` method will be to stop the animation. Note that the `stop` method is also called just before the applet is terminated (e.g., the user closes the web browser). The `destroy` method is called just before the applet is terminated by the web browser.

Consider the above program. It creates a panel and adds it to the applet. The `paintComponent` method of the panel displays the current value of `i` and the last method that is called. Note that the value of `i` starts at 0 and is incremented by 1 every time one of the four methods is called. As expected, our applet application does not have a `main` method, methods that make the applet window visible, or methods that set the title or size of the applet. All these parameters are specified from the HTML file. In NetBeans, one can just select the applet file, right-click on it, and run it. NetBeans will emulate a web browser and start the applet. NetBeans also automatically creates a `.html` file in the `build` subdirectory of the project. We can launch this file from a web browser to see the look and feel of our applet in different web browsers.

15.3   Creating Popup Windows

One may get the impression that a Java Applet is stuck inside a web browser. That is, we cannot create our own windows, set their size, and so on. This is not the case. The following code demonstrates how we can incorporate our Calculator program inside a web browser. The applet launches the Calculator program in a new window.

```java
import java.awt.event.*;
import javax.swing.*;

public class MyApplet extends JApplet {
  public void init(){
    JButton calcButton = new JButton("Calculator");
    final JFrame frame = new JFrame();
    frame.setTitle("Calculator");
    frame.setSize(200,200);
    frame.add(new CalculatorPanel());
    calcButton.addActionListener(new ActionListener(){
      public void actionPerformed(ActionEvent e){
        frame.setVisible(!frame.isVisible());
      }});
```

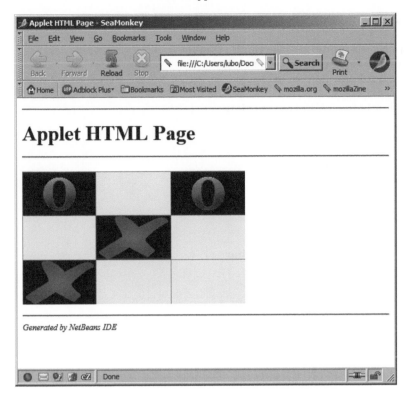

FIGURE 15.2: The Tic-Tac-Toe applet inside a web browser.

```
    add(calcButton);
  }
}
```

The applet will have a single button inside the web browser. When the button is pressed, a new calculator window will appear. When the button is pressed again, the window will hide. The advantage of this approach is that the program can set the size and title of the new window.

15.4   The Tic-Tac-Toe Game

Figure 15.2 shows a snapshot of an example run of the Tic-Tac-Toe game. Note that the program runs inside a web browser and a new window for the program is not created.

We will show a simple design that implements the applet in about 200 lines of code. We will create two classes: `TicTacToe` and `Square`. Every object of type `Square` will be responsible for one of the nine squares of the game. When asked to display the square, the object will display a rectangle and a possible picture inside the rectangle. If the rectangle is an X, then a picture of the letter X will be displayed. Similarly, if the square is an O, then a picture of the letter O will be displayed.

Here is a possible implementation of the `Square` class.

```
import java.awt.*;
```

```java
import java.awt.geom.*;

class Square extends Rectangle2D.Double {
  private boolean isX = false;
  private boolean isO = false;

  public boolean isCharacter(char c) {
    if (c == 'x') {
      return isX;
    }
    if (c == 'o') {
      return isO;
    }
    return false;
  }

  public void placeCharacter(char c) {
    if (c == 'x') {
      isX = true;
      isO = false;
    }
    if (c == 'o') {
      isO = true;
      isX = false;
    }
  }

  public void clear() {
    isX = false;
    isO = false;
  }

  public boolean hasValue() {
    return (isX || isO);
  }

  public Square(double x, double y, double dx, double dy) {
    super(x, y, dx, dy);
  }

  public void draw(Graphics2D g2, Image xImage, Image oImage) {
    g2.draw(super.getBounds2D());
    if (isX) {
      g2.drawImage(xImage, (int) getX()+1 ,(int) getY()+1, (int)
          getWidth()-2, (int) getHeight()-2, null);
    }
    if (isO) {
      g2.drawImage(oImage, (int) getX()+1,(int) getY() +1, (int)
          getWidth()-2, (int) getHeight()-2, null);
    }
  }
}
```

The class keeps track of two Boolean variables that determine if the square is an X and if the square is an O. Note that we could not have created just a single Boolean variable because we have three states: the square is an X, it is an O, and it is empty. The isCharacter method can check if the square is an X or an O, while the `placeCharacter` method changes the value of the square. Note that it is impossible that a square is both an X and an O at the same time. Since the variables `isX` and `isO` are `private`, we can guarantee that at no point both of them are set. The `clear` method simply resets the value of the rectangle, while the `hasValue` method returns `true` if the square is an X or an O, that is, it has a value.

Note that the `Square` class inherits from the `Rectangle2D.Double` class. Therefore, the `Square` class will have inside it a rectangular object (as a super object) and we can call methods, such as `getX`, `getWidth` and so on, to retrieve the parameters of the rectangle. As expected, the constructor of the `Square` class starts by calling the constructor of the `Rectangle2D.Double` class. This sets the top left corner and the width and height of the rectangle.

Lastly, let us examine the `draw` method. The paintbrush (an object of type `Graphics2D`) and the possible images to be displayed are passed as parameters. The call `g2.draw(super.getBounds2D())` draws the surrounding rectangle. Next, the `drawImage` method is used to display the character X or the character O. Note that the `drawImage` method expects the coordinates of the rectangle as integers and therefore we need to cast the coordinates of our rectangle to integers. Note as well that we have added one to the second and third parameters in order for the image to not intersect the border. The fourth and fifth parameters are the size of the image that will be displayed (can be different from the size of the original image). In our case, we calculate the dimensions as the size of the rectangle minus two in order to fit the image inside the surrounding rectangular frame.

Next, let us start examining the main class: `TicTacToe`. We will only override the `init` method from the `JApplet` class in it.

```java
import java.awt.*;
import java.net.*;
import java.util.*;
import javax.imageio.*;
import javax.swing.*;

public class TicTacToe extends JApplet {
  private ArrayList<Square> squares = new ArrayList<>();
  private Image xImage, oImage;

  public void initBoard() {
    squares = new ArrayList<>();
    Dimension d = getSize();
    double dx = d.getWidth() / 3.0;
    double dy = d.getHeight() / 3.0;
    for (int x = 0; x < 3; x++) {
      for (int y = 0; y < 3; y++) {
        squares.add(new Square(x * dx, y * dy, dx, dy));
      }
    }
    repaint();
  }

  public void init() {
    try {
      xImage = ImageIO.read(new URL(getCodeBase(), "images/x.jpg"));
      oImage = ImageIO.read(new URL(getCodeBase(), "images/o.jpg"));
    } catch (Exception exception) {
    }
    initBoard();
```

0	1	2
3	4	5
6	7	8

FIGURE 15.3: The index of the squares in the Tic-Tac-Toe game.

```
    addMouseListener(new MyMouseListener());
  }
  ...
}
```

Note that we did not define the number of rows and columns in the grid as constants. The reason is that our code is very specific and it works only for the 3x3 version of the game. The class has two variables: for the images and for the squares. The `init` method creates the board and the images and adds a mouse listener. The code of the `initBoard` method is moved into a separate method because it will be called multiple times. For example, we will need to call the method after every win, lost, or tie. This will allow the user to play multiple games without having to reload the applet. Note the `getCodeBase` method.

> The `getCodeBase` method can be called on a `JApplet` object. It returns the URL location of applet files.

The method is used to find the code base directory. Note that we set this directory in the HTML file with the line.

```
<APPLET codebase="classes" code="TicTacToe.class" width=350 height
    =200></APPLET>
```

This means that there is a subdirectory `classes` of the directory that contains the HTML file. This is the code base directory. The call `new URL(getCodeBase(), "images/x.jpg")` specifies the remote location from which the image can be downloaded. URL stands for *uniform resource locator* and specifies the Internet location of a resource, such as a file. In order for this to work, we need to create a subdirectory in the folder `classes` with name `images` and place the two image files there. Note that the `getCodeBase` method only applies to Java Applets. Since there is extra security when running a Java applet, we cannot specify an arbitrary file location. We can only access files from the code base directory and its subdirectories. Note that the actual file `x.jpg` is not saved on the client's side. Instead, it is read from the server and stored in the main memory of the client. The `ImageIO.read` method reads the file in the main memory of the client.

The `initBoard` method creates the nine squares of the game. Examine Figure 15.3 to see the index of each square. Note that we do not initially know the dimensions of the applet window because these are set from the HTML file. However, we can use the `getSize` method to get the size of the applet window. The applet window is then divided into nine equal parts. After the board is created, we call the `repaint` method to repaint the applet.

Next, let us examine the `paint` method inside the `TicTacToe` class.

...

```
public void paint(Graphics g) {
  super.paint(g);
  Graphics2D g2 = (Graphics2D) g;
  g2.setColor(Color.RED);
  for (Square r : squares) {
    r.draw(g2, xImage, oImage);
  }
}
  ...
```

The method is similar to the **paintComponent** method. However, since an applet is not a **JPanel**, the **paint** method needs to be called. An object of type **JApplet** has a default panel that does not need to be created. The **paint** method is called to draw on it. Our implementation starts by clearing the window by calling **super.paint(g)**. Then we set the brush color to red and we draw the squares. Note that it is the responsibility of each square to display both its boarders and the image inside it (when present).

Next, let us examine the inner **MousePressed** class.

```
public class TicTacToe extends JApplet {
  class MyMouseListener extends MouseAdapter {
    public void mousePressed(MouseEvent e) {
      for (Square r : squares) {
        if (r.contains(e.getPoint())) {
          if (!r.hasValue()) {
            r.placeCharacter('x');
            repaint();
            if (isGameOver()) {
              return;
            }
            computerMove();
            repaint();
            if (isGameOver()) {
              return;
            }
          }
        }
      }
    }
  }
  ...
}
```

The method iterates over all the squares of the board. The expression **e.getPoint()** returns the coordinates of where the mouse was pressed. If these coordinates are inside a square, then we interpret this as the player trying to put an **X** in the square. Note that the **contains** method checks if a point is inside a rectangle. If the square already has value, then we do not need to do anything. Otherwise, the program places an **X** in the square and repaints the canvas. If the game is over, then the method terminates. Otherwise, the computer makes a move and the program checks again if the game is over.

Next, let us start developing the logic of the **isGameOver** and **computerMove** methods. The first method checks to see if there is a line by the player or the computer. The second method determines the best possible move for the computer. We will start by creating several auxiliary methods.

```
public boolean isLine(int i, int j, int k, char c) {
  return (squares.get(i).isCharacter(c)
```

```
        && squares.get(j).isCharacter(c) && squares.get(k).isCharacter(c));
}
```

The method checks if the squares i, j, and k are all marked as the character c. Note that we assume that the method is only called on an actual line on the board. Next we create a method that checks to see if there is a winning combination with the character c.

```java
public boolean wins(char c) {
    for (int i = 0; i < 3; i++) {
        if (isLine(3 * i, 3 * i + 1, 3 * i + 2, c) || // horizontal line
                isLine(i, i + 3, i + 6, c))) { //vertical line
            return true;
        }
    }
    if (isLine(0, 4, 8, c) || isLine(2, 4, 6, c)) { //diagonal
        return true;
    }
    return false;
}
```

The method first checks all horizontal and vertical lines. If there is a line in which all squares are marked with the character c, then this is a winning combination and true is returned. Otherwise, the two diagonals are checked. If the method is unable to find a winning combination with the character c, then the value false is returned.

We next present the isBoardFull method. It simply checks to see if the board is full. It will be used by the isGameOver method to determine if we have reached a tie.

```java
public boolean isBoardFull() {
    for (Square r : squares) {
        if (!r.hasValue()) {
            return false;
        }
    }
    return true;
}
```

The method examines all the squares. If one of them is empty, then it returns false. Otherwise, if all the squares are full, the method returns true.

The isGameOver method is presented next. It first checks to see if one of the players wins. Then it checks if the board is full. If neither of these conditions are true, then the method returns false. Otherwise, the method displays an appropriate message to inform the user that the current game is over. After that, the initBoard method is called to start a new game.

```java
public boolean isGameOver() {
    if (wins('o')) {
        JOptionPane.showMessageDialog(this, "I win!");
        initBoard();
        return true;
    }
    if (wins('x')) {
        JOptionPane.showMessageDialog(this, "You win!");
        initBoard();
        return true;
    }
    if (isBoardFull()) {
        JOptionPane.showMessageDialog(this, "It's a tie!");
```

```
    initBoard();
    return true;
  }
  return false;
}
```

Note that the `JOptionPane.showMessageDialog(window, s)` method displays the string `s` in a pop-up window (a.k.a., a dialog box). The parameter `window` is the parent window, which in this case is the `JApplet` object. The dialog box that is created is modal, that is, no other window can be accessed until the window is closed. Fortunately, the dialog window will have an `OK` button that can be used to close the window. Note that it does not matter whether the `isGameOver` method first checks to see if `X` wins or whether it first checks to see if `Y` wins. The reason is that the program logic prevents both players from winning at the same time.

Next, let us examine the `computerMove` method. It first checks the middle square. If it is empty, then it always places the letter `O` there. Otherwise, the method goes through all the squares and calls the `computeScore` method on each square. The `computeScore` method evaluates the score for placing a symbol in the square. The square with the greatest score is then chosen and the character `o` is placed there.

```
public void computerMove() {
  if (!squares.get(4).hasValue()) { // if middle is empty
    squares.get(4).placeCharacter('o');
    return;
  }
  Square bestRectangle = squares.get(0);
  int best = computeScore(bestRectangle);
  for (Square r : squares) {
    if (computeScore(r) > best) {
      best = computeScore(r);
      bestRectangle = r;
    }
  }
  bestRectangle.placeCharacter('o');
}
```

The real magic or the AI (stands for *artificial intelligence*) of the program happens in the `computeScore` method. The method is smart enough to access the benefits of choosing between different squares of the board. Below is our implementation.

```
public int computeScore(Square r) {
  if (r.hasValue()) {
    return 0;
  }
  if (winsWithNextMove(r, 'o')) {
    return 4;
  }
  if (winsWithNextMove(r, 'x')) {
    return 3;
  }
  return 2;
}
```

The method first checks to see if the square is occupied. An occupied square is a terrible choice and therefore a score of 0 is returned. Next, the method checks to see if the computer can win if it places its sign in the square. If this is the case, then this is an automatic win and a score of 4 is returned. Next, the method checks to see if it can prevent the player from completing a line. If it can, then this is the next best alternative and a score of 3 is returned. In all other cases, a score of 2 is returned. As the reader can probably guess, this is a very primitive method that does not always choose the best available move. It is left as an exercise for the reader to identify possible improvements. For example, the next move to consider may be a move that can win the game in two moves regardless of what the human player chooses to do.

The `winsWithNextMove` method is shown next.

```java
public boolean winsWithNextMove(Square r, char c) {
  r.placeCharacter(c);
  if (wins(c)) {
    r.clear();
    return true;
  }
  r.clear();
  return false;
}
```

The method needs to check if placing the character c at the square r is a winning move. It first places the character on the board. It then checks if it is a winning move. As a final step, the character is removed from the board. This is a very common practice in board games. A move is made (e.g., a character is placed). We evaluate the position and the move is undone if necessary.

The complete code of the game, including imports, is shown next. Connect the program with the .html file that is shown at the beginning of this chapter. Open the web page and see if you can beat the game.

```java
import java.awt.*;
import java.awt.event.*;
import java.awt.geom.*;
import java.io.File;
import java.net.URL;
import java.util.*;
import javax.imageio.ImageIO;
import javax.swing.*;

public class TicTacToe extends JApplet {
  private ArrayList<Square> squares = new ArrayList<>();
  private Image xImage, oImage;

  public void initBoard() {
    squares = new ArrayList<>();
    Dimension d = getSize();
    double dx = d.getWidth() / 3.0;
    double dy = d.getHeight() / 3.0;
    for (int x = 0; x < 3; x++) {
      for (double y = 0; y < 3; y++) {
        squares.add(new Square(x * dx, y * dy, dx, dy));
      }
    }
    repaint();
  }

  public void init() {
    try {
```

```java
    xImage = ImageIO.read(new URL(getCodeBase(), "images/x.jpg"));
    oImage = ImageIO.read(new URL(getCodeBase(), "images/o.jpg"));
  } catch (Exception exception) {
  }
  initBoard();
  addMouseListener(new MyMouseListener());
}

public void paint(Graphics g) {
  super.paint(g);
  Graphics2D g2 = (Graphics2D) g;
  g2.setColor(Color.RED);
  for (Square r : squares) {
    r.draw(g2, xImage, oImage);
  }
}

public void computerMove() {
  if (!squares.get(4).hasValue()) { // if middle is empty
    squares.get(4).placeCharacter('o');
    return;
  }
  Square bestRectangle = squares.get(0);
  int best = computeScore(bestRectangle);
  for (Square r : squares) {
    if (computeScore(r) > best) {
      best = computeScore(r);
      bestRectangle = r;
    }
  }
  bestRectangle.placeCharacter('o');
}

public boolean isLine(int i, int j, int k, char c) {
  return (squares.get(i).isCharacter(c)
          && squares.get(j).isCharacter(c) && squares.get(k).
             isCharacter(c));
}

public boolean wins(char c) {
  for (int i = 0; i < 3; i++) {
    if (isLine(3 * i, 3 * i + 1, 3 * i + 2, c) || // horizontal line
        (isLine(i, i + 3, i + 6, c))) { //vertical line
      return true;
    }
  }
  if (isLine(0, 4, 8, c) || isLine(2, 4, 6, c)) { //diagonal
    return true;
  }
  return false;
}

public boolean winsWithNextMove(Square r, char c) {
  r.placeCharacter(c);
  if (wins(c)) {
```

```java
        r.clear();
        return true;
    }
    r.clear();
    return false;
}

public int computeScore(Square r) {
    if (r.hasValue()) {
        return 0;
    }
    if (winsWithNextMove(r, 'o')) {
        return 4;
    }
    if (winsWithNextMove(r, 'x')) {
        return 3;
    }
    return 2;
}

public boolean isGameOver() {
    if (wins('o')) {
        JOptionPane.showMessageDialog(this, "I win!");
        initBoard();
        return true;
    }
    if (wins('x')) {
        JOptionPane.showMessageDialog(this, "You win!");
        initBoard();
        return true;
    }
    if (isBoardFull()) {
        JOptionPane.showMessageDialog(this, "It's a tie!");
        initBoard();
        return true;
    }
    return false;
}

public boolean isBoardFull() {
    for (Square r : squares) {
        if (!r.hasValue()) {
            return false;
        }
    }
    return true;
}

class MyMouseListener extends MouseAdapter {
    public void mousePressed(MouseEvent e) {
        for (Square r : squares) {
            if (r.contains(e.getPoint())) {
                if (!r.hasValue()) {
                    r.placeCharacter('x');
                    repaint();
```

```java
          if (isGameOver()) {
            return;
          }
          computerMove();
          repaint();
          if (isGameOver()) {
            return;
          }
        }
      }
    }
  }
}

class Square extends Rectangle2D.Double {
  private boolean isX = false;
  private boolean isO = false;

  public boolean isCharacter(char c) {
    if (c == 'x') {
      return isX;
    }
    if (c == 'o') {
      return isO;
    }
    return false;
  }

  public void placeCharacter(char c) {
    if (c == 'x') {
      isX = true;
    }
    if (c == 'o') {
      isO = true;
    }
  }

  public void clear() {
    isX = false;
    isO = false;
  }

  public boolean hasValue() {
    return (isX || isO);
  }

  public Square(double x, double y, double dx, double dy) {
    super(x, y, dx, dy);
  }

  public void draw(Graphics2D g2, Image xImage, Image oImage) {
    g2.draw(super.getBounds2D());
    if (isX) {
```

```
      g2.drawImage(xImage, (int) getX() + 1, (int) getY() + 1, (int)
          getWidth() - 2, (int) getHeight() - 2, null);
    }
    if (isO) {
      g2.drawImage(oImage, (int) getX() + 1, (int) getY() + 1, (int)
          getWidth() - 2, (int) getHeight() - 2, null);
    }
  }
}
```

Examine once again all the methods. Every method is simple, easy to understand, and performs a single task. Many of the methods are called multiple times, which shortens the overall code size. Comments are used sparingly. The method and variable names are chosen appropriately to describe what the methods do and the purpose of the variables. The design is elegant and easy to understand, change, and maintain. This is what we should always strive to achieve when writing computer programs. We said it before, we will say it again. As Martin Fowler once famously wrote, "Any fool can write code that a computer can understand. Good programmers write code that humans can understand." Never forget to follow this principle, and happy programming!

15.5   Summary

The chapter presented the main principles of creating a Java Applet. Unlike regular applications, there are security concerns associated with Java Applets. For example, a Java Applet cannot open an arbitrary file, it cannot execute an arbitrary program, and cannot access information about the host computer. The chapter showed an example of how the Tic-Tac-Toe game can be coded as a Java Applet and placed inside a web browser. The AI of the game is very simple and the computer can lose. However, the purpose of the chapter is to give an example of a well-designed code that implements a Java Applet. The reader could learn more about how to design the AI of a computer game by reading an introductory book on artificial intelligence. The material on alphabeta pruning is particularly relevant to designing the AI of a computer game.

15.6   Syntax

- `class MyApplet extends JApplet { ... }` ⇒ Creates the main JApplet class.

- `init` ⇒ Method of the `JApplet` class that is called first.

- `start` ⇒ Method of the `JApplet` class that is called every time the applet is started, including immediately after the `init` method.

- `stop` ⇒ Method of the `JApplet` class that is called every time the applet is stopped, including immediately before the applet is destroyed.

- `destroy` ⇒ Method of the `JApplet` class that is called before the applet is destroyed.

- `getCodeBase()` ⇒ Returns a URL object of the code base directory.

- `URL url = new URL(getCodeBase(), "images/x.jpg");` ⇒ Creates a URL that points to the file `x.jpg` of the subdirectory `images` of the code base directory.

- `Image image = ImageIO.read(url);` ⇒ Reads the image from the URL and saves it in the `image` object.

- `g2.drawImage(oImage, x,y, w, h, null);` ⇒ Draws an image with the specified dimensions. The point `(x,y)` is the top left corner of the image, while `w` and `h` are the width and height of the image, respectively.

- `paint(Graphics g){ ... }` ⇒ Replaces the `paintComponent` method for drawing in a JApplet.

- `JOptionPane.showMessageDialog(..., "I win!");` ⇒ Shows the message `I win!` in a dialog box. The first parameter is a reference to the parent window.

- `<HTML> ... </HTML>` ⇒ Start and end of an HTML file.

- `<HEAD> ... </HEAD>` ⇒ Creates the HEAD part of an HTML document.

- `<HEAD> <TITLE> TITLE </TITLE> </HEAD>` ⇒ Sets the title of the document to be TITLE.

- `<H3> ... </H3>` ⇒ Creates text with size H3.

- `<P> ... </P>` ⇒ Creates a paragraph that is separated by lines.

15.7 Important Points

1. When Java files are compiled, Java binary code is created in the form of .class files. For an applet, these files are shipped and executed at the client. The client must have the Java Virtual Machine (JVM) software to execute the .class files.

2. An applet does not have a main method. Instead, it overrides the `init` method of the `JApplet` class.

3. The code of a Java Applet cannot set applet title, size, location, and so on. All these parameters are set in the HTML file.

4. Only the web browser can close an applet. Therefore, an applet should not have code that terminates the applet.

5. Use the `codebase` property to define the directory of the `.class` files. Resource files, such as images, can be created in a subdirectory of the `codebase` directory.

6. The HTML code `<APPLET codebase="classes" code="TicTacToe.class" width = 350 height=200></APPLET>` inserts an applet with code base directory `classes` (relative to the directory that contains the `.html` file). The code of the applet is in the file `TicTacToe.class`. The applet will be displayed in a 350 x 200 pixels rectangular area inside the web browser.

15.8 Exercises

1. Transform the calculator program from Chapter 12 into a Java Applet. The applet should appear inside a web browser without a new window being opened. You can use the HTML file that is generated by NetBeans.

2. Create a Java Applet that converts Celsius to Fahrenheit. The applet should appear inside a web browser without a new window being opened. You can use the HTML file that is generated by NetBeans.

3. Create a Java Applet for the `Breakout` game. The applet should appear inside a web browser without a new window being opened. Create your own HTML file.

15.9 Lab

Modify the `Tic-Tac-Toe` game by making the AI stronger. See if you can make the computer player so good that the program never loses.

15.10 Project

Extend the `Tic-Tac-Toe` game to work on a 15 x 15 board, where you need a line of 5 characters to win. Your AI will first check if the computer can win. Then it will check if the human player can be prevented from winning on the next move. Next, check if the computer can make a line of 4 characters that is open at both ends and that can be used to win the game on the next move. If such a line does not exist, your program should search to see if it can prevent the human player from creating such a line and so on. Your program does not need to be perfect, that is, it is expected that it will lose some games. Once the mouse cursor hovers over an empty square of the board, make the square green in order to indicate that the human player can play there. Display an appropriate message when the game ends. In the unlikely event that the board becomes full without anyone getting a line of 5 characters, the game should be declared a draw.

Index